Metaphysics of Goodness

Metaphysics of Goodness

Harmony and Form, Beauty and Art,
Obligation and Personhood, Flourishing and Civilization

ROBERT CUMMINGS NEVILLE

SUNY
PRESS

Cover design by Beth Neville

Published by State University of New York Press, Albany

© 2019 State University of New York

For information, contact State University of New York Press, Albany, NY
www.sunypress.edu

Library of Congress Cataloging-in-Publication Data

Name: Neville, Robert Cummings, author.
Title: Metaphysics of goodness : harmony and form, beauty and art, obligation and
    personhood, flourishing and civilization / Robert Cummings NevilleIdentifiers:
ISBN 9781438477435 (hardcover : alk. paper) | ISBN 9781438477428
        (pbk. : alk. paper) | ISBN 9781438477442 (ebook)
        Further information is available at the Library of Congress.

10 9 8 7 6 5 4 3 2 1

Dedicated to the legacies of Plato and Confucius

O Creator out of blank nothing of this universe whose immense reality, sublimity, and beauty so little thrilled me as it should, inspire me with the earnest desire to make this chapter useful to my brethren!

The earliest occupation of man is poetizing, is *feeling* and delighting in feeling. That is what the infant in his cradle seems mainly to be about.

But feeling generates dreams; dreams, desires; desires, impulses to do things. So the main business of a normal man's life is *Action.*

But any man that has any ability to ripen is soon made by active life to realize that his different acts must not stand each for itself unrelated to the others, that mere action is fatuous unless it accomplishes some thing and in some way affects the world; and that in order to affect the world the man must be affected by the world, that is, must know the facts of the case; that consideration is necessary to harmonize one's actions with each other and to harmonize them with the situation of the world; and without this harmony and systematization of efforts nothing can be accomplished. The longer a man lives the more he is impressed with the necessity of elaborate consideration to obtain basics and a plan for action. The longer he lives to and the more he becomes harmonized to the universe, deeper becomes his conviction of how little man can individually affect the world. A man is such a little thing, and is so imperfect; the universe is so immense and overwhelming. As old age creeps upon him he gets more and more to rate the search after the truth about man, about physical things, and about real potentialities, as that part of the business of life that lays up for us the greatest treasure . . .

—Fragment of a prayer by Charles S. Peirce
to begin his *Logic*, ms. 277

Contents

Part II
Goodness in Beauty and Art / 89

Part IV
Goodness in Flourishing and Civilization / 257

The cover art by Beth Neville for this volume is an oil painting of a sunset as seen from the sunset terrace at our house. Early in the text I introduce the example of a sunset to illustrate aspects of how its beauty lies within itself and yet also requires viewers with both the visual apparatus to see colors and the right vantage point on the meteorological events. Subsequent chapters embellish the sunset example to illustrate the social aspects of sunset viewing and how experiences of sunsets play roles within the larger lives of viewers. The book introduces a theory of harmony so complex as to make the cover painting look simple. But the painting shows how harmonies contain harmonies and are contained within harmonies. I thank Beth once again for artwork for the covers of my SUNY books. This is the twenty-first.

Preface

A Philosophy of Goodness

Can anything be more important to know than what is good in the world? Even in the worst of times, when it is important to understand the things that are bad, it is even more important to know what is good. For each of us, what is good and bad depends on our contexts, and we live in many contexts. To know something about the nature of goodness and its absence, or opposites, or near misses, is immensely practical. To understand tragedy, suffering, and evil without a philosophy of goodness is impossible. To know how, why, or whether we are happy, without at least a penumbral philosophy of goodness, is impossible. For this reason, with humble daring, I offer here a philosophy of goodness. Given the density and weight of the project, I hope everyone maintains a sense of humor and proportion.

A mature philosophy is a system of ideas that is relevant for engaging the world in its full reality. A philosophy is unlike a scientific theory or hypothesis. In science, you can set aside large swaths of reality as irrelevant to what you study. In philosophy, everything is relevant and any claim is vulnerable to correction by anything with which it connects. As a system, its parts interconnect so that you cannot articulate one part without implications for and qualifications from other parts. As engaging the whole world, a philosophical system operates on many levels and comes at its topics from many angles. So how can you express a philosophy of goodness that is systematic and universally applicable? You are always in the middle and cannot say everything at once.

A prior question arises, however. You cannot express a philosophy unless you have one. To be sure, you might not know what philosophy you have until you try to express it. How do you *have* a philosophy such that a possibility exists of expressing it to someone else? A philosophy consists of ideas that shape the most general ways you engage the world, the ways that affect just about everything you do. As ideas, you can think about them intellectually, which involves careful articulation, deep inquiry that takes you through arrays of topics, critical consideration of alternatives, constant checks for coherence and consistency, and a habit of thinking dialectically, not just linearly. You can undertake this kind of reasoning in philosophy building when you are relatively young and I strongly recommend that you start young. However, your philosophy is the deep hypothesis by which you live your life. You shape and correct it not only by argument but also by living with it. Living with a philosophy is the subtlest kind of argument, with the world correcting you in small ways every day. Your philosophy leads you to expect certain things, and expectations are sometimes frustrated, leading to corrective philosophical inquiry. Your philosophy leads you to pay attention to what is important in the world, and the world often reveals your own vanity and shows you other important things you had not imagined. You do not really *have* a philosophy until joys and sorrows of great depth have corrected it. Until you have lived an active life wrangling with birth and death, achievement and destruction, love and hate, commitment and betrayal, inexorable forces and chance accidents, and the passage of time and its eternal significance, you do not really have a philosophy. Experience cannot correct and enrich your philosophy unless it is the great hypothesis by which you live: it takes time and self-cultivation to live a philosophy. This fact comforts me enough about getting old to commend it to you.

You do not live your life alone nor do you develop your philosophy alone. From the beginning, philosophy has been dialogical, conversational, argumentative, and social. You develop your ideas through imaginative, inspiring, and critical conversations with others. These include the great philosophers you can read and discuss with people. If you are as fortunate as I, you have as companions in developing a philosophy other living philosophers of intelligence, wit, care for the truth, affection for you, and friendship. Philosophers come from many fields in many guises, not merely from academic philosophy. The philosophical life is a friendship association with webs of collaborators close and far, all developing your philosophies together. Furthermore, the people with whom you live your life, sharing families, careers, historical destinies, and fate's tragedies, are also internal to developing a philosophy through its vulnerable maturation, even when they are not philosophers. Living over half a century with my wife, Beth Neville, an artist with exquisite sensitivity and imagination, has been as important for my philosophy as all my other philosophical conversations. I hope you too have people with whom to build a life that embodies a philosophy to communicate.

Returning then to the question of how to express a philosophy of goodness, I hope we can conceive the expression as a sharing in the building of our philosophies, perhaps to some degree sharing the philosophical ideas that can guide our lives, or at least offering each other new ideas and corrections of old ones. I offer this philosophy of goodness as a way to live in our time and place, not the only way, but one deep philosophical hypothesis that might help you. If it is not to your taste, let it entertain you. What entertains you might then shape your taste.

Where shall I start? Can I plunge into the middle without putting you off? Here is the plan.

First, I will argue that everything is good in its way, a strong if unoriginal thesis. To argue this, we have to share in our conversation a "philosophy of everything," namely, a metaphysics. Hence the title of this book. The metaphysics I shall explain says that everything is determinate in its way and so the metaphysics takes the form of a theory of determinateness. The metaphysics proposes that to be a determinate thing is to be a harmony that relates to everything else with respect to which it is determinate. To be a harmony is to have form, and to have form is to embody goodness. This is my first major thesis. The thesis is extremely abstract, which is the virtue of a good metaphysics: it applies to everything equally. It applies to any world that is determinate, even a nontemporal world.

This is a "strong" thesis because it seems ridiculously false in light of so many bad things in the world. Bad things include more forms of human evil than can be catalogued, the suffering of sentient beings great and small, social injustices such as racism, unnecessary poverty, multiple kinds of oppression, and the destruction of all sorts of high achievements of value in ecologies, planets as ecosystems sustaining life, and even supernovas. Nevertheless, I want to say, with many philosophers including Plato and Confucius, whom I will discuss later, that all these bads consist in the misplacement of things and what they do to each other, not in themselves. What things are "in themselves," of course, is the deep metaphysical question we shall explore in this book. My answer is that things in themselves are harmonies and, as harmonies, they relate in multiple ways to other things. Therefore, things are never in themselves "by themselves." They are always also related to other things. Some of those relations might be bad for those others, and it is even metaphysically possible for every harmony to be good but also bad for something else. The strength of my theory of determinateness as harmony is that it is thoroughly relational.

The use of the word "harmony," however, is likely to get me into more trouble with those of you who read it as a treacly word. Everything is harmony and light! Nonsense! Some things are wretched, like a comet about to hit the earth and blow away the life-sustaining atmosphere, or a disease germ, or a racist institution. Many things are extremely destructive and explosive of good things. Can they be called "harmonies"? For many people, "harmony" has a primary connotation of voices singing together as in a choir, which necessarily suggests something good and beautiful, and this connotation stays in the background of how people hear my discussion of harmony. Nevertheless, what I mean by "harmony" is things just fitting together. This connotation comes from the Greek *harmos*, meaning a joint, and from the Latin *harmonia*, meaning a joining or concord. The components of a determinate thing just fit together, join, relate in concord, so that the thing has an identity relative to other things with respect to which it is determinate. A composer might write in a discord, according to musical expectations, that provides just the discordant harmony the composer wants; at a deeper level, the discord is the concord of things not expected to fit together, but that do fit together to produce the heard discord.

My rhetorical problem is even deeper than this, however. In my analysis of harmony in chapters 1 and 2, I will argue that getting the components of a determinate thing together with its form and relative to the things with respect to which the thing is determinate constitutes the value of the thing "in itself." So, I do want to say that being a harmony is to have goodness or value because of the way its form joins together its components, some of which are relations to other things. I do want to say that to be determinate is to have value and that the things of the universe are at base good, no matter how bad they might be for one another. You are right to be suspicious that my rhetoric might blind you to the tragedy of a "perfect storm." Hold that suspicion in mind as you follow my arguments that goodness consists in how the form of a harmony composes the joining of its components in its existential context. In the long run, my argument will be, in what other than harmony could value or goodness consist? Or is there no real goodness at all, only the human propensity to value some things and disvalue others?

How can I convince you that everything has a goodness just in having a form if I cannot show you that this is how you experience goodness and badness, and all the other value traits? Therefore, my argument needs to supplement the abstract metaphysics with a theory of aesthetic experience, or the experience of things as having goodness each in its own way. A theory of experience deals with concrete examples of good and bad things, not only with the experience of all goods and bads of all things. My conversation with you then must jump dialectically from abstract postulations and reasonings to examples and appeals to experience. It cannot first develop a theory of determinateness and then a theory of experience, or vice versa, but must interweave these. I apologize for the nonlinearity of this kind of argument, but it is more fun than most other kinds of philosophical plots. Expect surprises as well as confusions when I seem to switch topics.

To complicate this dialectic between metaphysics and examples is the fact that the metaphysics of determinateness applies to any possible cosmos, temporal or not. It is vague with respect to whether any harmonies are temporal. The metaphysics of determinateness would be true for a temporal cosmos and also for a nontemporal cosmos. Yet our cosmos in fact *is* temporal and my examples come from that realm. Any description of our actual temporal cosmos makes the metaphysics more specific than the metaphysics would be alone. The temporal cosmology

I shall develop does not derive from the metaphysics, although it must be understandable as a specification of the metaphysics. Other considerations need to come into play to give a cosmological description of the cosmos we have. Among those considerations are the findings of the sciences in the sense that the cosmology must allow the sciences to be true; because the sciences often involve conflict and contradiction, the cosmology needs to be vague in accepting any plausible scientific position. Science is a rather narrow approach to interpreting the cosmos, privileging order and regularity and limited to our scientific theories. Many other aspects of the cosmos need articulation in order to flesh out a cosmology.

My own philosophy here develops a process cosmos rather than a substance cosmos, following in the general train of process philosophies and pragmatisms, as will be apparent shortly. More than Western process philosophy and pragmatism, however, I aim to highlight in my cosmology senses of process, change, and depth of existence that are prominent in the last three millennia of Chinese thought, in what we know now as Daoism, Confucianism, and Chinese versions of Buddhism. I have learned greatly from James Miller's splendid *China's Green Religion*.[1] His interpretations of the ancient and medieval Daoist texts in terms of contemporary ecological issues are very close to the relational cosmologies of fluid harmonies I shall put forward here.

My second major thesis is that beauty is the good any harmony has in itself. By a "harmony in itself," I mean to include its relations to others as components within itself but to exclude how it can be components in other things. I also exclude from a harmony in itself some of the own-being of the things to which it is related; the other terms in the relations are not all internal to the harmony related to them. I propose to define beauty as the good each thing has in itself. This is another metaphysical point, and it reflects some religious intuitions that everything is good in its way, however bad or harmful a thing might be in the ways it affects other things. We can understand beauty more concretely, however, by examining human-made beauty, namely, art. Art is the way people delight in things for their own sakes, for their beauty, for their goodness in themselves, and seek to stabilize these intrinsic enjoyments, making more and preserving them. I shall endeavor to articulate this theory of art with many examples. We also can discuss both how to appreciate art and how to create it. Beauty and art have to do with how things are good as such.

My third major thesis is that a kind of goodness exists in harmonies that relates persons to the world with obligation. I call this the "goodness in relations of obligation." These harmonies are special two-term relations, with the world or some part of it being one term and the person relating to the world or to that part being the other. On the one hand, the obligation relations define what we ought to do in the world and, on the other hand, what we do in those relations defines us as persons. I shall try to persuade you of four kinds of obligation relations. The first is how we relate to the world by interpreting it and the things in it. The obligation here is to be as true in our interpretations as we can be and not false. The second is how we relate to the world in the decisions we make about it, choosing the better versus worse possibilities. The obligation here is to be as moral as we can. (I admit this is an extended use of "moral.") The third is how we conform our lives to the world, or to its most important dimensions, such as family, society, economy, and work, and what we should do about those dimensions. This kind of obligation relates not only to individual decisions but to what we make of ourselves relative to the important dimensions of life. This is an obligation to comport ourselves to the world rightly. The fourth is how we relate to the world in developing a character that is relevant for living well within the world. We have an obligation to make ourselves virtuous. To be a person, I shall suggest, is to be under obligation to be true, moral, right, and virtuous. To be good as a person is to be good in these respects. These discussions will parse many of the notions of value philosophers have discussed concerning human life. Surely, you cannot be against truth, morality, rightness, and virtue! But can you accept my interpretations of them?

My fourth major thesis is that harmonic structures of society exist that set the conditions for human flourishing. These social structures link people to one another, groups to groups, institutions to individuals, nature, and other institutions, and societies to the natural environments within which they exist. These social structures are harmonies that embrace their components, which are also harmonies. Individuals and groups relate differentially within these social structures, some flourishing and others suffering sometimes. The structures have values that we should improve where possible. The civilizational structures for flourishing are diverse and undergird many kinds of goodness, for instance, justice, freedom, equality, opportunity, abundance, and the like. Some if not most civilizational structures have ambiguous goodness, some aspects positively good and others, or negative value, that we would call bad rather than good. Together they make up the texture of kinds of goods, and their lacks, that constitute a civilization. A philosophy of goodness needs to direct reflection on the complex goods involved in civilization and I shall try to do so.

For the most part, the harmonies of form, beauty/art, obligation/personhood, and flourishing/civilization are harmonies of changes. The harmonies play out over time with much spontaneity of emergence. So many of the topics have to do with goodness in changes, emergences, and transformations. By the same token, the experiences of things as good are also temporally dynamic. So my philosophy of goodness is less about "what is" than about "what happens," or better yet "happenings."

All this is ambitious for a philosophy of goodness. Nevertheless, it is only a beginning.

Philosophical Background and Context

My philosophy of goodness is not original. For me personally, it comes from two main traditions reflected in the dedication of this book. In the West, Plato began systematic philosophical thinking by asking about the nature of goodness, the Form of the Good, what makes things good, how we know what is good, and how we need to understand goodness in order to guide our lives. Plato's reflections on goodness influenced all subsequent Western philosophy, including Islamic thought. Gottfried Leibniz and Alfred North Whitehead, along with Charles S. Peirce and John Dewey, developed Plato's philosophy of goodness in ways that I incorporate. The other main source of my philosophy of goodness is East Asia where Confucius, Mengzi, and Xunzi, along with other classic writers of their era, especially Laozi and Zhuangzi, inaugurated a quite similar tradition regarding goodness.[2] Neo-Confucian philosophers from Zhou Dunyi to Wang Yangming developed that classical

Confucian tradition in ways that I also incorporate.[3] You do not have
to be an expert in any of these philosophies, however, to understand
the philosophy of goodness I shall put forward.

Despite the hoary legacies of Confucius and Plato, their philosophical lines on goodness are not popular today, either with professional philosophers or with most people's philosophies. Those two
traditions agree that some good inheres in anything that has form or
determinate character, however much the goodness of one thing might
be bad for another. They agree also in saying that this goodness can
be known to a degree, under some kind of interpretation or other: to
have any grasp of something is to have some feel for its worth, however
accurate or inaccurate. Yet modern Western science has taught itself
that to know nature is to know it as a set of facts, ideally expressible
in mathematical terms. John Locke stated this scientific viewpoint with
influential precision, and many other philosophers, including especially
Immanuel Kant, developed it with a wide range of applications. For
them, the goodness of things is something imputed to the things by
the mind and so, even in knowing the goodness attributed to things,
we only know some characters of our experience, not of the things
themselves. As Western science became influential in the East, so did
its radical distinction between facts and values. The Confucian tradition, which has always said that understanding the world is necessarily
aesthetic, began to lose its influence in China, Korea, and Japan in the
late nineteenth century when Western fact/value scientism gradually
became popular. So the philosophy of goodness for which I shall
argue runs against the grain of these contemporary philosophical and
cultural assumptions.

These common assumptions have caused particular difficulty for
my language. I had first thought to entitle this book *Metaphysics of Value*
rather than *Goodness*, because "value" is a good philosophical word and
"goodness" is a clumsy noun made from the adjective "good." But
"value" has become so closely associated with valuation, evaluation,
and "our own values" in the sense of things we prize that it betrays
my intent to say that value lies in the things that have value, that are
good. I want to say that when we value something, we take in its
value and make it part of our own reality, although how we value it
might not do justice to the thing. When we evaluate something, we

consider what its value is relative to how we evaluate other things, often noting that this evaluation might be mistaken. When we have "our own values," these are our attempts to articulate what is valuable in things, particularly what values we would like to see instantiated in things. These articulations guide how we interpret our world, especially our possibilities, even when our values are misplaced or just dead wrong. How can we think we have valued a person unjustly if there is no value in the person about which to be just? How can we come to realize that we have been mistaken in our evaluation of something if there is no value in the thing to be wrong about? How can we be wrong about value if there is nothing about which to be wrong? Is not our experience shot through with pellets of rude awakening about being wrong about the value of something? The ambiguities in the word "value," which for many has come to mean little more than the price for which a commodity might sell, confuse the point I want to make. Therefore, I now call mine a "philosophy of goodness," which does not have this ambiguity. Having completed a rough draft of sixteen chapters, I pressed the "replace" button and changed 814 "value" mentions to "goodness."

How shall I address you as a reader? I am accustomed to writing in an academic style, mostly in the third person. Academics feel themselves surrounded by a cloud of critics against whom they defend themselves with storm cellars of footnotes and walls of preemptive qualifications. That has been my style. Having done that for many years, however, now I simply want to write for you reading this book. This means explaining myself to you, wondering what you think and who you are. I hope you can read in the spirit of telling me how you respond. If you explain to yourself your response to me, you probably will understand my point. On the one hand, I worry that this first- and second-person dialogue might seem frivolous or contrived. On the other hand, the heavy technical detail of the coming argument quickly will banish any thought that I am trying to be cute.

The Plot

The plot of this book is not what you might expect, which would be to move inductively from the concrete to the abstract. Rather, it begins with an abstract metaphysics of goodness in harmony and form and then moves to illustrate and concretize the theory in discussions of goodness in beauty and art, obligation and personhood, and flourishing and civilization. Discussions of the general nature of art, personhood, and civilization might not be your frontline candidates for concreteness. I do give many examples, however, and even embellish some examples from chapter to chapter.

The book here comprises four main parts, one devoted to each of the primary theses mentioned earlier. Each part has four chapters. Part I is an analysis of goodness itself that puts forward the hypothesis that goodness is a trait of anything that has form. Anything that has form is a harmony and, in addition to its form, any harmony has components that are formed, existential location in a field constituted by its relations with other harmonies, and the goodness achieved by getting these components together with this form in this location relative to other harmonies. I shall exfoliate these formulaic points throughout the rest of this book.[4] The hypothesis here concerning harmony is an analysis of what it means to be determinate at all. Hence, to be determinate is to have goodness or value.

My analysis of determinateness as harmony rejects the notion that things are substances that have their own properties. Instead, I claim that the components of harmonies are other harmonies that influence them and thus internally relate to them, if also remaining somewhat external. If a harmony is determinate with respect to other harmonies, directly or indirectly, those other harmonies are among its components. Consequently, my hypothesis affirms that everything relates internally to everything else with respect to which it is determinately different, although most of those relations are either trivial or vague (technical terms I shall define later). This hypothesis is not immediately plausible to people with an Aristotelian common sense. I need to elaborate it and open it to evaluation.

Although I have been writing about harmony for over half a century, only in this book have I discovered just how radical it is to say that anything at all determinate is a harmony that includes all the other things with respect to which it is determinate as its components. I am making an astonishingly strong claim that all things are in relation to the extent they are determinate with respect to one another. My claim is more metaphysically general than Whitehead's similar claim. Furthermore, I elaborate the metaphysical structure of harmony through topics in which that had been vague in my previous writings. For instance, in several of the following chapters I elaborate the beauty of a sunset in terms of a kind of harmony that I call a "situation," in which the beauty of the meteorological events exists in harmonic relation with potential viewers with the right angle to the horizon and with the visual apparatus to see colors, shapes, and movement. From the meteorological horizon to the viewing platform, millions of causal harmonies are themselves harmonized within the situational harmony. Interpretive cultures also affect the experience of the potential viewers. Actual persons include situations of admiring a beautiful sunset among the many other components they need to harmonize within their own individual lives; or, they might actually have been in such a situation but have forgotten about it so as to trivialize it in their lives. All this facilitates building a naturalistic theory of experience that makes no appeal to "inner" experience of things "out there."

Part of the evaluation of my theory of harmony has to do with demonstrating its usefulness for understanding the goodness in form, art, persons, and civilization, although many other domains provide for its probation as well. I suspect you will find that the claim that things are harmonies, not substances, will seem stranger and farther-reaching, and yet more plausible, as the questions of those domains unfold.

I need to forestall a misunderstanding about the term "harmony" as I use it. Many people hear that word as connoting that everything nicely hangs together and that my philosophical use of the term papers over the chaos and evil in the world. Chaos and evil are not the same thing, although some evil is the introduction of chaos into a desirable, otherwise harmonious process. Arrigo Boito's *Mefistofele* treats evil incarnate as the bringer of chaos and love as the restoration of harmony. Chaos as such, however, is the opposite of form, order, or harmony. It is the lack of determinateness. "As such," chaos is nothing, pure nothing, neither good nor evil. Of course, there is no chaos as such, only chaos as relative lack of connection, often a breakdown of harmony. Plato envisioned concrete process as a near-chaos of diverse processes or changes without much order. Whereas Aristotle saw the universe as basically stable, Plato saw it as fragile in its order, often near to unraveling and self-destruction. Particularly in human affairs, Plato saw the fragile bonds of human sociality under constant threat, not from evil, but from things just not hanging together, from unanticipated accidental change. Therefore, Plato emphasized that the forms of things that are in jeopardy are ideals. Much of the human task both personally and socially is to find ways to bring ideal form or order out of real or threatened chaos, Plato argued in the *Republic*. John Dewey, in *Experience and Nature*, said that precariousness is one of the generic traits of existence, even more basic than order; precariousness is the stimulus to investing human experience in the pursuit of "ideal ends." The Confucians saw the chaotic processes of Earth as needing the ordering principles of Heaven. The metaphysical Neo-Confucians thought the stuff of things, *qi*, to be energetic processes that have minimal form but that need principle, *li*, to bring them under control and into connection. John Berthrong likens *qi* to an energetic but untrained puppy. In his *Sagehood*, Stephen C. Angle provides an acute analysis of the Neo-Confucian concern for coherence, *li*, and its related harmony, *he*.[5] Angle shows how the education of the sage is to discern what makes things harmonize, what makes things not harmonize, how to break up evil patterns of harmony, and how to imagine unrecognized opportunities for harmony, all in the face of threats of dissolution from unanticipated quarters. Tragedy, for Confucians, is being unable to harmonize harmful conflicts. I agree with these Platonic, pragmatic, and Confucian sensibilities about harmony under threat by chaos. Chaos is not a philosophical or natural principle balanced off against harmony: it is not a principle at all.

Evil, on the other hand, is the condition in which one harmony is bad for another harmony, as when a healthy germ infects an animal's body. Some harmonies, such as the HIV virus, are perfectly good in themselves, even beautiful to microbiologists, but perfectly horrible for what they do to the things in which they become components. Concern for your group's welfare, good in itself, can lead to evil bigotry against others and even to war. Capitalism usually produces increase in wealth, but often a decrease in equitable distribution of wealth. The theory of harmony I am proposing emphasizes not only the integrity of each harmony but the many ways in which harmonies can be components in other harmonies, some of which are quite destructive or bad for those other harmonies. I shall argue in part IV that many things that are good in themselves are evil with regard to human flourishing.

Part II is an analysis of beauty generally and of art as humanly produced beauty. Beauty I define as that which is good in itself as a harmony, regardless of how something might be good or bad for something else. Any harmony is beautiful if you can just regard it in itself, although in real life the determinate harmonies intertwine. Beauty is humanly relevant when we can enjoy it, and I follow John Dewey in giving primacy in human life to such enjoyment. Art is the human production of things for the sake of their enjoyment potential, whether it is simply the organized repetition of something that is enjoyable or the making of a potentially pleasing artifact. Just about any art object or artful activity has all sorts of values other than its enjoyable goodness in itself. The arts as we know them are complex developments of simple things of pleasure. In part II, which illustrates its points with many kinds of art, I consider gardening to be an art form, as well as sport or athletics, whether or not it is competitive.

Part III is an analysis of certain kinds of goodness in persons that have to do with how they relate with obligation to their environment. These kinds are truth, morality, rightness, and virtue of personal character. As I said earlier, each is a kind of harmony that is dominantly a two-term relation between a person on the one hand and something in the environment on the other. In common parlance we say that the persons are (or are not) true, moral, right in relation to their environment, and virtuous as persons in their environment. Each of those two-term relations includes the environment as well as the persons. The persons define themselves by how those relations are conditions within their own harmonies. But the relations themselves are not wholly contained within the persons. The environmental terms in the relations have their own external reality within which the persons are only components. The relations involved in truth, morality, rightness, and virtue are harmonies embracing both the persons' experiences and the environmental things' ongoing natures. Thus, my hypothesis is a naturalistic one, treating persons as "organisms interacting with an environment," to use John Dewey's phrase. With this move, I mean to reject the transcendental turn in philosophy, as will be explained in what follows. Many if not most contemporary Western philosophers are transcendental philosophers in one or another of the many ways transcendental thinking has developed since Kant.

Part IV explores the kind of goodness associated with human flourishing. I am especially interested in civilization in the highfalutin sense of the word. These kinds of goodness are characteristic of the structures of social life within which human beings can flourish. I shall reflect on these goods of flourishing in terms of social context, especially as defined by ritual practice. The crowning kinds of goodness in civilization are creativity and spirit construed as ways that harmonize the society, not merely the ways by which individuals are creative or spirited. The ideas in this part play off the considerations of the values in civilization articulated so beautifully by Alfred North Whitehead in his *Adventures of Ideas*.

Each of the parts has two levels of analysis, sometimes not well distinguished. At the lower level is some theoretical philosophical point about goodness. At higher levels are less theoretical points that build on goodness relative to human interests. Part I has the metaphysics of harmony as its lower-level theory, and the discussion of form as a function of harmony in which we can appreciate goodness as its higher level. Part II has the metaphysics of beauty as its lower level and the discussion of art, its appreciation and creation, as its high levels. Part III has a metaphysics of obligation as its lower level and discussions of obligations to truth, morality, rightness, and virtue as its higher levels. Part IV has the metaphysics of flourishing as its lower level and discussions of ritual, creativity, and civilization as its higher levels. The first chapter in each part introduces the lower-level theory and the others elaborate the higher levels, although there are anticipations, restatements, and interweavings throughout.

Behind the choice to study goodness in beauty and art, obligation and personhood, and flourishing and civilization is an architectonic philosophical idea developed from Charles Peirce.[6] Goodness in beauty is goodness sustained in a harmony considered in itself. He would call this Firstness, the nature a thing has in itself irrespective of anything else. The goodness on which I focus in the obligations of personhood relates persons to what is at least partly external to them, other than them, which Peirce would call Secondness, involving sheer otherness.

The goodness in civilized flourishing characterizes the social structures that mediate between persons and their environments of various sorts, which Peirce would have called Thirdness, or that which is what it is by virtue of mediating between at least two other things. I will explain Peirce's ideas in more detail later. My theory of determinateness as harmony, of course, does not let me say that anything is only itself, because its harmony includes relations to other harmonies as components; nor does *sheer* otherness exist, though at least *some* robust otherness exists. Peirce's plan still serves as a structural guide to the complex hypotheses I put forward here.

Gary Slater, a recent interpreter of Peirce who extends his categories in an original way, would say that Peirce would diagram kinds of relations among inquiries in religion and philosophy generally in terms of a series of concentric circles, or "nested continua." An inner circle rests within the larger continuum of the next outer circle, which rests within the continuum of the next, and so forth. In Slater's terms, my discussion of beauty and form nests within the larger circle of the discussion of personhood and obligation, which nests within the circle of flourishing and civilization. On a different set of continua relating to the specificity of inquiry, the discussion of harmony and form nests within the larger circle of beauty and art, which nests within obligation and personhood, which nests within flourishing and civilization. On yet a different set of continua, the discussion of form nests within the larger circle of harmony, art within the larger circle of beauty, personhood within the larger circle of obligation, and civilization within the larger circle of flourishing.[7] If you do not know Peirce, do not worry about it. If you do know Peirce and do not like his ideas of Firstness, Secondness, and Thirdness, I hope the argument ahead will change your mind: the more you like Peirce, the more you will be comfortable with the architectonic of my philosophy of goodness.

Nevertheless, David Rohr has made me realize that I am not just a sloppy Peircean but at the metaphysical level profoundly reject Peirce. For Peirce, the harmonization of things comes from a third term (which of course he calls a Third) whose determinate character mediates the things. His treatment of goodness, therefore, is Aristotelian in the sense that the good is what completes or realizes a thing's integration. My sense of harmony, however, is that it is a "just fitting together" of things in consistent forms of possibility. Harmony is the just fitting together of what Peirce would call Seconds because their separate determinate natures simply cohere. Harmony is an aesthetic integration of things that still contrast, not a fulfillment of a final cause. So I am a Platonist appealing to coherence rather than an Aristotelian appealing, as Peirce does, to the good as completing concrete reasonableness. Whitehead rather than Peirce is my inspiration in the metaphysics of harmony and goodness, although I also reject many of Whitehead's ideas.

Acknowledgments

Whatever is good in this book arises out of decades of conversations and interactions with philosophers and others I acknowledged in my earlier books, especially Wesley Wildman. I am grateful for my good fortune to have had such a rich, intelligent, and supportive crowd of people who have sought to improve my thinking. Here I want to single out three voices for special thanks. Steve Odin was my student many years ago at SUNY Purchase and then at SUNY Stony Brook where he took his doctorate. I have always learned more from him than I taught him and recently have been inspired again by his *Tragic Beauty in Whitehead and Japanese Aesthetics*. James Miller was my student at Boston University and has gone on to become a major figure in Daoist studies. In particular, he has developed a contemporary Daoist philosophy that profoundly alters the way we should think about the environment and ecology. When I contemplate the radical extent to which my philosophy here emphasizes relational harmonies, he is the only one I know who would say "of course!" Tyler Tritten is a new friend who has graciously advised me on the orientation of this present book, reading and commenting on the whole. We encountered one another at the 2017 Metaphysical Society of America meeting where we agreed on the rarely recognized truth that intelligibility is contingent; we developed a friendship from there. See his book, *The Contingency of Necessity: Reason and God as Matters of Fact*. New thanks go to him.

I want to mention my class on axiology in the fall of 2017 at Boston University that helpfully addressed a draft of this book. Its members were Christie Brophy, Ari Brouwer, Jason Cabitac, Jesse

Cicotti, Greylyn Hydinger, Xiyan Sun, Siyoung Sung, Yuling Wang, and Xinyi Zhou. Greylyn Hydinger and Jason Cabitac gave especially helpful seminar presentations on the book. Wesley Wildman, as usual, discussed just about every aspect of this book with me, especially its rhetorical orientation. Most particularly, I want to thank David Rohr, who made page-by-page suggestions, nearly all of which I have incorporated. He even made suggestions for better wording that I have adopted with his blessing. He has vastly improved this book.

PART I

Goodness in Harmony and Form

Would it not be helpful if we could be clear at the beginning of our inquiry? Would it not be helpful if we could just define our terms clearly and build on that beginning? Mathematics works this way, clear step by clear step. Philosophy, however, gains clarity only toward the end of inquiry. Even at the end of a philosophical inquiry, clarity is not exactly the end in view. Rather we should hope for an enlarged and highly complicated feel for what connects with what and why certain things are more important than others. Nevertheless, in order to begin I can counterfeit the helpful feeling of clarity by establishing a contrast between what I intend to argue for and what I shall argue against. Let me begin by contrasting two large, thematic, models of goodness.

The one I shall argue *for* is the aesthetic model according to which goodness is some kind of harmonious togetherness of things with balance, proportion, and measure, things that "just fit together," as I mentioned earlier. It deserves the label "aesthetic" because it holds that goodness is something grasped or appreciated in a kind of aesthetic vision or judgment, a matter of coherent perception ("aesthetic" derives from the Greek word for perception). The grasp is itself a harmony that connects the goodness in the thing with the goodness in the perception. The large model of goodness *against* which I shall argue is the realization or fulfillment model according to which goodness is the realization, fulfillment, or completion of a thing's nature; this model usually supposes that things are substances that can bear unrealized

1

realizations. That something is good means that it is finished in its realization, or on the way to finishing, according to the realization model.

By virtue of thoroughness, clarity might develop in the maturation of inquiry. Thoroughness of inquiry overcomes the dichotomies
that provide initial clarity and integrates the truth in both sides. I hope
to show along the way that something is true in both the aesthetic
and the realization models of goodness. Nevertheless, I will argue that
the second is subordinate to and accounted for within the first.

In the West, Plato is associated with the aesthetic model of goodness. His fundamental vision was that the cosmos is a maelstrom of
changing processes that have determinateness only insofar as they pass
through formal structures. The processes cohere, when they do, because
their forms cohere. Because the processes are always passing through
forms on the way to other forms, Plato called the concrete world
the realm of *becoming*. Everything is always becoming something else.
The stability of the world, for Plato, derives from the stability of the
forms through which things pass repeatedly. In the human sphere are
forms that are necessary and precious for human life, and these become
the ideals that we strive to preserve or achieve. The understanding
of goodness then is the understanding of what makes forms cohere.
Evil or disaster happen when the forms important to embody in the
processes of human life break up by accident, collision, or entropy.
Plato's abstract analysis of goodness appealed to what he called the
Form of the Good, that which makes good things good because they
have internal coherence. In the *Republic* where he talked about the
Form of the Good, he said that it gives coherence of different sorts
to images, concrete processes, theoretical ideas that might apply to
those processes, and to what he called the "dialectic" of weighing
what theories take in or leave out in their account of processes. He
also said the Form of the Good gives aesthetic judgmental faculties to
imagination, to common sense for dealing with concrete processes, to
theoretical rationality, and to dialectical speculation. The Form of the
Good is not itself a determinate form, and hence we cannot know it
in a theory or conceptual picture. It gives coherence to the forms of
things in process, and in the *Philebus* Plato characterized "that which
gives coherence" as balance, proportion, measure, beauty, and things of
this sort, all matters of aesthetic appreciation. In the *Statesman* Plato said

that a good politician has an aesthetic sense of "normative measure" for just how much of this or that to promote and how far to go, this all in contrast with "standard measure" or rules that tell you how much and how many. In the preface, I listed some of the major Platonic contributors to the aesthetic model of goodness, coming down to Charles Peirce and Alfred North Whitehead, my own patrons. Robert S. Brumbaugh is the extraordinary interpreter of Plato on goodness whom I follow in my reading.

In the West, Aristotle is associated with the realization model of goodness. Goodness lies in the achievement of a final cause, "that for the sake of which" a thing acts. The ultimate final cause for Aristotle is self-sufficiency, that which needs nothing else and cannot change because any change would be for the worse. For him, the ultimate Good is "thought thinking itself," which is pure act with no potency; Thomas Aquinas developed this into his idea of God. Next most perfect in itself to thought thinking itself, for Aristotle, is a fixed star spinning in place; next best is a spinning star moving in orbit; next best is the rotation of the seasons; next best is the reproductive cycle in plants and animals. Human beings need to find the balance between extremes, the Golden Mean, in moral life; but the highest good for human beings, according to Aristotle in book 10 of the *Nicomachean Ethics*, is contemplation of eternal truths in imitation of thought thinking itself.[1]

Chapter 1 of this part introduces many of the important concepts concerning goodness that I will develop throughout this volume. The claim basic to this whole project is that anything with form has goodness by virtue of that form. The first argument for this is experiential, namely, that we experience everything as having some good or other. To make out this argument I need to introduce the notion of form as such, which I will articulate theoretically in the first and second chapters. Crucial to the notion of form is that of harmony, which I shall develop abstractly in the second and third sections of the first chapter. In order to experience goodness appreciatively, the form of that which is good needs to relate to the appreciators. I shall elaborate a conception of a "situation" in which the intentions and attentions of experiencers relate through harmonies to that which is appreciated. Throughout the volume, I will embroider the example of appreciating a sunset.

The most revolutionary contribution of this book, I dare to think, is its systematic development of the hypothesis that anything that is determinate is a harmony, including as components within itself relations with all other things with respect to which the thing is determinate. We cannot fully define things by "properties" they possess, but by how they compose in their forms all the other things to which they relate without making those things lose their own external integrity. In my language, things have components rather than properties, and many of these components are relations to other things. Relations themselves are harmonies. This is an extreme relational metaphysics undergirding a relational axiology.

Chapter 2 extends the argument by asking, in a preliminary way prior to the full-blown discussion in chapter 4, why we should identify goodness with form. The first answer is that goodness is a kind of "density of being," as in the philosophy of Leibniz. The denser the being of something, the better it is. The chapter elaborates the theory of harmony to explain density of being. This elaboration requires the further elucidation of the notion of an existential field in which harmonies are related. A situation as defined in chapter 1 is one kind of existential field and is "situated" within a larger environing existential field. I justify the goodness of density of being in two stages. First, I explain how the elegant optimization of complexity and simplicity constitutes goodness. Second, I explain how the composition of the form of a harmony arranges its components so that they function in one or several of four ways: as having narrowness, width, vagueness, or triviality. Though borrowed from Whitehead, I nevertheless develop these notions here according to my view of harmony, not his. Finally, chapter 2 articulates the experiential terms of intensity and immediacy for the situational grasp of the goodness in density of being.

Chapter 3 deepens the discussion of the previous two chapters by developing a more formal but concrete cosmology to show the grounds for their claims. The metaphysical theory of determinateness as harmony applies to any possible cosmos. Our particular cosmos is temporal, and so a temporal cosmology needs articulation. It includes a theory of the future as a structured field of possibilities, often including alternative possibilities. I introduce and complicate Aristotle's famous example (in *De Interpretatione* 19a30, chapter 9) of admirals contemplating a sea battle on the morrow to illustrate alternatives in the future that have different values. The chapter discusses a theory of actuality and actualization with an analysis of becoming. Acts of becoming take place in the overlap of a field of actualized things and a field of possibilities. Goodness is present wherever there is form, in possibility or actuality. The perspectives in which things are good include their own harmonies and their functions in all the harmonies in which they become components. The cosmology articulates some of the complex ways in which things are good in themselves and good for or in other things.

The fourth chapter steps back to ask why we should identify what I have described in the complex theory of form with what we mean by goodness or value. The preliminary discussion treats and rejects several arguments to the effect that goodness is not really in things but is just in the projections of valuations onto things. Then I argue that we distinguish between greater and lesser goods, and different kinds of goods, by contemplating imagined possibilities, as when an artist contemplates how to compose a work. The chapter begins the sketch of a theory of aesthetic judgment so that we can see how aesthetic valuation, on the one hand, is immediate, and, on the other hand, is mediated to be critical. All of this immediate appreciation and critical judgment takes place within the processes of engaging things in the world that have goodness in one perspective or another.

The argument plot of this part is like successive waves washing over the beach, each bringing in new material, adding layers of sediment. It is like climbing a hill from many different approaches, each with its special tracks. It is like the five parts of Whitehead's *Process and Reality* that are radically different ways of approaching the same general topic. Although some sections here have the form of a sequential argument, like a mathematical argument, with steps building upon what has been suggested earlier, the overall plot of this part is a deepening of the hypothesis about harmony, form, and goodness by adding new dimensions to what was articulated earlier.

CHAPTER I

Goodness in Experience

Ubiquity, Evolution, and Aesthetic Perception

Anything with form has goodness. At least, this is the hypothesis of which I hope to persuade you in this book. We shall begin with the most abstract considerations in the first part and then treat more concrete kinds of goodness in the parts on beauty and art, obligation and personhood, and flourishing and civilization. Art is an example of goodness as beauty, which is goodness ready for appreciation through special humanly constructed symbolic artifacts. Persons under obligation illustrate goodness as appreciable and ready to be acted upon, defining the actor in relation to goodness. Civilization is the bearer of goodness in relation to human flourishing, and it exemplifies a larger reach of goodness across the cosmos. I shall articulate these abstract declarations from many angles as a complex hypothesis made vulnerable to correction and justified to some extent throughout this book.

You might think that to account for goodness by reference to form is to explain the obscure by the more obscure. What is form? That is an ancient question in the West, beginning with Parmenides, Pythagoras, Plato, and Aristotle. In China, it is even more ancient, with speculations on the hexagrams of the *Yijing*. In South Asia, concern for form is at least as early as the Samkhya philosophy that tried to distinguish the content of consciousness from consciousness itself. A central project of this book is to understand form as one of four transcendental traits of any harmony; I mean "transcendental" in the

7

Western medieval sense of a trait found in everything, not the Kantian sense of "transcendental philosophy" as the study of the conditions for the possibility of knowledge.

The claim that anything with form has goodness is by no means new, as I affirmed earlier. Plato claimed it in his theory that the Form of the Good gives goodness to anything with form. Augustine maintained that all beings are good because of their formed nature, although their goodness might be misplaced or misdirected. The Confucians said that what Heaven imparts to each person is an inner "heart-mind" that includes a capacity to grasp the worth of each thing in its forms or coherences and to respond appropriately; the Confucians debated how to cultivate this heart-mind and what might distort it. The South Asian traditions have a paradoxical history. On the one hand, form as the content of consciousness exhibits goodness that attracts or repels, either way putting a consciousness in bondage; freedom is to detach oneself from the attractions and repulsions of what passes through consciousness. On the other hand, parts of those traditions consider the movement of the universe to be like delightful play, Shiva dancing, Krishna flirting and playing the flute: human fulfillment is to couple with the dance.

Nevertheless, the thesis of this book, that anything with form bears goodness because of its form, is not popular today, as I already confessed. Many reasons exist for this unpopularity. One is the cultural trickle-down of the modern scientific distinction between fact and value. What is knowable, according to that distinction, are only facts, and value or goodness is what we subjectively project onto facts. Another reason, possibly related to the first, is the democratic impulse to say that anyone's value judgments are as good as anyone else's and should be limited only when they cause harm. The thesis that goodness is the result of form runs against the common sense of much of the late modern world.

My thesis here is strongly realistic in the philosophic sense. Its claim is that goodness is resident in things and that we need to discern what it is. The human capacities to discern goodness in things are among the most important results of evolutionary processes and they need constant enhancement through education. Also, among the most important elements of culture are signs for discerning and interpreting what is good. What we notice as good is what we have experiential signs to recognize. What we notice is also a function of our interests and purposes. Nevertheless, the heart of goodness lies in the characters that the forms of things have, my hypothesis says, not in our judgment. Is it not common to think we know what is valuable about something, positive or negative, and then learn that we are mistaken? You cannot be mistaken without there being something about which to be mistaken.

If this goodness-realism thesis is correct, then perceptions of goodness approximately appropriate to the things experienced must pervade the entirety of human experience. The ubiquity of goodness in experience was a hallmark of John Dewey's philosophy. And was he not correct? Before thinking of all the reasons why human interests might be the sole source of goodness, do you not admit that appreciations, negative, positive, and of different kinds, fill your experience? They do mine. I want to insist on this as a naïve, precritical reading of experience and then give a critical justification for the reading.

The main point of this part is the explication and justification of the thesis that having form makes things valuable in ways borne by their forms. In order to make this case, we have to deal with the human recognition of goodness in formed things. My characterization of goodness in things cannot justify itself without appealing to your appreciation of them as something like what I characterize. Therefore, another and intrinsically related project is the investigation of human valuation on the many levels in which valuation takes place. The present project relates systematically to an earlier project, my *Axiology of Thinking* trilogy.[1] That project studied valuation in four families of thinking: imagination, interpretation, theorizing, and the pursuit of responsibility or practical reason. The present book involves some rethinking of those claims.

It is useful to look at some of the diverse ways in which the experiential side focuses on the goodness experienced. The experience of something good is itself a relational harmony brought to focus essentially by the intentionality of the experiencer. As a harmony, the experiencing of something as good is itself something good. At perhaps the most basic level, elementary animal life-forms have mechanisms of moving toward edibles they discriminate as nourishing and away from what they recognize as toxic. Within the limits of mobility, things move away from environments that are too hot or cold and toward those environments that are just right in temperature. "Just right" means what supports the harmony of the various components of the organism. Higher animals perceive greater varieties of things as to nourishment and poison, greater ranges of environmental adaptation; and they possess other instincts for defense against predators and hostile conditions, for the protection of young and other group members, for winning the protection of potential helpers, and so forth. Higher animals move from sheer instinct to the employment of signaling systems for warning their fellows of predators, indicating sources of food and water, and other tools of group life. With the development of signs, semiotic systems come into play that lead into rudimentary cultures. Signaling behavior is somewhat instinctual in a purely biological sense, but also cultural in the sense that young need to see the signals at work to master behavior according to them.

Evolutionary biologists are quick to point out that instincts for what is good and bad for animal life in various contexts develop according to biological adaptability. Those animals that are good at distinguishing nourishing food from toxins are more likely to pass on their genes for doing that instinctively. Evolutionary arguments such as this explain a great deal. Nevertheless, we should be careful to remember that what is being explained is the capacity to discriminate what is good and bad for the animal. The biological behavior being explained is not reproductive success or failure but the instincts to judge and respond appropriately to what is good and bad food, good and bad environmental temperatures, what beasts and conditions to fear, and the rest. These pragmatic considerations of what is good or harmful are relative to the needs of the organisms and animals themselves; different animals need different foods, different temperatures. The goodness, relative to the discerning animal, lies in the chemical composition of the potential food and the degree of warmth or coolness. Valuation of these factors is not a subjective projection of emotional opinion onto pure facts that have no goodness. The fact is the foods and environing conditions are really good or bad for the organism that might be mistaken in its assessments.

As animals develop more complicated kinds of semiotic systems of signals, cultures come to play important roles in the discernment of what is good. Social groups develop complex interactions of instinct and lore about what is valuable. Ants, bees, wolves, herds of antelopes, and primates have complex social behaviors that involve sharing a semiotic system and making sure that the relevant members learn it. Division of labor and articulation of authority structures come to be perceived as valuable, according to the kinds of animals and environments at hand. Whether a yearling should challenge the alpha male is a life-and-death matter of goodness discrimination.

Animals with a complex social life also develop signs within semiotic systems for nonpragmatic goodness. Primates grooming one another might contribute to family solidarity, and thus to evolutionary adaptability, but also it just feels good. Growling out musical sounds might be adaptive, too, but it also heightens the aesthetic appreciation of music. The earliest humans decorated their graves and likely much else. Human tattooing and distinctive hairstyles might have evolutionary goodness in facilitating the identification of boundaries of ingroups. Nevertheless, an aesthetic quality to those markers exists that is pragmatically gratuitous. People admire beautiful tattoos and dress. Primitive human groups need to engage in economic, protective, and domestic behavior in order to survive and they develop cultures that discern what is good for all this. Nevertheless, they also spend a lot of time dancing, drinking intoxicants, and telling stories around the campfire. These celebrations might enhance group solidarity and, hence, are evolutionarily adaptive. Nevertheless, people engage in them for the fun of it. As John Dewey pointed out, although people need to work, they develop work songs to make the tasks more enjoyable. I will quote Dewey on this at length in chapter 6.

In dealing with human life, we need to make complicated distinctions in order to understand the character of real goods as they are experienced. We experience some things as having a kind of goodness because we foreground them against a background and they stand out as objects. We experience other things as valuable in the background when we expand attention. A farmer can be working outside, concentrating on plowing a field, and then suddenly realize what great weather it is that day. The greatness of the weather is a combination of climatic factors that harmonizes beautifully with the combination of biological and personal factors in the farmer's life. The plow and field are foreground elements against the weather background, and then the focus shifts to foreground the weather and the plowing becomes an incidental element in the farmer's attention.

If everything that has form has goodness, then there is a vast intermixing of goods corresponding to the formal relations among things with forms. A person tightly focusing attention on a small thing against the background environment is likely not to notice the goodness in the background. Attention can shift to foreground one thing in the background, and then another thing, and then another. The nature of experiential attention is extremely important for understanding human discernment of goodness. One thing that causes attention to shift is the frustration of our expectations that drive largely unconscious behavior, as Charles S. Peirce pointed out. This is reality saying No to our expectations and causing us to pay attention to why. Another thing that causes shifts in attention is the aesthetic characters of things in the environment. A beautiful scene, or person, or a play in an athletic game, or sunset, or squall, can attract attention that otherwise would be elsewhere. We will reflect on the power of art to focus attention at length in part II.

Developments in the semiotic systems of human cultures give rise to expansions in the forms of things that people can notice as having the value of locating them in their largest imagined environment. A person or social group can have a story, for instance, even a large narrative within mythic or historical time. Early on, human cultures learned to imagine cosmic epochs with symbols that articulated the formal beauty of the cultures, or their tragedy. Now we have the narratives of scientific evolution and astrophysical expansiveness. Metaphysical schemes in various cultures for millennia have called for the interpretation of the human place in the shape of the cosmos.

Within all these culturally diverse ways of articulating the forms and hence the goods of things are biological variations such as between genders, age and developmental variations from early childhood to old age, social class distinctions and social role distinctions in a group. These and a host of other variations affect what parts of the world can come to attention, when, and in relation to what other social and natural interactions according to which specific forms in the worldly environment appear and disappear.

The point of this section is that, even without general agreement on what is good, everywhere anyone looks, from whatever perspective, various foci of attention articulate formal harmonies that are apprehended as having worth of some sort or another. Some of these are pragmatic in the sense of detecting first the instrumental worths of things for the people engaging the world. Others have to do with things that just seem fine or discordant in themselves relatively unhinged to human need. Most things focusing attention combine both extremes and lie between them.

Harmonies Defined, and Ecosystems

The previous section introduced the discussion of goodness mainly from the standpoint of human experience. Concerning the difference between goodness in things and our experiencing the goodness in things, an important distinction needs constantly to be borne in mind. Each thing has its own goodness, however complex, because of the harmony it has; I shall argue in the next two chapters that this complexity is infinite though determinate. An experiencer never appreciates the whole of the thing's goodness, however, only that part of the thing's goodness that the experiencer can interpret; this interpretation is limited by the experiencer's signs and biased by purposes and limited modes of engagement. Therefore, the experiencing relation includes both the experiencer's interpretive orientation on the one hand and the object interpreted on the other; but the object interpreted has elements of its own harmony that are not interpreted.

The object interpreted is partly external to the experiencer. This is the condition for a real pluralism of things. The object interpreted might have all sorts of causal connections with the experiencer over and above being interpreted. Peirce thought that all causal connections have the general form of interpretation; I agree with most of his account of experiential interpretation. Nevertheless, I hold more with Whitehead that temporal process involves the spontaneous achievement of simplification of novelty against an infinite background. That infinite background, not merely the interpreted elements of the background, is the causal environment for the temporal emergence of a harmony. I will spell this out in the next two chapters.

From the standpoint of the experience of the goodness of things, within the Western philosophical tradition especially, the frame of the discussion has to do with discriminating focal forms bearing goodness within a larger environmental background field. Distinguishing field and focus is an important element of experience, relating to changing attention. Nevertheless, a crucial part of the nature of form itself is that it is a pattern harmonizing components. Because a form is itself determinate, it is a harmony with components and a form of its own. Therefore, the nature of form as harmonizing components, rather than as a focus within a field, is also important and is our topic in this section. At this point in our discussion, I am approaching goodness as form in the most abstract way possible. I am not talking here about goodness as form in human experience, or even goodness as form in actual things. Subsequent chapters will develop those topics. Here I mean to lay the theoretical groundwork by discussing forms as harmonies.

Any determinate thing is a harmony. To be determinate is to be a harmony that is what it is, is not nothing, and is not some other thing. In order to be different from some other things, a harmony needs some components that condition it with regard to those other things. I call those "conditional components." Thus, every harmony relates to everything in the cosmos with respect to which it is determinate. Some determinate relations are extremely complex, as I will discuss in this and the next two chapters. Other relations are much simpler, perhaps even indirect. Perhaps the indirection is so great that the things for all practical purposes do not relate at all in any significant way. Some harmonies are determinately indeterminate. For instance, today is somewhat indeterminate as to which of today's future possibilities tomorrow will actualize; this indeterminacy today stems from a determinate relation of today to tomorrow's alternative possibilities. Any determinate harmony relates to any other harmony with respect to which it is determinate. Those relations are internal components of the harmony's identity. Nevertheless, the things to which a determinate harmony relates are partly external to it with their own essential components and conditional relations with other things.

A determinate harmony (that is, any harmony whatsoever) cannot be only its component relations. If it were, it would be nothing but the things to which it is related, which would mean that there would be no relations, only the other things. A harmony needs some "essential components" of its own in order to give it its own-being. It needs essential components in order to have the standing to itself be a term in relations with other things. Therefore, to be determinate a thing must be a harmony of both conditional and essential components. Without conditional components, a thing would not be determinate with respect to anything else. Without essential components, a thing would not integrate the conditional components into being a thing of its own so as to be able to be in a relation with other things. Please bear with this terribly abstract argument about determinateness a bit longer.

Given that a determinate thing is a harmony with multiple components, both conditional and essential, relating it to the other things with respect to which it is determinate, we know four more traits of harmonies. First, a harmony has a multiplicity of components, conditional and essential, that it integrates so that they harmonize together. Second, a harmony has a form or pattern according to which the components harmonize. Third, a harmony has a location in an existential field including all the other harmonies with respect to which it is determinately differentiated. The various conditional components of the related harmonies constitute a field, and the mix of conditional components involved determines its character as a field. I will say more about this shortly. Fourth, a harmony has the goodness, or goodness-identity, of integrating these components with this form in this location in the existential field. This is the basic sense of goodness that I mean to explicate and defend.

This abstract account should be valid for all determinate things whatsoever. Consider, for instance, an actual thing in space-time. Of course, what one means by such an actual thing depends on one's cosmology. Aristotle's substance cosmology would give one kind of account and the ancient Chinese yin/yang cosmology another. The cosmology I develop in this book is much like Alfred North Whitehead's and close also to the cosmologies of Charles S. Peirce and John Dewey, as I explained in *Recovery of the Measure*. According to this cosmology, an actual thing in space-time would have as conditional components all the past things that are its causal conditions, configured in the complex ways that causation takes place across space-time. It would also have conditional components from future possibilities and anticipations. Its essential components would consist in whatever spontaneous or creative supplementations the thing makes in its present moments to integrate the conditions into its new reality or self. If the actual thing has the complex of conditional components sufficient for it to be intentional, its present can be a matter of choosing among alternative possibilities in the future, actualizing some and excluding others from actualization. Understanding goodness in human experience will require a more exact account of this.

Forms as such are determinate, and we can prescind from how they ingress in temporal things to consider what they are in themselves. I need to do this in order to give an account of forms in temporal things. Forms have components to integrate together. These components can be of many types, for instance, relations to temporal actualities for which the form is a possibility. Consider only those components that themselves are purely formal, for instance, the separate elements in an equation or the three lines of a triangle in a plane. The form by which the formal components fit together is the form's form. The existential field of a form is constituted by the other formal elements with respect to which the form is determinate, for instance, $2 + 2 = 4$ is in an existential field with $4 + 4 = 8$ in respect of doubling. The goodness–identity of the form is the goodness achieved by getting these components together in this formal pattern in the existential field. For instance, there is an elegant balance to an equation, $2 + 2 = 4$, and there is an even deeper elegant balance in the harmony that is the existential field of doubles.

Metaphors help to get our heads around such abstract notions. The metaphor of a simple hierarchy is appealing, and I will bring in the metaphor of a more complex hierarchy later. We can say that a given harmony has components that themselves are harmonies with components, whose components are harmonies all the way down. Similarly, the given harmony is itself a component in a higher harmony, or in an existential field that is itself a harmony, on up and up. But, that metaphor is too rigid for connoting the kinds of relations in and around a harmony.

A better metaphor is that a determinate harmony, such as a form as such, is an ecosystem ecosystemically related to other harmonies as ecosystems.[2] The components of a harmony harmonize with the harmony's form in the context of other harmonies with respect to which the harmony is determinate. Like a biological ecosystem, a pond, say, a harmony has just the right components to fit together with the ecology's pattern or form. But the components of the pond are changing. Some changes do not affect the other components or the form of the whole. Other changes make a difference to some components but not others. Some changes are devastating to the form of the pond as a whole, for instance, causing it to dry up. Each of the components of the pond ecology is also an ecology, members of a species of fish, for instance, that require water of a certain temperature, nutrients, hiding places, and so forth. Although it might seem strange to call members of a species an ecology, those members have ecological relations with each other that require larger ecologies. Some ecological conditions are necessary, such as those just mentioned, while others are adventitious, such as the presence of other species of fish that need to be taken into account in sharing the pond but that the first species can do without.

The pond itself is a component in many larger ecologies, such as a landscape in which it receives runoff water and in turn drains into a stream; perhaps the pond is a component in the ecology of a farm, with its water used for cattle and irrigation. The pond is determinate with regard to the land along its banks, and its inlet and outlet streams. Those are all ecologies that relate to the pond in mutually conditioning ways. In tracing out the causal patterns of those various conditionings, one needs to look at how the components play roles in the ecologies at hand. Thus the notion of ecology is not limited to biological things but to any things in relation that have systematic connections like biological systematic connections.

The form of an ecology contains other forms as ecologies as components, relates indirectly to forms as ecologies, and itself plays component roles in other ecologies. Thus, the ways by which a determinate form contains components are not just those of the hierarchies of components within component within components. Nor should we construe the ways of conditioning mainly as straight-line causation with earlier conditioning later conditioning still later components of an overarching harmony. Rather, the form of a harmony is like ecological systems conditioning systems conditioning systems. A change in one place might resonate throughout many different systems, having effects of different sorts depending on the form of the various ecosystems through which it resonates.

Now the metaphor of an ecosystem is biological and therefore involves spatiotemporal changes. The reference to changes does not apply directly to the form of a form itself, only to form that has spatiotemporal changes as some of its components. The metaphor applies to the form of form as such, however, by asking what difference a formal component makes in the various formal ecologies in which it plays formal roles. The form of a formal harmony contains systems within systems within systems and itself is a formal component in other formal systems. Chapter 2 will elaborate this in detail.

Situations, Perspectives, and Sunsets

Consider a beautiful sunset. Sometimes people say that the beauty is in the eye of the beholder. For these people, the sunset itself is just a set of meteorological facts. This observation reflects an unfortunate philosophical dualism between objective facts and minds. Rather, the sunset is beautiful in a situation that includes not only the clouds and light but also potential viewers with a capacity for vision of a certain sort located at a certain angle to the clouds and light. This situation is itself a harmony with meteorological, visioning, placement, and other components. The sunset would not be seen as beautiful, or even as a "sunset," without the other components of the situation. Nevertheless, given the other components, the form of the meteorological components is what makes the sunset beautiful. If the clouds were so thick as to block out all light, or if there were no clouds to reflect the light, there would be no beautiful sunset no matter who was looking and from what angle. This is what I mean by the realistic claim in my hypothesis that goodness is resident in form: that the beauty is in the form of the sunset, not only in the viewer or in the viewer's position relative to the meteorological elements. The reference within the situation is to the sunset. However, if by contrast the reference within the situation were to the aesthetic and other emotional pleasure the viewer might have, the question would be whether the viewer has the right kind of visual apparatus and is in the right place with the right angle on the sun and clouds. All reference is internal to a situation, which is itself a determinate harmony.

The cosmos is a great maelstrom of harmonies, ecosystemically relating to one another through resonating changes. One subset of harmonies within the cosmos is what I, following Whitehead, call a "situation." John Dewey used the notion of situation in much the same way. I define a situation as a certain harmony of harmonies that takes the essential components of its form from the *perspective* of one or several of the situation's components. That perspective determines the scope of harmonies to be included within the situation. The components of the situation, of course, are involved in many harmonic relations beyond the situation. However, as components within the situation, their main relevance to the perspective defining the situation is the roles they play in the form of the situation as a harmony. The situation of the beautiful sunset includes the meteorological conditions, the potential viewers with their visual capacities, their location and angle of vision, and a host of other harmonies that connect them.

Whitehead almost held to this naturalistic view. For him, the sunset situation would be a nexus of causal occasions beginning with the meteorological events that subsequent occasions prehend in a causal chain to the viewers who see colors, shapes, and movements of clouds. The resulting internal experience of the viewers is the only place where the sunset is beautiful. In this account, the sunset as object is located only in the subjectivity of the viewing occasions, not in the nexus or situation as a whole. My theory is that the situation itself is a harmony with the integrity of its own form that integrates the whole nexus so that the meteorological events are beautiful from the standpoint of the viewers. The beauty is in the whole situation, not merely in the vision of the viewers. Whereas Whitehead can be interpreted as holding that the meteorological events pass away and have no subsequent reality except in the vision of the viewers, I say that situational connections taking time, perhaps with a significant duration, have a temporal reality of their own that does not reduce to the last moment. The situation has a significant temporal thickness. Whitehead was not sufficiently emancipated from the Kantian transcendental point of view.

The perspective of the potential viewer essentially defines the situation of the beautiful sunset. That the perspective of the meteorological elements defines any special situation with respect to the viewer or the place of vantage is doubtful. Within the situation, the viewer's perspective might focus reference on the sunset consisting of light, clouds, wind, and so forth, and we say that the sunset is beautiful. In the same situation, the perspective of the viewer might focus reference on the viewer's enjoyment of the sunset. The relevant perspective might be a group of viewers gathered to watch the sunset. The situation might have a more complex perspective than simply viewing the sunset. In my family, we like sunset viewing so much that we have constructed a masonry sunset terrace on the west side of our house. We have deepened the situation to include habits of watching the sunset whenever the weather is right and our schedule permits. We make it the time of day when we relax with beverages and talk to neighbors as they walk by. The situation of our sunset watching includes part of our neighborhood socializing. The perspectives of some of our neighbors define a new situation for them that includes walking by our sunset terrace.

Many different kinds of things can provide perspectives that define a situation. From the perspective of Americans, the situation of balance of trade between America and other nations has to do with America's import-export ratio. From the perspective of the Chinese, there is a similar economic situation, except that the Chinese import-export ratio is what is important. From the perspective of people cultured in the visual and sculptural arts, the situation of museum going is an important part of life; from the standpoint of people uncultured in those ways, no situation exists in which museum going is important. Nevertheless, the power of good art is such that a chance encounter with it might cause them to look for situations in which they visit museums.

In a situation, the perspective provides essential components delimiting the harmony of the situation, marking what is or might be relevant. A perspective might allow of many different foci of attention, as the sunset watcher might focus on the sunset itself, or on personal enjoyment of the sunset, or on both, or on the constructed components in the situation of the architectural terrace and the social habits of regular watching. We need to understand many things that condition the focus of attention if we are to unpack the notion mentioned earlier about how the goodness of something is apprehended as a focal point against a background field. One thing that focuses attention is reality frustrating our expectations. Another thing that focuses our attention is the pursuit of our own purposes, where we need to attend first to this and then to that. Yet a third component of attention focus is the aesthetic appeal of a form whose beauty or goodness draws attention. Sunsets can command our attention by their beauty. Because of the attractiveness of regularizing the pleasure of enjoying beautiful sunsets, we then can shift attention to the building of sunset-viewing places and working that activity into the routines of life. All these components of attention focus are important to bear in mind.

Where in a situation is the goodness? According to my hypothesis, every harmony in the situation is the achievement of the goodness of getting its components together with its form in that existential location relative to other things within and without the situation. In this general sense, any harmony of meteorological conditions situated west of a vantage point with capable viewers is the achievement of its own goodness, harmonizing its components just so. A different kind of goodness is achieved by a totally fogged in sky and another of a cloudless sky, different from the conditions of light and clouds we name a beautiful sunset relative to the vantage point. There is also the intrinsic goodness achieved in the harmony of the viewers at the vantage point. The good achieved in the form of any harmony also affects the goods of the other things that harmony conditions. The goodness achieved by total fog is not likely to incite the interest of anyone at the vantage point, and its contribution to the viewers is minimal. A cloudless sky might incite a bit more interest, but the viewers would not call their friends to watch. The meteorological condition of the sunset, however, enters into the viewers as an important component of their pleasure and attention. Given the conditions for viewing sunsets, including the right clouds and light, the harmony of the situation as a whole is such that the goodness in the sunset carries over through myriads of intervening ecosystems of harmony into the viewers and their friends. Indirectly, this appreciation of the sunset influences the architecture of their garden, their habits of social life, and the quality of life in the neighborhood.

Is the sunset beautiful even if nobody is in a position to notice? The sunset in that circumstance would not be enjoyed by anyone. Nevertheless, in contrast to too thick a cloudbank or no clouds at all, the meteorological conditions are right for having a beautiful sunset. Therefore, we should say it is a beautiful sunset and not a fogbank or a cloudless sky, though the fog and clear sky might have their own kinds of beauty. This is the sense in which the goodness is resident in the form of the harmony to which reference is made, namely, the meteorological events as seen. If the vantage point of that situation were missing, then we would say that there is no situation for beautiful sunsets despite the right meteorological conditions. But there would be a situation for beautiful sunsets if the meteorological conditions and vantage point were present such that a viewer would be able to see the sunset if the viewer were there. If no viewer were there, we still would say there is a beautiful sunset that could be seen if someone were in the right place. There is a beautiful sunset but no one sees or appreciates it. The beautiful sunset is subjunctive, as it were. It is what would be appreciated if there were someone there to see it. My wife and I often rush to see a sunset before it is over. The subjunctive character of beauty, or just about any kind of goodness, is true for all kinds of appreciation. The beautiful paintings in a museum do not suddenly become nonbeautiful when the janitor turns the lights out for the night. Without the viewer, the ecology of the situation might have all the right component harmonies for carrying across the visual materials to the viewing place. Lacking those crucial carryover components, the situation is not one for beautiful sunsets. Given those components, the sunset *is* beautiful and its beauty would be seen *if* the situation were to include viewers at the right place. Because we can think about how harmonies would be different if they had different components or different forms integrating the components, we can imagine subjunctive situations: what the situations would be if they were a little different. So we can think of sunsets that are beautiful and would be appreciated as such if the right viewers were in the right place. To ask whether a sunset is beautiful if there is no one to see it is to suppose that someone could be there to see it. As far as the sunset goes, it is what it is whether or not it is viewed, and so it is appropriate to call it beautiful. We imagine the situation as if it includes the viewer.

Goodness Experienced

I have introduced so many abstract ideas, and illustrated them so complexly, that you must be frustrated and confused. The moral in that is that you should be frustrated and confused because goodness in experience is frustrating in its vulnerability to mistaken appreciation and confusing in the ways that goods play within each other's ecologies. I have proposed several things in this chapter for understanding our common sense that goodness is ubiquitous in our experience and it is time to summarize them, noting that they still need much further explication. Here are the proposals.

First is that this commonsense appreciation of all things as having goodness of some sort can receive a philosophical explication and justification. In fact, I have already introduced several of the important hypotheses for that explication, although the theory is by no means complete. The experience of things as good is extraordinarily complex. Skeptics can easily refute the simple explanations of goodness in experience. When we recognize the complexity of the experience of things as good, I hope to persuade you that we are justified to take that experience at face value.

Second is the observation, based on the initial pass at explaining how to have form is to have goodness, that things such as good things and the experiencers of them are themselves harmonic ecosystems of components relating to other ecosystems in ways that connect the good things with the experience of them as good. Rarely is there a straight-line causation from the good object to the valuational experience of it. The causation moves through many mediating ecosystemic harmonies. Each of those mediating harmonies is subject to systematic conditioning by elements from outside the scope of harmonies within the situation of experiencing the thing as good. Changes in those mediating systematic harmonies resonate throughout those systems, sometimes affecting how the systems condition one another.

Third is the point that the experience of goodness always supposes a situation linking the thing valued as a kind of harmony, such as a sunset, with the experiencer who values it. Because everything in the cosmos relates to everything else with respect to which it is determinate, to indicate the peculiar kinds of harmonic relations that involve the experience of things as good is important. The peculiar kind of harmony that includes among its components both the good thing and the experiential appreciator I dub a situation. The situation's components include all the ecosystemic harmonies linking object and experiencer.

Fourth is that the form of the situation is determined in its main essential components by the perspective of the experiencer. That perspective on the experienced object determines much of the scope of the situation, indicating what other harmonies are relevant to mediate that experience of the object and what harmonies are not so relevant, although they still might condition the relevant harmonies.

Fifth is that within a situation of experiencing something as good, attention focuses on the object as experienced, or on the experience of it, or on any number of other components within the situation. Moreover, attention can focus on the whole situation as such from the perspective of the experiencer within it.

Sixth is that we have discovered two senses in which an object can be a foreground focal point against a background. One is that something within a situation can be the focus of attention with the rest of the situation as highly relevant background. The second is that the rest of the cosmos outside the harmonies within the scope of the situation is a less relevant background. The elements in the extra-situational groups of harmonies have varying degrees of relevance to the experience. Moreover, as we say, situations change. The extra-situational background elements might become decisive for situational component harmonies, and might join them.

Seventh is that we now have good reason to reject and abandon the dualistic thinking that says experience is contained within the experiencer, in the mind or brain. Dualists say that there is a material, perhaps mechanistic, chain of causes from the meteorological elements across the land and atmosphere to the eyes and optical nervous system of the experiencer on the sunset terrace, who somehow turns that into a mental vision of the sunset. Consistent dualists will keep this turning a mystery. Mechanists will try to reduce the mental vision to neurological elements. We can reject all this. The experience is the whole situation from sunset to the experiencer. The experience is not within the head of the experiencer but rather within the complex of systematic interactions of the harmonies in the situation. The meteorological elements are as much part of the experience as the eyes and habits of seeing shapes and colors. The experiencer does not "contain" the experience in isolation but rather takes into the experiencer's own harmony the real other things that enter as conditioning components. This has been the lesson of American philosophy beginning with Emerson, who thought that to see something is to expand the self to include the thing seen. Dewey said that experience is a transaction between an experiencer and the things experienced, not a property of the experiencer. No neurological examination of the brain can explain experience until we include and understand the connections of the brain with the meteorological conditions that account for the enjoyment of the sunset, as well as the cultural components of the viewers interpreting the meteorological conditions as a sunset.

Eighth is that, although I have not yet shown that form as such is good, the discussion has shown that all things in a situation of the experience of things as having goodness have form; any form is a harmony. A form harmonizes its components in a pattern; some of its components come from the other things with respect to which the form is determinate, with the result that there is an existential field constituted by the ways things condition one another and each form or harmony has a location within that field. The hypothesis that form bears goodness can be expressed by saying that a harmony is good as the result of getting its components harmonized with its form or pattern in its location in the existential field.

Ninth is the beginning of an analysis of form as harmony. The most abstract thing that we can say of anything and everything is that to be a thing is to be determinate. Something determinate relates to the other things with respect to which it is determinate, and those relations are its conditional components. A determinate thing also has essential components that integrate themselves with the conditional components so that the thing has its own being. As an integration of components, a determinate thing is a harmony and, as such, a harmony has its form, its components formed, its existential location, and its goodness-identity.

Tenth is that the form of a harmony is itself determinate and so we can analyze it in terms of its own form, components, existential location, and goodness. Much of chapter 2 will be devoted to this metaphysical level of analysis. In the present chapter, however, the focus has been on the human experience of things as valuable, and so we have been concerned with forms in things that we can experience as having goodness and with forms in the experiencing of them, and in the forms of the situation of experiencing and in the other harmonies within the situation.

Eleventh is that when a thing such as a sunset or sunset watcher comes to be, it can be said to be or achieve the harmony that is itself. You and I can become sunset watchers. If that harmony has goodness, as my hypothesis supposes, then each temporal harmony is an achievement of goodness in itself. Because those harmonies condition other harmonies, including each other in various ways, we can distinguish intrinsic goodness from conditioning goodness. The meteorological conditions of the sunset have their own intrinsic goodness. In addition, they condition the experiencer so as to be beautiful to the experiencer. The experiencer then can achieve the intrinsic goodness of great pleasure and aesthetic depth in sunset watching. Taking time out for sunset watching, however, might cause us to neglect a greater good, therefore making the sunset leisure a bad thing for the other good. As nature's history has evolved at least for human beings, situations have developed for allowing human beings to experience a blessed array of the great goodness of things. That evolution itself is a great good for human beings.

Twelfth is that in a situation two senses of goodness exist: the intrinsic goodness achieved in a harmony by getting its components together in its existential location with its form and the goodness that it has when it is a component in other harmonies, resonating through ecosystems of harmonies of harmonies. In a situation in which a beau-

tiful sunset is experienced, the sunset itself—as a harmony of meteorological components, and so forth—is intrinsically beautiful, and that
intrinsic beauty must precede the appreciation of the sunset's beauty
in the experience of a viewer.

Thirteenth is a reminder that a thing experienced has a harmony
of its own and that the experience of it interprets only certain aspects
of that harmony, only certain aspects of its goodness. You know your
friends in only certain aspects of their lives. Furthermore, the experience of a thing, because it is a harmony in which the thing is one pole
in a complex relation, involves the thing functioning as a component
in a harmony beyond itself. The meteorological events in a sunset are
enhanced in goodness by being in relation to sunset viewers so that
a situation of sunset viewing is created.

Having exhibited some of the confusing complexity of goodness
in form, I now turn to giving a more theoretical account.

Chapter 2

A Metaphysics of Form as Goodness

Density of Being and Existential Fields

The line of analysis I shall develop here extends the tradition that identifies goodness with density of being. The phrase, "density of being," comes from Leibniz who interpreted it with his new theory of infinitesimals. However, the idea goes back to Plato for whom the greater reality has greater goodness. For Plato, "being" had two meanings. On the one hand, it meant that which is what it is and does not change; he contrasted it with "becoming," in which he was chiefly interested. (Contrary to the depiction in Raphael's fresco *The School of Athens*, Plato was interested in ideas and theories for the sake of guiding the life of becoming, whereas Aristotle was interested in stabilizing the processes of life to be able to contemplate eternal truths in peace.)[1] In Plato's first meaning, being refers to the static forms by which changes in becoming pass, are recognized, and measured. This is not a major theme in my account of being. On the other hand, by "being" Plato also meant the power to make a difference. In this second usage, which he developed in the *Sophist*, things within time make a difference to one another and have being both in themselves and in the things they affect. This is very much a major theme in my account.

The density of being notion means something like getting more being in a harmonic unit than it might otherwise have. Plato and his tradition interpreted this in an aesthetic way. Plato in the *Philebus* said that the Good as cause of mixture is that which balances out the limited and the unlimited, creating finite beings. In that context he said that the Good is something like balance, measure, due proportion, as I noted earlier. He appealed to an aesthetic sense for getting it just right, or for telling when the balance is off. Aristotle did not pick up this Platonic theme except in matters of morals when the goal is to find the Golden Mean between extremes. For Aristotle, rather, reality consists of substances, and goodness is the fulfilling of the final causes of substances. Aristotle's tradition of goodness-theory has to do with the completion or perfection of things. In my account, the interest in perfection or self-realization is a subset of considerations about goodness, though important in its place.

The language about goodness here comes from Western philosophy. Nevertheless, strong parallels exist in both Confucianism and Daoism that appeal to Platonic-like aesthetic sensibilities. The same thing is true of South Asian traditions that emphasize the metaphor of dance.

In my own account, harmonies are loci of goodness in the existential fields within which they come to be. Each harmony has a density of a kind particular to itself. Because a harmony has conditional components from other things in the fields in which it is located, it relates internally and intrinsically to those other things. A harmony is always itself, with its own form according to which its components are integrated. Internal to itself, however, are its relations with other things that contribute conditional components.

The components of a harmony each have their own densities, and those densities register in the containing harmony. This is true for the densities of the components of the components all the way down and around. The densities (or goods) are what they are as the achievement of the component harmony. Yet, the *way* they register in the other harmonies in which they are components depends on the essential components of the other harmonies they condition. They can have greater or lesser importance depending on how the other harmonies integrate them with their other components.

The density of a harmony also plays roles in other harmonies that it conditions. However those harmonies take it up and value it, it affects further harmonies conditioned by its conditioning. An existential field consists of many loci of density or goodness (as I shall argue) in all sorts of conditioning relations. Each harmony is an ecology of harmonies, conditioned by and conditioning ecologies of harmonies. The density of being thus is lumpy across an existential field, with each harmony having its own density of being or goodness, and each also conditioning others, contributing to the others' densities, on and on.

In the discussion so far, it has been appropriate to speak most often as if there is only one existential field for the cosmos and, in a strict sense, this is correct. Insofar as anything is determinate with respect to anything else, it is in an existential field with the other thing, a field constituted by the conditional components anything receives from or contributes to another. This is so whether the other things are directly or indirectly related; earlier, later, or simultaneous in time; of a physical order in some scientifically defined sense or of a social or political order; or whether they are different melodies in a complex musical composition; or the intermix of characters and locales in a novel. In this sense, a singular existential field exists for the whole cosmos, however changing in its temporal dynamics. Nevertheless, it is not necessary that there be a unity or harmony of the singular existential field, only some unities here and other unities there. There are no component essential features turning the singular cosmic existential field into a harmony itself. The cosmos seems to be filled with pockets of dense order loosely connected by minimal cross-conditioning. Only some portions of the singular existential field have harmonic unities.

Therefore, to speak of a plurality of delimited existential fields with harmonies that indicate their scope is appropriate. We have already encountered one kind of delimited existential field, that of a situation in which a person perceives an object, such as a sunset. In a situation, the perspective of the perceiver determines the form of its harmony. But, the imaginative world of a novel is also a delimited existential field of its own, united by the form of the harmony of the novel as a whole. Even if the novel is not very good, it has the imaginative existential field of beginning and ending with some kind of development in between. Some characters might be poorly developed, the plot might have outrageous gaps, the setting might be vacuous, and yet there is some harmony there, albeit with a low density of being or goodness. To the extent the characters are brilliantly developed, the plot thick and surprising, and the setting a sharp evocation of a world, the novel has high density of being as a whole, albeit with a lumpy set of internal components, each with its own density of being or goodness. The delimited existential field of the novel, of course, relates to things outside of it by virtue, for instance, of being the product of the author who has a family, lives somewhere, and so forth. The later parts of this book, on art, persons, and civilization, will develop a much more complicated array of distinguishable delimited existential fields.

A delimited existential field has a harmony of its own with a form that unifies the components of the field. This form exists within two kinds of perspective, as I have mentioned before.

In a static thing, the first kind of perspective is simply the actualization of the harmony itself, its self-satisfaction, as Whitehead would say. In a more dynamic temporal thing, such as the performance of a musical symphony, the harmony of the whole is in the growing perspective of the parts coming together in time, with anticipations early for the later harmony of the whole. The harmony itself constitutes this first kind of perspective.

The second kind of perspective is that of a harmony within the existential field that takes in the harmony of the existential field as a condition of or within its own harmony. A human perceiver can take in the harmony of sunset watching as well as the harmony of the sunset and the harmony of his or her own enjoyment of the sunset. Human beings generally parse the environment in which they live as situations of various sorts defined by the nature and interests of their personal perspectives. Most adults need to make a living or be part of a living arrangement where some people make a living for the group. Thus, an economic situation exists consisting in part of the various jobs and talents available, placed within a larger economic setting. An educational situation for raising children in the neighborhood exists, set within a larger educational situation. A governance situation exists for a town, a larger one for a nation, and a larger global situation defined differently by different political bodies and actors. Human individuals and groups are not the only kinds of perspective that define situations. Corn growing in southern Wisconsin defines a situation of conditions for success, including soil with nutrients, water in a range of amounts, numbers of days of sun, and so forth. A similar breed of corn growing in Asia or Africa might have similar situations, but the growing situation for corn in Wisconsin is relatively independent of the situations for corn elsewhere. Each of these kinds of situations, and countless others, has a kind of harmonic unifying form that determines the scope of relevant components in the existential field it delimits, a form containing components of perhaps many different kinds of density.

Is there a harmony of the singular existential field of the cosmos containing everything determinate in all respects in which things are determinate with respect to one another? As mentioned earlier, I think not. For such a harmony to be determinate, it would have to be determinate with respect to something outside itself from which it receives conditioning components. Then, it is not itself the harmony integrating everything. Therefore, no perspective exists of totalization achieving a harmony of the whole. There is no totality, only everything determinately related to something else, a cosmos of pockets of order, with lumpy density. We ourselves can think of the existential field of the entire cosmos by using philosophical symbols or concepts, as in this argument here. Religious people signify "everything" in an astonishing array of different ways. Many philosophers and theologians of different traditions emphasize unity or oneness and attribute a totality label or oneness to the cosmos. However, this is misleading insofar as the cosmos consists of determinate things conditioning one another. I suspect it is far better to refer to everything in the cosmos in the traditional Chinese way: the Ten Thousand Things. Only delimited existential fields within the larger singular field have harmonies of their own.

That the cosmos is not a total harmony does not mean that there is no sense in which the cosmos is singular. Because the last word is that the cosmos is a plurality in which things are determinate only through mutually conditioning and being conditioned by other things, we have to ask about the context in which things ultimately are together. They are together in the existential field, but this is a function only of their conditional components, not of their essential ones. I have argued extensively in *Ultimates*, part III, that the existence (in all the different senses of existence) of the plural cosmos is the result or terminus of a nontemporal and nonspatial ontological creative act. This act is sheerly productive, creating totally novel determinate things; the act has no determinate character of its own save for what it creates. The act has no possibilities, potentialities, or nature prior to the creating. This is not the place to elaborate this argument, although it will be important for the analysis of art in part II.

This section has developed the metaphor that goodness is density of being according to which goodness is in the form of a harmony that packs in harmonies. The more harmonies packed into a harmony, the better, and the more elegantly they are packed in, better yet. There is no goodness of the cosmos as a whole because there is no harmony of the cosmos as a whole. Now is the time to unpack the claim that form in harmony contains harmonies so as to show how being can be dense.

Quantity, Complexity, Simplicity, and Elegance

In order to see how forms have density of being, imagine a universe with five things in it, A, B, C, D, and E. Forget for a moment that each of these is a harmony with many components that themselves have components and so forth. Forget also that among these components are those that make the five things determinate with respect to one another, and just consider that they are five things, five harmonies. These five together, with minimal distinction and conjunction, constitute a kind of baseline form that has the goodness of having these five together. Suppose now we have a form that combines A and B to get F, and C and D to get G. This two-level form has the density of being and goodness of getting A, B, C, D, E, F, and G together with F and G being on a higher level in a hierarchy. A three-level form could combine F and G with E on the third level to form H, and so forth. In this form, E functions on the first and third levels but not the second.

How the baseline reality of the five things is supplemented by the addition of their combinations that add new harmonies is apparent. In the hierarchy, the form has the goodness of getting not only the baseline things but also their various combinations together. The more the original things combine to produce new things, the greater density of being and goodness the form has. Of course, this example is extremely simplified. The five things have their own forms and might not be able to combine in the ways suggested. Things on the baseline level might have to be transformed somewhat to combine on higher levels. Indeed, the hierarchy might require the elimination of the baseline things in their pure baseline form so that they remain in the formal hierarchy only on higher levels and as modified. A formal hierarchy of levels is likely to be much more complicated than the model here suggests. Nevertheless, this model indicates, on a first pass, how form integrates elements to produce new kinds of components; those forms that integrate more components produce harmonies with greater density of being and greater goodness.

To take a second pass at understanding form as goodness and density of being, consider complexity and simplicity. For the sake of argument, I take complexity here to mean the different kinds of things to be included within the form—the more kinds of things, the more complex the form. The baseline form has the complexity of A + B + C + D + E, mere conjunction, however that fits together. None of the things combine to produce a new thing that has the baseline things within it. This would be like a Whiteheadian actual occasion that has only initial data and no combination; Whitehead called that conjunction a function of mere "subjective unity," with no subjective harmony that adds something to the initial data. He would say that such a form could not be actual.[2]

Simplicity, in my usage, is when the components of a form are the same. This is interesting when the form has a hierarchy in which a higher level contains elements from the direct lower levels pretty much unchanged. In the preceding example, A and B combine on the second level of the formal hierarchy to become F. Assuming A and B do not have to change to be combined in F, they function on both levels. F contains A and B. We can represent it as F (A, B). In the previous example, H on the third level contains F and G, so that within H there are A and B as on the first level and A and B as on the second level. The hierarchy is thus simple with regard to having A and B homogeneous on three levels. Homogeneity obtains to the extent that a form has a unity of traits existing on several levels. Pure homogeneity or simplicity would be the case if a form had only one trait through its whole hierarchy, which would be impossible because such a trait could not be determinate unless it were with something else with respect to which it would be determinate. Thinkers such as Thomas Aquinas have argued that God, being simple, cannot be determinate, cannot have internal complexity, and cannot enter into relations with things outside the divine simple substance.

Any form must have both complexity and simplicity. Without simplicity, there could not be more than a baseline level. I said that the baseline was the mere conjunction of A, B, C, D, and E. Nevertheless, there is a difference between those things not conjoined and those things conjoined, and the latter is already the building of a second level. Each of those things is within the harmony as not conjoined and also as conjoined, which is to say that the idea of a baseline of only those things is impossible, though I prompted you to imagine it. To be within the form at all, the baseline things must have their conjunction added to them.

Without complexity, on the other hand, there would be pure simplicity or homogeneity, which would not be determinate. Therefore, any form has both complexity and simplicity. The goodness of the form is measured by its particular way of balancing complexity and simplicity. The form of the form is the pattern by which complexity and simplicity are integrated. There may be many ways of expressing both, some perhaps emphasizing complexity and others emphasizing simplicity, some emphasizing complexity here and simplicity there, and so on.

The density of being or goodness in a form is greater when both complexity and simplicity are optimized. Yet, there are many ways of optimizing complexity and simplicity. The higher levels in a formal hierarchy can differ radically in how they integrate the lower levels into themselves. Bach, Beethoven, and Brahms have the same notes and rather much the same conventions of harmony, but they have radically different forms of music. The optimizing of complexity and simplicity I call "elegance." Music in a sense is noise with syntax, and Bach, Beethoven, and Brahms are all extremely elegant with their music, though in different ways.

"Elegance" is an explicitly aesthetic category. It denotes things fitting together just right and there can be many "just right" ways of fitting the same things together. Plato's balance, measure, and proportion are ways of characterizing elegance. "Elegance" also connotes the appreciation of the elegant balance of complexity and simplicity, as when mathematicians prefer the more elegant proofs even when all the proofs are logically valid. Here I mean to call attention to what is appreciated when something is called elegant. It is the appreciation of the particular ways in which a form, relative to its alternatives, integrates its components with an optimization of complexity and simplicity.

Whitehead pointed out that there is a particular way to achieve elegance, and that is through contrast.[3] Contrast exists when two or more pyramids in a formal hierarchy develop with structures that each have their own character as different from the other and yet that harmonize together. The harmony of the different structures at a higher level is the contrast, the togetherness of radically different things. Imagine a form with A, B, and C organizing themselves at many levels, maintaining their complex diversity but achieving depth of simplicity or homogeneity. On the other hand, imagine that D and E organize themselves at many levels, also maintaining their diverse complexity and deep simplicity. The form that harmonizes both of these two deep structures is a contrast, with the contrast being greater the greater the differences between the two organizations internal to the form. Density of being, or goodness, is greater the more the organization of the form on many levels exhibits contrast, indeed contrasts within contrast. Any form is a hierarchy of patterns by which elements combine to produce new elements. A form has greater structure to the extent its hierarchy exhibits contrasts that draw deeply articulated characters into harmony with one another.

I asked you at the beginning of this section to prescind from the fact that the baseline elements in a form are themselves forms with components that have components, and so forth. Now bring that fact back into consideration. A, B, C, D, and E themselves are all harmonies whose forms have components that are formal harmonies, whose own components have their own components, and so on. The cosmos exhibits relatedness in terms of the hierarchies within forms as such. This calls for a new level of analysis of goodness or density of being.

Narrowness, Width, Vagueness, and Triviality

How does a form order the various trajectories of components within components? I follow Whitehead in analyzing this in terms of narrowness, width, vagueness, and triviality.[4] The perspective of analysis here is that of a harmony composing its components, especially though not exclusively conditional components with their components, and so on, reaching out through the existential field in which the harmony is located. The question is to understand how the structure of a harmony makes some of its components important or highly valued, and others of its components less important. Triviality, vagueness, narrowness, and width are types of functions of components within a harmony, and there are degrees and middle grounds among them.

Triviality is the function of a component that makes no difference, or hardly any, to the harmony. For instance, in the sunset in the western sky, light presumably from the planet Jupiter causally affects what we see. However, for all practical purposes, that light makes no difference discernable by our eyes or current instruments to how the sunset looks from our viewing position. Surely, the light from the third planet out from Alpha Centauri is trivial if Jupiter's is not. To take another example, consider the form of the future as contemplated by Aristotle's admirals debating whether to enter into a sea battle the next day. The light from distant planets would be trivial to the admirals except perhaps for whether the future allows for navigating by them. For most of the forms of harmony that we name and discuss, although they relate to components if they are in any way determinate with respect to them, most of those components are trivial and need not be taken into account in analyzing the form of the harmony.

Vagueness is the function of a harmony's components that comprise within them many other components that the harmony's form does not distinguish. Its form transmutes them, to use Whitehead's term, into just the vague component within its own form. For instance, the sky consists of zillions of events of light reflecting off particulate matter, but in the form of our vision, we see the sky as blue. Blue, in our visual experience, vaguely presents the sky to us. The sunset is more complex. The colors seen themselves vaguely contain as their own components a vast array of meteorological events, which we do not see. However, in the sunset, the contrast between the light and dark blues, the crimsons, scarlets, and purples are vague ways of containing the meteorological events. Shapes that are constantly shifting as the sun sets relative to our viewpoint and as winds move the clouds contour the colors we see. If we are paying attention to the harmony of the moving sunset, the color components vaguely contain the meteorological events but harmonize among themselves with narrowness and width. In the sea battle example, the form of the future contemplated by the admirals includes the numbers and types of the enemy's ships and their own but is vague with respect to the precise forests from which the ships' timbers were hewn. The admirals contemplate the winds, tides, and weather for the morrow, but they take those nautical calculations to be vague about the exact meteorological events that might take place.

Narrowness is the function of components to provide high-level contrast in forms of harmony. It results from structures that emphasize depth and simplicity. Contrast consists in the harmonic togetherness of parts that are radically different from one another, such as the silhouette of a building contrasted with another building or a bright sky. Narrowness in the form of a sunset consists in the different colors changing place with one another and changing hue. Narrowness in the form of the future contemplated by the admirals consists most obviously in the choice of whether to fight. That future also has narrow components in the future conditions of tide and wind, relative strength of the fleets, and anticipations of the enemy's strategies. The overall future debated by the admirals contains many points of narrow focus. One of their chief concerns is whether their categories of analysis can pick out the genuinely important narrow turning points. The future might contain, unbeknownst to them, an earthquake that will produce a tsunami that suddenly annihilates both fleets. The narrow components in a form are the decisive things that make a huge difference to the form.

Width is the function of components that bring together a wide array of components with narrowness and vagueness. A sunset at a moment might have extraordinary narrow beauty. Over time, that configuration changes, and wide components allow for continuity of change of colors, shapes, and so forth. A sunset is always in a situation relative to a potential viewer, and there might be components of the sunset that connect the beauty in the sky with the awe and pleasure

in the viewer. The future for the admirals worrying about the morrow
has width-giving components connecting many things that they should
take into account, some beyond their ken, such as the future shift in
tectonic plates. Surely the admirals know, however, to think about the
politics behind the war of which the battle is part, the geography of
the sea and coastline that offers alternative positions for the ships, the
likely thinking of the admirals on the other side, the readiness of the
fighting men and sailors on both sides, and many other things. The
implicit agenda of a meeting to plan about a battle is very wide in
its inclusion of many different kinds of factors. The real future for the
admirals has special width in that there are alternative forms within the
future that contradict one another, any of which they can actualize by
their choices and orders to their commanders. Commanding a battle
requires exquisite attention to the shifting widths of elements in the
future as it comes to actualization, moment by moment.

The form of a harmony thus has both a focus and a field. The
components in the form that give narrowness and width provide the
focus. Those that give triviality and vagueness provide the field. The
form of a harmony grades all of its components as to their functions
as trivial, vague, narrow, or wide. The form of a dynamic thing, such
as a group of admirals deciding whether to attack the enemy tomorrow, continually shifts its grading of the components of the future. Of
course, as the morrow approaches, its form itself is shifting in terms
of what is important about the outcome.

Each of the components of a harmony is itself a harmony, with a
form that contains its components functioning as trivial, vague, narrow,
and wide. Each of the components of the components is also such
a harmony. The form of a harmony achieves great narrowness when
that narrow structure comes from a component that contains itself as
a component, and so on down reinforcing simplicity and homogeneity. Great width comes in the form of a harmony when it contains a
broad structure with a complexity of different kinds of components,
and such width in some of the components of the components, and so
on down, reinforcing differences among the things joined. Narrowness
comes in contrasting simplicities, and width in connected differences
in complexity. A form is more or less elegant depending on the optimization of complexity and simplicity, or width and narrowness. The

kind of elegance a form has determines the kind of goodness the form has because it is its particular way of achieving density of being, which is what I argue constitutes goodness.

A form contains within itself all the things that are its components, with some things functioning trivially, vaguely, narrowly, or widely. Nevertheless, the form does not reduce to all the things to which it is related, its conditional components. It has its own essential components that give it its own harmony, its own being, over and against its conditions or relations. If it did not have its essential components, it would not be a form at all, only the things formed together as components, although without forming them together. The essential components contribute to the grading of the whole of the components as trivial, vague, narrow, and wide, as limited by the harmonic structures of the components that allow them to be so integrated. The essential components of the sunset are those that achieve getting the light, clouds, movement, and other elements together during a duration, say ten minutes, of the setting sun. The future possibilities for the sea battle contain essential components that determine not only the wind, water, the navies' relative strengths, but also the deliberations of the admirals, the outcome of which is an essential component of the form of the future.

I conclude that every form is a harmony whose components function with triviality, vagueness, narrowness, and width, giving rise to the form's complexity and simplicity constituting its elegance. Every form has density of being, and its internal structure is lumpy with the densities of beings of its various components, especially those functioning in its focal structures with narrowness and width. This amounts to saying, as I shall argue further in the fourth chapter, that every form has goodness and every form values its components with regard to their triviality, vagueness, narrowness, and width, manifesting as the form's elegant achievement of complexity and simplicity.

Focus, Field, Intensity, and Immediacy

The language of focus and field comes from phenomenological philosophy and philosophy of culture that use it to describe experience.

We experience things as focal elements against a background field. The focus/field language in this section, however, I use to characterize the internal composition of the form of a harmony. A form itself is a harmony. We can treat human experience as a metaphor for a form composing itself, integrating its components with its formal pattern. Some forms do compose themselves over time, such as the performance of a symphony, a sun setting over a duration of ten minutes, or the admirals actually directing a sea battle as it takes place. Whitehead thought that every actual occasion itself is a concrescence that aims at its own satisfied form that grades all the things it prehends regarding triviality, vagueness, narrowness, and width. I will embrace some of Whitehead's cosmology in the next chapter, but I think my own analysis of form, indeed of determinateness as harmony, is more general and abstract than the things that interested Whitehead. A purely static form with no temporal or concrescent forming can be regarded as composing its components within itself as functioning with triviality, vagueness, narrowness, and width. Even a purely static form as imagined by a mathematician, unrelated to actual temporal change and formation, has a compositional structure that gives it connections with all other forms with respect to which it is determinate.

The sections of this chapter have laid out successively more complicated articulations of how form constructs density of being, which I argue means goodness. A form is the pattern of a harmony. A form considered by itself also is a harmony because it is a determinate thing. Harmonies relate to one another so as to be determinate with regard to one another and they contain those relations as components of themselves. Thus, a form contains within itself relations to all other forms, and other things with forms, with respect to which it is determinate. A form also contains essential components that make its patterning of its components different from the ways other forms pattern pretty much the same components.

My discussion has attempted to speak about form as such, or density of being as such, or goodness as such. Nevertheless, I can hardly discuss this "as suchness" without bringing in the fact that we know form and form's goodness through experience. We know goodness by valuing it in something. We know form by grasping its formal character. I will try to connect the discussion of the appreciation of goodness to that of the formal nature of goodness, although chapter 4 will be the principal discussion of experiential appreciation.

The grasp of form, the apprehension of a being as being, the appreciation of goodness, is always from a perspective. I have followed Whitehead in taking a form to be itself a perspective on itself, particularly in dynamic forms, as well as being the object or components in the perspective of another form or harmony. It is necessary to acknowledge that the metaphors and signs used to articulate form as constructing density of being inevitably have an aesthetic reference. For the ancient Greeks and Confucians, to perceive something is to grasp it as having a form with some goodness. I mean "aesthetic" in this broad sense.

We experience the density of a thing's being, with all the lumpy density of its components functioning trivially, vaguely, narrowly, and with width, as intensity. Chapter 3 will sketch a cosmology that shows how the density of a thing's being registers as intensity of experience, insofar as that thing is brought unmodified into the harmony of the experiencer. The experiencer needs to integrate that thing with all the other elements that go into the harmony of the experiencer. In doing this, the experiencer might alter the original density of being of the things to fit into the harmony with the other things and their densities of being. Many kinds of intensity exist, varying according to the form of the thing experienced and according to the functioning of the thing as trivial, vague, narrow, or wide within the experiencer. An aesthetically perceived thing relegated to triviality in the experiencer will have little or no intensity. A thing transmuted to enter the experience only vaguely will have only the intensity of its transformed self. A thing reinforced with simplicity so as to function in a narrow contrast will have sharply focused intensity. A thing functioning widely in a set of complex connections with other things will contribute to wide intensity.

These senses of intensity belong intrinsically to the things perceived with their goodness or density of being. How the experiencer composes them together in the experience is what determines their triviality, vagueness, narrowness, and width in the experience of them. This affects the intensity with which they function in the experience. Factors quite unrelated to the perceived objects at hand might cause

the experience of them to be inattentive to their intrinsic intensity.
How often do we fail to experience things in their existentially relevant intrinsic intensity because we are distracted, bored, or uneducated
about how to bring the density of being of something perceived into
its rightful intensity in experience? Anyone with good hearing can
hear the notes in the performance of a Bach prelude and fugue, but
without some musical education, a person will hear less, grasp less, feel
less of the intensity of the piece than will a connoisseur.

Related to intensity in experience is immediacy. A form is a
harmony that just hangs together. Its parts just fit and that fit is their
pattern. This "just fitting" is something grasped immediately. Of course,
human experience is all highly mediated. I have barely begun to discuss
the signs and semiotic systems that allow us to organize things in our
experience. All experience is interpretation in one or several of many
senses. Things enter into experience as components of components
of components, ad infinitum, with many ecosystems of ecosystems of
mediation. Moreover, once the components of human intentionality
enter into experience, we can interpret the things experienced quite
wrongly. Nevertheless, no matter how wrongly interpreted, a thing
grasped in experience is taken to have its components immediately
fitting together. To experience the form of a thing is to experience
its perceived components as immediately together according to the
form's pattern.

Intensity and immediacy are two components of aesthetic experience that derive directly from the nature of the form of anything
perceived. They have to do with how anything with form can enter
into experience. Experience is at base aesthetic and thus carries the
being of things experienced, with their densities of being, into the
experiencer according to the experiencer's own form. I hope you
can hold these abstract remarks about goodness and its experiential
appreciation in mind while I move to flesh out more of the nature
of goodness in harmony.

CHAPTER 3

A Cosmology of Form as Goodness

Because of the extraordinary generality and abstractness of the claim that anything with form has goodness, my discussion too has been very abstract. This abstractness is extraordinary because of its utmost practicality: the claim applies to everything that has form. Nevertheless, my discussion has prescinded from all concrete locations of form and from the actual interactions of things that have form, except in the illustrative examples of people experiencing goodness. Although all forms bear goodness, I have not yet said much about how goodness is located in the world, except in terms of examples and illustrative situations.

Any discussion of the *locus* of goodness in the world, however, still will be abstract. If goodness is as ultimately constitutive of any-thing determinate, as I claim here, then it is a trait of anything in the cosmos insofar it has form. Therefore, how form bears goodness is a question with the generality of philosophical cosmology. My aim in this chapter is to present you elements of a cosmology that makes sense of the interrelations of goodness in the spatially and temporally extended world we have. A lot more is cosmologically specific to our world than just space and time. The cosmology further articulates dimensions of harmony presupposed in my earlier attempts to develop an hypothesis about goodness.

What is cosmology? The beginning place for metaphysics, as I noted earlier, is the study of determinateness. The characters of deter-minateness would apply in any cosmology whatsoever. For this reason, we can consider the study of determinateness itself to be metaphysics, the development of hypotheses about the conditions of any world whatsoever that is determinate or contains determinate things. (On the matter of labels for inquiries, I shall argue in chapter 6 that the study of determinateness is also the way to understand being, and so it can be called ontology as well as metaphysics.) Cosmology is more than the study of determinateness, however, because it extends to the general traits of this cosmos, for instance, that it contains temporal things. This chapter is about goodness as form in a temporally changing world. From the standpoint of a theory of determinateness as harmonies that might apply to any possible world, it is not necessary that the world be temporal. But in fact the world we have is indeed temporal and changing, or at least I shall assume so for the sake of the argument.

To distinguish the logical levels of vagueness and specificity in my argument is extremely important. A level of analysis is vague if it can be made more specific in various ways. Those ways might contradict one another. For instance, the metaphysics of determinateness is vague with respect to what kinds of determinate things exist. The ontological creative act can create any kinds of determinate things and we just have to see what kinds of things are created. I have argued that any world, with any kinds of things, needs to have harmonies with forms, components formed, existential location relative to other harmonies, and the value of getting these components together in this form in this location relative to the rest of the world. This level of metaphysical analysis of harmony and its ultimate conditions is vague with respect to whether the world that actually exists is temporal or not. At the vague metaphysical level, there might be a world with no temporality. Nevertheless, in our actual world, temporal things exist, so we can and must specify our otherwise vague metaphysics of determinate harmonies so as to account cosmologically for temporal harmonies. Assuming we affirm that this world is temporal, our analysis is still vague with respect to what kind of temporality the world has, with different theories of time vying to specify the temporality we have. Platonic, Aristotelian, Samkhya, and yin/yang theories have been advanced since ancient times. Contemporary physicists debate about a block universe sense of temporality versus linear asymmetrical views. In this chapter, I shall specify temporality with a particular theory of time with real temporal causation. From the standpoint of the theory in this chapter, the ontological act of creation makes this kind of temporal world.[1]

Cosmology is not what many people would expect in a book on the nature of goodness in harmony and form, beauty and art, obligation and personhood, and flourishing and civilization. Nevertheless, suppose the pragmatists are right that value or goodness of one sort or other permeates human experience throughout. Suppose the Confucians are right that everything we perceive or grasp in any situation has a goodness of some sort. Suppose the Platonic tradition is right that anything that is determinate in any way is good. These are cosmic claims and need to be articulated and justified in a cosmology.

Form as bearing goodness is a universal trait of all determinate things in any kind of cosmos, a metaphysical hypothesis. The discussion in chapter 2 addressed form as goodness with that orientation. Nevertheless, we need to discuss something of our own cosmos and thus elaborate cosmological hypotheses. Many cosmologies exist that attempt to describe our world. Whitehead subtitled his major work, *Process and Reality, An Essay in Cosmology*, and yet he claimed it applied only to our "cosmic epoch" and perhaps not to others. Although my discussion to come will have to deal with some technical cosmological issues, largely the discussion will proceed with what we commonly accept as traits of our world, such as that it is temporal.

What I need to explain by cosmological hypotheses in this chapter is how a present creation of changes takes harmonies that have actualized in the past and changes them into something new according to what is possible. The present creation of a harmony is the actualization of what had previously been only a future possibility out of what had been actualized in the past. The past actual things are harmonies and so are the future possibilities. A present creative change is a harmony that actualizes the future possibilities and joins them in some continuity or other with the actual past. The harmony of the present actualizing has both past and future components and turns the latter into the temporal mode of the actualized past. The present harmony thus has both conditional components and the essential components of actualizing or creative becoming. On the one hand, a creative changing harmonizes continuities between past and future. On the other hand, a creative changing brings about emergent novelties as measured by the distinction between finished past and merely possible future. A creative change of long duration, such as the emergence of a melody, contains lesser creative changes within it, such as the successive notes in the melody. The notes themselves have harmonies that contain attack, resonance, and cessation perhaps. While it is tempting to identify a creative harmony of changing with what can be contained within the specious present of human experience, obviously some creative harmonies are of much longer duration, and those harmonies have essential components that emerge through time to define that duration. All of these elements are what a theory of temporality must explain with its various hypotheses. I shall now begin to unfold the hypotheses.

Possibilities, Determinism, Indeterminism, and Temporality

The first cosmological hypothesis I shall lay out is that some forms are possibilities for actualization. Possibilities are forms. Some possible forms get actualized and others are excluded from actualization. In a temporal cosmos, the future is the form of what can unify the present creative processes and things when the future date comes to be present.

Stated most generally, however, form schematizes pure unity to a plurality of things yielding consistency or harmony among them. Many forms might exist that would unify a given plurality, and each would have the goodness of harmonizing that plurality its way, with its balances of complexity and simplicity and with its composing of things to have triviality, vagueness, narrowness, and width. A given form is a harmony whose conditional components are the multiplicity or plurality of things it has to unify and whose essential components are how pure unity applies to that plurality.

The notion of pure unity is complex (pun intended, please groan) and receives attention from nearly all the world's philosophical and theological traditions. Plato in the *Republic* pointed out that the Form of the Good transcends being and all forms of determinate objects and epistemic judgments and visions.[2] Daoist and Confucian traditions emphasize a unity that lies behind or transcends all things that manifest determinate unity.[3] The ancient Vedic Hymn of Creation (x.129) says that the One precedes the distinction between nonbeing and being. In diverse ways, the Upanishads pursue a unity behind consciousness and its objects, behind differences among persons (atman), behind Brahman with qualities and down to Brahman without qualities. Buddhists tend to shy away from metaphysical speculation but emphasize the unity of Enlightenment while emphasizing the utter plurality of the things that are such as they are.[4]

My position is that we cannot grasp pure unity as anything in itself but rather as part of the condition for unified plurality, that is, for form integrating components. As one of four cosmological ultimates upon which any determinate world depends, form is the harmony of unity and plurality; any form schematizes unity to some plurality. The determinate world (however we characterize it cosmologically or locally) has as one of its ultimate conditions that there be forms for all determinate things. Any form is a finite/infinite contrast between its components and pure unity: it has its determinate character as a unified plurality. The finite side of the finite/infinite contrast of form is the determinate form itself. The infinite side is what there would be (the not-finite) if there were not the plurality. Of course, without the plurality, there would be nothing determinate. Pure unity is not different from pure nothingness, the lack of any existence or contrast between existence and nonexistence.[5] This is why many traditions characterize the one or primordial state as nothingness, or that which transcends the distinction between being and nonbeing: that distinction itself is determinate.

The ontological act of creation mentioned in chapter 2, in creating determinate things, creates forms for those things that on the one hand integrate a created plurality and that on the other hand exhibit unity. There is no such thing as pure unity. It never exists by itself. It is not a trait of the ontological act of creation apart from the determinate things created, including the determinate forms. It is manifest only in the determinate forms that unify pluralities. Were there no determinate forms, there would be no pure unity. Were there no determinate forms, there would be no plurality either. The ontological creative act creates determinate things as such, all bearing the ultimate conditions of form, plural components, relations with others, and achieved value identity.[6]

Nevertheless, given the creation of determinate things, determinate forms exist that are harmonies unifying pluralities. The essential components that bring unity to the plurality of things otherwise dis-joined are the sorts of things Plato mentions—measure, balance, proportion, and the like. These give goodness to all the things that Plato characterized as "mixtures of the unlimited and limited." Chapter 2 gave an elaborate, if still preliminary and barely illustrated, account of those essential components, involving the elegance of simplicity and complexity and the relational functions of triviality, vagueness, narrowness, and width. Whatever the given plurality might be, pure unity manifests itself in those components that achieve the goodness of getting that plurality together with its specific density of being or goodness.

Form as possibility in the future is relative to the plurality of things in the present that need integration as the dates in the future advance toward their time of actualization. Any region of present reality relates to all the other regions, insofar as it is determinate and contains determinate things. Nevertheless, as will be spelled out more in the next section, for a given region there is a determinate set of realities for which possibilities exist. The future possibilities are constrained by the actualities that need to be composed in the present, which is only to say that the future needs to schematize the present plurality with unity.

Ours does not appear to be a wholly deterministic world as Laplace envisioned. Aristotle's example of the admirals debating whether to engage the enemy in battle tomorrow models a common situation in the human condition. We frequently need to choose among alternatives within tomorrow's possibility. The relevant factors for the admirals include the enemy's forces and their own, their estimates of those enemy forces and their own, the geography within which the battle might take place, the winds and tides of the morrow and their estimate of the weather, their abilities to communicate with their commanders, the parallel abilities of the enemy, and so forth. The structure of the future possibility is constantly changing with the advance of time. Suppose the admirals gather at 5 p.m. to make their plan and by 6 p.m. have decided to attack the next morning. At that point, the future that had held to the inclusive possibility of sea battle or no sea battle drops most dimensions of the latter alternative, although there is still the possibility that an overnight tsunami will occur to wipe out both fleets before they can engage. Suppose at first light on the morrow the admirals take their fleet out of anchorage for battle. At this point, they have the possibility of attacking from the north or the west, and they decide on the west because that gives them the weather gage. A northern attack is then impossible once the attack begins. All throughout the battle, the possibilities shift. New possibilities present themselves because of the strategy of the enemy, perhaps. The shape of possibilities for the day of battle is a kaleidoscope of constant changes as the course of events eliminates original alternatives and opens up others as the march of time changes the plurality at hand that needs integration.

Within the temporal sphere, possibilities are always changing as the conditions that their forms must integrate change. Insofar as inexorable forces running through the present do not wholly determine the possibilities, the alternatives within the possibilities are constantly shifting. Therefore, the shape of future possibilities has a temporal depth dimension, from the immediate future as determinable by the admirals' decisions at 6 p.m. to each subsequent moment. Even the meaning of "subsequent moment" is complicated by the theories of modern physics that have conceptions of temporal lines and simultaneity that differ from the common sense of Aristotle's admirals (and most of us). In addition to the conditional components from the plurality for the future possibilities that come from present actualities that they need to integrate, conditional components exist that consist in the different possible consequences in the farther future, a point of great importance for the admirals. Future possibilities are structured in depth by alternatives among farther future consequences.

Philosophers in the West have differed over the status of these forms of future possibilities, whether static forms like states of affairs or dynamic forms with the depth dimension of consequences. Plato treated them as myths or likely stories, and in the *Parmenides* he refuted the claim that we should take them literally as existents. Whitehead believed the forms are eternal objects and are primordially real in the mind of God as he conceived God.[7] Charles Hartshorne said that the forms are only the temporal possibilities of the future and that if there were no time and no future there would be no forms. I am inclined to give a temporalist interpretation like Hartshorne's.[8] Nevertheless, we can imagine forms, and we can imagine them with any kind of plurality whatsoever, a plurality that has nothing to do with what is actual in some present time. Mathematicians imagine forms that have nothing to do with what is actual, with pluralities that have forms that are not actual. Perhaps Kant was right that mathematics is all constructed in this sense; Stephan Koerner lays out the issues.[9] Nevertheless, whereas Kant said the a priori quality of mathematics comes from the given structure of inner and outer sense (conditions of transcendental human subjectivity), it seems clear that $2 + 2 = 4$ is true whether or not there is any transcendental subjectivity. We need not solve this problem in philosophy of mathematics to note that intricacies of form can be abstracted from any real forms functioning as future possibilities. The elegance mathematicians see in form resides in the density of being of the forms with their formal pluralities of formal components.

Actuality, Becoming, Conditions, and Loci of Goodness

To make much sense of possibilities without an understanding of actualities and actualization is impossible. This section aims to remedy this with a discussion of how the temporal actualization of possibilities gives specific goodness to the actual state of affairs. The place to begin is with some observations on the nature of time, commonly understood.

The past is all the things that are actual, including the goodness actualized in them and the structures that relate them. Most often, these structures are ecosystems of harmonies within and among others. The future consists of all the possibilities that are not yet actual. The present consists of the events that come to be actualizing the possibilities, selecting among alternative possibilities where the future allows alternatives. Any plausible account must be able to acknowledge that a present event is creative in the senses that (1) it takes past, finished, actualities as the material or potentials with which to make something new; (2) it grasps the form of the future as the limits within which it can make something new out of the past actualities; (3) it constitutes a new reality out of the finished past and future possibilities such that the actual past is added to by the present event and the future that had been has been actualized in some decisive way by the present.

Whereas the past has the being of actuality that has become fixed and the future has the kind of reality form has, the present has the reality of becoming. However we might delimit a present moment, we understand it as the becoming of something.

We can analyze any becoming as a harmony with two poles and a process of becoming connecting them. One pole is when only the past actualities exist as potentials for becoming and the future possibilities are not yet actualized. The other pole is the novel actuality of what has become, thus turned into a past actuality. The process of the becoming is the coming to be of a new harmony, the event that becomes. That harmony has conditional components both from the past and from the future. The conditional components from the past are the past actualities that enter relationally into the emergent becoming. The conditional components from the future are the formal structures of possibility for combining the conditional components from the past plus the essential components of the present. The essential components of the present include at least some that involve spontaneity within the moment that brings about something new. In this sense, each present moment is creative, adding something novel that is not contained in that moment's past. Even if the past is structured by highly stable trajectories and the future allows only one possible way of integrating those trajectories, so that what becomes in the present is wholly determined to be like the past in some sense, still the novelty exists of one more moment than had been actualized before. Most likely, much more randomness exists than that in the possibilities open for any given present moment. For moments of human experiential life, there are importantly structured possibilities that depend on the choice of the moment, as Aristotle's admirals knew.

Although this is not the place for me to lay out a whole systematic cosmology, I do want to affirm my commitment for the time being to an East Asian sensibility that construes the basic elements of the actual world to be changes, not substances. A present existent is a harmony that changes its actual fixed conditions from the past and its open future possibilities into a new actual thing. The present harmony includes both past and future within it as well as the essential spontaneous creativity that makes something new. Such a change is not merely present, in a sense that excludes past and future. Rather it is a changing that begins with past actuality and concludes with new actuality. The spontaneous act of changing constitutes the continuity between old and new. A past actual harmony is a past changing. A future possibility is a future form of a changing. This sense of change is not the only story of actuality to be told. Nevertheless, I think it is the dominant one.

According to the thesis that anything with form has goodness, a future possibility has the goodness of getting its components together with a certain density of goodness, as analyzed in the previous chapter, with the elegance of simplicity and complexity and the disposition of components having triviality, vagueness, narrowness, and width. The future relevant to a present becoming is purely formal, with its components being the forms of determinate harmonies that the present becoming might actualize. However, the past relevant to a present becoming is the actuality of all that has happened, as connected by the conditional components of the past's existential field. Therefore, the past provides the actualities whose forms are those that are formally integrated in the form of the future for that event of becoming. The future possibility is the form of the goodness that actualizing that possibility would achieve. The creative becoming of a present event is the coming to be of a harmony that includes as some of its components the actualities of the past, as others of its components the possibilities for integrating those actualized components, and as yet others of its components the essential components that make the new actuality become out of the becoming process.

Thus a moment of becoming, when it has become, has the goodness of integrating its past with its future so as to be something new. Because each becoming is the becoming of an actuality with goodness, the past is permeated with valuable things as those have been actualized in the past. Each actual thing in the past is a harmony with components relating to other things in the ecological systemic sense that I have described. Each valuable thing in the past has components with specific goodness or density of being, lumpily laid out according to the functions of triviality, vagueness, narrowness, and width. The emerging becoming is the composing of itself as having all the valuable things of the past as laid out within its own form in the functional patterns of triviality, vagueness, narrowness, and width. The becoming is the achieving of the goodness of getting its past together in just its own way that becomes. Because the becoming event has the real actual past within it as needing integration into a novel harmony, there is actual continuity with the past. Because the becoming event is limited to what is possible as formed by the future, there is continuity with the future. Because of these continuities, time flows.[10]

Therefore, the goodness that consists in the form of the future for articulating possible density of being becomes actualized in the present, thereby being actual as part of the past. The past has the goodness of all the things that have been actualized, which of course are defined in terms of one another through the ecologies of harmonies. Each thing in the past has the goodness of harmonizing its components, each of which has the goodness of harmonizing its components, and so on around the relations of the various ecosystems of the existential field. The actual universe is thus a vast tissue of actual things in relations with goods in relation. A present becoming within the universe is the actualization of a possible goodness. The future is the formal possibility of goodness to be actualized. That formal possibility bears goodness because it is the way, or perhaps alternative ways, by which things can be integrated to achieve density of being. The past has goodness because it is the actualization of future possibilities that have goodness.

Because the goodness of the actualized world often is the actualization of only some of the things that were possible, part of its goodness is the peculiar kind of goodness of having excluded some possibility that might have been good. Thus, part of the reality of the past is that it is not what it might have been. Various decision points in present moments determined that those possibilities that might have been actualized were not. The admirals at the end of the morrow might have rued the decision to go to battle, because what became actual was their defeat; on the other hand, if victory had gone their way, they might have rejoiced. Human affairs are particularly poignant with "might have beens."

Perhaps it would be helpful to indicate some similarities and differences between my theory of time's flow and Alfred North Whitehead's because obviously mine is a kind of process philosophy. Whitehead's theory has been interpreted in two different directions. One direction, taken in different ways by Charles Hartshorne and Lewis

Ford, emphasizes that present moments of becoming, actual occasions, are very small, such that you do not get anything recognizable except as a society of such occasions.[11] They emphasize that the past is not real except insofar as it is prehended into an actual occasion that is becoming, and that the future is not real except insofar as it is antici-pated or superjected by an actual occasion in its becoming. The other direction of interpretation gives more solid, real weight to inclusive actual occasions that unfold through time and include subordinate actual occasions within them, a direction pioneered by F. Bradford Wallach in 1980 and developed in a different way by Randall E. Aux-ier and Gary L. Herstein more recently.[12] I take the latter direction in my own way. You might think that only the present is real or is more real than the past and future. Nevertheless, "reality" is anything that is what it is and that you can be mistaken about; such realities include changes. I construe the future, present, and past as equally real as harmonized together in temporal flow. Flow would not be possible without changes that involve future and past as well as present together. Moreover, I hold that becoming is itself a harmony with past and future poles and that time's flow can contain a succession of earlier and later moments. Consider a symphony being performed, an example to which I shall return in part II. It has chords, which are notes of different pitches struck together and resonating for a time, and melo-dies, each of which is a harmony of several notes. The symphony has four movements, each of which is a durational harmony on its own, and, if the symphony is good, the four movements constitute a larger harmony for the piece as a whole. Each of these items is a harmony in itself with its own essential components that give it its own-being. Moreover, each of these kinds of harmonies functions as a component in the others, modifying each other. The resonating mechanisms of the different instruments are also harmonies, and components in other parts of the symphony, as are the players themselves, the acoustical space, and the social occasion. The hearing of the symphony involves yet another array of harmonies in the listeners. The unity of these durational har-monies comes from their various kinds of essential components and those essential components might be present only over the duration, not at an instant or in a single actual occasion of Whitehead's sort. The relationality of harmonies across space as well as time is not limited to that which Whitehead found for actual occasions.

We now are in a position to see how things that can be experienced as valuable permeate the cosmos, as the pragmatists and Confucians argued. Everything experienced as real in our environment is
valuable, both in its own achievement and in how each thing functions in other things with the goods it carries there. Of course, our
experience might be mistaken in how it values things, as a function
of how it lays out its pattern composing its components regarding
triviality, vagueness, narrowness, and width. How often do we miss out
on what would really be delightful, for instance a sunset, because we
are distracted by something else, for instance grousing about a paper
that we have not finished in time for a deadline? How often have we
overly prized something, such as a sumptuous diet, when really we
should have valued a healthy diet more?

It is far better to say that everything in the cosmos has some
goodness, relationally good with respect to all the other components of
the harmonies in the cosmos, than to say nothing has goodness except
what we subjectively project upon it. We now have a theory for saying
that everything has real goodness and that we can be mistaken about
it. Our theory allows us to see how the goods of things intertwine
as the components of the components of the things that we experience. Each achieved actual goodness existing in its own right and in
its function as a component in other harmonies. Indeed, our theory
allows us to understand how human experience itself takes the form
of harmonizing components in which we dismiss some good things
as trivial (perhaps when we should have paid attention), smush others
together vaguely, make others the sharp narrow focus of attention, and
yet connect others with a width of existential field.

I have needed to give technical analysis of the process of becoming to determine in what sense an event of becoming is a harmony of
its own. Whitehead thought that at least two kinds of analysis must be
given, how the becoming generates its determinate actual conclusion
and how the becoming inherits and includes the lines of causation
contained within its ecosystem of components.[13] We do not need to
pursue this matter here, except in the discussions of human experiences
of creativity that will come later.

For any act of becoming that actualizes something of goodness,
its own past is a field of previously actualized things in their myriad
structures that also can be components of other acts of becoming. All

the things that become "at once" share this field of past actual things, although how the things happening simultaneously compose them in triviality, vagueness, narrowness, and width can differ enormously. Similarly, all the things happening "at once" share a common field of possibilities, although they variously relate to the formal field of possibilities in regional ways. The admirals do not have to take into account the possibilities for the third planet out from Alpha Centauri and the folks on that planet do not have to relate to the admirals' concerns. The notion of the simultaneity of present events is far more complicated than our commonsense image that is sufficient for the admirals.

We now have three more dimensions of the existential field in terms of which things as harmonies mutually condition one another, symmetrically or asymmetrically. One dimension is the field of the past relative to any given present perspective of emergence. Other events of present, spontaneous, emergence share some or all of this field. The field of the existential past is temporally, historically, thick; earlier ecological harmonies condition later ones but not vice versa in any direct sense.

Another dimension is the field of future possibilities relative to any given present perspective of emergence. The field of the future is relevant to many events of present decision making, and its coherence with internal alternative possibilities takes structure in part by having to integrate all the possible present decision-making points. Aristotle's admirals were pondering a future field of possibilities that they assumed the enemy admirals were also pondering. The field of the future is thick with a succession of dates in which the structure of the future at any one date shifts by what happens at earlier dates.

A third dimension of the existential field is that of the present of a different emergent relative to a given present event of emergence. That dimension is systematically indirect. All the present moments of emergence that are simultaneous with one another are conditioned, perhaps, by the actual finished actualities in their common past and also by the future field of which they all, or at least some of them, can actualize parts or regions. However, in their present coming-to-be, they do not condition one another because they are only becoming determinate enough to be different from or determinate with respect to one another. After they have achieved determinateness, they of course are determinate, at least in part, with respect to one another, whether or not known to us in any conscious way. As past to us, it has nodal points of goodness that have importance in our present lives: those of us with arthritis and diabetes have Neanderthal ancestors, whether we know it or not. However wonderful the lives of those Neanderthal ancestors might have been for them, celebrating around the fire, the value of their genes for arthritis and diabetes, as they have come down through eons of harmonic ecosystems of genetic inheritance, is painfully negative for us who suffer (and for our health insurance companies). Not only do we experience the narrow nodal points of the past, we experience them as connected with one another through forms of width. Not just isolated narrow points of focus exist but connected achieved goods, whose connections also have goodness.

Some of us make a point of knowing as much of our history as we can. This means we seek out as many of the important perspectives in the past that achieved actual harmonization as we can learn about and grasp the goodness of the things in their world from those perspectives. We cannot help but experience most of the world that is actual by our time as trivial and much of the rest of that world as only vaguely grasped. Nevertheless, with learning, inquiry, and appreciative attention, we can experience the actual world as filled with goods from a very great many perspectives, putting those perspectives into place in the construction of our own perspective. How vast and various are the lumpy densities of being of the actual world that we can experience!

To put this point formally, the goods are disposed in the actual world from the perspectives of the harmonies achieving them and from the perspective of the harmonies that take in the goods of other harmonies as components, each with its own formal pattern of valuing itself and others.

The loci of goodness in the future are from the perspective of some emergent present or from the perspective of future moments considered as if they were present actualizations. There is a perspective in each of the emerging occasions that share a present defined both (1) by having a more or less common past that each composes within its components in its own way and (2) by sharing a more or less common field of future possibilities. (The temporal relations among simultaneous emergents are more complicated than this, but not to the point of this discussion.) The field of possibilities with all the goods in its forms, alternative and otherwise, is shared by all the emerging occasions that can actualize one or another of the possibilities in it. Philosophers commonly think of individual agents actualizing future possibilities and being responsible for the goods ingredient in their choices. However, because there is a common field of future possibilities, nearly all individual actions are conjoint actions. In the natural world, including the human, this means that there is a constantly moving rush of present emergences simultaneously achieving actual harmonies by actualizing the field of possibilities in the perspectives of each of the emergences. Each harmony emerging as actual has its own perspective on the field of future possibilities, dismissing some as trivial, massing others as vague, sharpening others as narrow, and broaching yet others as connecting things widely. The structure of the future, as said earlier, is not just a proximate moment in time unactualized as yet but also a kaleidoscope of stages of future actualization. Each stage in the possible future is a perspective on later stages or moments when it is considered as actually made determinate. As human agents, we think of the future often like a branching of decision points. It really is this way. However, we must remember that because many simultaneous decisive emergents exist, the whole kaleidoscope of future stages is different from the perspective of each, taking into account their joint actions on the future. Each possibility at any place in the future, from the perspective of any emergent position of decision, including future possibilities of emergent decisions, has a goodness.

The goods in the future can be identified from the perspective of just their own form, which essentially integrates its formal components with triviality, vagueness, narrowness, and width embodying some kind of elegant balance of simplicity and complexity. They also can be appreciated from the perspective of the present emergent whose future they are. For human experience, the appreciation of the assorted goods in the kaleidoscope of future possibilities is twofold. Like any natural thing, human beings have a real future about which they and their field of simultaneous actors will be making decisions. Human beings participate in the ongoing rush of time where successive present emergent moments jointly carry on the actuality of the past into integrations that actualize the common future field. Nevertheless, human beings, and perhaps nearly all animals, *interpret* their future possibilities so that they can use those interpretations to guide their decision. Human semiotically shaped interpretation is part of nature, not some subjective consciousness that is apart from nature. Human beings with actual semiotic systems and learned skills at interpretation have much more complex possibilities for actualization than emergent harmonies that have not inherited a culture. For Aristotle's admirals, most of what will happen on the morrow moves by natural forces that do not register their decisions about the battle. Some elements of the morrow, however, will indeed be determined by the semiotically shaped interpretations of the goods approaching in the future that the admirals can figure out and upon which they can act.

Goods located in the past become components in subsequent actualizations and thus can change as they are located in the subsequent harmonies. Athens's defeat in Sicily has been the component of zillions of subsequent harmonies, taking perhaps a different form in each of those zillion according to the pattern of triviality, vagueness, narrowness, and width of each harmony. It was anguish for the Athenians at the time, and joy for the Sicilians (mainly Carthaginians). Its importance has been modified by centuries of subsequent history so that it was of little importance for the battles in Sicily between the Axis and Allies in World War II. Our present time allows us a perspective on perspectives on perspectives, each of which grasps its components as having some goodness within it.

Nevertheless, the Sicilian battle of the Athenians achieved a complex set of goods in its own coming to actuality. This goodness emerged as the battle came to actual determinate resolution. We can think of this as the goodness of the battle in itself, in its own perspective as the combatants waged it. The battle was not simply located, however, as Whitehead said in *Science and the Modern World* when he complained about what he called the "fallacy of simple location." The battle subsequently became a component in a zillion subsequent actualizations of harmonies. It was transformed as a component in each of these. The battle with its goodness is multiply located—this is how we acknowledge actual continuity through time—with many transformations. The form of the actual battle, with its goodness, is transformed as it is heard as news by the Athenians at home, and then by each event of subsequent history. All of those goods of the battle, in itself and in each of the subsequent events in which it becomes a component, can become a distinctive goodness. Most of the time in human experience we trivialize many of the goods of that battle for the distant stretch of history and think only of its goods in recent events; stories of the battle are important for contemporary Mediterranean cruise ships docking in Sicily with the narrow densities of goodness of recent narrative. In Athens, the battle is largely part of the vague past, remembered only by historians. The multiple locations of the battle in itself and in its component functions in other subsequent events are what give the actual world such a rich supply of interweaving goods.

The lesson of this section is that goodness always exists or is located in perspective: the perspective of the emerging event coming to actualization of that goodness or the perspective of another emergent harmony making the goodness one of its components with triviality, vagueness, narrowness, and width, elegantly disposed. We can ask whether a transcendent perspective on the whole exists as a complex cosmic goodness, a cosmic harmony. Is there a transcendent perspective on the whole goodness–identity of a sunset, or a painting, or a person? To answer these questions requires another foray into the metaphysics of determinateness.

Goodness–Identity

The goodness–identity of a determinate thing is the goodness it has as getting its components together according to its form in its place relative to other things in the existential field. Alternatively, thinking more regionally, its various goodness–identities are the goods it has relative to other things in its various existential fields. The phrase "goodness–identity" is redundant, at least if the thesis identifying goodness with form is correct. To have a formal identity—an identity as actualizing a form in relation to others in existential fields—is to have that goodness, the density of goodness achieved by the actualized form. I need to distinguish and connect two elements of goodness–identity, which I call the subjective and the objective, respectively.

The subjective goodness-identity a determinate thing has is its identity as constituted by the form of its harmony, how it puts together its components with what pattern of elegance, composing its harmony by giving triviality, vagueness, narrowness, and width to its components. This is "subjective" because it is the goodness of the harmony as a subject. Nothing walls off the harmony's subjectivity from the things with respect to which it is determinate. The subjective identity includes relations with those things as among its own components. Hence, very distant things can be components of a harmony as they are components of components of components of the components that are prominent in the shape of the harmony itself. Most distant things, of course, are trivial or vaguely represented components, but still everything relates internally to any harmony that is determinate with respect to them in some sense or other.

For instance, the subjective goodness-identity of the sunset consists in the harmony of the situation in which the viewer sees or might see the meteorological events. This harmony is determined in large part by the perspective of the viewer's attention, visual apparatus, cultural affinity for beauty on the horizon, and so forth, although the meteorological events have to be there for the situation to occur. The goodness-identity of the harmony of the sunset is what comes of getting those elements together with the form of the harmony in that place in the existential field.

Consider the instance of a painting. Its subjective goodness-identity consists in what is achieved by getting its composition or design together with the colors with which it is painted, together with a representational subject matter (if it has one), in a cultural context within which its style is meaningful, and so forth. In part II, I shall discuss the elements in a work of art in more detail. A painting is a little like a sunset in that its goodness-identity requires a situation in which a viewer might exist. A painting that could not be seen would be a chemical state of affairs of paint on canvas (or whatever the painting is made of, perhaps egg tempera colors embedded in plaster). Part of the subjective identity of a painting is the painter's intention or hope that it be seen, at least by the artist. A good art critic or art historian can explain a lot about how the elements of a painting harmonize to achieve the goodness-identity it has. Untrained people can see something of the harmony or goodness-identity of a painting, its "beauty," although they might not see as much as a critic. This is like all of us being able to listen to Bach but not hear as much in the music as an expert critic or musician would hear. The subjective goodness-identity of a work of art is not a "mere fact"—which might be just a bunch of materials with a certain arrangement and chemistry. Like a beautiful sunset, it exists in a situation in which there is a subjunctive viewer: its goodness-identity is what a properly cultured and visually capable viewer "would" see if the viewer were there. Artists paint for the subjunctive viewer.

Consider the subjective goodness-identity of you as a human person. It consists of all the harmonies that make up your life, composed together in the achievement of the temporal harmony making up your life from birth to death, something you do not achieve fully until death. Personal identity is vastly more complex than can be articulated in a brief illustration. It includes what you make of your genetic makeup, inherited family situation, the social and historical circumstances in which you live, the issues that turn up moment by moment on your watch, your maturation and development through time, plus all the breakages, disasters, failures, frustrations, and discontinuities to which you respond. Much is given by your environments and circumstances, but what counts most in your subjective harmony over time is how you respond to those things that are given, how they are taken up in the harmonies of your moments and in how you add up those moments. All this is within your subjective goodness-identity, and it reflects our sense that personhood has to do with self-reflexive responsibility, a matter that involves lying under obligation. The high points of personal identity are what you do with what you are given.

The subjective side of goodness-identity is what most people think of first when they consider in what identity consists. Nevertheless, in addition is the objective side of goodness-identity, namely, the identity a thing has insofar as it is a component in something else. Although the harmonies that take in the thing as a component need to cope with the subjective goodness-identity of what they take in, what they do with those components is a function of their own harmony, their own subjective identities. They can give the component this place or that within their elegant pattern of complexity and simplicity, as trivial, vague, narrow, or wide in function. The component does not control how it is a component beyond being the thing it is that has to be integrated somehow or other into the harmony within which it is a component.

For instance, the sunset has the subjective goodness-identity of the situation in which the meteorological elements might be viewed as a sunset. Its objective goodness-identity, however, includes its roles in larger weather patterns in that area, inclusive of the position in which it is delightfully viewed, and weather patterns across the globe to which it might contribute nontrivially. It also has the objective goodness-identity of forming the aesthetic memories of the viewers, of contributing to their emotional lives, of being a way by which they spend part of their day in the economic and domestic situations of their lives, and in countless other ways. The harmony of the sunset situation does not control the other harmonies in which that situation can be a component. The larger weather patterns, the biographies of the viewers and their roles in larger societies, and a host of other things, control how the sunset is taken up. Nevertheless, they are also part of the sunset's objective identity as influencing those other things. If the sunset were different, those other things would be different unless given trivial or vague functions.

In the case of a painting, its objective identity consists in how it affects, for instance, its various viewers. It might be a life-transforming experience for some viewers, ho hum for others. Part of its objective identity is to constitute some of the wealth of the museum, institutions, or person who owns it. Part of its objective goodness-identity consists in the various roles it plays in the art history of its culture, in the political history that uses it as a symbol, and so forth. These many kinds of objective goodness-identity would not be what they are without the subjective goodness-identity of the painting. However, they consist in the goodness the painting has outside or over and above its subjective situation of being composed as it is relative to a viewer who might see it. Sometimes the particularly subjective identity of a painting might not make much of a difference to, say, the good it has for a museum; any painting by Picasso might be as good as any other. Still, any subjective goodness-identity of any Picasso has some objective goodness-identity for the museum that own it. The objective goodness-identity is just as much part of the goodness-identity of a painting as its subjective goodness-identity.

The objective goodness-identity of a person consists in all the ways that person influences other things. For instance, each person has an environmental footprint. This is part of who we are. Perhaps most interesting is the influence we have on other people. I am a teacher and have influenced many students over the years, for better and worse. My objective goodness-identity as a teacher includes all those influences. I try hard to have certain good influences and present my teachings and myself in ways that I hope will have good effect; these intentions and practices are parts of my subjective goodness-identity. Yet I do not control how the students respond to my teachings. That is part of their subjective identities and a function of their biographies, their interests, and the course of their lives. My personal identity includes those objective elements as much as my subjective ones. The concrete personal goodness-identity of the Buddha, Confucius, Ashoka, Genghis Khan, Julius Caesar, Jesus, Mohammed, Plato, Pope Leo X, Martin Luther, George Washington, and Abraham Lincoln, to list only some political and religious figures, is as much in how they have influenced history as in their subjective lives. Who they are includes the objective influences as well as the subjective achievements.

In what perspective is there a registration, if any, of the integrated goodness-identity of a person, painting, sunset, or any determinate thing whatsoever? The subjective goodness-identity of a thing registers in its own harmony: it constitutes the goodness of its own harmony. Nevertheless, the objective goodness identity of a thing registers only in the different subjective harmonies of the things in which it is a component. Each of those other things registers part of a given harmony's objective goodness-identity, but only a part. Is there a super perspective, which would be a super harmony, in whose subjective goodness-identity all of the objective identity of me as a teacher, or the objective roles of a painting, or the influences of the sunset on global weather, or the viewer's long-term biography could register? I think not, and for important reasons.

Here is one reason. The super harmony would have to be determinate, and this means it must be determinate with respect to something else different from itself. It has to be itself and not something else. With respect to what could the super harmony be determinate, if all other determinate things were components within itself? Nothing. Therefore, there could not exist a super harmony that is a perspective within which all the objective elements of the identity of anything could be registered.

Here is another reason. Any ordinary determinate thing, for instance a sunset, a painting, or a person, needs anything with respect to which it is determinate to be partly external to itself. In the language developed earlier, those other things need to have essential components of their own that do not reduce to the harmonies that they condition. If a harmony with respect to which a given harmony is determinate were only the conditions within the given harmony, it would not have its own being with respect to which the given harmony is determinate. Determinateness in a harmony requires some otherness in the things with respect to which it is determinate. If a harmony were by itself, and its components were wholly internal to itself, it could not have its own essential components over against its conditional components so as to be determinate over against them.

Could it not be the case, however, that a harmony is like an organism with internal organs, internal organs that have no existence outside itself? Yes, such an organism could be like an existential field that includes its internal organs as things within the field. Then each of those internal organs needs its own essential components over against the others and against the containing organism in order to have their existence. In the human body, for instance, the liver is dependent on the circulatory and many other systems to exist. Nevertheless, it needs to have its own essential components in order to function within the larger whole. Think in causal terms. The liver cells need to have their own harmony in order to function holistically within the liver, and the liver needs its own harmony that makes components of those cells in order to contribute to the circulatory system, and vice versa. Even when functioning within a larger harmony as conditioning causes, the causes need their own harmonization in order to function in later or larger harmonies as component causes.

All this is to say that each harmony in itself and as it functions as a component in other harmonies needs to have its own essential components, its own act of existence in achieving or being itself, or its own part of a larger act of existence. Indeed, each determinate harmony exists as part of the ontological act of creation, to use my technical terms, insofar as it ontologically relates to but does not reduce to the other things with respect to which it is determinate. The ontological act of creation is not a super harmony, because that would be determinate. The ontological act of creation is simply a producer of novelty: the novelty has to be determinate: a determinate product has to be together with the other things with respect to which it is determinate. Therefore, any part of the existential reality of a harmony is within the context of an ontological act that creates all of them together. The act of creation is not in time. Nevertheless, it is presupposed as what allows things to differ in time. It is not more in any whole than in any of its parts. Within time, a temporal cause must have its own harmonic reality before it can enter as a component into a temporal effect.

Thus, no transcendent perspective exists that registers in its subjective form all the plurality of elements of the identity of any determinate thing. All the elements of identity are contained within the terminus of the ontological creative act. However, no superdeterminate integration of them exists. The goodness–identity of any determinate thing, including both subject and objective sides, is ineluctably plural. Many unities exist within the world, but each also supposes a plurality.

The thinking about goodness in nearly every culture has associated goodness with unity, Oneness. This is a mistake, however, if the analysis here is on the mark. Rather, goodness should be associated with harmony, for which the plurality harmonized is as vital as the unity of the plurality achieved.

CHAPTER 4

Testing the Theory

The Question of the Meaning of Goodness

The thesis that anything that has form has goodness because of its form requires saying what we mean by goodness and then showing that this is what we find in form. My strategy in the first three chapters of this part has been to describe form as such and as we encounter it in experience. I hope, and have confidently asserted, that you will recognize the description of form to be also a description of goodness, but I have not argued that yet. Between the study of form as such and the study of form as situated in experience as goodness is a series of cosmological considerations, made necessary by the cosmological implication of the thesis. If a thing that has form bears goodness, then goodness is a characteristic of anything in the cosmos that has form. Goodness is not a mere construction of human experience. Nor is it something in the cosmos that is valuable only when it is experienced as such. The cosmos has goods insofar as it has forms in things. Cosmological considerations have pervaded all the chapters so far and will continue to do so because of my realist axiological naturalism.

Nevertheless, "what we mean by goodness" is a function of human experience and meaning. Therefore, we need to look at human experience more than I did in chapter 1 to see whether what I have described as form and its relations through ecologies of harmony and modalities of harmonic composition is what we take goodness to be.

This chapter undertakes to show that form, as analyzed briefly so far, is what we mean by goodness. Then, part II on goodness in beauty and art, part III on goodness in obligation and persons, and part IV on goodness in flourishing and civilization will add depth and detail to the claims about form and goodness. We will not resolve the issue of whether what we mean by goodness is a function of form by a single neat argument, but only by a rich hypothesis that proves its worth by how it weaves together a host of observations. As Charles Peirce said, a good argument is not like a chain that is no stronger than its weakest link but rather like a rope with many strands interweaving and tightening against each other.[1] You can consider the plot of this book to be twisting and braiding a rope.

We can begin in this section with some negative considerations of positions, touched on earlier, that would reject the hypothesis that goodness is a function of form and that anything with form has goodness.

The first is the extreme position that there is no such thing as real goodness in any sense. We might believe some things have goodness and we might engage in valuing behaviors. Nevertheless, for this position, these things are only the mechanical results of mechanical processes. This was Thomas Hobbes's view, for instance, although it is inconsistent with his claim that we ought to believe it. We are forced to think valuational thoughts and behave in valuational ways by antecedent brain processes and organic interaction processes. This position denies any human intentionality. For such an extreme mechanistic philosophy, speaking is like burping, not a matter of trying to express a meaningful thought.[2] Many sciences have models of causation such that anything that happens is an effect of a mechanical process. Extreme mechanism is somewhat out of fashion in the sciences these days. Nevertheless, an analogue has currency in evolutionary biology where some scientists think that the reason people say and prize things is that those who do so have more adaptive reproductive powers than those who do not, not because they believe the things they say are true or that their choices reflect good valuational discrimination.

No one would believe such a position, however, unless he or she thought it had good reason behind it. This point is in direct contradiction to the position itself that says there is no reason to distinguish better and worse theories, that there is no such thing as truth, only mentation that is blurted out or is caused to pass through the mind. Philosophers have understood the self-referential contradiction in this kind of mechanistic position for a long while. Nevertheless, its defenders can make the mechanistic position more sophisticated by claiming that mechanism should be assumed as a heuristic scientific program. By assuming that there are only mechanistic processes that have no values, only factual traits, we can make great strides in understanding human nature. Considering the progress made in early modern science, this heuristic argument has merit. Strict deterministic mechanism gave way to statistical mechanism in the nineteenth century, but still there was no reason to explore causes other than antecedent efficient causes, according to many scientists. They of course recognized that they thought their theories and arguments were better, hence more valuable, than the alternatives, and that this recognition stands in self-referential contradiction to their causal theory itself. In fact, they are making a valuational heuristic argument for the heuristic goodness of value-free factual descriptions of nature. This heuristic argument for the fact/value dichotomy has limited goodness, like the limited goodness of retaining Linnaeus's biological classification system when it comes to "preserving species." However, it has in fact abandoned the claim that nature itself is value free. This opens inquiry to pursuing just what nature holds by way of goods when we are not trying to reduce it to its mechanistic dimensions.

Another position that denies that anything with form has goodness claims that all valuation is human projection. Of course, human beings do project their values onto things and the question is whether this is for good or bad reasons. This extreme subjectivist position has its historical beginnings in the West with Protagoras's claim that "man is the measure of all things." Early modern science formulated it with the distinction between primary, secondary, and tertiary qualities. John Locke and others thought that real nature has only physical properties such as spatial and temporal dimensionality; these are the primary qualities of things. The secondary qualities are those of the human senses in knowing the corporeal properties of the primary qualities. The tertiary qualities are the goods that people superimpose on the world of their sensible experience. This distinction of layers of qualities no longer holds much sway. Nevertheless, its legacy of subjectivizing valuation lingers on. No one disputes that human beings subjectively value and disvalue things that they encounter. The question, however, is whether there is reason in the nature of the things valued or disvalued for doing so.

I have made an extensive argument in the three volumes of *Axiology of Thinking* that all thinking is valuation in some sense and that it is all based on the way things are and on whether the interpretation of the way things are is accurate. In *Reconstruction of Thinking*, I argued that human processes become experiential when images are developed. An image is a form that integrates a multiplicity of factors in the environment that it is valuable to apprehend together. An image by itself, outside of any interpretation, is neither true nor false. Nevertheless, it is a good image if it picks up for discrimination the things in the environment that are important to know. In *Recovery of the Measure*, I argued that human beings engage the environment by interpreting it, and among the valuational elements are those concerning what is important to know. The function of interpretation is to guide life, often issuing in action. Intentionality is a form of valuing based on the coordination of purpose with what the environment has worth interpreting. In *Normative Cultures*, I argued two theses about thinking. First is that thinking involves getting theoretical overviews of things so that life can be coordinated well. Theorizing has its own goods—consistency, coherence, adequacy, and applicability, to cite Whitehead's famous list.[3] Nevertheless, its aim is to see what I have called the lumpy character of goods located across an existential field. The second thesis is that all thinking—imagination, interpretation, and theorizing—is ordered to guide life, practical reason. What is really and truly important to take into account concerning the cosmos is inextricably bound up with what we need to know in order to guide our lives. The goods that are really in things justify, or challenge, our projected valuations of them.

I need to bring up one more position that is negative to my thesis, namely, the view that there is real goodness but that it is not connected with form. The clearest expression of this is that of G. E. Moore's argument that goodness is a nonnatural property.[4] All sorts of natural properties exist, and he listed what Locke would call primary and secondary qualities. Goodness is not like these. It is just itself, knowable, but not connected to the characters or forms of things. This position has the virtue of being realistic about goodness. However, it does not explain much. As I shall attempt to persuade you in the next section, the goodness of something changes when its form changes. Moore was wedded to the notion that nature consists of what science knows, and what science knows is facts, not values. He only added to the mystery of goodness by saying it is a nonnatural property that adheres to some things.

Having rejected some reasons to think that goodness is not a function of form, let us now consider how we think about the goods of things when we deliberate.

Imaginative Analytic of Goodness

To argue for the identification of goodness with form in the ways developed so far, in this section I shall consider three examples in which we deliberate about how to make things better or worse. I am asking you to reflect on how we make judgments as to making things better or more valuable: Do we not take into account just the things I have talked about—the cultivation of elegance through the composition of components in functions of narrowness, width, vagueness, and triviality? The examples are an artist's thinking about a painting while executing it, the analysis of a personal character-defining situation, and reflections on the goods embodied in civilization. These are examples within the main topics of parts two, three, and four of this volume. In each of these considerations, imaginative deliberation varies the formal elements in ways discussed by the formal and situational analyses of form, with aesthetic judgment as to what variations make things better or worse. If this point rings true across the examples, then we have gone a long way toward identifying having goodness with having form.

By contrast with a personal character-defining dilemma in which most of the important things to reconcile are simply given, an artist has a great deal of freedom to choose what the baseline factors are going to be for a painting. For instance, the artist can choose the size and shape of the canvas, the medium (oil, acrylic, watercolor, etc.), the visual compositional elements, the colors, the subject matter if there is one, the reason for making the painting, and so forth. Notice that each of these baseline factors needs harmonization with the others. If the ostensible subject matter is a battlefield scene, the canvas should not be too small, and it probably should be horizontal. If the scene is to have many details, watercolor is not likely to be the best medium. Acrylic paint dries fast, which might be an advantage if there is a time pressure to finish the painting quickly for a buyer or exhibit; oil paints can be overpainted much more easily than acrylics if the artist thinks the details might evolve. The composition of a large, detail-filled painting needs to have overall compositional structure to give coherence to the canvas, but it also needs to have smaller compositional units, perhaps many of them, to integrate the details. The artist's initial imagining of the painting and procurement of the canvas, paints, brushes, and so forth, needs to think of these things in rough harmonic relations with one another. Of course, it is possible to paint a small, even a miniature, vertical canvas of a battlefield scene, but that would require simplifying the composition greatly, choosing very fine brushes, and selecting colors that harmonize in close proximity to one another.

Having selected a preliminary set of baseline conditions, suppose the artist begins a series of sketches of the compositional elements, say with chalk or pencil. Some artists even make quick preliminary sketches in oil or pastels to play with color as well as composition. The artist might try out two compositional sketches, one emphasizing a wealth of detail of many parts of the battle, the other a few focal points such as individual combat while vaguely rendering the rest of the two armies and the natural environment. The former approach emphasizes complexity, and the difficulty will be to integrate the whole with a few simple compositional elements. The latter approach emphasizes simplicity and the difficulty will be to suggest enough detail without losing the focus. Artists adjust the complexity and simplicity of a composition to optimize elegance in composition, although many different emphases exist that they need to bring into harmony. Several sketches can help the artist visualize alternative ways of composing the painting, though some artists can do the whole thing in the imagination. Artists can also imagine or sketch out preliminary color palettes.

Creating a painting is a dynamic process, and changes in composition, color, and the painting of sections continually can be adjusted to one another during the process. These changes occur as the artist sees what happens when the elements are developed. A constant set of evaluations happen concerning how things are fitting together or are not. The artist can see how a variation in this or that element affects the other elements and the harmony of the whole.

The baseline elements in the painting are themselves harmonies that have all sorts of components with many kinds of relations. Suppose the artist intends the painting simply to illustrate battlefield warfare, with no particular historical or literary battle in mind. Then the artist can emphasize the conflictual elements of the composition, render the identities of the combatants more vaguely, and reduce the historical setting to near triviality. If the artist wants to indicate the horrors of war, he or she paints the figures one way, but another way of painting is appropriate to indicate the glories of martial heroism. If the battle is an historical one, then it might be important to indicate the identities of the forces and their leaders, and the leading incidents within the battle. Perhaps the artist wants to please the victor or console the loser; suppose the purchaser wants to stress an ideological commitment. Symbols of many kinds can come into play. All these are factors that the artist varies in imagination in the attempt to find a very valuable way of painting the scene.

For many paintings, the composition is the main way by which the concrete form of the painting harmonizes its elements. Strong compositional lines and focal points develop the many elements of narrowness in the painting. The ways by which the compositional lines and focal points relate to one another across space develop the many elements of width. Most compositions create positive and negative spaces. The negative spaces function to fill the space trivially, the positive spaces vaguely. The composition can render all sorts of potential elements in the painting trivial. The painter imaginatively, and then physically with the brush, adjusts all these things as the painting is created.

The general upshot about the painting is that the artist imaginatively as well as experimentally tries out variations on complexity and simplicity, with different compositions of narrowness and width, vagueness and triviality, to see what leads to greater harmony. The internal harmony of the painting has to do with what is on the canvas, and the external harmony has to do with how the painting relates to its purpose and monetary goodness, to its referencing of history or not, its roles in the development of the artist's own craft and career, and so forth. The imaginative and experimental variations that the artist employs are variations on the important elements of form I described earlier. Throughout the imaginative contemplations, the artist grasps the imagined or experimental harmony with an intuitive aesthetic judgment of its harmoniousness of form, with the internal and external landscapes of lumpy densities of being, made coherent in a single more or less unified overall harmonious quality. It helps to have taught painting to children or inept adults to see the many ways in which the sought-after harmony of a painting can fail. Connoisseurship confined to museums skips the experience of understanding how harmonies can be less good than they could be.

The case with reasoning about relating to the world in ways that determine the agent's character is similar to that of art with the very important exception that the baseline components to harmonize are given rather than chosen as in the case of painting. Sometimes the dilemma is to choose the least evil possible outcomes. Other times it is to choose among goods that are exclusive of one another or diminish one another. Sometimes these intermix, as in the case of Aristotle's admirals debating whether to go to battle on the morrow and how exactly to act on their decision. More than in the case of painting, a personal dilemma has proximate baseline factors, such as whether to put to sea in such and such anticipated weather, that themselves bear the cumulative goods of recent and indeed more remote past history. What the admirals decide to do will add to history for better or worse, or rather, for better in some respects and worse in others. Moreover, there are consequences that follow from the possible configurations of the baseline components, consequences both proximate and remote. The contexts of character-forming reasoning are much denser and more intricately entwined across a broad existential field than are the typical contexts of painting. In addition to thinking about whether and how they might win on the morrow, the admirals need to reflect on what this battle means for the history and fortune of their city-state. What do they lose or gain by not fighting and saving their ships? What are the consequences of winning the battle at great cost that will impoverish their city-state and perhaps lose the larger war? What are the consequences of defeat? How do these remoter motives and consequences adjust the risks the admirals are willing to make? The admirals need to factor all of this through the field of future possibilities that include more than the battle site, and the actions of others not related to the battle directly. Aristotle would have understood that Themistocles and his admirals knew that fighting at Salamis against the Persian fleet was a way to lessen the pain of the defeat of the Greeks by Xerxes at Thermopylae a bit earlier in 480 BCE. Themistocles, the great politician, would have imagined the variables in the sea battle decision to extend very far into the historical and geographic context. His imaginative reasoning envisioned a great many of the contextual relations involved in the disposition of his ships on the morrow.

Although I shall not get more specific about contextual personhood reasoning and its appeal to the aesthetic intuition of the better and worse until part III, I can remark on one distinguishing mark of the personal, namely, that its imaginative possibilities relate to one another as better and worse, a kind of dyadic relation. The admirals need to figure out the best thing to do as accurately as they can. Most decisions among possibilities where significant decisions are required, however, are not just matters of dyadic moral judgment. They involve choosing different kinds of outcomes with different kinds of goodness. Choosing to eat chicken or fish on a given day is usually not a moral decision except in terms of remote economics of supply, fairness to animals, and the like. A young person's decision about what career to pursue is not particularly moral, although it might have moral components. Postponing more consideration of personal decisions among kinds of goodness until part III, however, let me consider reasoning about the kinds of goodness that are important in civilizations.

Civilizations are vastly complex kinds of harmonies, changing harmonies, with many different kinds of densities of goodness, in economics, the arts, tradition, coping with weather and geography, educational institutions, changing interactions among social and governmental elements within the civilization and in other civilizations, political authority, and many more kinds of things. Unlike the example of a painting where an artist decides, and unlike a personal situation where the choices rest with particular agents and determine the personal character of the agents, no one in particular decides to determine the existential field of goods that constitute the harmonic goodness of a civilization.

Nevertheless, within a situation in a civilization, countless decisions are made and careers followed that affect its balance of harmonic elements. For instance, European and North American civilizations have achieved great accomplishments in science, the arts, and letters, with a generally high economic base for most of us (for nearly all of us compared with many other civilizations). Nevertheless, the heritages of slavery and colonialism have negative values in a great many dimensions of life. What we do, wittingly and unwittingly, affects those negative goods that most of us would like to change. Nearly all civilizations on Earth in our time make many kinds of impact on climate change, one of the most consequential processes taking place in natural and social spheres of civilizations. The practices of quotidian life we follow, as much as the decisions of our large corporations, affect how civilizations influence climate change.

One of the most important dimensions of any civilization is how its educational practices and institutions shape the consciousness of various groups of people regarding the positive and negative things within their civilization. We need to be educated to appreciate, as accurately as possible, how our civilization manifests the valuable elements it does. We need to see how our lives enact, reinforce, or diminish various lumps of dense goodness in their civilization. This means we need to envision what the different goods resident in a civilization are. Part IV will explore this in detail. Here we can observe, however, that the map of the value-laden institutions, practices, achievements, and evils in a civilization needs to be imagined, something deeply difficult to do. To the extent that we do this, we imagine different ways to conceive the relations among the components of a civilization. How we imagine the goods of certain institutions, for instance, depends on the perspective from which we imagine. Attaining to fair perspectives for appreciating the goods in a civilization is itself an achievement that is rare in any civilization. I submit that how to conceive the goods in a civilization is a matter of imagining different forms of harmony for that civilization, noting that the harmony and its components are always in dynamic interaction. I will advance this case in part IV.

Immediacy and Mediacy in Framing Intensity

The previous section used examples from art, personal choice in the world, and goodness in civilization to illustrate the fact that in real life, we make decisions in part by imaginatively varying the elements of form in harmony and seeing what different kinds of harmony result, with different kinds of goodness. The aesthetic judgment, by which we appreciate the various imaginative projects, or actual things and situations before us, has a kind of immediacy. This is to say, we just grasp how the components of the harmony fit together with the harmony's form. The interpretive grasp not only sees how the things just fit; it also appreciates the goodness in the harmony grasped immediately. The grasp is a feeling of the weight of goodness in the harmony. It is an appreciation. It is a feeling of goodness-laden quality.

Nevertheless, such an act of aesthetic judgment is an interpretation and therefore signs mediate it. For the moment, call these signs "images." The painter interprets the canvas, paints, purpose of the painting, and all the rest with an imaginative visualized image of what the painting might look like. The process of painting evolves through many such imagined visual scenes that might interpret the intended painting so as to integrate the artistic materials into a plan for the next steps in the creative process. The imagined image can be a sign in an interpretation of the future with respect to doing something with the paints, and so forth. The image itself has to have an immediate hang-togetherness of its components in its form and relative to place in the existential field, beginning with the easel and amounting to something in the end when the painter imagines the painting to be finished. The interpretive judgment itself has the immediacy of taking the artistic materials as integrated by the image that refers to it. The act of taking is itself a harmony that just fits together. The interpretation has a qualitative unity of taking the elements to be harmonizable in ways that fit into the imagined visual image. Interpretations are constantly changing, of course, if the artist is creative, but each interpretation, each stage of interpretation, has the immediacy of taking the world to be the way the image refers to the elements. The aesthetic judgments in moral deliberation and in reflections on civilization are also immediate in that the judgments are concretely made, however fleeting.

This point about the immediacy of aesthetic judgment is universal in experience rather than limited to the artistic creative dimensions of experience, or to such judgment in personhood or civilization. The difference between an interpretive organism's reactive response to environmental elements and the experiencing of those elements consists in the interpreter using an image to integrate the elements. When we use imagistic signs to respond to the environment, we experience the environment. Without the imagistic signs, we are merely conditioned by the environment and condition it.[5]

Images are determinate—forms for integrating components—and as such related determinately to other images. Thus, a semiotic code or system comes into play when people begin to parse their environment and their drives in terms of images. A culture begins by developing systems of images for elementary interpretation of the world as a world experienced. These images function in experience often without being recognized as images. Rather, the experience takes the environment to be as the images say. The images themselves are neither true nor false except as used in interpretive judgments to experience the environment and one's engagements of the environment. In fact, the very possibility of interpretations concerned with the truth of how things exist supposes a reservoir of images so that people can wonder whether the world is like this image rather than that one. Whitehead rightly said the basic consciousness requires an interpretation that includes an "affirmation-negation" contrast: the world is as this image takes it rather than as that one would.[6] Basic consciousness is that the world is this way, interpreted by this image, rather than that way, interpreted by that image.

Most basic experience is not conscious of the images as such. Conscious interpretations have an immediate unity of the world taken as organized by the image functioning as sign. The act of interpretation, the "taking of the world to be as this image articulates it," is an immediate unity. Of course, we can also step back and interpret the image itself, and interpret its alternatives. A person in the jungle hears a rustling in the bush, interprets it with the image of a tiger waiting to pounce, and runs away fast. Such a person interprets the rustling as a tiger-situation. A more reflective person might think that it could be either a tiger or wind rustling the bush and stop to investigate which image works best—tiger-situation or wind-situation. Most of the time it will be wind. Nevertheless, enough times it is not, and humans evolved to use the danger-detecting images first; reflective inquirers in tiger territory tend to reproduce less. Our basic ways of experiencing the world develop from pragmatic practices of survival, finding food and water, and so forth.

Yet, a sense exists in which images can be true or false. They can be false by misidentifying the components in the world. For instance, it might be the wind, or it might be a tiger, and the image that is true is the one that gets it right. Moreover, most images integrate a number of things, for instance, a possible predator and the predicament of the prey; the image is false if it cannot integrate them. In ordinary experience, we employ many images at once, making many interpretations, integrating the interpretations with other interpretations, and so forth. At many levels in complex experience, we question and evaluate the signs that we employ, asking whether they are true within the interpretations within which we employ them.

The form of an image has the goodness of integrating its components. What is important to see in the world together and what can we treat as trivial or vaguely push away? How should we see the things in the world as connected or unconnected? Images are proposals or resources for answering those questions. The person in the jungle should have a tiger image that includes the tiger as predator and inclined to wait along paths for prey to come by; that tiger image is far more valuable than a visual picture of a tiger in an array of cats in a biology book. Both tiger images have their place, and their appropriateness for their respective places consists in them unifying the right elements.

As a sign, an image in experience imputes a goodness to the components of the environment or object interpreted. That goodness might not be correct about the environment. So experiential interpretations are always fallible. Our semiotic system of images and habits of interpretation might take the world to be immediately as the interpretive images say, when in fact other things ought to have gone into the interpretation because they too are important. The structure of images might simply ignore what they should have as components because the world contains relevant important things they miss. Moreover, any image has a form expressing narrowness and width in its composition but also dismissing other elements as vaguely unimportant or even trivial. The form of the image contains an existential field of densities arranged in the modes of triviality, vagueness, narrowness, and width. When an image functions in experience to articulate the environment or object for engagement, it proposes (immediately) that the environment or object has that form for the modes of triviality, vagueness, narrowness, and width. In this way, experience takes the world to have the goods it imagines it to have.

Of course, the images can be wrong, incoherent as harmonies, or missing what is important. This is particularly obvious in responding aesthetically to a work of art. What a person sees, looking at a painting, is what the person has the semiotic system and habits of interpretation to see. Some people look at paintings to see only familiar objects in them, scenes of a vase of flowers or a battle. They might never get around to interpreting the lines and structures of the composition or notice the palette of colors. An art critic will see much more in a painting than a person uncultured in that kind of art. Assuming that their eyes are equally good biologically, the untrained person will employ only interpretive images that push compositional and color elements into the vague or even trivial background, not noticing them or being affected by them. The critic will know to look for many dimensions of the work of art and will have images that lift all these things into importance. The critic will feel levels of value in the painting (and perhaps disvalues!) that the untrained person will not experience.

So experience is an achievement that involves, among other things, developing images that discern what is valuable in what is experienced. Experience is also recursive so that we experience ourselves experiencing. Experience is always mediated by signs, including images of the sort described. Experience is also shaped by purposes and interests and is responsive to shocks and frustrations. Nevertheless, it is always immediate in that there is an aesthetic judgment in any experiential interpretation that takes something to be a certain way.

Goodness, Engagement, Relations, and Experience

In the pragmatic tradition from which I have learned so much, experience is an affair of engaging with the world experienced. This seems obvious enough. Nevertheless, it stands in direct contrast with much of the Western philosophical tradition for which experience is an affair of human subjectivity. Generally, for most of the Western tradition influenced by Aristotle, people are substances and their experiences are among their properties. With the addition of Descartes's sharp distinction between mind and body, many in the tradition have confined experience to affairs of human mentality. The standard epistemological problem for modern philosophy has been whether, and if so how, you could know that the subjective experience in mind rightly represents the real world. Hume said we cannot know the external world, only the impressions and ideas that passed through mind, and he tried to define experience in terms of the force and vivacity of those impressions. This seemed to fly in the face of the fact that science was discovering all sorts of real and important things about the world. Kant argued that subjective experience could indeed be about objective reality by redefining objective reality as the appearances of the world constructed by subjective mind when it followed certain rules of investigation and critical judgment. Still, on Kant's view, the objective world known by science is only the subjective representations of mind as ordered by the rules governing spatial, temporal, and logical imagination and inference. Nothing real in the sense of transcending subjective representations is ever engaged, for Kant and his highly influential tradition. The pragmatic movement is a decisive rejection of this modern tradition of experience as that which can be described in consciousness only; perceptions of what is genuinely other than our subjective syntheses are constantly filled with surprise on our part.

Experience as engagement obviously includes the objects engaged as part of the experience. "Engagement" has a range of interpretations along a continuum. On one side are perceptions, which are largely forced upon us by physical kinds of interpretation, grabbing our attention. The goodness or beauty in the object perceived shapes out attention. On the other side are deliberate intentions to do something in and with the environment and its contents. The experience-situation of the sunset includes the meteorological events and the physical angle of vision as much as it does the interpretive experiencers with their visual apparatus, semiotic systems of color, shape, and movement discrimination, and emotional associations. The experience is a dynamic harmony that lasts several minutes. The interpreters' intentional orientation sets the contours of the situation of experience, but the distant horizon is as much a part of the experience as the subjective appreciations of the experiencers.

The theory of harmony developed here makes room for including within the harmony of the sunset experience both the meteorological events and the experiencers watching from the sunset terrace and all the relevant things in between. I can now supplement our previous discussion by saying that in the harmony that is the experience of the sunset, the form of the harmony gives great narrow focal weight to the meteorological events and the visual registration of this and semiotic interpretation in the experiencers, with much of the form coming from the intentionality of the experiencers. The form of the experience also gives great weight to the factors of width that allow (a) the visual orientation to events on the far horizon and (b) the transformation of meteorological events into a visual show of color, shape, and movement with great emotional or valuational impact on the experiencers who exclaim, "Wow! What a beautiful sunset!" Focused on the sunset, the experiencers still have a vague sense of place and orientation; perhaps they also vaguely transmute the stresses of a hard day into a sense of peace, all vague elements in the sunset experience. Given the "Wow" quality of the experience, the harmony of the sunset experience makes a great many things trivial, hardly counting if at all.

I have now placed a new level of analytical meaning on the notion of the "situation" of experience introduced in the first chapter. The human experience of goodness in the world consists of many experiences, each with its own kinds of harmony appropriate for its assorted situations. Experiences transform into experience of other things. They are included within larger experiences, and they contain more focused experiences. Some experiential situations harmonize sharply, others are fuzzier. In some, the objects in the experience forcefully shape the experiencers; in others, the experiencers are more active in forming the harmony. Sometimes the orientations that shape the experiencers' intentionality, which in turn forms the harmonic situation of the experience, come from antecedent, perhaps cultural expectations. Other times, the specific purposes of the experiencers make the most important differences. All these and countless other variations in experience register within this model of harmonies of experience.

This point, that the experience of something is a harmony that includes as components the object of the experience (the meteorological events) and the delighted appreciation of the colors and movement in the experiencers, and incalculably many intervening ecosystems of harmonic conditioning, is the philosophical ground for the conception of truth I shall defend in chapter 9. There I shall claim that truth is the carryover of value or what is important, given the interests and purposes of the interpreter, from the object to the interpreter as modified by intervening physical conditions, including the biology of the interpreter, as well as by the culture and semiotic systems.[7] The interpretation is true if the value in the object registers appropriately in the interpreter. Do not worry about the technicalities in that definition yet. My point about the carryover of value contrasts explicitly with Aristotle's claim that what carries over is form: true knowledge of, say, a cup consists in getting the form of the cup out of its ceramic matter into the mental matter of the knower. My theory stresses that what carries over is goodness, value, or importance, and that its form can change radically, say, from meteorological events to the vision of beautiful colors, shapes, and movements. Nevertheless, there is a conundrum with my theory. If goodness or value is born by the form of a harmony, then if the form is changed in the carryover, must not the value itself then be changed as well? If so, then the goodness cannot be carried over. On the contrary, I answer that each of the relevant ecosystemic harmonies intervening between the meteorological events (the object) and the delighted appreciation of people on the sunset terrace (the subjective interpretation) takes in the value of the antecedent conditioning ecosystem in its own way. Each intervening ecosystemic harmony composes the antecedents' goods in forms with narrowness, width, vagueness, and triviality. Each passes the value on with its own transformations. The interpretive experience is a vastly complex harmony that includes all the carryovers from the meteorological events to the mental image that one of the viewers might paint by embodying it in oil on canvas. You can see how vastly complex and minutely intricate the evolution of life on earth must be to give rise to beings that can experience and enjoy sunsets. Science is only beginning to articulate the ecosystems of causal carryover. Regarding sunsets, we are usually more interested in beauty than in truth. Nevertheless, we can say that the viewer's visual image is true of the meteorological events if those events are not too foggy or too cloudless and the sun is in the right position relative to the viewing platform. The real object, the meteorological events, is included in the harmony of its being a sunset for the viewers, and that harmony includes as its composed components all the relevant intervening harmonies. Interpretation is far more complex than I have indicated so far, especially regarding the respects in which an object is interpreted as selected by the interpreters' purposes. It can be true to say, however, that truth is the carryover of what is good or important (for the interpreter) from the object to the interpreter's interpretation, as mediated by the vast complexity of the experience itself including the object.

Another legacy of Kant is called into question by this model, namely, his emphasis on the unity of the self, his construction of experience on the basis of the transcendental unity of apperception, his claim that the "I think" automatically accompanies any subjective (and objective) representation. I would say rather that the unity of the self is something achieved. It is a harmony whose components consist, among other things, of the experiences that the self makes its own. Those experiences are harmonies that include the real objects experienced. How a self harmonizes experiences to contribute to its own harmony is extraordinarily complex and worthy of careful inquiry. Kant was hiding those questions when he appealed to the transcendental unity of apperception as automatic. Of course, Kant would accuse me of mistaking his transcendental logical point with a genetic psychological one. For him, the transcendental unity of apperception is part of the logical apparatus to which experiential thinking must conform if it is to have objective experience and knowledge. Empirical selves need not conform to this at all, which happens often enough when we make mistakes. Even more important for Kant is that the empirical self is known empirically, that is, as determined under the conditions of objective knowledge, and must appear as an automaton experiencing mechanistically. Because the theory of pragmatic engagement does not need a transcendental apparatus of subjectivity to ascertain objectivity, we can ignore his objection. The genetic psychological account of the development of the harmony of the self, such as it is, takes precedence over transcendental logic.

When we think of the experiencers watching the sunset, we assume that they are selves and that what they are experiencing of the sunset is one of the experiences that they harmonize into their cumulative personal experience. Moreover, we assume that those experiencers have a significant history of experiences that they have already integrated into their harmony of the sunset moment. This history of experiences so integrated sets them up to notice sunsets, to revel in that kind of beauty, to get themselves to the sunset terrace on time, and to have a deep goodness–laden character into which this experience comes as a potential new element. The development of selves, of persons, is a matter of very high goodness. Persons are valuable, and our art, our fulfillment of obligations, and our civilizations are devoted to fostering the development, among other things, of those harmonies that constitute selves. So many things of goodness need to be harmonized into a self! Consider the goods in bodily life and health, of personal psychological growth, achievement, and promise, of coming to terms with family and social situations, and of whatever we can imagine as part of a person's life. The harmonies definitive of persons are special kinds of harmonies, four of which I shall discuss at length in part III. The harmonies definitive of experiences are other special kinds of harmonies. The harmonies that consist of experiences require as components the harmonies of selves to give them intentional orientation. The harmonies in which selves consist require many experiential harmonies because so much of human personal harmony involves interpretations of experiences in light of interpretations of what they mean for the person.

Many if not most experiences are had by persons together, as my wife and I enjoy the sunsets from our sunset terrace together. Many modern philosophers follow Descartes and Kant in thinking that there are two experiences of the same sunset, hers and mine.

On the contrary: we jointly experience the sunset. She integrates that sunset experience into herself as part of her person, and I integrate it into myself as part of my person. Nevertheless, we are together in experiencing the sunset, and it is one harmonious situation of experience with two experiencers. The bias of modern subjectivism should not mislead us here. The joint character of many experiences is very important for understanding human community and sociality. It is important for morality and civilization. Social life is not an aggregate of individual subjective experiences. It is an aggregate of conjoint experiences that might or might not be also harmonized into the personal selves of individuals. A community's experience of racism is what it is, even when many individuals within that community deny that experience as a component within their personal lives. In the case of the experience of racism, such denial of the importance of that experience in the life of the racist is very harmful. The experience of racism has at least two if not more kinds of experiencers bound together conjointly, the racists and the victims. That experience has a harmonic form shaped by both intentional perspectives of experiencers. Thinking this through would reveal a vast array of loci of goodness. However, the legacy of subjective individualism in experience manages to hide many of those loci of goodness.

The complicated argument of this and the preceding three chapters has laid the groundwork in cosmology, theory of form, and theory of goodness for a complex understanding of how goodness is laced throughout human experience. Do you begin to see how goodness is a dimension of anything that has form? The theory should prove its worth in discussing goodness in beauty and art, in obligation and personhood, and in flourishing and civilization, weaving together more strands of evidence, twisting and braiding as in a rope. We are now prepared to reflect on aesthetic goodness in its most basic form, as beauty, and as acknowledged and enhanced in art.

PART II

———————

Goodness in Beauty and Art

Beauty is the most fundamental and important trait of existence. At least this is the hypothesis about beauty that I shall elaborate and of which I hope to persuade you. Without a form that gives it beauty, a harmony could not exist. If a harmony exists, its form is beautiful in its own way. No matter what other kinds of goodness a thing might have, and indeed many other kinds exist, for a harmony to be itself is for it to have beauty. A harmony achieves beauty by its essential components that compose the totality of the components, conditional and essential, so that they have narrowness, width, vagueness, and triviality, balancing simplicity and complexity with some elegance. "Existence," in the sense encompassed here, includes possibilities as well as actual things and moments of creative becoming, and it includes all the things that people might imagine or know.

Beauty is the goodness a thing has in itself, as opposed to the kind of good it has as a component of other things or as an organizer of the fates of other things in the world. For the theory of harmony and relatedness I have been developing here, "in itselfness" is weird. Any harmony has among its components all the other things to which it relates by virtue of being determinate with respect to them. Therefore, a thing has no nature by itself, no properties that define it by itself. Nevertheless, any harmony *is its own way* of harmonizing its components, and other harmonies with many of the same conditional components harmonize them differently. What makes each harmony unique in its way are its essential components that give it its own-being, hence its existence. Its unique existence is not the essential components themselves but what those essential components do to harmonize all the components.

Because things exist by bearing at least the goodness of beauty, beauty is an especially important kind of goodness for religion. What the ontological act of creation creates is determinate things with beauty. They might also have many other kinds of goodness, but at least they have beauty. In this important sense, appreciation of beauty is the appreciation of creation at its most ultimate and intimate levels. If your metaphors for the ontological creative act are personifications, then appreciating beauty is appreciating the handiwork of God. If your metaphors have more to do with consciousness, appreciating beauty is blissing out on the suchness of things that arise in consciousness. If your metaphors have little to do with personlike agency or the fundamental consciousness in which all things have form, then per-haps appreciating beauty is delighting in the spontaneity of the sheer emergence of things.

Art is the human production of beauty, or at least the attempt to produce something that the artist intends to be beautiful. Of course, any art production, like any determinate thing, is beautiful in its way. The kind of beauty produced might be of such low quality, however, that we would judge the artwork to be a near miss, or a far miss. We should understand art, I shall argue, as what people would delight in for its own sake under the right circumstances. Art has many other kinds of goodness than what is delightful in itself, such as monetary value, the enhancement of an artist's career, and so forth. What gives an artwork the prima facie claim to be art, however, is that it is appreciable for its beauty.

To the extent art is the human production of beauty, artists are little creators, miniature versions of the ontological creative act. Of course, they are created as that by and within the ontological creative act. Nevertheless, artists have the special goodness of being creators, creators of the existential reality of beautiful things. This makes artists of interest to religion.

Is not all of this outrageous? Is not beauty just a condition that sometimes obtains in nature and in human productions, but that is rare in both places? Nature is hard and most human productions are ugly and often destructive, dangerous, and regrettable. Besides, they say that beauty is in the eye of the beholder, not in the things to which their eye ascribes beauty. How can I convince you to tie beauty to the metaphysical conditions of harmony and determinateness? In the chapters of this part I attempt to domesticate the outrage of these claims and open your sensibilities to perceive their truth.

The first chapter in this part addresses the nature of beauty itself and how we perceive it. Building on the analysis of goodness in part I, it explains the metaphysics of existence as depending on the essential integration of any determinate thing's components in a harmonic form. It argues that the best way to use the notion of beauty is to see it as characteristic of all things that have harmony (which includes any determinate thing whatsoever) and to interpret this as an ultimate condition of existence. Beauty in an actual thing is the simplification both of the multitude of alternative possibilities for that thing and of the many potentials in the actual things that need integration in a moment of creative becoming. Both kinds of simplification lead to actualities that we can characterize as haecceities, "thises," to use Duns Scotus's language. The chapter also sets up the discussion of how we can experience beauty by drawing on the concept of a "situation of experience" that I introduced in part I.

Chapter 6 moves to make all the preceding plausible and persuasive through the analysis of art. It starts with a hauntingly beautiful passage from John Dewey (who says Dewey could not write poetically?) about the priority of the human longing for enjoyment over the need for work. We act, he said, for the sake of art, especially the humble arts rather than the fine arts (a distinction he deconstructed). From this longing for enjoyments, the chapter moves to the impulses of creativity to make steady and available things to enjoy, namely, artworks. The chapter then argues in more detail that this simple impulse to enjoy is at root a celebration of existence, even when existence is what Hobbes called "solitary, poor, nasty, brutish, and short."[1] This leads into a complex discussion of some of the connections of art with religion.

Chapter 7 examines the appreciation of art. I intend to deepen the argument that beauty consists in the goodness peculiar to the form of a harmony considered in itself by dealing in this case with harmonies

that are works of art. Three principal topics occupy this chapter: what
the form of art works is, what the situations of appreciation are, and
how art works have their beauty even when not appreciated, art "in
repose" as I call it. The chapter introduces discussions of many examples of art, such as painting, sculpture, and architecture as "static" arts;
music, dance, theater, sports, and other performance arts as "dynamic"
arts; and poetry, stories, novels, and other literature that are static in the
sense of being there all at once but dynamic in the sense that their
forms essentially unfold in the reading of them. Of course, we take
time to walk through a building to appreciate its architecture. We take
time to analyze and come to appreciate a painting. Furthermore, all
art appreciation can change over time as a given person engages the
work in new circumstances, with new critical appreciation. Gardens
are among the most complicated kinds of art in terms of their own
form and the situations of those who appreciate them.

Chapter 8 discusses the creation of art and takes its clue from
John Dewey's notion of "an end in view." The relevant end in view
for artists is the creation of a work of art. How the artist imagines the
end is part of the process of artistic creativity, as the end is a form that
needs to take enough shape that an actual work of art can embody it.
The other side of this is the creativity of working with the materials
of the art, taking "materials" in a broad sense, to see how the artist
can make them coherent or not with this or that form. Thus, the
creativity of the artist works dialectically between imagination of ever
more determinate form as possibility and mastery of the materials.
Imagination and mastery are yoked powers of artists. Choreographers
or composers produce one kind of form in their art works, whereas
dancers or musicians introduce different kinds of form such as performance styles and the singularity of actualization itself. The chapter
finally introduces the topic of the particular kind of beauty in the
artistic life, the life dedicated to artistic creativity. The last discussion
is only introductory, however, awaiting analysis of the goodness of
persons and civilizations in parts 3 and 4.

CHAPTER 5

Beauty in Form

Beauty as What Is Good in Itself

Western thought has thematized goodness under many labels, including the medieval transcendentals Goodness, Beauty, Truth, and Unity, to which I would immediately attach Diversity. This set of associations goes back at least to Plato and the tradition has treated them from many angles. East and South Asian thought, and Islamic philosophy, have made similar associations. The Perennial Philosophy, found in many different cultures with the international influence of Neo-Platonism, has united many of these different traditional associations, giving special prominence to Unity. Huston Smith and Seyyed Hossein Nasr are distinguished and well-known representatives of Perennial Philosophy.[1] I do not share their philosophy's emphasis on unity and hierarchy, insisting as I do that unity means nothing without a diverse plurality unified.[2] Yet I appreciate the complexity of the different themes for understanding goodness.

Beauty is hard to define because we can approach its definition in two ways. One is to be open and faithful to the plethora of forms in which we speak of beauty in our experience and in the cultural traditions that provide the background for our discussion. The other is to give a heuristic definition that can order and direct our inquiry. The advantage of the former is that it is a venue for saying that the way I describe beauty is true and accurate, resonating with various

usages. Its disadvantage is that the uses of the term "beauty" are chaotic and disorganized (unless brought together in a beautiful way!).
The advantage of the latter is that we can begin our discussion with
a definition and then see whether that has been fruitful at the end
of inquiry. Its disadvantage is that it will seem arbitrary, especially to
those who prefer to define beauty in some other way. I will begin
with a heuristic definition and then see whether I can use enough
examples to rake in at least a great many of the ways by which we
speak of beauty in experience.

Let me begin with the heuristic claim that beauty is that which is
good insofar as it is good in itself and needs no further qualification for
having the goodness it does. Sometimes we call this intrinsic goodness.
Beautiful things also have goodness as components in other things, as
my theory of harmony hypothesizes from many angles. Sometimes
we call these instrumental goods, as when a beautiful painting also
is valuable because of its contribution to the wealth of its owner or
the fame of its artist. Sometimes, something beautiful can become a
component in another thing and be appreciated precisely because of
its intrinsic worth or beauty, as when a connoisseur appreciates the
painting for its beauty as well as its financial worth or contribution
to a career.

Beautiful things also have goodness other than beauty by virtue of
what they do with things that are their components. Sometimes they
enhance those things and sometimes they degrade them. The other
things of course have their own beauty in themselves, but their natures
might be modified as they are incorporated into a harmony among
its components. What I shall mean by beauty here is the goodness a
thing has simply as being itself.

This point derives from the discussion of goodness as form in part
I of this book. Beauty is the goodness a form achieves that harmonizes
the components of a harmony in its place relative to other harmonies
in an existential field. For a form to harmonize the components of
a harmony in an existential location is to achieve the goodness I call
beauty. The harmony itself might be a component in countless other
harmonies, and it might be appreciated as beautiful, but its being
valued as narrow, wide, vague, or trivial in those other things is not
necessarily a function of its beauty. You might say that the beauty of
a harmony is the Firstness of its form.

Charles Peirce, who thought that aesthetic goodness is the norm for all other kinds of goodness, said things can be classified as Firsts, Seconds, and Thirds. I introduced this point in the preface by way of giving a rationale for the organization of this volume. Firstness is a thing's being what it is without regard for anything else. Secondness is a thing's being what it is by virtue of being not something else, different as such, perhaps in opposition. Thirdness is a thing's being what it is by virtue of mediating between a multiplicity of things, or at least two of them. Any determinate thing is a harmony of components and so it must be a Third that unites its components that are what they are, Firsts, and that are different from one another, Seconds. In Peirce's terms, beauty is the Firstness of Thirdness, the quality a harmony has as just being itself as a Third harmonizing components. Whereas Peirce thought of a Third as something on its own that brings other things into relation, I stress that harmonies are the just fitting together of things in forms of togetherness. Peirce would likely counter that the form of the harmony is precisely the Third that mediates all the components. I would answer that, yes, the form of the harmony is a Third that mediates the components, but nevertheless form is not something more than the components fitting together.

Extending Peirce's categories in anticipation of later parts of this book, obligation in personhood is based fundamentally on a relation between two things: one thing is obligated about something else. Perhaps the signs in an interpretation are true about the object interpreted, or perhaps they are wrong. Perhaps one harmony should embrace another as a component without distortion, or not. Human obligation lies on a large vague class of actions. Truth is a species of obligation that has to do with being right in propositions about their object. Morality in the usual sense is making the right choice in a situation. Moral deliberation is a matter of seeking truth about the moral situation to be resolved. Rightness is the Secondness of a situation in which harmonies, Thirds, are in a relation that obligates one to others in an appropriate way. Rightness is the Firstness of the Secondness of a situation normatively relating things in right or wrong ways. Something that is right or wrong is always in a relation of "aboutness" to something else. Beauty is not right or wrong: it just is, in the form of a thing being what it is.

Flourishing is the goodness of a field of things such that the harmony of the field enhances the goods of the things in some way. A civilization is the harmony of a field of individuals and institutions in certain relations. It is the Firstness of the Thirdness of a culturally integrated group, integrated in certain respects and only up to a point.

In Peirce's terms, part II of this book studies the Firstness of the world's things, part III the Secondness of the relations between persons and the world's things, and part IV the Thirdness of the world's things. Of course, at this stage in the argument, these remarks only explain the obscure by the more obscure, though by the end you will say, "Aha!" I hope.

To grasp the beauty of something requires some kind of aesthetic experience. In fact, the term "beauty" has become associated with aesthetics. We sometimes say that nature is beautiful, using the language of aesthetic experience, and the beauty found in art in some ways defines the field of aesthetics. The Greek root of aesthetics and its cognates means perception and has come to mean the beauty of something *as perceived*. By beauty in this book, however, I mean the quality of a harmony that has the intrinsic goodness of harmonizing the components as such, whatever other goodness or badness it has for other things. This is my heuristic definition of beauty. The immediate togetherness in the harmony is a goodness that we can grasp in a perception that focuses on the harmony. Because of the immediacy of the grasp of the togetherness in perception, we call the harmony "aesthetic" or beautiful. Nevertheless, many times it happens that something is beautiful and we miss it, only to discover its beauty later. Sometimes we mistakenly believe something is beautiful in a certain way because we impose a false image of togetherness upon it. Sometimes the perception that we believe grasps the beauty of something has so misidentified its components or even its form that we say, upon discovering these mistakes, that the thing is not beautiful after all. Of course, if everything with form has the intrinsic beauty given by the form itself, then everything has its own beauty. David Rohr (in a personal communication) quotes Peirce from an unpublished manuscript: "As a matter of Opinion, I believe that Glory shines out in everything like the sun and that any aesthetic odiousness is merely our Unfeelingness resulting from obscurations due to our own moral and intellectual aberrations." We might perceive a thing to have such a low level of beauty that we call it ugly from a human standpoint. What we perceive in aesthetic experience is beauty as interpreted, and that interpretation might be wrong. It is always at least partial, for reasons I shall explore.

To make my case for defining beauty, of course I must appeal to how we perceive things as beautiful. How else could I persuade you? Nevertheless, the beauty is in the harmony perceived, or misperceived. The very fact that our personal experience of something as beautiful can turn out to be wrong indicates that the reality of the harmony perceived as beautiful measures the perception.

To be sure, the study of aesthetic *experience* needs to account for how we experience things as beautiful in a way even when they are not beautiful in that way. We need to account for the role of images in experience that have the intrinsic hang-togetherness of aesthetic experience, regardless of whether they are iconic of that of which they are images. Sunsets, songs, or statues have intrinsic beauty because of the form of their harmony. To perceive these things as aesthetically beautiful requires that the perceiver in the "situation" of each be able to interpret the hang-togetherness in the objects. This involves many long processes of harmonies embracing components and in turn being embraced by subsequent interpreting harmonies. Our semiotic systems of signs can transmute those processes to distort what we need to grasp in order aesthetically to perceive the beautiful things. Perhaps the sunset viewers are more interested in each other, or in the wine, than in the sunset, and so miss most of it. Perhaps the listeners do not know how to discriminate the important elements in the song and thus cannot hear its harmony. Perhaps the statue's viewers are so trained that they can see only kitsch in the statue. I shall return to beauty as experienced in the last section of this chapter and in the discussions of art in subsequent chapters.

Beauty as Ubiquitous and Ultimate

Before focusing on aesthetic experience, however, I shall exercise my strategy of switching back and forth from the experience of beauty to the nature of beauty, laying out more of the complexities of the metaphysics and cosmology of beauty, braiding more strands into the rope of my major hypothesis.

To be a determinate thing at all is to have a form according to which its components are integrated and, because of this form, to be beautiful. Beauty is the goodness that consists in being determinate at all. To be determinate is to be beautiful. To be determinate is to have the particular beauty of that determinate thing. Without being determinate, a thing would have no existence, no existence as a possibility or an actuality, no existence as real or as imaginable. Beauty is the primitive goodness of existence as such. All this I have said or implied since the beginning.

Given the ecological complexities of harmonies, however, a determinate thing that has its own beauty can be extraordinarily destructive of the beauty of its components. It can be terrible for the harmonies that in turn include it as a component. As a determinate thing enters into other harmonies in many directions across an existential field, it takes on many goods other than that of its intrinsic beauty. Its intrinsic beauty might be completely lost if the thing is decomposed so as to lose its formal harmony, or is transmuted into vagueness by a very different kind of harmony, or is dismissed into triviality. Therefore, the simple claim that a thing is beautiful because it has an integrating form if it is determinate at all is not for a moment to suggest that there is no ugliness in the world. Ugliness is the condition in which components ought to harmonize a certain way for some reason but the form that they have together does not achieve that harmony. To say that everything is beautiful by virtue of having a determinate form is not at all to suggest that there is not horrendous violence and destruction in the world. Earthquakes cause environmental ecologies to dissolve, societies to collapse, and people to die and suffer. Natural forces are heedless of much of the harmonic structures needed for human life and civilization. The dinosaurs were vulnerable to radical climate change caused by at least one huge comet hitting the Earth. Supernovas destroy most harmonies among their components. Black holes suck in everything that comes too close.

Societies are harmonies that sustain human life for as long as they last. Nevertheless, they can be vicious and oppressive to many people within them. Their agriculture and industry can destroy the natural environment. Their organization can lead to horrendous war and violence. Human beings can possess many beautifully organized components, such as a strong body or a sharp wit. Nevertheless, they can use the strength to cause suffering and the wit to make suffering worse. Such harmonies as there might be in racism and bigotry, greed, and power mongering are highly destructive of human flourishing, and surely any decent human society ought to oppose them in all their particularities.

Although nature is red in tooth and claw, and human life is often "solitary, poor, nasty, brutish, and short," much of this is among the vital conditions for the harmonies that make up complex biological existence and the necessities of human society. Animals are predators of what they eat and plants break down chemicals in the soil. Organized societies employ force to limit harmful (and sometimes helpful) social practices, and that force may not be equally beneficial to all the people affected. Money corrupts, but it also allows for the production of wealth that can help things flourish. Given the relations that make things harmonious, horror, violence, and indefinitely many dimensions of negative goodness riddle many aspects of life, and existence itself.

Therefore, it is with good reason that many people complain about my use of the term "harmony" to mean determinate things. Harmony is good, of course, and suggests that everything might be just fine. In Confucian thought, harmony is what makes things coherent and hence determinate.[3] The ancient Confucian classic *The Doctrine of the Mean* (Zhong-Yong) said:

> Before the feelings of pleasure, anger, sorrow, and joy are aroused, it is called equilibrium. When these feelings are aroused and each and all attain due measure and degree, it is called harmony. Equilibrium is the great foundation of the world, and harmony its universal path. When equilibrium and harmony are realized to the highest degree, heaven and earth will attain their proper order and all things will flourish.[4]

When things go wrong, it is because things do not harmonize and they exist in destructive conflict. Nevertheless, as the Confucians also know, sometimes things simply cannot harmonize. The very meaning of harmony is that things with their own goods play many roles in other things, with very different goods, to their weal or woe. "Harmony" should not connote treacly goodness. In fact, it is what explains how things that are all good in some sense, at least beautiful when looked at exclusively on their own terms, can be in destructive conflict with one another. Sometimes the things that are greater goods are destroyed by things of lesser good. In the actual world, harmonies usually do not last, no matter how good they are. Such is the nature of harmonies, at least in the world we live in. Harmonies, in their ecological harmonic structures, cause ugliness, destruction, and evil as well as all the other kinds of goodness.[5]

Nevertheless, each harmonious thing has the glorious beauty of the integrity of its form integrating its components. Taken by itself, each form is beautiful, making the harmony beautiful. Intrinsic beauty is ubiquitous. Beauty defines the definiteness of any determinate thing. Of course, we cannot take harmonies out of context. Each defines its location in existential fields relative to other things, and it achieves its own goodness identity within the Ten Thousand Things. Nevertheless, in its own form itself, each harmony is beautiful.

This is the inspiration behind the widespread, though by no means universal, view that everything positive is good and that evil or badness is only a function of limitation or misplacement of being. Augustine said that everything God creates is good insofar as it has being, is limited in its goodness by not being something else, and diminishes in goodness when nonbeing, destructiveness, or antibeing infects it. Augustine and many others worked with a Neo-Platonic hierarchy with greater reality or being at the top identified with oneness and lesser reality arranged in levels characterized by increasing kinds of limitation or nonbeing. Seyyed Hossein Nasr beautifully expresses this view today. This is not my supposition, however. I do signal agreement with Augustine and his tradition that anything that has determinate existence at all is good in the sense defined here as being beautiful.

Therefore, the ubiquity of beauty is a universal condition of existence. To exist is to have form, which is to have beauty. This is an ultimate condition of existence. Not to have beauty is not to have form, and therefore not to be anything. Evil, destruction, violence, and all the other negatively valuable things in the universe are determinate and therefore are beautiful in their way.

Most of the time we attend to the beautiful things that are pragmatically important and for which we have semiotic resources for grasping. Many things are narrowly and widely important for us regarding their beauty. Many more things are vaguely transmuted or trivially dismissed in their beauty. In the next chapter, I shall discuss the role of art in fashioning our matrices for construing the beautiful things in the world as beautiful. Here I want to note that, in common experience, we do not recognize everything as beautiful. Our common experience is pragmatically alert to all the harms that stem from the constitutions of the universe through harmonies. Many people live lives that are so bereft of what we commonly recognize as beautiful that they are wretched.

Despite this, the great religions of the world suggest that experience can be cultivated into spiritual depths so that adepts can recognize something close to the ubiquity of beauty. They have cultivated many spiritual paths for this. Most of these paths have to do with detaching ourselves from favoring certain harmonies over others so that we do not mourn their passing. This is a Buddhist way of putting it. Steve Odin has shown how the Japanese sense of tragic beauty focuses on letting each thing pass, each harmony or determinate thing, each dharma as the Buddhists would say.[6] What is left in the celebration of passing is only that each thing is beautiful in itself, and that its passing is the loss of its existence. This is a tough posture for moral vitality in which striving to achieve goods and avoid evils is an ultimate condition. Nevertheless, it underscores the ubiquity of beauty as an ultimate condition of life.

The religious recognition of the ubiquity of beauty as an ultimate condition shows up in Western religions as well, although detachment from craving is not the motif as much as the identification with creation as such. The Twenty-Third Psalm, common to Jews, Christians, and Muslims, says that God is our shepherd who protects, improves, and makes us flourish, which is manifestly false. Paradoxically, in some religious groups this psalm is a favorite at funerals that celebrate the ending of life. I think this means that at some level, the psalm communicates that everything is beautiful despite death, sickness, loss, destruction, violence, and the ambiguities of even the most fortunate lives. Its peace passes understanding, precisely because its images indicate the beauty of things where much else overshadows the beauty.

Beauty as Simplification

Another dimension of beauty is that it is a simplification. Any beautiful form is a possible or actual simplification of all the components that might function within it. These include all the things that relate to the form with respect to which it is determinate and all the essential components that constitute the own-being of the form's harmony. Any determinate beautiful form constitutes a decisive selection of its own way of composing its components. They might be composed some other way, with a different disposition of narrowness, width, vagueness, and triviality. The unique ontological reality, the thisness or haecceity, is how a form as beautiful simplifies the world that consists of the things that might be its components.

This dimension of beauty stands in preliminary contrast with that described in the previous section, which pertains to the goodness that obtains in the beautiful form itself. The form in itself has the intrinsic beauty of putting its components into a certain pattern, and this is true of all forms. The perspective of the achieved form looks back, as it were, on the components, and components of components, that the form composes in trivial, vague, narrow, and wide functions. From the perspective of the components, however, indefinitely dense and various as they are with myriad relations constituting the basic cosmic existential field, the achievement of the form of the harmony is a simplification. It is a simplification in two senses.

First, any given set of possible components might be harmonizable in a number of different ways, and the determinate harmonization of them in one harmony simplifies that range of possibilities. In human terms, this can be a conscious choice among many envisioned possibilities. Although in principle any given harmonization with a form relates directly or indirectly with all other harmonies with respect to which it is determinate, the relevant existential field of components is finite, dismissing most relations into triviality. Groups can determine their structure in many different ways. Politicians can offer competing visions for what to do. Personal choices, group drift, or electoral victory for one kind of political vision all involve the simplification of possibilities for integrating the given components (including possibilities) in some one determinate harmonious outcome (remembering that the harmony might be very bad and destructive of other valuable things). In this first sense of simplification, any simplification that achieves a harmony has its own particular beauty.

The second sense of simplification is that each harmony is the achievement of something novel over and above the possible components as unharmonized. We understand this easily in temporal terms. In fact, Whitehead's Category of the Ultimate says that creativity integrates any given many into a new entity, thus increasing the many by one. You do not have to accept his interpretation of ultimacy to see that it illustrates my point. A new event within natural time integrates all its antecedents into its own form, adding something more to the past. Even if it merely repeats a harmony in its immediate past, it differs at least in relating to things in time differently from its predecessor, minimally by coming after it. In this way, every moment in a mountain is new, though very much unchanged in other ways. Every novel unique harmony has a particular achieved identity.

This second sense of simplification of possible components is what gives each harmony its own-being. A harmony is determinate not only because it relates to all the other harmonies with respect to which it is determinate but also because it has its own essential components that integrate all its components into its unique form. Many kinds of essential components can exist. For instance, a person can take out a mortgage on a house; until the mortgage is paid off, every subsequent phase of the person's life is essentially obligated by the past deal to pay off the mortgage in the future. Most of the important continuities of human life, in morals and even more in the creative making of a particular life, including making art, involve essential components in which the past obligates the future.

Here I want to stress that essential components give the harmony a standing to relate to other harmonies. In a strict sense, there is no "given" set of possible components to be harmonized except from an existential perspective to which they can be given. The existential essential components must be present for the harmony to be a term in relations with other things in the existential field. The harmony cannot have existential location in that field without the existential essential components that integrate its conditional components into a location or position. The conditional components are necessary for other things to be related, and the existential essential components are necessary for those relations to be integrated into the harmony that bears them. A harmony must integrate its conditional components into its own being. Without the existential essential components, the components would not be integrated, or they would be integrated only into a different harmony with a different form.

Whitehead saw the deep metaphysical issues with this sense of simplification. As he put it, there is no such thing as a simple multiplicity except from a perspective. For him, an emerging event has to begin with subjective unity that is enough of a perspective to determine what things are in the past, what things are simultaneous, and what things are future possibilities, for the event to occur.[7] This would be, for him, what I am calling existential essential components giving the emerging event its own-being relative to what it can incorporate and to which it can relate. Whitehead gave a genetic account of how an event can emerge, beginning with the things it can incorporate plus the subjective unity. The process of emergence, "concrescence" in his language, has many phases that result in what he called "subjective harmony," the completely determinate new event that is a new simplification of all the antecedent resources for harmonization. How does Whitehead account for the novel arising of subjective unity, which is necessary for the emergence of subjective harmony? He said that it is an envisionment of a possible emergence in God, and that every event begins by grasping that envisionment. This first grasp is how events incorporate God into their most basic structure. Once grasped, that divine envisionment functions as a lure for how the event can and perhaps should emerge into a determinate harmony. With this in mind, Whitehead called God the "Poet of the World," who creates things all of which have goodness because of the form actualized.[8]

I find Whitehead's account unsatisfactory, however. How does an emerging event have the standing to grasp God's envisionment in the first place, if having that envisionment is a necessary condition for grasping anything? Whitehead's theory begs the question at this point. Furthermore, Whitehead's account of God says that at no finite time is God determinate enough for things in the world to grasp. Whitehead acknowledged that God apart from the world is deficient in actuality. Charles Hartshorne recognized this and reconceived God, in *The Divine Relativity*, as a society of strictly connected emergent events, each one of which is determinate and thus graspable by a subsequent finite emergent event. Hartshorne's concept of God has its own difficulties, as I have argued.[9] Moreover, it does not solve the problem of how a finite emergent event has the standing to grasp a determinate divine event if that divine event is what would have to give it such standing.

My preferred solution is to scrap Whitehead and Hartshorne's appeals to a finite God interacting with things within time and say instead that the necessary existential essential components of any harmony are elements of that harmony's portion of the terminus of the ontological creative act. God (or Brahman, the Dao, or however we symbolize that act) creates everything determinate in a singular ontological creative act. That act is eternal in the sense of not being in time. Time is created along with all temporal things. Nevertheless, within time, the creation of a determinate harmony occurs in a duration of present moments. Its components include things now past that, in their own present moments, had divinely created existential essential components; its components include future possibilities whose intrinsic form is nontemporal or eternal, but whose form relevant for actual things can become actual if chosen. The ontological creative act is eternal in its creating, but its created products locate the creativity relevant to them in their temporal positions.

Of course, the essential components of harmonies are not the only created products of the ontological act. The act creates all the components of harmonies as well. Harmonies include their components through their forms composing things with triviality, vagueness, narrowness, and width. Therefore, in this sense, all determinate things are created within an ontological context of mutual relevance. Within that context, there is a cosmological context of mutual relations constituted by the assorted conditionings, and these conditionings give the structure to the temporal world.

Mystical religions find various ways to symbolize this dependence on the ontological creative act. Some find the symbols for appreciating the internal existential essential components. Others find symbols for appreciating the unity in the world, or in the Ten Thousand Things, or in however broad an expanse they symbolize the existential field. Other religious mysticisms focus on divine plenitude, while yet others focus on the freedom or arbitrariness of the creation. The creative act has no character at all, nothing determinate, that is not itself its product.

With regard to beauty, this sense of simplification marks the beauty of sheer particular existence. *What* the harmony is depends on what form it has for its components. *That* it is depends on its being created, with its unique haecceity arising from its existential essential components. To exist at all is simply to be beautiful, which is what I have been arguing throughout this chapter. There is beauty in novel identity. Not all novelty need be temporal. Anything that is what it is over and above its unintegrated components has the beauty of novelty. Novelty is always a unique "this," an haecceity.

Beauty as Experienced

I have introduced the case, with preliminary justification, that any form is beautiful and has the beauty particular to that form. Anything with form is beautiful. This claim presupposes the analysis of form begun in part I in terms of elegant blends of complexity and simplicity with patterns that arrange components in functions of narrowness and width, vagueness and triviality. According to this analysis, any form, or harmony with form, connects internally, directly or indirectly, to all the things with respect to which the form is determinate. All this goes to support the thesis that the goodness of beauty is a necessary, ubiquitous, universal condition of determinateness.

The topic of this part, however, includes more than this metaphysical claim about beauty as a transcendental. It includes as well the experience of beauty, and of other dimensions of goodness, in human life, at least in art, personal obligation, and civilization. My argument now returns to the nature of aesthetic experience, where "aesthetic" means at least the experience of beauty, that is, the experience of something as beautiful.

Though complicated, an important distinction needs to be made between the beauty of a harmonious thing in itself and the experience of that thing as beautiful by aesthetic perceivers. If we were to conceive of objects as substances, bearing their own properties, we could distinguish neatly between the beautiful form of the object and the form in the experiencer and ask whether there is an iconic relation between them. But things are harmonies and among their components are their relations with other harmonies. The sunset is a harmony with many relational components, including the situation relative to viewers to whom it is related as a play of moving colors and shapes. The meteorological elements in the sunset harmony also are related to the city directly beneath the sun in a situation that gives noonday light, and it is related to the horizon opposite the sunset terrace that is, say, open water of an ocean in a situation of sunrise that no one is in a position to observe, say. Therefore, the viewers on the sunset terrace get only one aspect of the whole harmony that is the sunset in their experience. The sunset itself is infinitely complex as a harmony, even though it is named in our example by its situational relation to potential sunset viewers. The people in the city and the fish near the surface of the ocean who feel warmed by the sunrise do not experience what we call the sunset as a sunset. Essential components of the sunset include the meteorological conditions on the horizon relative to the sunset terrace and its conditional components include all its situational relations to the terrace, the city, and the ocean. The meteorological elements of the sunset are the structured harmonies that make the sunset appreciable as a sunset from the terrace, as noontide from the city, and as warming sunrise rays in the ocean. Change those meteorological elements and there may be no sunset, noontide, or sunrise. That is why we say that the sunset is on the horizon relative to the sunset terrace, even though the situation necessary for appreciating it as a sunset, and so naming it, requires the relational connections between the meteorological elements and the potential viewers in the right place at the right time. The harmony that is the sunset itself, inclusive of all its relations, is different from the harmony that is the viewers on the sunset terrace, although the latter also includes the sunset situation relating to the meteorological events.

The experience of the beauty of the sunset from the sunset terrace includes many interpretations. An obvious line of interpretations includes the series of photonic events, which are interpretations themselves of predecessor photonic events, that convey something of the form of the meteorological events down the line to the retinas and optic nerves of the viewers (or that would do so if there were viewers in place). The harmony of the retinal events is very different from the harmony of the photonic events, but something of the form of the latter becomes a component of the retinal events so that the retinal events are somewhat iconic of the pattern conveyed through the line of photonic events. Also, the line of photonic events involves some modification of predecessor components as the light passes through light clouds and other intervening meteorological events. This view of "lines of interpretation" is by no means a commitment to panpsychism: physical processes such as the movement of photons can have the structure of interpretation.

The line of photonic interpretations is not the only line of interpretations involved in the experience of the sunset. There also are lines of interpretation that convey the geography of the horizon, the hills in the middle distance, our neighbors' garden and trees, and the physical setting of the sunset terrace; insofar as lines have to do with visual perception, iconic transfer across the distances is involved. Other physical lines of causal interpretation are also part of the situational harmony and these are not necessarily mainly iconic but also indexical. Much of the experience of the sunset involves interpretations focusing on the viewers' bodies, their personal histories, their semiotic ways of discriminating color, shape, and movement, and all the social relations involved in spending fifteen minutes with friends, wine glasses in hand, with many glances at the horizon. The experience of the sunset is far more than just the visual perception of its colors and patterns as registered in the viewers. The harmony of the situation defined by the actual or potential viewers' attention includes both the meteorological events and the actual or potential enjoyment of the sunset by the viewers. The situation is included as a component of the full harmony of the sunset, including the meteorological events, and also as a component in the personal developing identity of the viewers. The sunset in its own harmonic beauty includes many components that are not relevant to the sunset's appreciation as a sunset, and that harmony has its own essential features. Likewise, the harmonies of the viewers' personal identity include many elements that are not relevant to the harmony of the sunset in its inclusive self. The situation as a component of the sunset's larger harmony always includes the possibility of its being appreciated from the sunset terrace by people who bring the apparatus and other interpretative histories of my wife, our friends, and myself. Sometimes that possibility is actualized and the harmonic identity of the sunset includes actually being appreciated. The meteorological aspects of the sunset is the same whether it is actually appreciated or not, although the sunset's full identity includes whether or not it is actually appreciated. Although both the sunset in itself and the viewers are involved in the situation of sunset appreciation, only the viewers *experience* the sunset. The sunset does not experience the viewers except insofar as it includes the whole situation of being appreciated.

In human experience, among the mediators between the experiencer and the object experienced are signs defined in part within some human semiotic system. An experience has the form of a bundle of interpretations, usually including perceptual interpretations. The experiencer takes the object to be as the interpretive signs represents it to be. The interpretive interests of the experiencer to interpret the object in some respect form the situation. The intentionality of the experiencer to interpret the object in some respect determines the respects in which the signs refer to the object. This sense of intentionality is very broad, running from conscious purposes to perceptions that involve signs nested in semiotic systems because of the things valued in those semiotic systems, such as color or sound discrimination. Perceptual interpretations seem to occur to people who are passive with respect to them. But in fact even perceptions are shaped by the intentionality built into the interests of perceptual discrimination in the person's semiotic systems.

The experience of something is itself a harmony with a form. The experience of anything thus has a kind of beauty appropriate for the *experience* of that thing in that respect with that sign. Nevertheless, it is also possible to experience the *object* as beautiful. For this, the experiencer needs one or more signs to indicate the beauty in the object. These signs need to be integrated together to have a harmony of signification that is itself beautiful. Moreover, the signs need to be icons of the beauty in the object in the respects in which the object is experienced. This is more complicated than it seems. Let us reconsider some of our familiar examples.

In the situation of experiencing the sunset on the western horizon from the vantage point of our sunset terrace, all sorts of causal mediators are involved, such as geography, light, atmosphere, and meteorological events. However, the signs are those of colors, the articulation of shapes, the observations of movement, and so forth, all of which are functions of the experiencer's biological and cultural capabilities. The experience itself is a complex, developing interpretant of those colors and shapes. The droplets of moisture in the clouds are not colored close up the way they are from the vantage of the sunset terrace. If we were in the clouds themselves, we would not see the sunset. Moreover, the relevant causal factors in the clouds, wind, and light are not those the color of which is relevant to the sunset experience. The visual array of light, cloud shapes, and movement is itself harmonized in a beautiful complex of signs. We might remember, dream about, or even construct in our imagination that visual array of signs. In any of these forms, it would have its particular beauty. Nevertheless, if we employ that array to interpret the real sunset, the harmony that includes the meteorological events on the horizon as viewed from the sunset terrace, then the array functions iconically to represent some similar harmony in the events on the horizon as involved in the situation inclusive of the vantage point and the experiencer. The beauty *of the situation* of experiencing the sunset includes the signs of the visual array in the capabilities of a potential experiencer as well as the meteorological events, the potential experiencers, the architecture and location of the terrace, and all the other causal components. All this is to say that within the situation of the sunset experience, an array of signs within the semiotic capabilities of the experiencer is employed to experience the sunset as an object. A different array of signs is involved in experiencing the situation of experiencing, how it is enjoyable, and why it is worthwhile spending money to build the sunset terrace.

This section has argued the point familiar to pragmatists that all experience is interpretive and that it involves an interaction of the object, interpreter, and signs. What is important to stress is that the form of the aesthetic experience is the situation with those three elements plus many other mediators. The form of the aesthetic experience includes the capacity to experience the object as beautiful insofar as it is experienced in the situation as beautiful. Insofar as the object experienced has a form, at that metaphysical level it is beautiful both as intrinsically achieving the beauty its form bears and as a simplification of the components it harmonizes. For that beauty in the object to be experienced, however, requires an array of interpretive signs afforded the experiencer, and those signs must cohere in some way to be iconic, in some sense, of the beauty in the object. Only some aspects of the beauty of the sunset as a whole object, harmonizing many things beyond the situation with the viewers, enter into the experience of the sunset by viewers.

In this chapter, I have argued the general point that every harmony is not only good but also beautiful. I have also elaborated some of the conditions for the aesthetic judgment that can appreciate this beauty everywhere. Now I want to turn from the general scope of beauty across nature to the beauty in art.

CHAPTER 6

Beauty in Art

Art as an Elementary Human Process

In one of his most beautiful and powerful passages, John Dewey wrote:

> Human experience in the large, in its coarse and con-
> spicuous features, has for one of its most striking features
> preoccupation with direct enjoyment: feasting and festivities,
> ornamentation, dance, song, dramatic pantomime, telling
> yarns and enacting stories. In comparison with intellec-
> tual and moral endeavor, this trait of experience has hardly
> received the attention from philosophers that it demands.
> Even philosophers who have conceived that pleasure is the
> sole motive and man and the attainment of happiness his
> whole aim, have given a curiously sober, drab, account of
> the working of pleasure and the search for happiness. Con-
> sider the utilitarians how they toiled, spun and wove, but
> who never saw man arrayed in joy as the lilies of the field.
> Happiness was to them a matter of calculation and effort of
> industry guided by mathematical book-keeping. The history
> of man shows however that man takes his enjoyment neat,
> and at as short range as possible.
>
> Direct appropriations and satisfactions were prior to
> anything but the most elementary and exigent prudence,

just as the useful arts preceded the sciences. The body is decked before it is clothed. While homes are still hovels, temples and palaces are embellished. Luxuries prevail over necessities except when necessities can be festally celebrated. Men make a game of their fishing and hunting, and turn to the periodic and disciplinary labor of agriculture only when inferiors, women and slaves, cannot be had to do the work. Useful labor is, whenever possible, transformed by ceremonial and ritual accompaniments, subordinated to art that yields immediate enjoyment; otherwise it is attended to under the compulsion of circumstance during abbreviated surrenders of leisure. For leisure permits of festivity, in revery, ceremonies and conversation. The pressure of necessity is, however, never wholly lost, and the sense of it led men, as if with uneasy conscience at the respite from work, to impute practical efficacy to play and rites, endowing them with power to coerce events and to purchase the favor of rulers of events.[1]

This passage should dispel decisively the common assumption that pragmatism is the attempt to get what is practical. In concert with Peirce and James, Dewey asserted that we first want to play, to do things for the sake of the enjoyment of doing them. He went on to write:

Reflected upon, this phase of experience manifests objects which are final. The attitude involved in their appreciation is esthetic. The operations entering into their production is fine art, distinguished from useful art. It is dangerous however to give names, especially in discourse that is far aloof from the things named—direct enjoyment of the interplay of the contingent and the effective, purged of practical risks and penalties. Esthetic, fine art, appreciation, drama have an eulogistic flavor. We hesitate to call the penny-dreadful of fiction artistic, so we call it debased fiction or a travesty on art. Most sources of direct enjoyment for the masses are not art to the cultivated, but perverted art, an unworthy indulgence. Thus we miss the point. A passion of anger, a dream, relaxation of the limbs after effort, swapping of jokes, horse-play, beating of drums, blowing of tin whistles, explosion of firecrackers and walking on stilts, have the same quality of immediate and absorbing finality that is possessed by things and acts dignified by the title of esthetic. For man is more preoccupied with enhancing life than with bare living; so that a sense of living when it attends labor and utility is borrowed not intrinsic, having been generated in those periods of relief when activity was dramatic.[2]

Dewey's point is that immediate pleasure and satisfaction have priority in experience over calculated effort to achieve goals. Experience gives priority to what we enjoy in itself, or for itself. I identified this in the previous chapter as beauty, though in that discussion I treated it with metaphysical generality, not for its role in art. In *Art as Experience*, Dewey gave more sophisticated interpretations of the roles of beauty and art in experience. He said in *The Quest for Certainty* that human experience aims at "consummatory experience," experience that consummates previous processes. This is what I called beauty as "simplification," though again at the level of metaphysical generality. He accounted for inquiry and thinking, even conscious effort itself, in terms of trying to organize experience to achieve the consummatory enjoyment of something worthwhile in itself. He counseled people to calculate the consequences of a consummatory experience, as well as the cost of achieving it, into the goodness of the experience enjoyed in itself. While insisting on the immediacy of consummatory experience, its "quality," he also recognized change, the transformation of phases of experience that are not consummatory into those that are, and the deformation of the consummatory into what happens after. The upshot of *Art as Experience* is that experience itself is the art of cultivating and enjoying what is enjoyable in itself.

To recover Dewey's point in our own time is important. These days it is common for the human sciences to think of human beings in terms of ideal types who can be understood by seeing how they can optimize their goals by rational calculation, or who are understood as flawed because they do not act for their own benefit. For many students of human nature, it is hard to understand why people would be altruistic to their own detriment, because it is assumed that they are always acting for their own interest. We cling to this assumption of selfishness by supposing that people somehow enlarge their own interest to include the others' interests or take the good of the group as a whole as their interest. Dewey would point out, to the contrary, that we find great pleasure or satisfaction in being good to others, even to the point of self-sacrifice: helping others often is just plain fun, enjoyable in itself.

Consider another popular way of thinking about human beings, namely, in terms of the traits that give them an evolutionary advantage. Dewey of course recognized the importance of taking care of the necessities of life, including staying alive in evolutionary competition. People who danced too much perhaps did not survive. Dancing on the other hand strengthened group solidarity and thus had an evolutionary adaptive advantage. Dewey could admit that evolution selected for people who naturally liked to dance because of its adaptive advantage. Nevertheless, those who did not survive to pass on their genes and those who did often danced for the sake of the dance, Dewey would say. As they evolved more complicated societies, people were able to take on more complicated dances. Dewey's enthusiasm for evolution as the overall context in which to understand nature, human nature, and social institutions exceeded just about any other philosopher; see his *The Influence of Darwin on Philosophy*. Yet he never made the mistake of thinking that evolutionary advantage explains why people do things. Evolutionary observations can explain why people who do certain things thrive in evolutionary competition where others do not, and why evolutionary adaptive advantage might increase the prevalence of certain adaptive behaviors in the population as if the motivations for the behavior do not count. Nevertheless, where motivations do count, as they always should in understanding human experience, Dewey is surely right that we first off enjoy the things that seem good in themselves, the enjoyment of which is then motivation to do it again, to secure the enjoyable against destruction, and to enhance what is enjoyable in more intense ways.

Dewey's point reinforces the claim I have been making that human experience is redolent with goodness and, in this case, with beauty as that goodness that we experience as good in itself, a "final" goodness, as Dewey said. There are of course other goods in experience, those of inquiry into what is worth valuing, the negative values of loss, the positive ones of striving for goals, and so forth. As Dewey pointed out, suffering is a kind of goodness, one that can be so intense as to be strangely good in itself. We can also experience suffering as loss of other goods. The previous chapter detailed how a harmony is beautiful, at whatever grade or kind, insofar as we consider it in itself. Some harmonies are those constituted with regard to humanly oriented situations, and we can experience these as immediately enjoyed in themselves. Of course, not all things that are beautiful in themselves register as such in human experience. Human experience depends on many conditions and these might not be present is situations where a certain immediate goodness might be expected. However, when there is a consummatory experience, its harmonic quality in itself is the enjoyed experience.

The mention of consummatory experience recalls the argument of the previous chapter that any beauty, including any experience of beauty, is a simplification of antecedents calling for harmony. Dewey's treatment of consummatory experiences focuses mainly on the human contribution to the consummation, although many other elements can be involved.

The experience of something as beautiful in itself does not have to be sophisticated. Dewey's attack, in the passage quoted earlier, on the distinction between the experience of fine art and the experience of low-grade or kitsch art makes the point. Whatever the people find delightful and satisfying is "final" or intrinsically good for them, however much there might be deeper satisfactions in the fine arts. Philosophy enters into the experience of beauty insofar as it judges what things are beautiful and why, and for whom. For some people, listening to Beethoven's Ninth Symphony might be no better than walking on stilts.

Dewey rightly stresses the fact that people beautify all sorts of things and activities that need not be intrinsically satisfying. All the crazy things people do on holidays, such as the celebration of the Fourth of July in the United States (which is what Dewey had in mind in the quote about tin whistles and walking on stilts), are not just for paying proper honor to the thing celebrated. They are for having fun. Dewey makes a great deal of the fact that many parts of ritual are invented for the fun of it. This is an inadequate account of the personal and social functions of ritual, although it is true as far as it goes. The reason that those rituals that have become irrelevant to their original functions are still celebrated, sometimes, is that they are just fun. We preserve primitive legends and myths because they are interesting to rehearse and tell, and if they happen also to allay fears of the unknown, provide a sense of group identity, give some proto-scientific explanation for a natural anomaly, so much the better. None of those legends and myths would last if they were not first interesting and fascinating. The fact that we sophisticates know that they are not "true" does not mean that we cannot enjoy them too.

That we human beings add fun finalities to ordinary happenings, work, and business brings up the topic of human creativity in art.

Art in Motivation and Creativity

Two principal topics emerge concerning art and creativity. One is the natural urge to be creative, as illustrated in the quotation from Dewey. The other is how to be creative when art requires advancing beyond the ordinary.

Art is the production of something aimed to have experienceable beauty in the senses expressed in the previous section. In all those senses, the artful thing is produced or practiced primarily for the good-ness experienced in itself, whatever other positive or negative goods it might have or serve. The range of artistic practices and productions stretches from the most primitive, perhaps shared with other animals, to the fine arts of museums, concert halls, and libraries.

To assign an evolutionary beginning to art is difficult and perhaps fruitless. Rhythmic behavior, for instance, beating time, drumming, or moving in cadence, might begin as an unconscious effort to repro-duce the comforting feeling of a mother's heartbeat from the womb. It might come also from instinctive sexual movements. Rhythm leads to dance, where different rhythms intertwine and motions take on complex patterns. Rhythm can unite people into shared experience,

dancing together. Dancing is enjoyable in itself, not because it necessarily does something practical for the necessities of living. As Dewey
pointed out, dancing adds to menial work to make it more bearable.
As I remarked earlier, societies that dance together might have greater
solidarity and hence greater evolutionary adaptive goodness, but that
is not why people dance. Dance is for its own sake.

People and higher animals can make noise that becomes singing
when it has patterns. Anthropologists have shown that in all the cultures
studied in this regard, caretakers of infants sing to the babies in higher
tones and with more exaggerated rhythms than is customary in those
cultures; if this does not happen for some reason, the children find it
difficult to learn to talk later on. Therefore, singing is evolutionarily
prior to speech, at least in the sense of grammatical conversation. The
motive for singing is not to prepare babies for language but because the
babies seem to like it. Singing becomes codified into songs that many
people can enjoy, singing themselves, or together, or just listening like
the babies. The development of speech obviously has some practical
advantage for communicating in times of crisis and in organizing an
economy and household. Nevertheless, speech probably developed its
nuance and continuity of thought in yarns told around the campfire, in
the festivities to which Dewey alluded. They recounted the hunt, not
just the events of the hunt but the emotions felt and the character of
the prey. They recounted tales of ancestors and group identity in terms
of place and narrative continuity, regardless of whether those tales are
true in the modern historical sense. Stories can be told about natural
phenomena such as storms, the sea, changes of seasons, fertility, or death
by personifying them as gods. Human intentions can be understood
more easily (if imperfectly) than meteorology in primitive conditions,
and so the affairs of the gods can be hymned to add a sense of delight
concerning the world, especially its inhospitable parts. We can look back
on the early tales of gods as proto-science, as if their motive were an
attempt to explain. Nevertheless, the motive at the time was also, if not
rather, to enjoy a good story. There is an entrancing beauty in a story,
as in a novel; the novel is not a "true" story any more than the affairs
of Zeus's lovers are "true" stories, but it is fascinating and delightful
nonetheless and may carry a different kind of truth, as we shall explore
later. These are among the beginnings of the performing arts.

Along with verbal tales of the hunt is the delight in simplifying the prey as having a character of its own bracketed from the actual events of the hunt. Hunters can imagine a bison or deer with a persona that can be drawn on cave walls or sculpted. So also with the great hunters. Over and above the sheer practicalities of killing a deer for meat is the delight in imagining a special character to the deer, perhaps a spirit inhabiting a body that itself is not eaten. So also with the hunters. Animals can artistically be enhanced as totems, and people as heroes, perhaps even quasi-divine ones. Female sexuality can be simplified and beautified with images of wombs and pregnant women; male sexuality is simplified and enhanced with phallic symbols. What an interesting way to simplify the meaning of a human life by thinking of, and perhaps drawing, or singing about, the image of a person's spirit! The idea of a soul or spirit might be primitive proto-psychology. However, the motive for elaborating such an idea is that it is a beautiful way to think about the whole of a person and the person's role in the community when the person dies, or becomes nasty or demented. Perhaps some practical benefit comes from the artful representation of animals and people; pictures can be used to advise young hunters to avoid the horns; representations of people as having large, not-entirely material spirits might encourage more general respect for authorities when they do not seem so authoritative, which is good for group solidarity. Ideas of immortality might assuage grief, but they also are beautiful ways of thinking about what life adds up to. Those ideas are beautiful ways to think about the whole of a person or animal in enjoyable, simplified ways. The same thing can be said about glorifying wholly fictitious images of one's group. Filling experience with these elementary art forms makes it more beautiful, regardless of how true it is. Of course, nowadays we are acutely aware of the downsides of many of these ideas, leading to ingroup–outgroup war and preventing people from facing up to realities. Artistic images of this sort do affect behavior as well as entertain immediately, and sometimes that behavior is counterproductive.

Dewey said, in the passage quoted earlier, "the body is decked before it is clothed. While homes are still hovels, temples and palaces are embellished." Decoration is adding something nonutilitarian but of aesthetic delight to what otherwise might be merely utilitarian.

Scarification and tattooing in primitive societies might serve prac- tically as signals to distinguish between tribes and social status, but their elaborateness points to their sheerly aesthetic qualities. Fancy hairdos might serve practically to keep hair out of the eyes, but their beauty is its own justification. Artful dress might serve to woo sex- ual partners, but it is also beautiful, which helps in the wooing. The ancient Egyptians tied bundles of reeds together to make posts to hold up dwellings; the Greeks thought they were so beautiful that they carved marble columns in fluted patterns to look like reeds, or like the beautiful vertical pattern that bundled reeds have. Buildings have utilitarian purposes, of course, but we enhance them with decorative ornaments. Decorations are visual, tactile, olfactory, and other sensible pleasing images that we take out of their natural or original context and apply to something else that does not need them to perform its function. A box can hold your pencils without inlaid woods, but it is so much more beautiful when it has those decorations. There have been periods in history when art and architecture have attempted to eschew decoration, an extreme case being the modernist architectural principle that form should follow function. What happened in that architecture, however, was that the abstract ideas of formal beauty in shape, line, color, and volume functioned as a kind of antidecoration decoration, often to the detriment of function. To walk through a beautiful building unadorned but magnificent as a space is a delightful experience regardless of function. The Hartford Theological Seminary building by Richard Meier is a case in point: beautiful modernist shapes that are ruined if someone places a printer in an office that needs uncluttered space.

Dewey's argument was that art arises in practice and in produc- tion in the earliest and even now unsophisticated human experience. To be sure, these practices and works of art and architecture develop forms that are more elaborate and become objects of intention them- selves. We not only appreciated their intrinsic or "final" delight but we appreciated the fact that they give delight. Fireside storytellers go into training and become bards, then authors of novels and poems of linguistic creativity. Specialists in dance become professionals as forms of dance themselves separate from what comes easily to just about anyone. Building becomes a business and architects learn a specialized craft. Imhotep, who lived in the twenty-seventh century before the Common Era, was famous as the architect of a step pyramid, perhaps the first named architect. The move from the art of everyone to the art of experts began early.

Reflection on the development of trained and perhaps professional artists raises the other main question of this section, how to understand creativity. Creativity involves artistic practices and production of artifacts that is innovative, producing something new over and above inherited practices and styles of products. Creativity is a virtue much lauded in large parts of contemporary cultures, particularly elite cultures. Even when some cultures are "conservative" in the sense of wanting to revive older forms of the arts, a recognition exists that someone in the past had brought the previously inherited arts to a higher level of development and excellence.

We need to acknowledge immediately some ambiguities concerning the appreciation of creativity. First, no creative advance in art is wholly new; each builds upon previous practices and forms even as it changes them. Modern dance differs from classical ballet in many ways but still involves movement and music shaped by the old styles. Abstract expressionism in art has been direct in rejecting the roles of pictorial representation in painting but still focused attention on elements of painting that had been present all along, for instance shape, color, and line; it has made these as such the focal points of paintings.

Second, we recognize creativity as novelty only in contrast with what had gone before. This we presuppose in looking for novelty as the measure of advancement in art.

Third, while creativity as novelty has become at least one of the criteria for appreciating contemporary art in both high and low cultures, novelty is not the only criterion and often other criteria outweigh novelty. Many novel advances in the arts do not last. Many drop out as people go back to older forms. The rise of high modernism in architectures was itself a rejection of the heavy decoration of Victorian building in the West, but it in turn evoked a return to postmodern architecture that often used Victorian decorations in new ways.

Fourth, whereas creativity as novelty sometimes holds an important place in the arts, it is not a universal virtue. For instance, Chinese landscape (shanshui, mountain-water) painting reached a high level

of development by the late Tong dynasty and flourished throughout the Song. While the style slowly modified in accordance with
more general cultural and political changes, it has lasted until today.
I visited a famous art school in Chongjing in 1986 that overlooked
the fantastically rugged landscape of the Three Gorges but whose
students were intent on copying with their own minor modifications
the landscape paintings of the Li River valley, far away, with its gentle
and mystical karst mountains. Perhaps in part the school crassly aimed
the twentieth-century version of the ninth-century style at tourists
who associate Chinese painting with the landscape. Nevertheless, there
were some brilliant contemporary painters practicing that ancient art.
Consider Byzantine icon painting that reached its mature style in the
sixth century and that has continued with only the subtlest changes
in style down to the present time. The Eastern Orthodox painters did
not prize novelty so much as deepening in each generation the art of
the previous generation.

Fifth, and perhaps most important, because social, climatic, political, and cultural conditions are always changing, for an art form to
remain relatively constant requires constant adjustment. The artistic
meaning, that is, its immediate qualities as subject to analysis and
revised appreciation, is always under changing conditions and it has to
change to approximate its earlier experience. Creativity as novelty is
required even to stay the same, as it were. Of course, nothing stays the
same. The performance style for Beethoven's sonatas has changed many
times since he played them himself. Because the beauty or artfulness
of an artifact includes the situation in which it is appreciated, even
a building that changes very little in itself changes many times over
in its artfulness. Imhotep's Step Pyramid has taken on many different
experiential artistic meanings since its original building.

These ambiguities or failures of sharp distinctions noted, what can
we say about creativity in the sense of the artistic creation of novelty?
What is it that allows some people to have the imagination to create
something new, or to adapt old forms to new contexts? Two things
need to be mentioned, musing and skillful means.

"Musement" is the word Charles Peirce used to describe what
the phrase "thinking outside the box" captures.[3] Thinking in the box
is the result of habit, often trained habit, and the failure to think

within the habits of the box is subject to normative correction. We teach children to color within the lines. Dancers are taught how to hold their hands. Architects learn how to achieve a given style with a variety of buildings. Peirce said that musement is letting the imagination wander freely, explicitly pushing back some of the learned habits of what is good and bad thinking. He thought that with practiced musement, freely playing with ideas, any properly formulated problem could be solved in forty minutes; he was a faster thinker than most. In art, musement does not have to be limited to thinking, although thinking in advance is important. It can be more like random movement, random application of paints, random playing with sculptural forms, free-association writing. Musement is the capacity to imagine possibilities that do not naturally occur to habituated ways of thinking.

By "skillful means" (a Buddhist phrase), I mean adeptness at pursing novel alternatives, the capacity to think through to clarity, to paint in a novel way, to move in a new way, or to make new rhythms and sounds, and to recognize the character of the novelty. The sheer randomness of musement is extremely inefficient, although it sometimes is sufficient to make something new, as if by accident. An artist of skillful means understands and can quickly adopt and improve upon a novel practice or product. Musicians who are adept in the performance style current for their musical instrument are better able spontaneously to invent new ways to play than musicians who have not well mastered their instrument. Spontaneous creativity in most of the arts comes only when many of the moves, methods, and anticipations of what results have been honed in old ways. Of course, when Peirce talked about musement, he did not have in mind the undisciplined thought of the addled, however much that might be outside the box; he had in mind himself, a highly disciplined logical thinker who could see the consequences of a new line of thought in a flash. Bursts of creative insight combine the freedom from habitual thinking with the skill at seeing how a novel approach adds up. Creativity also involves frequent experiments to see in real trials what the significance of novelty is for the beauty of harmony in a resulting practice or product. Creativity shall be a recurrent theme throughout this volume, especially in part IV as a trait of a civilization.

Art as a Basic Response to Existence

I want to offer a fundamental theological point about art. You might not be aware of this idea in the cultural climate where everyone says art is good but many think religion is suspect. Nevertheless, it is an old point, related to the transcendentals. Art is a basic human response to existence as such and thus has a religious dimension and contributes to religion. The reason that art is a basic response to existence as such is that it is an affirmation of the beautiful particularity of things that exist, their haecceity or particular thisness. Art is an affirmation of beauty by the creation of something intended to be beautiful. No particular "this" exists without being a particular "what." "This particular what" is their beauty, the goodness they have simply by virtue of having their form, irrespective of what other goods they have. As I argued earlier, we grasp this beauty both as that which is good in itself and that which is good as a simplification (out of possibly many simplifications) of its potential components. Among actual things in time, beauty is the particular goodness achieved in each advance into novelty. Art is a human response to this beauty, insofar as it is amenable to human experience, first by imitating it after a fashion, then by augmenting it in creative human symbols, and finally by affirming the process of making novel, beautiful things as human artifacts and practices. Art as imitative representation is an affirmation of the beauty of the imitated by attempting to make something like it, similarly beautiful just in its existence. Art frequently augments representative imitation of particular beauty by elaborating humanly meaningful forms with new particulars of beauty, good in themselves and as simplifications. Art for art's sake is an affirmation of the creativity in nature, the cosmos, and society by epitomizing it in the task of art, or making beauty, as a basic human enterprise.

Of course, this interpretation of art rests upon the fundamental thesis of this book that anything with form has goodness, and that goodness is a characteristic of form itself as harmonizing components. In part I, I developed a theory of determinateness in which any determinate thing has form, components formed, location in an existential field, and the goodness-identity of getting these components together with this form in this existential location. I analyzed goodness itself as the density achieved by the unification of many components, each of which has goodness, into a new harmony that contains the goodness of having them together. The togetherness of components has elegance of balancing complexity and simplicity and composing the components according to their functions as trivial, vague, narrow, and wide. The integration of narrowness and width constitutes contrast or intensity of being. The integration of triviality and vagueness constitutes background or environment. The integration of contrast and background constitutes depth. The integration of all the preceding constitutes density of being for each harmony in an existential field as well as in the ontological context in which all determinate things are mutually relevant to whatever else there is with respect to which they are determinate. The beauty in a harmony is not something that applies to it as a property to an Aristotelian substance. Rather, each harmony is the integration of all the things in the cosmos that might condition it from its own perspective as defined by its form. Its form has the particular beauty of the harmony's own existence. Nevertheless, its form also includes, according to the functions of narrowness, width, vagueness, and triviality, all the other things in the world that could condition the harmony; all those potential conditions are components internal to the harmony, however much they are external also by virtue of their own essential components. This is my hypothesis about the metaphysical structure of beauty as the goodness of form: it underlies the claim that art is the affirmation of the goodness of existence itself. Although only an hypothesis, I hope that it is justified by the cumulative arguments of this book and its various component traditions.

To say that art is the human response to beauty notes that such response depends on our semiotic capacities. Human beings have physical limitations. Some things are too small or too big to engage, or they have resonant frequencies to which we cannot relate without mediating instruments. Human song might imitate the sounds of birds, animals, storms, or animal grunts and groans, but only within the forms available for making human sounds. Human movement might imitate that of bears or herons, but people are not as strong as bears, or as furry, and cannot fly like herons. The animal forms transmute into human forms of movement in, say, the Chinese ancient taiji movements and postures and other early elements of dance and semiotically repeatable movements. Representational arts are limited to what can be transmuted into the human capacities to see movement, shape, color, line, and the rest. The visual, plastic, architectural, and musical arts take place with a semiotic vocabulary that can be developed out of human capacities. The arts themselves, as well as the sciences, extend human capacities, sometimes to a remarkable degree. The point to recognize here, however, is that the experience of beauty, presupposed in the human response to experienceable beauty, is limited to what lies within human semiotic capacities.

The three levels of art mentioned here—imitation, augmentation, and creativity for its own sake—are "emergent properties." Imitation emerges out of human activities and production as it takes on repeatable forms with semiotic meaning, and there is no clear line when that happens. Augmentation so that the art takes on a trajectory of its own emerges from semiotically structured imitation. Creativity for its own sake emerges out of the creativity of developing art as we prize it more and more for the beauty in its own process. By no means does this entail that the lower levels are not present in the higher. The art-for-art's-sake paintings of the Pre-Raphaelites were both representational and self-conscious about cultivating the novel resources of their media.

The artistic response of imitation is extremely elemental, however sophisticated it might become. Imitation of things in movement, sound such as singing and drumming, drawing and painting, sculpting, and the building of artificial caves, happen for many reasons. Among the most obvious are the communication of warnings, instruction as to what to watch out for, and organization of activities in economic and domestic life. Imitation bears many kinds of goodness. However, I say that it becomes artistic when the activity or artistic product is valued for its own sake, its pleasure or fun, in addition to or regardless of any other goodness it might have. Beyond a single bit of fun, the artistic activity or product is given a semiotic code so that it is recognizable by oneself and especially by others. Repeatability arises from this semiotic form. This includes repeatability of recognition, as when an artist says that a cliff face looks like a human face and people thereafter see that as so. Activities such as planting or digging, or undertaking an organized hunt, or preparing dinner, become more efficient when coded with a semiotic structure and this is not art as such. They become art, however, when those activities are ritualized so that participation in the ritual, digging in rhythm, singing while hauling, role-playing while hunting, are also appreciated for their own sakes. They are art forms when we pursue them for pleasure even when the ritualized activity might be inefficient for "practical purposes." Given the avail-ability of food, eating can be simply functional, but with art, it turns into feasting, with stipulations regarding who eats what, stories to tell, toasting, dancing, singing, and more toasting. Feasting is what art can do with mere nutrition.

In artistic imitation, two beauties are involved, that of the thing imitated and that in the imitation. Artistic representation identifies a harmonic character in that which it imitates. Moving like a bear identifies bears out of the background of the rest of nature and calls attention to certain ways in which they move. Imitation of a heron selects out the quick movement down and forward of the bird as it feeds. Singing might call attention to the comforting sounds a mother makes for her babies, or to the screams of delight of hunters on making a kill. An extremely important form of artistic imitation is a person imitating another's speech, calling attention to the meaning in the original speech by meaning something like it in imitation. Imitation in speech is not just for the sake of learning how to speak when young, but also for taking delight in the meanings conveyed by speech. Speech expressing "please" and "thank you" imitates the delight, as well as utility, in request and gratitude.

On the other hand, the imitation itself has a beauty that we can appreciate for its intrinsic goodness. The movements in taijiquan, which are mostly imitations of movements of animals, have their own beauty of form that relates strictly to the possibilities and symmetries of human movement. They are codified in a semiotic system that emphasizes extension and recovery in due balance, as articulated in the elementary Chinese philosophy in the *Yijing*. A drawing has beauty of line and color that is different in part from what the drawing represents. The sounds of a human voice have a beauty different from what they imi-tate. Dewey was right to emphasize that the activities and productions, laid on top of the things with which we interact, are prized for their own sake and constitute art because of their own beauty.

Art that augments imitation does so by virtue of the fact that the semiotic structure of the imitation has a life of its own that can develop in beautiful ways. Moving like a bear extends into moving with grace in all sorts of semiotically structured dance. Song can move far beyond the codification of cooing to baby, grunting while hauling, or calling out the cadence in a march. Kabuki theater and grand opera exhibit vastly complicated semiotics of movement, drama, and music beyond what begins as elementary imitation. Of course, both of those are still highly representative, articulating contours of an imagined world as well as exploiting the beauty of their sensuous and dramatic expressions. Nevertheless, as art, the development of augmentations through complicating semiotic practices creates new kinds of harmonies that are beautiful in themselves.

The art of augmentation has developed in many different ways. Paul Weiss, an unduly neglected American philosopher, distinguished nine basic arts: architecture, sculpture, painting, musicry (the artistic creation of a common time), story, poetry, music, theater, and dance.[4] Brilliant as his analysis is, it reflects a very Western sense of the genres of art. We can characterize the arts in other ways. I would include sport as art that begins as imitation but quickly extends into highly ritualized games of individual and collective activity aimed at excellence in itself.[5] The following two chapters will discuss the arts as augmentation of beauty by new beauty in more detail. The arts do not have to be classified. They can just be illustrated.

Art for art's sake augments the production of beautiful artifacts and beautiful activities with an appreciation of the human process of creating artful beauty. It recognizes that one of the beauties of being human is being creators of beautiful things, in the senses defined here. We cannot separate the artistic life from the products of art. Nevertheless, we can celebrate the processes of being artistic. This happens perhaps all along the line, as those listening at the feast appreciate a talented bard for his or her talent. The augmentation of art takes on special needs for training in skills, expertise at the performance or production of art works, and finally the development of artistry as a profession where the sophistication and cultivation of connoisseurs is required for the appreciation of its beauty. Guilds of artists can be stultifying for the creativity of artistic augmentation. Perhaps for this reason, those appreciating art for art's sake sometimes break out of the guild guidelines and embrace novelty in the sense of distancing art from its models. In our time, art has come to be appreciated for something that is good as art as well as for providing beauty that can be appreciated in itself for what it is.

At all three levels, art is the appreciation and affirmation of the beauty of form as such. Form is a crucial element in determinateness and without form things would not exist. Anything that has form exists. Human beings can appreciate the beauty of the sheer existence of things within the limits of their semiotic and perceptive capacities. Art is the response to this appreciation, or perhaps the very enabling of the appreciation, by making new beautiful things in imitation, in augmentation of the imitations, and in the celebration of art for the sake of its own making.

Art and Religion

The best way to define religion is the human engagement of ulti-macy in cognitive, existential, and practical ways.[6] The heart of this definition is the issue of ultimacy. What is ultimate? Philosophical and theological cultures have taken many different approaches to this question. Many would emphasize the ultimacy of the ground of things, what I have called here the ontological creative act. Here is not the place to argue for this conception. Nevertheless, it is clear that whatever this ontological ground is, what makes it ultimate is that it is the source of all determinate things. It would not be the ultimate ground if there were not determinate things that it grounds. There-fore, the conditions of determinateness are equally ultimate with the ontological creative act (or its alternatives). They "derive" from it, but it would not be ultimate if they did not exist. Therefore, in matters of ultimacy, the conditions of determinateness are just as ultimate as their indeterminate ground. We have seen in the discussion of goodness so far that there are at least four conditions of ultimacy: form, com-ponents formed, existential location relative to others, and achieved goodness identity. Thus, there are five ultimate realities, individually, and many more of those in combination: contingency on the onto-logical ground, form, components formed, location in an existential field, and goodness–identity.

Art is a human response to the beauty in form that affirms, appropriates in imitation, augments, and celebrates art as such. There are many ways to engage form as an ultimate condition of human life, and art is only one. However, it is an important one. Art is a special celebration of beauty as the mark of existence as such.

I have been arguing that anything that is determinate is a har-mony, with components harmonized, relating to other things, and achieving a goodness. Religion is a harmony, and so is art.

Religion is whatever harmonizes any human responses to what is ultimate. Its components include the signs and semiotic systems that cultures and individuals employ to represent the ultimate realities, the interpretation of these semiotic systems in the experience, behavior, and thought of religious people, the social settings in which those interpretations are made, the institutions and organizations that are venues for those interpretations, the psychological states involved in those interpretations, and a whole host of other components, some necessary to any response to ultimacy and some accidental or particular to certain interpretations.

Art functions as a component in religion in many ways. First, art as the celebration and affirmation of beauty is itself a primary kind of response to the ultimacy of goodness in form, which is the mark of existence itself. Art is a response to the ultimacy of con-tingent existence as that is a function of form. Not all people are artists, of course, and so might not take part in this way of engaging ultimacy. Some people are even deaf, dumb, and blind to art and so do not participate in the art process in any way that directly cele-brates existence. However, most people do respond positively to art. Anyone who practices or produces something for the sake of its own self, whatever its utilitarian goodness or negative value, is making a religious response to art. Who would have thought that walking on stilts is a holy practice!? But if I myself dared to walk on stilts, I would surely count it as a challenging affirmation of existence. If we remember to count as art the range of "low art" activities to which

Dewey called attention, then anyone who does semiotically structured things to have fun is worshipping the contingency of existence in beauty, regardless of the intentionality of the person's consciousness (for instance, not to fall off the stilts).

In addition, art is a component of religion by way of providing beautiful and therefore captivating articulations of many of religions' symbols for other kinds of ultimate engagement. The Bhagavad Gita articulates and conveys a great many classical theological concepts in South Asian religions, but its power consists in the fact that it is a great narrative and an artful discussion. Judaism and Christianity form, in part, around stories that have their power in their beauty. Islam is less about narrative, but the verses of the Qur'an are themselves beautiful.

Religious practices such as ritual ceremonies are not only functional to relate people to what is ultimate but also beautiful. Without the beauty, they probably would not function so well. Religious architecture is not only functional but also beautiful as a product of architectural art. That beauty contributes to engagements with ultimate realities that otherwise have little if anything to do with the beauty of form.

Although some people might be able to engage ultimate matters with little art, and some religious practices and communities might have art on a very low level, art is present in just about all religious traditions and communities. We cannot understand the religion of a person, community, or place without understanding their art and how the art functions. Art functions also in ethnic communities to help define the ethnic culture, and sometimes those ethnic communities are important components of religion. So art's involvement in religion can be indirect. But it is massive and ubiquitous.

Art too is a harmony, and religion is very often an important component of the practice of art. The religious impulse to engage ultimacy can be a primary motive in artistic activity and the appreciation of art. For many artists, the practice of their art is a primary way of being religious. In addition, religious people, interests, cultures, and communities have been primary sponsors of art. They provide the venues within which art can be practiced, not to speak of the funds to support it!

My discussion here of the institutions of art, namely, those practices of the human creation of beauty, and the institutions of religion,
namely, those practices of the engagement of ultimacy, are harmonies
that bear each other as components. Further study of those institutional
harmonies might trace out how each functions with narrowness, width,
vagueness, and triviality in the other.

CHAPTER 7

To Appreciate Arts

Beauty for Appreciation

This chapter and the next deal respectively with the appreciation and creation of artworks, illustrated with specific kinds of art. As always, the underlying theme is how goodness as beauty functions in the arts. The justification for the order of these two chapters may not be obvious. To inquire first into creativity in the various arts, into the issues involved in how art is created, would make a great deal of sense. However, it makes more sense to inquire first into the art that is created to see what the ideal or intention is for which artists strive.

By the "arts" in this and the next chapter, I mean artful beauty with a high degree of excellence. Up to this point, I have stressed Dewey's point that any regular creation, practice, and appreciation of what people take to be beautiful and worth enjoying for its own sake should be recognized as art, though not necessarily good art. Now I want to focus on art as refined: great poetry, not enjoyable doggerel; great songs, not cheapened music; great choreographed dancing, not amateur square dance; highly trained voices singing transcendent music, not the local choir; magnificent architecture, not cheap replicas; painting and sculpture with both creative imagination and profound depth, not the art of gift shops; great gardens, not just what looks good as informed by popular catalogues. These distinctions, of course, are not dichotomies but continua. Remember that all of these should be considered to be art insofar as they are made or practiced as sources of intrinsic appreciation; we appreciate good art, bad art, and all in between as art in the right circumstances for the right people. However, I mean to talk now about the good art, the art exhibiting beauty with excellence.

Many people have objected to this distinction between "good" refined art and "bad" vulgar or common art, and Dewey seems at times to be one of them. The objection sometimes takes the form of assigning that distinction to the perspectives of social class: the upper or so-called educated classes identify high arts or fine arts because they have been taught to do so, just as the culture of the lower classes teaches them to appreciate as art what the others call kitsch. There is some truth to this, especially when the upper classes merely identify certain things as high art from custom without knowing what makes them so good, just as the lower classes are taught to "know what they like" as a matter of their class culture. Nevertheless, the distinction between upper and lower classes, with the middle class in the middle, is far more complicated than this simple distinction requires. People from the lower and middle classes obviously are capable of enjoying and appreciating great art, and rich people can be wholly blind to it. This objection, however, might generalize to say that what one thinks of as good art is wholly dependent on one's perspective—social class, education, ethnic culture, and other perspectival loci. This objection surely is valid in some circumstances: what we can appreciate depends on our perspective that is formed by many elements, and sometimes this disposes us to perceptiveness or blindness concerning forms of art.

Nevertheless, this observation should not prevent us also from recognizing some elements of greatness in art that I exposed in the analysis of beauty in art in the previous chapter. A work of art is great to the degree and in the ways it has contrast and depth, I argue. Contrast is a function of narrowness and width, and depth is a function of vagueness and triviality. These categories mean different things in different arts, of course. Furthermore, they are mediated by human capacities to engage art interpretively with some semiotic apparatus. The critical experience of art involves the capacity to experience the overall quality of the art with a discernment of how its elements function regarding what is trivialized, included in a vague way, brought to narrow clarity, and broadly integrated. To be a connoisseur is to be able to discern these functions and to appreciate qualitatively, in the immediacy of enjoyment, how the complexity and simplicity of those functions balance with some elegance.

The cultivation of the capacities to discern the kinds and degrees of contrast and depth does indeed depend on the culture of cultivation. A sophisticated person from India might have great appreciation for the Mahabharata, including the Bhagavad Gita, while not being able to see why Dostoyevsky's *The Brothers Karamazov* is a great novel. Most Western readers of Dostoyevsky, even those with great sophistication, are at a loss to appreciate the Mahabharata. Indeed, one is tempted to employ the clues for interpretation that work well in one culture to interpret another, missing what truly is relevant in the other. The Indian lover of the Mahabharata might overestimate Henry Wadsworth Longfellow's *The Song of Hiawatha* because it has largely the same meter and rhyme scheme. Although *The Song of Hiawatha* might present itself as an epic, it does not come close to the epic depth and sweep of the Mahabharata.

Many cases exist in which the quality of certain kinds of art and artists clearly transcend classification schemes based on social location. Some of Martin Luther's hymn tunes came from barroom music of his day. Recently the American pop singer-songwriter Bob Dylan received the Nobel Prize for Literature. He had been at the center of popular protest music in his early career in the 1960s and always has been widely popular. Nevertheless, people who identified more with the songs of Schubert than pop music came to appreciate him. No one ever said he had a beautiful voice, though he could sing in the "performance tradition" of several kinds of pop music. However, his lyrics are often of the very highest poetic quality and serious critics of poetry such as Christopher Ricks have analyzed them in detail.[1] His lyrics, though they stand on their own, are enhanced by being sung. His music, as musical literature, transcends social, educational, and class distinctions and is appreciated as just *excellent*. It is *good* art, not doggerel or nostalgia.

The very wide appreciation for Bob Dylan comes in large measure from the fact that it does not make demands on people for that of which they might be ignorant. T. S. Eliot and Geoffrey Hill are also

great poets in the English language, but only people with a sophisticated education can appreciate their allusions; maybe a dictionary or
commentary would help, but even then, their poetry loses its force
unless people have been cultivated to live with their language and
allusions. Dylan's language is common English, and he wrote about
events and conditions that everyone knows about firsthand or through
popular media such as television. We must take seriously the point that
the appreciation of art is limited by the capacity of potential appreciators to grasp what is going on. Art from a different culture might
be opaque to some potential appreciators, though its quality of art is
high for those of the other culture. Art that is appreciated by those
with deep cultural training might not be appreciated by those who are
ignorant of that training. In some cases, those who are ignorant can
acquire the training, and in other cases not where the training requires
immersion in an unavailable culture. Given the goodness to human life
of the appreciation of artistic beauty, the goodness of enjoying things
of great beauty in depth and contrast, this simple point is a powerful
argument for education in the cultivation of the arts.

The argument I shall make in this chapter is that beauty in
art is to be appreciated in terms of its excellence because of how it
enhances the elegance of complexity and simplicity and composes in
its form the functions of its elements in narrowness, width, vagueness,
and triviality. This claim for the appreciation of art with critical acu-
men, built into the immediacy of aesthetic appreciation, comes from
the larger metaphysical or philosophical scheme I adumbrated in the
previous chapters. This differs radically from the approach of most
philosophers of art who begin with what they can learn from the
critical, historical, and social analyses. Those approaches are all valuable
and I incorporate some of them here; but they are not my approach.
One of the other of the few philosophers in recent years to take this
metaphysical tack was Paul Weiss (my teacher). In his "middle period,"
he thought that reality consists of four fundamental modes: actuality,
ideality, existence, and God.[2] Here is not the place to explain these
modes; but, roughly, actuality means Aristotelian-like substances, ideality
means what is good, existence is a field of temporal and spatial pulsing
extensionality, and God means unity. Each of these affects the others;
for instance, God is pure unity and gives the kind of unity appro-

priate to actualities, ideals in a field, and coherent space-time. Weiss accounted for many domains of human experience as specializations of certain of these modes. Art, he thought, was a mixture of ideality and existence: art creates a new world that explores its own forms of excellence in the structures of space-time. He classified nine basic arts, plus some compound arts. The first three arts, architecture, sculpture, and painting, primarily are creative structures of space. Musicry (discussed earlier), story, and poetry primarily articulate a world of time, exploring and creating temporal structures. Music, theater, and dance involve both time and space. His books, *The World of Art* and *Nine Basic Arts*, are treasure troves of insights into the arts that flourished in the mid-twentieth century. He threw himself into artistic work and became a rather good painter of portraits. He came to know many of the great artists of his time, and their great critics, all of whom enriched his work. However, the source of his originality and new vision was his metaphysics that caused him to ask questions that had not been asked before and to view art from perspectives that had not been built within the various art worlds. I would hope that my own analysis would have at least this last virtue. I do not agree with Weiss's metaphysics, although I appreciate him as the greatest American metaphysician after Whitehead. Whereas he focused on the artistic rendering of extensionality, I focus on the metaphysical conditions for beauty that I have been elaborating. Weiss himself was a student of Whitehead, and among his earliest publications were the (coedited with Charles Hartshorne) papers of Charles Peirce. Nevertheless, he rejected too much of Whitehead's insights on relationality and goodness. I shall attempt to rescue as many of Weiss's insights into art as I can, grafting them onto my metaphysics.[3]

To follow Weiss by classifying the arts is tempting. Despite their professionalization in our time, however, too many crossovers exist. The scheme for analysis I shall follow comes rather from consideration of processes of actualization. First, I shall consider the appreciation of art as form; form is ambiguous as to whether it means future form or a future form that is being actualized in the present and remains the form of something actual. Second, I shall consider the appreciation of art as form being actualized, as in performances of various sorts and other artistic activities. Third, I shall consider the appreciation of art as a body of work, as something finished and adorning the actual world. This scheme allows for an initial discussion of the appreciation of art. It is incomplete without the following chapter that shall supplement this discussion with considerations of the processes of creating art and making artists.

Beauty in Form

The appreciation of artistic beauty in form is basic to all appreciations of artful things and processes because beauty resides in the form itself, as I have argued from the beginning of this book. The appreciation of beauty in nature, and the beauty in social institutions, and in a great many other things besides art, is fundamental, and the appreciation of beauty in art is a subset of the appreciation of beauty in form generally.

One of the distinctive marks of the appreciation of beauty in art concerns the configuration of the "situation" of appreciation. Earlier, we reflected on how to understand the situation of appreciating a sunset, which is not a work of art. The sunset situation consists of all the elements from the meteorological events to the viewing platform with people whose biological apparatus includes color vision and the capacities to discern shape, movement, and so forth. The people also need to have visual and emotional semiotic resources for interpreting the sunset. The form of the situation of sunset viewing relegates some things in the larger existential field to the vague or even trivial background and thus outside the relevant situation. The intentionality of the viewers determines the form of the sunset situation. The relevant elements in the situation, and the situation's own form, are determined by the interests of the viewers in taking pleasure in and appreciating the sunset. Those interests might include watching sunsets frequently, building a terrace specially oriented to sunset views, and even cultivating a lifestyle that includes watching sunsets. Complicated as the intentionality of the viewers might be in determining the sunset-appreciation situation, that locus of intentionality is what does the determining of the situation.

In the case of the appreciation of artful beauty, two loci of intentionality determine the situation for the appreciation of art, that of the appreciators and that of the artists. The intentionality of the appreciators is somewhat like that of the appreciators of sunsets. In addition, however, the intentionality of the artist to create a work of art (an artifact, a practice, a performance, whatever) also determines the situation of art appreciation. Moreover, this dual determination by intentionality reflexively imprints itself in both loci of intentionality. That is, the artist produces art to be appreciated by someone, if only by the artist's own self as appreciator. In addition, the appreciator of art recognizes that the artist intends appreciation of the artwork.

Because of the dual loci for determining a situation of the appreciation of artful beauty, such situations are most often vague, perhaps even confused. Artists rarely know much about who might appreciate their work. A painter might have an advantage when painting for a patron who is explicit about what he or she wants; but the patron's heirs might have very different tastes and the painting ends up in a museum for viewing by people very different from the patron. An architect designs a building for certain uses (not necessarily the artistic part of the creating) with artistic elements that have special meaning for the people imagined to use the building and for the fit or misfit with the local setting. Although walking on stilts might not be an art form that gets much refinement, acrobatics surely can be a great art, and the acrobat does not know much about the people who watch in a circus, on television, or through a computer. A priest performing a religious ritual with great beauty probably knows much about the people attending for religious reasons but might not know much about the capacities of the attendees to grasp ritual beauty. In general, artists producing beautiful artifacts or practices might have vague senses of what the relevant people can appreciate, but that still leaves the situation perhaps confused, especially when the artist's sense of capacities for appreciation is simply mistaken regarding specific audiences.

On the other side, the appreciator of artistic beauty obviously has some sense that the art is created to be appreciated for its beauty (however that is understood) and sometimes knows quite specifically what the artist was intending. Nevertheless, there are long-standing issues concerning the knowability and relevance of artists' intentions. Some form critics say that the artist's intentions, especially in literature, are wholly irrelevant to grasping the work of art, whereas others say that the work of art is itself merely a sign of the artist's intention, where that intention is the real work of art whose beauty needs to be discerned. When the art involves "found objects," or commonplace objects unexpectedly hung on a museum wall, the artist's intent is understood to be about the placement or recontextualization of the artifact, not with the composition of the artifact itself.

All that I said earlier about the difficulty of interpreting art across cultures or cultural milieus applies here. The situation of appreciating beauty in art often involves a disconnection between the cultural resources for appreciation that the artist presupposes and those of the potential appreciators. Hans-Georg Gadamer's discussions of the difficulties of fusing the cultural horizons of different cultures are highly relevant for understanding diverse situations of appreciating beauty in art.[4] Nevertheless, let me reinforce the point that the appreciation of beauty in a work of art (however much its monetary worth, memorial value, or contribution to a decorating scheme is also appreciated) is not something only in the mind of the appreciator. The appreciation of a work of art is a harmony that consists in the situation of appreciation with its own harmonic form. The harmonic form of the situation includes as components the artwork, the appreciator, and the artist as creator (though the last might be long forgotten). The situation with its own harmony is itself a component in the appreciator who integrates it with the rest of life.

The appreciation of beauty in the form of art is involved in the appreciation of beauty in any art whatsoever. This includes the art of performance that unfolds its form through time, the topic of the next section. Here the focus is on the appreciation of form in art as such. This involves two modes, form as aesthetically beautiful possibility and form as aesthetically beautiful structure in actual artworks and practices.

Form as aesthetically beautiful possibility is, of course, extraordinarily important for artists in imagining and then executing works of art of various sorts. I will examine this more in chapter 8. Beautiful possible artwork, however, is important for appreciators of art as well. Many artworks, such as buildings, paintings, and musical pieces, never become actualized, and yet their plans can be appreciated. Architects imagine their buildings and describe them to clients. They can also sketch them and attempt to render what the building would look like in its local environment. Architects can draw up detailed plans as blueprints from which engineers and builders might work, and all of these have their aesthetic qualities. Presumably, Imhotep had some kind of plans for his Step Pyramid that he showed to the pharaoh for approval and used to direct the engineers who moved the stone blocks in place. The engineers might not have appreciated the beauty in the plans, but the pharaoh and his financiers must have. The main architect of the Taj Mahal, Ustad Ahmad Lahauri, must have made many plans for his building. Shah Jahan, who ordered it built, is reported to have met almost daily with architects and builders as they designed and built the mausoleum and temple complex over the years from 1632 to 1653. They must have considered possible alterations given contingent matters arising. Painters also can imagine and describe prospective paintings, draw sketches, and the like. Composers can do the same with music. Imagined but unwritten music is one kind of hopefully beautiful formal possibility. A written score by itself is another kind of possibility. Musicians and musically "literate" people can read scores and appreciate their formal beauty. Dance notation is less developed than musical notation, although to a degree experts can appreciate a dance "score."

Tradition and cultural habit can also produce a possible form that someone can appreciate for its beauty. People can commission a Song dynasty–style landscape painting based on their familiarity with the genre; that familiarity can lead them to look for paintings based on their appreciation of the "kind" of beauty they might have. People can imagine a painting, piece of music, a building, or an urban plan, based on their knowledge of elements that such a work might harmonize, motifs, figures, traditional elements, movements of thematic development, and so forth.

The important thing to remember about a form as a possibility is that it is vague with respect to the details of its actualization as well as to what is vague in the form itself. Set aside consideration of how a possibility changes in the course of production. It still is the case that a plan is vague with respect to just how the materials can be arranged with its construction. The form in an actual artwork is completely definite with regard to how the artist actualizes it in the haecceity or "thisness" of the art itself. This point is especially complex because the nature of form itself involves vagueness and triviality among its functional components. Consider a geometric form, such as a cross in a plane with equal legs, or an arithmetical equation such as $2 + 2 = 4$. Those forms are vague with respect to anything that might be in a plane in the first instance, and any things that are countable in the second. Given this vagueness, all else in the world is trivially neglected or excluded except insofar as it might show up in the subdetermination of the vague elements.

In the plans for a building, the form needs to reflect the potential materials, the visual and utilitarian locale, and the purposes to which the building is to be put. The rest can be vague. There is a beauty in the form of the building's possibilities at this stage. Most art appreciation courses would not press for the appreciation of beautiful elements beyond this sort of thing. Now we know to plan ahead, that is, include within the architectural plans, issues such as the stability of the land and the atmosphere. The Taj Mahal is being undermined because the water table of the land it is on is sinking; industrial smog is yellowing its bright white surfaces. Architects today design buildings with this environmental site concern in mind, and the cleverness of dealing with these elements is part of their buildings' beauty.

To stress the structural analysis of form in artwork is important. The beauty in any form for artwork is an elegant mixture of simplicity and complexity, and it composes its elements in functions of narrowness, width, vagueness, and triviality. The form treats many things in the world that in principle relate to the art as trivial. It treats hosts of background elements as vague. It has compositional elements that focus narrow contrasts and it has compositional elements that make the whole hang together. Consider, for instance, Constantin Brancusi's *Bird in Space*. It is a sculpture with a thin swelling arc a couple of feet tall, beginning and ending with points, the bottom of which is fixed to a stand. It swells out several inches in the middle and is mounted to incline a bit in the direction of the top point. The beautiful shape itself is a narrow and sharply focused element, highly polished. It occupies a volume that functions as negative space and the arc it cuts through this volume constitutes much of its width, defining the whole volume. The sculpture is usually seen in some kind of display setting, a museum or home, which constitutes a vague setting for the overall space defined by the shape. The viewer sees this first as an abstract shape in a volume, despite the figurative title, a shape of extraordinary grace, and gracefully defining the larger volume. Brancusi himself intended this to be abstract in the sense of depicting the flight of the bird while leaving off the wings, feathers, head, tail, and other elements that would represent the body of a bird flying. This was part of his intent, and his way of participating in the general modernist movement of abstraction during his time. However, without knowing that intent, we can appreciate it as a pure sculptural abstraction that symbolizes a special beauty for abstraction as such. Part of its form is thus its historical importance regarding abstraction and modernism that flourished between the two world wars of the twentieth century. The form of *Bird in Space* was realized in various media. Brancusi himself made several in bronze and several in marble, and of different sizes. The history of modernism is treated vaguely in the form, and the form has a specific place in that vague history. Connoisseurs who know this history will see this in the form itself. When a bronze version was shipped to the United States, the customs officials taxed it as not art, which was duty-free, but as an industrial piece; a subsequent trial justified abstract art in general as being art, not as an industrial something or other. All this is part of the form. The situation of viewing the form of *Bird in Space* includes both the perspective of Brancusi and that of viewers, some of whom know its importance in art history. The beauty of the form, especially for the connoisseurs, includes its adventitious power of staking out a place in the history of modernism and American customs law. The beauty is not merely in the superbly graceful shape that meets the eye.

The form of *Bird in Space* includes its vague capacity to be realized in several media, especially in bronze and marble. That form is made more specific when it is in bronze and even then more specific for each casting of bronze; this same is true for each piece of marble. The form also includes the specific ambient exhibition space, one thing for big museums, another for small spaces, and one thing for exhibition in sunlight, another for carefully slanted lighting. Each specific sculpture is a "this," but it also has the form that is vaguely common to the other authentic sculptures, to knock-offs by popularizers, and to use as a motif on airline advertisements and pictures in magazines and books.

Beauty in Actualizing Form

The formal beauty of a work of art that actualizes itself through space and time, such as a performance or hearing/reading a story, requires capacities for cumulative appreciation on the part of the person experiencing its beauty. To be sure, it takes time to appreciate a sculpture, looking from afar and close up, ranging the eye around its parts and sides, reflecting on how it relates to its exhibitive environment, and to its history and other matters of cultural and social definition. Significant appreciation of the beauty of a building requires walking around it and through it. But some works of art such as sculptures, buildings, and paintings have a location in a duration of space-time. Often the order in which the aspects of such works are experienced is not very significant.

However, works whose form is dynamic have an essential temporal order. Performances exist as spread out in time (and usually significant space as successively occupied in different ways). It is possible, of course, to experience recordings of performances backward, but part of that experience is then reconstructing the temporal progression as an important factor in defining the form of the performance. We can read literary works backward as well, although that might seem strange. We can read a mystery novel by starting at the end in which all things are revealed and working back into the complications of the plot; a serious critic might do that methodologically in addition to reading the book from beginning to end. Serious analysis of literary works often means considering their parts in various relations and orders. Plato's famous discussion in the *Phaedrus* of the inscription on King Midas's tomb comes to mind:

> A maid of bronze I stand on Midas' tomb,
> So long as waters flow and trees grow tall,
> Abiding here on his lamented grace,
> It tells the traveler Midas here is laid.[5]

You can read those four lines in any order, said Plato, and make just as much sense in any order. He took that to be a mark of their aesthetic deficiency: in that context, there should be something important to the sequence in which they are read. Any narrative in a poem, story, or longer work such as a novel has a dynamic order of unfolding.

From the standpoint of the perception of the artistic beauty of temporally unfolding art, the experience itself requires semiotic capacities for memory and integration. Kant, in the "A Deduction" to his *Critique of Pure Reason*, gave a brilliant genetic account of how a temporal series requires the reproduction of the past in present experience to get a sense of temporal cumulative flow. Unfortunately, he abandoned that account in the "B Deduction" precisely because it was genetic, reminiscent of John Locke's "historical plain method" of describing the formation of experience. Nowadays the topic of experience through time is important in experimental psychology. Given the diversity of kinds of dynamic art, and the many neurological elements involved in different kinds of perception, and interpretation in terms of other elements of experience, many different kinds of memory and integration are likely to be involved.

The quality of immediate feeling that unfolds through time necessarily involves changes: the quality is not just one thing but also a quality of changing. A simple model for the classical Western symphony is that the first movement is dramatic, the second slower and more meditative, the third peppy, and the fourth majestic. Of course, very many ways exist to achieve these qualitative effects and many important symphonies of the classical and romantic periods do not follow them with much faithfulness. Nevertheless, the aesthetic experience of the symphony needs to be able qualitatively to integrate the different qualities of the movements. The form of a symphony sometimes involves something like pictorial representation, as in Beethoven's Pastoral Symphony (Symphony No. 6 in F major, Op. 68) that critics agree is a reflective depiction of nature. To hear this, the listener needs to integrate experiences of nature with the music heard. Many kinds of music, indeed for some critics, all kinds of music, are evocative of human emotions, and such emotional states need integration with the musical sounds with their own forms. The form of beauty appreciated in music, like other dynamic forms of art, includes many dimensions of experiences from the listener in addition to the notes and chords heard in order. That larger integrated quality to the situation of experiencing dynamic art has to be understood in terms of the quality of feeling the harmony, whose various components are composed with narrowness and width, vagueness and triviality.

The experience of the symphony is not just something in the subjective feelings of the listener, but the whole situation involving the orchestra or sound system, the setting, and the listener with semiotic capacities of particular sorts. The aesthetic form lies in that harmony of the situation, not in the harmony of subjective feelings only. As I have argued, the situation of artistic aesthetic experience has two intentional centers that define the situation. For instance, the listener to Beethoven's Pastoral Symphony can consider Beethoven's own intentions. In one sense, this is easy because Beethoven's artistic intent is obvious in the pictorial qualities of that symphony. It would be much harder to understand Beethoven's intent with regard to the Hammerklavier Sonata, however, which has little if any pictorial quality (despite its title). In addition, part of a deep appreciation of the Pastoral Symphony would involve knowing that he composed it while also composing the Fifth Symphony and he premiered them on the same program. The contrast between the aggressive, majestic, Sturm und Drang quality of the Fifth and the happy harmonics of the Sixth is part of the form of each of them when it comes to authorial intent, a point not easily heard in the music alone but part of the experience of the deep and informed listener.

Think now about just how complex the aesthetic grasp of an artistic harmony through time must be. Perhaps two kinds of aesthetic attention take place through the duration. First, there might be the continuous immediacy moment through moment of the appreciation of the continuous quality. Reading a page-turner or immersing oneself in the immediate flow of the music can be like this. This might be only an ideal. In most dynamic aesthetic appreciative experiences, moments of break in immediacy occur, even if the immediate flow quickly picks up again. Listening at home or reading a thrilling story can be interrupted by taking sips of coffee that diminish, if not introduce gaps in, aesthetic attention, even when the immediate line is returned to quickly.

Second, in most dynamic artistic appreciative experiences, moments exist when the appreciation takes stock of where things have come and what they have come to. Listening to the symphony, one reflects quickly on the fact that there has been a transition from the first to the second movement, with appreciation and anticipation according to somewhat finished interpretations. Reading a story, one recollects what has gone before and how the plot is unfolding; this is different from following the unfolding of the plot and settings of scenes pell-mell. Without the moments of taking stock, it is difficult to keep the memory necessary for appreciation through time in sufficient felt focus. Without the immediacy of felt movement on to the next, the continuity of the experience is hard to feel in a focused way. The experience needs both.

You might think that in a continuous dynamic appreciation of a performance or reading there must be an aesthetic harmony at each slice of time. Perhaps at many slices there are harmonies—otherwise the slice could not exist on its own—but not harmonies that have any artful aesthetic quality. They might be analytical moments of the sort just mentioned, whose aesthetic unity is not of the artistic sort, as when one reflects on different characters in the story or the shifts in emotional mood in the music. They might be comparative moments when earlier and later elements of what is remembered and anticipated are brought to consciousness, having the unity of a comparison but not of a work of art. Rather, the formal unity of a spatiotemporally dynamic work of art has to do with the harmonic connections through that dynamic. The music might contain beautiful sections, interrupted by far less beautiful sections. Parts of the story might be artful and other parts just bad. Not all pieces of music hang together as wholes, and not all stories add up to more than vignettes. However, for most works of art, the aesthetic experience of them aims at grasping an overall beautiful form of the whole. The dynamic works have an extensive or wide density of being, itself punctuated in lumpy fashion by internal lumps of dense being, appreciated as art.

Therefore, the unfolding of a dynamic work of art in the experience of it is an overall harmony that has within it as components many moments of harmony, some of which themselves are artful and others perhaps not. The unfolding itself might have the regularity of a rule, as musicians performing faithfully from a score play the notes as written. On the other hand, the unfolding might have many moments of hitherto undetermined spontaneity, as in jazz improvisation. Many dynamic performances involve spontaneous improvisation, the whole aesthetic worth of which does not arise until the end. In all cases of temporally dynamic art, the possibilities of the form to be unfolded in the future, even the near future, are vague at least in part with respect to how those possibilities will be actualized. Musicians follow the score but play the notes uniquely. The musicians might train in certain performance traditions so that even how they play the notes is partly determined by habits that limit their possibilities for playing the notes beyond what is on the score. Still, there is a reduction of possible form to form actually made wholly determinate in the unfolding.

How do we judge artistic quality in dynamic works of art? We do it the same way as in nondynamic works: by tracing out whether they end up trivializing those things that would only compromise narrowness and width, by tracing out the pregnant depth of what is formed vaguely, by noting the sharpness of the narrow elements, and by appreciating the unifying roles of the elements shaping width or connection. These functions include the complexity and simplicity of the notes or story line and also the depth of emotions evoked, the relevance to the deep issues in life, the poignancy of the work of art in the personal life of the appreciator, and all the rest that go into the harmony of the situation of the appreciation of a dynamic work of art.

Beauty in Repose

The organization of this chapter follows a line on temporal actualization, focusing first on the aesthetic appreciation of beauty in the form of art that might be only future possibility, although a form that might also become actualized. The second focus is on art as experience coming into actuality in time. The third focus is the appreciation of art as actually existing. As actually existing, works of art have an existential locus of their own as actualities structured by artistic form.

As actual, works of art have the appreciable goodness of being potentials for situations of their appreciation. An actual building has the aesthetic goodness or beauty it does regardless of whether anyone is appreciating it, although part of that aesthetic beauty is its potential relevance for being in a situation in which its appreciation is possible. People can walk away from a building at night, leaving no one there actually appreciating it, and can return to it the next morning. The beauty of the building does not change overnight, but it consists in the mode of potentiality for being in a situation of aesthetic appreciation. The work is not beautiful if it does not have the actual or possible relations with things that make it appreciable from some appreciator's standpoint. The beauty consists in the work's capacity, by virtue of its own form, to be in a situation where it is appreciable, a situation defined both by the potential appreciator's intentionality and by the intentionality of the artist. The form of the work of art is not limited to physical shape and color or to the acoustical sounds of notes played; the form of a work of art includes whatever might be involved in a situation in which it might be appreciated. A painting hung in a museum where the lights are turned off at night does not cease to be beautiful when no one sees it.

An actualized painting or sculpture has beauty relative to a great many situations in which it can be appreciated, and appreciated in different ways by different appreciators because of their interpretation of it in terms of their own experience. Its being a term in these potential situations is part of its intrinsic form. The painting is subjunctively beautiful in the sense (among other senses) that anyone who sees it in the museum in good light can appreciate it, given the required semiotic capabilities in the viewer. The potential for the situation of appreciation of a painting allows the appreciators to come and go. To appreciate a performance, however, requires that the experiencer be present throughout the duration of the symphony's actualization. That particular performance does not have the capacity to be appreciated after it has been actualized because it is no longer present to be engaged by the interpreter. A recording of the performance, however, can make at least certain aspects of the performance capable of being present to the appreciator after the duration of the initial performance. One might also regard the symphony as potentially being performed as the work of art, not a particular performance of it; most of the time when we discuss performance art, that is what we have in mind. The beauty in the symphony then comes from its form that allows performances on different occasions. The capacity for multiple performances is the potential in the symphony to be in multiple situations of appreciation, and that is its actualized form.

The beauty in the actualized work of art includes its capacity to be in situations of appreciation; all that is involved in that capacity counts among the elements of the form of the work itself. The beauty of the art as appreciated lies in the situation, actual or potential, in which it is appreciated, and the beautiful harmony here is a function of the situation inclusive both of the work and the appreciator, plus all the mediating factors. A distinction exists, then, between the beauty in the work of art itself, because of its form that includes potential situations of appreciation, and the beauty of the art as actually or potentially appreciated in the situation. The former beauty includes all the alternative potential situations of appreciation, and that beauty includes many different ways of appreciation. The latter beauty does not register those alternative situations, only the situation at hand for appreciating the work with the specific position and semiotic resources of the particular appreciators. When we think of the beauty or aesthetic goodness of a work of art, we most commonly have in mind how we can appreciate it. Thus, its beauty registers only in terms of the situations we have at hand. However, the artwork might have many potential situations of appreciation of which we are unaware. This appears repeatedly when later generations see, hear, or engage with things an earlier set of appreciators could not do. The beauty of an artwork is one thing in one culture, somewhat different in other cultures. The beauty of the work itself is its inclusive set of potential situations for appreciation, something in terms of which perhaps no artwork can be fully appreciated. David Tracy has nicely defined a "classic" as something that can be deeply and widely appreciated in many contexts and cultures.[6]

The upshot of this reflection on art as actualized is to appreciate it in terms of its range of potentials for appreciation, directly and singularly. In part IV, I shall consider the aesthetic goods important for civilization: surely having an environment of art is one of them. A house filled with paintings and sculptures is a repository of beautiful art (though just how beautiful depends on the various pieces) even when no one is looking at all the art at once. A neighborhood of beautiful houses and public buildings is beautiful as a repository of potentials for appreciation of beautiful architecture.

I call this dimension of actualized art "art in repose." The art is there, ready for particular appreciations. Moreover, there is beauty in each work of art in repose as ready for appreciation. This beauty in each work of art itself can be appreciated by engaging the art in the situation in which it might be directly engaged. The art is beautiful because its intrinsic form includes its being actualized in a culture that includes its potential appreciation. Such an art-filled culture has its own beauty, and it is not exactly the same kind of beauty as the beauty of art because there are few agents who aim at creating culture as a work of art. For the most part, there are artists for the art works but not for the culture as such. Of course, there are exceptions to this. Great artists can affect whole cultures, giving them an artful quality perhaps. However, there are so many other dynamics within a culture about which, except in the case of the great Sage Kings of Chinese myth, we do not say that the culture itself is the product of artful creativity, our next topic.

CHAPTER 8

To Create Arts

To Seek Beauty

The fundamental structure of artistic creativity is the process of actualizing an ideal. It is a species of what John Dewey called the pursuit of "an end in view."[1] This was Dewey's general term for any intentional activity within human experience, such as taking out the trash, cooking a meal, building a piece of furniture, resolving a neighborhood conflict, running a race, trying to understand a book, inquiring about a curiosity, cultivating a family, ordering up one's life, pursuing a career, working for a political goal, or creating a work of art. Pursuit of an end in view was Dewey's version of what I have called a "situation," selecting out of all the things in an existential field only those things and connections that are relevant to a person's intentions. The situations defined through the pursuit of an end in view are those in which human intentionality and often agency are important; Dewey liked to emphasize experience as interaction, or more strongly, transaction.[2] I often use the even stronger word, engagement, where the connection with what is engaged is very much a function of intentionality, habitual or conscious. The situation of enjoying a sunset reflects a more passive intentionality in which the beauty of the sunset attracts the viewer's attention and prompts a more deliberate focus on the sunset and, in the example, cultivates habits of sunset viewing and even the construction of a viewing station. In the complicated situation of the beautiful sunset, only when the situation advances to deliberate plans to enjoy the sunset would it fall under what Dewey called an end in view, the end of sunset enjoyment. The sunset situation grows into one with an end in view when the sky arrests the viewer's attention and the intention forms to pay attention because of the beauty of it.

The situation of creating a work of art is a much more deliberate intentionality, not merely arrested attention with the intention of paying attention. Such a situation in a way parallels the situation of appreciating a work of art in that it has two centers of intentionality defining what is relevant, that of the viewer and that of the artist. The situation of artistic creativity can be vague with respect to the prospective viewer. An artist can create an artwork for a very specific appreciator, such as a client, a typical audience in a concert hall or art gallery, or a certain readership. Or, the appreciators as the artist imagines them might be vague, perhaps assuming a culture in which the artist is so much a part that the question of differential appreciation does not come up. Or, perhaps the artist creates in explicit rejection of an assumed public, wanting to assert his or her own authority exclusively to determine and appreciate what is beautiful; the artist anticipates that the work will not be appreciated. Perhaps the artist creates only for self-enjoyment, works that appeal only to the artist's own appreciation. Most of the time, artists who have an interest in originality over and above making something beautiful hope the beauty of their art will be seductive enough to bring a public around to a new way of appreciation.

However vague an artist might be in imagining the appreciating public for the work under way, the artist is specific about the resources and means for creating the artwork. A poet or novelist feels the sensuosity of the words, the subtle levels and twists of meanings, and the uniqueness of the ways of perception and life emerging in the artistic entity. The dancer is specific about the powers of the body, the meanings of the dance forms, the ways movement shapes space negatively and positively, as well as possible symbolic content. The painter deals with pigments and canvas, decisions about line and color, and many other aspects of representation or nonrepresentation. Two centers of intention define a situation of artistic creativity, the specific workmanship of the artist and the artist's imagination of the public that might appreciate the art.

The *ideal* the artist has of creating something appreciable as beautiful also determines a situation of artistic creativity. The ideal is an end in view toward which the creative process works. Unlike many kinds of ends in view, such as resolution of a moral problem or the funding of a community health complex, an artistic end in view begins somewhat vaguely and becomes more determinate as the artist works with the materials. A painter might go through a number of sketches and color experiments before achieving the end. A musical composer might contemplate variations on a melody, different sound combinations, and the like. A choreographer might sort through many steps and moves in order to find the ideal coherence. A performer such as a dancer or musician might not treat the overall plan as an ideal, but in a given performance feel with wonder how to instantiate that plan with the next move.

In one sense, the ideal for a creative process is something like a human imaginative or experimental representation of a future possibility. The artist seeks to actualize the ideal possibility. In a deeper sense, the relation of the artist's work to the ideal is a matter of resolving issues of coherence for the artistic material at hand. This is a dialectical process. On the one hand, the structure of the ideal keeps changing as the artist works the matter. On the other hand, the artist seeks out or rejects different material resources, such as paints for the painter and different muscular moves for the dancer, as the demands of the ideal take shape. Sometimes a predetermined form for the ideal takes precedence, as when a client approaches an architect with an idea. Other times the resources at hand, such as paints, a canvas, and a scene take precedence and an ideal is sought that would make them coherent with beauty. With most artistic processes, there is give and take both ways, with ideas for the ideal emerging as the artist feels potentials in the resources and with a modification of what can be found as resources as new ideas for the ideal call for new elements. Perhaps formal garden design offers the best drawn-out example of the creative process. Several seasons are required to see what plants flourish in a given environment and how they grow together. The plans for their combination have to evolve as their growing potential is learned, as my wife and I have learned from experience. At the same time, visions of the garden call up suggestions for other plants that might be appropriate. The artistic gardener needs to experiment with the soil, weather conditions, and length of daylight per season to see what goes together in the various moments of the growing season. Then, of course, the gardening itself changes the soil and moisture conditions, even the ambient insects and underground microbes, worms, and other creatures. To be sure, plants of different kinds have their emotional association. The location of the garden means something with regard to the surroundings; a garden structure that is beautiful in one setting might be discordant in another, even with nearly identical growing conditions. Whereas a dancer has almost no time to wonder whether a leap of a certain sort will work today, and a water colorist needs some patience to let one coat dry before adding another, a garden designer needs the patience of Job. Or Job's boss, whose original garden was ruined.

Given the back-and-forth movement between resources and ideal, the artistic process is drawn to the ideal as that which (tentatively) might give coherence to the material resources. A fundamental human attraction to coherence exists relative to what might cohere. The imagined ideal possibility is taken as ideal by the artist's feelings for what would resolve the various resources into a beautiful work. Despite all the dismissive things that some philosophers have said about human intentionality being a fiction because some kind of mechanistic conception of human nature is true, in artistic creativity, the ideal is a drawing power that determines the artist to do something to achieve the actualization of beauty in the materials at hand. To be sure, the artist can sort through many arrays of materials. The artist can reconceive the ideal repeatedly. Nevertheless, the artistic process is lured by the ideal for the materials comprising the resources for the artwork at hand. Some philosophers, including me, argue that any act of human intentionality and agency aims toward some ideal of coherence of all the disparate things impinging on that act. However, in the work of artistic creation, the ideal is set within the larger class of ideals as focused on bringing about a work of art as enjoyable in itself and for itself.

Layers upon layers of coherence exist in an artwork. Indeed, layers upon layers of incoherence need reordering to cohere in the creation of an artwork. The Confucian conception of *li*, often translated "principle" or "coherence," emphasizes the multidimensionality of coherence, from the making coherent of the artist's original tentative impulses to the arrangement of the material elements to the production of the completed actual artwork.[3] Better than the Western traditions, the Confucian has deeply acknowledged this multidimensionality, including connections and disconnections that cut across other dimensions. Because in human life, especially social and personal life, so many things *cannot* be made coherent, Confucians are particularly sensitive to the frustrations and tragedies of living.[4] In the art associated with Confucianism, such as the landscape paintings discussed earlier, the issues of making disparate elements coherent are front and center, as in the landscape composition that emphasizes foreground, middle ground, and background as floating around each other.

Bringing artistic elements to coherence calls attention to what an artist tries to do in creating a work of art out of the material resources. But of course, it is a kind of process of harmonization, bringing the resources to harmony with a beautiful form. So we ought not to think of coherence just as making things fit together, as different patterns in a drawing might do. That would simply be to create a work with narrowness of contrast. A contrast is the fitting together of very different things, each of which has its own depth. The ideal for a work of art also needs to have width that unites many points of narrow contrast. As I have said repeatedly, most of the components in the artistic harmony are disposed to function vaguely. The form of the work excludes from the artwork the relations to things that the form trivializes. The form that constitutes the ideal for the artistic process is not merely some highlights brought to consciousness. The ideal form includes also the functions of narrowness, width, vagueness, and triviality in the potential resources, even when these elements do not rise to the artist's consciousness. It also exhibits some element of elegance balancing its complexity and simplicity.

In what does an artist's creativity consist? Although this is a huge question, I believe that part of the answer is that it is a species of what Aristotle called wit, the art of hitting upon the third term. The "third term" is something that brings other things into coherence. By themselves, the other things do not cohere, and to stick with the other things leads to an impasse. However, an artist is able to bring in some new element that makes the rest cohere. Some people think of this as random spontaneity. Surely, accidents of life—an apple dropping from a tree—can function as third terms, prompting Newton's theory of gravity (if you believe that story). Sometimes, otherwise random ideas can lead to just the right stroke, note, architectural shadow, or garden accent. I suspect, however, that most of the time the creative intervention comes from an artist's vast store of learned habits of gesture, experience with different paints, unconscious habits of performance style, and experience with what works architecturally versus what leads to further problems. Rarely is an artist so preoccupied with pursuit of a single ideal with a fixed palette of resources as to exclude all the other artistic experiences. Those whose artistic skills are most honed, so as to become virtually unconscious, are most able to call upon them to achieve spontaneity in a given creative process. Thinking outside the box usually means that the artist has many boxes.

To Seek Beauty in Form

We can look at the creative artistic process in at least two ways. This section examines the way the creative process searches for just the right form that bears beauty. The next section examines how the artist actualizes the form in the resources at hand, whether the artwork is an artifact, a performance, or a garden. These two ways reflect the dialectical back and forth of the creative process discussed in the previous section.

The search for the right form in artistic creation has at least five related kinds of variables in addition to the structure of harmonic form itself: potentials, possibilities, imaginative representation, aesthetic inventiveness, and aesthetic judgment. Because the arts are so different from one another, with so many crossover kinds, these terms fit better and more obviously with some than others.

By *potentials*, I mean the actual things that are resources to be combined into the artwork. To give you a sense of their range, I can mention several senses of such potentials. For painters the material potentials include the paints, canvases, brushes, thinners, rags, and such; for sculptors, blocks of marble, pieces of wood, lumps of clay, and the chiseling, shaping, and polishing tools; for architects the building materials. In addition are all the actual examples of the genre produced in the past that serve as tradition and models. The various publics for the works of art are potentials that enter into calculations of the appreciators' perspectives. The training of the artists and the traditions in which they work, their own personal experiences, and their motivations and artistic impulses are among the potentials to be actualized in the artwork. Perhaps most elusive is the actual culture with its symbol systems that provide the resources for meaning. Composers and choreographers have their potential instruments and performers, senses of genres, traditions, and the like. Performers have their trained bodies and minds, performance styles to which they have achieved habituation, plus all the emotional and representational meanings at their disposal. A writer has the given resources of language, the potential allusions, models for story lines and language combination, long reflected on themes and impulses to write this or that, as well as the given character of their potential readership. Garden designers have their geographical location with its resources and limitations, plant materials, given ambitions for their gardens, the aesthetics of visual and emotional settings, and the like. The search for beauty in form has to do with combining all these potentials into a new actual work of art or performance.

Whereas potentialities are actual things in or from the past that can be made into something, *possibilities* are structures from the future that set limits to how the potentialities can be combined. In my cosmology, possibilities are harmonies whose forms mediate between the plurality of potentials and the unity that would unite them in various patterns of coherence. Only certain ways of combining the actual things into something new are possible. The form of a possibility is always relative to the things that are to be combined; not all combinations are possible. The goodness in a work of art has to do with the formal structure of its possibility, how it combines the potentials with complexity and simplicity in some kind of elegance, and how it composes those potentials with narrowness, width, vagueness, and triviality. A possibility always has that structure of form, not just a coherence of noncontradiction of narrow focal points but a coherence of such a complex composition as to have triviality, vagueness, narrowness, and width in respect to all the potentials for affecting the creative process and entering into the work.

Possibilities by themselves are relevant to the creative process only when they can be *represented in imagination* to lure the artist and make aesthetic judgment possible. Given the harmonic structure of natural materials, the real possibilities for a sculpture are indefinitely large. However, the sculptor needs to be able to think of them. For human experience, the structures of our interpretive semiotic systems vastly simplify the complex future. We recognize possibilities in terms of the signs we have for interpreting them. Many of these signs need to count among the potentialities available for the creative process, including especially the taste and imaginative categories that tradition and professional training imbue in artists. Nevertheless, over and above the given potentialities are the creative elements in interpreting. Artists see possibilities others do not and that they themselves have not seen before. Artists invent images as ways of seeing new dimensions of possibilities. The dialectical character of the artistic process always needs emphasis: new visions of what is possible call for revisions of what potentials can be called upon, and new understanding of the potentials prompts inquiry into new structures of possibilities. Artists have the freedom to select both which potentials are relevant and which ideal forms might integrate them, and this freedom is borne by the process of interpreting possibilities.

By *aesthetic inventiveness*, I mean the capacity to envision new ways of making things coherent, especially ways of harmonizing things that seem incoherent. This goes beyond understanding the potentials for a work of art, beyond the sheer field of possibilities, and beyond the ways to imagine and represent those possibilities relative to the potentials. Aesthetic inventiveness is the imagining of hitherto unimagined possibilities as ways of bringing coherent form to what had been missing in the previous imagination of the ideal form for the work of art. Of course, those possibilities have to be possible. However, what makes them aesthetic inventions is that the artist understands them in the context of adding to the richness of the form in the work of art. They are bits of aesthetic achievement created along the way in the process of producing the work of art. They are important not because they are possible—a zillion more things are possible—but because they contribute to the beauty of the whole, add something to the complexity, and integrate with some new devise of simplicity. Or, to put the point another way, in many cases the process of creating a work of art is to imagine an ideal form with very vague elements, and then engage in the dialectical process of relating that ideal to the potentials. This process fills in the vague elements with new structures of narrowness and width, or new ways of escaping incoherence by discovering how to render certain elements trivial or transform them with vague elements. The feeling of being creative that many artists of various genres enjoy comes from the practice of many acts of aesthetic inventiveness along the way. When an artist feels stuck, it is because those acts of aesthetic inventiveness are not happening.

Aesthetic judgment is the moment of evaluation in which the artist assesses how well the form of the artwork, imagined or actualized, achieves a kind of beauty relative to what is possible for the potentials, including social and traditional contexts among the potentials. In artwork that takes significant time to produce, such as writing a novel, painting a painting, or cultivating a garden, many moments of aesthetic judgment take place. Sometimes the artist sees what is good and knows just when to stop. Other times the artist is never satisfied or is satisfied only on Saturdays or in the company of wealthy clients. Most creative processes waffle between these two extremes. Brancusi made many versions of *Bird in Space*. Was that because none satisfied him? Or was it because each variation had its own positive evaluation?

One way of looking at the creative process is to see it as a search for the form that would give beauty to the project defined by its potentials. This process includes discovering new depths in the potentials and is limited by what is truly possible. The possibilities become relevant within the situation of the creative process only insofar as the artist can interpret them so as to do something in reference to them. The creation of works of art can be routinized and made so repetitious that no new problems arise. Nevertheless, the emphasis on creativity in art comes from the fact that, in at least certain kinds of art, each artistic process encounters new problems for coherence that aesthetic inventiveness needs to solve. Most artists insist on making new problems for themselves when they feel that repeating art productions—paintings, novels, dances, symphonies—has become routine.

Part of making artwork is creativity. Artists cannot reduce their activity to mere production if it is to feel like a creative process to the artist, however much the public might like cheap knock-offs of good artwork. On the simple level of audience satisfaction, a singer's concert that is entirely lip-synched with a good sound system might be just as beautiful and appreciable as a live concert. Nevertheless, for the singer, this is not creative, at least not creative in that concert however creative the time in the sound studio might have been. Moreover, part of the situation of appreciating art is the appreciator's sense that the artist was being creative. Two perspectives define a situation of appreciating art, I have argued, that of the appreciator and that of the artist. Just as the artist to some degree anticipates the audience, so those in the audience appreciate the creativity in the artist solving problems.

Sometimes "schools" of art, such as painting schools, can reach a level of high beauty in which the problems of the media and the setting are "solved" with formulae that skilled artists can follow. Nevertheless, "school" art usually seems flat after a while because the sense that the artists are still solving problems is missing. The sense of aesthetic innovation is missing and the artistic process is more about successful formulaic production than about creative production. As John Dewey said on a much larger scale, human experience does not rise to the level of conscious interest unless it involves what he called a "problematic situation." That is true in most genres of art: interest comes because of the problematic situation, even when the aesthetic judgment at the end might prefer productions with the problems solved.

To Seek Beauty in Actualizing Form

Whereas one way of understanding the creative process in art is to see it as the search for the ideal form that most magnifies beauty in the result, thus creating great density of being of an artful sort, another and somewhat opposite way is to see the process as embodying the ideal in the actualized materials. Whereas any natural and social process results in extraordinarily beautiful things, such as a sunset or a festival celebration, processes of artistic creation work to embody an imagined artful ideal in an actual thing. How can the actual resources be organized or manipulated to embody the ideal form sought?

Perhaps the art of garden design is the most obvious example of this point. The art does involve planning ahead regarding how the garden is supposed to look throughout the changes of seasons. Mainly, however, it has to do with cultivating the plants, grading terraces, arranging water and drainage, weeding, pruning, deadheading, mulching, manipulating light and shade, and countless other tasks of working with the actual materials and monitoring their transformations. When Kant called gardening one of the fine arts, he had in mind formal gardens such as were designed, planted, tended, and enjoyed in the Renaissance in Europe; he may have known of formal Persian gardens throughout the Islamic world. It is obvious how much care gardeners need to take to create and maintain through time such a formal garden. However, the naturalistic gardens of Kant's contemporary, Lancelot "Capability" Brown, require just as much work in order to make the plantings and settings look as if they "just happened."[5]

Most other creative artistic processes are not as inclusive as garden design. At one extreme are the processes that work to embody the intended ideal form into something that endures for a while once actualized. Creating paintings, sculptures, buildings, novels, poems, and other forms of literature are like this. In a way, the writing of a musical score and the development of a choreographic plan are like the once and for all actualization of an ideal form. At the other extreme are the arts of dynamic actualization of things through time such as a musical performance or a dance.

Although a painter might spend some time making sketches, most of the work involves the application of paint to canvas, reworking, overpainting, correcting mistakes, mixing new colors, and the like. How can the imagined ideal intent be actualized on the canvas? Inexperienced painters try many different ways and see how they turn out. This involves a lot of experimentation and guesswork, all monitored by aesthetic judgments along the way. More experienced painters know the potential effects of certain additions or subtractions and can make more deliberate forays into aesthetic invention. To be sure, many different kinds of painting processes exist. Chinese landscape painters finish a painting with an economy of brushstrokes, though the real potentials they emphasize are their years of experience in learning how to eliminate everything but the most essential. Painters of monumental battle scenes can work and rework every square inch of the canvas; or they can assign students in their studio to paint different parts of the canvas, following the artist's cartoon. Most painters work between these extremes.

Whereas the structure of an ideal form that an artist intends to embody in the actual work includes the compositional functioning of various components as trivial, vague, narrow, and width-giving, most of the time the artist focuses on embodying the narrow and wide elements. The narrow elements are the focal points that give high contrast. The elements of width are those that make the composition hang together, the balance of narrow elements across the canvas, creating relative positive and negative shapes. I doubt that many artists painting a battle scene think much about the elements of the scene that are out of sight, such as the road the army came down the day before. Even when the artist wants to paint the distant soldiers in some detail, most resort to rather vague suggestions of faces: those vague representations of soldiers stand for many individuals that the artist could have painted in detail had they been more in the foreground. The thousands of terra cotta soldiers entombed with the first Chin Chinese emperor, Shih Hsi Huang Ti, are remarkable for what they make narrow and vague. Among the thousands, there are only a few body forms, such as archers standing or kneeling, soldiers with spears or swords, and the like. These few body types are vague representations of the stances of soldiers that in real life would be individual for each person. By contrast, the head on each of these soldiers portrays some specific person. Each statue has a realistic portrait head of some individual. Artisans made the instances of the body types; genuine sculptors made the heads.

In the actual process of embodying the ideal form in the painting, the artist treats every part of the canvas singularly. Each brush stroke counts. Each exists in a harmonic relation with each other part of the canvas. This singularity of the brush strokes might be quite different from the functional roles that the brush strokes play in the painting as actualizing the artistic form. The effort of the artist is to lay down each brush stroke, singular as it is, in harmony with the strokes around it, to play its role in the functional composition of the painting. Of course, as the potential combinations of the strokes reveal hitherto unimagined coherences, the ideal form itself shifts. In fact, the imagined and unpainted ideal form for a painting is always a cartoon relative to its actual embodiment. The cartoon leaves vague what cannot be left vague in the haecceity of the painting itself.

Actualizing performances is more complicated. In theater, professional dance, and music, most often a script or score exists that the performer has mastered and perhaps performed many times before. The creation of the script as a work of art is a form of actualizing an ideal of the sort just discussed. However, the performance of the script, score, and so on, involves a dual form of creative harmonization. On the one hand, the next move is to actualize aims to fit into the script or score. It needs to be actual to play its role in the functioning of components in the script or score. On the other hand, the next move has to be made to harmonize with the previous moves, relating to what already has been actualized, building on or extending the past elements in the performance. With regard to the former, many ways of speaking the next line and moving appropriately are possible, all of which fall within the script; each way might have its own unique emotional tone or even conceptual meaning, different from the other ways but all falling within the script. There are many ways of playing or singing the note or phrase, all of which follow the score. In dance, many ways to make a leap are possible that fit the choreography; different dancers play the role differently, and even the same dancer does it a bit differently each time. Nevertheless, with regard to the latter element of creative harmonization, the next move needs to be in harmony with the past singular moves. The subtle interpretation of the previous elements of plot needs to follow harmoniously with what has been actualized; if the past had been actualized differently, albeit in conformation with the script, the next moves must follow up on that. In musical performance, there are different traditions of performance style, and the next note or phrase should be in conformity with what is already actual; even more subtly, each part of a performance has its own emotional dynamic that needs to be harmonized with the parts of the performance to come. In dance, the steps being enacted need to conform to those that lead to them. In all performance, the sense of temporal continuity through changes is as much the result of harmonizing with the actual past as it is with harmonizing according to the ideal script or score.

Performance is vastly complicated when several performers work together, as is usually though not always the case. In the cases of multiple performers, each needs to relate to the others according to the script or score, but also and more importantly according to what the others have been doing in the past to which they are attempting to conform now. Perhaps the most obvious example is singing in a chorus where each singer needs to tune with the others. Other kinds of performance also need rapport.

I have been writing here about performance where the ideal form is a future possibility embodied in a script, score, or choreographic form. Many arts forms, including theater, music, and dance, involve improvisational performances where the plan for the whole dynamic is lacking. In these instances, the performers quicken what they know from the past, like jazz performers picking up known riffs and licks. Improvisational theater employs meanings and situations that are recognizable from the past, and so does dance. Beautiful ballroom dancing, a great participatory art for many, combines basic steps and rhythms with splendid improvisation. In all group improvisation, the issue of rapport among the performers is important, working with the past moves, sensitivities, and emotional tones of the fellow performers. Improvisational rapport works not only to harmonize each performer's interpretation of the others' past moves but also with anticipation of the others' imagination of how the future might bring the dynamic of the whole performance together. Absent a script or score, the ideal form slowly emerges as the creative performers relate to one another in ways that can make a beautiful whole of the performance. The result, when the improvisation is good, is an embodied ideal form that was never disembodied or merely ideal, except insofar as the performers anticipated its elements at moments along the way. In the midst of the performance, no performer has an anticipation of the whole, because the variants of the others yet to come are unknown and unknowable. Improvisation requires extraordinary sensitivity to new possibilities opening up as the performers work together. In an important sense, any performance involving several performers requires improvisation to establish rapport, even when there is a script or score.

Beauty in Achieving Beauty: The Artistic Life

This chapter has been about the process of creating art. I have defined art roughly as the artifacts and practices that artists make to be beautiful in the sense that appropriate audiences can prize them for their own sake, whatever other kinds of goodness they might have. The discussion has added complexity and depth to the more formal theory of goodness that I developed earlier in this volume. Let me conclude this chapter with some reflections on the life of artistic creativity itself.

No one pattern for an artistic life exists. Some artists devote their whole lives to learning, perfecting, and producing from their art, with the other dimensions of life subordinated to that. Bach and Haydn had long lives with a constant production of musical compositions and performances. Mozart, Schubert, and Mendelssohn lived only into their thirties but still left massive oeuvres. The English romantic poets Keats, Shelley, and Byron died at ages twenty-five, twenty-nine, and thirty-six, respectively, whereas W. H. Auden lived to be sixty-six and T. S. Eliot seventy-six; all of them organized their lives around their art, although the first three made politics part of their art. Many artists produce only one, or a few, significant works of art, sometimes just barely fitting it into lives defined by other occupations. The places of artists in society vary greatly by culture, and each genre has a variety of places as its own. Throughout history and across cultures artists have found a variety of means of making a living for their art.

Yet to an important degree, the making of a creative artist's life can itself be a work of art, though not always so. An artist who develops artistic excellence is making his or her own character a kind of artwork. Romantics are the cheerleaders for making the life of an artist, but this holds for many kinds of artistic life. Why be an artist? Perhaps it is a way of making a living. Perhaps it comes from following a family tradition. Perhaps it is in response to a great need for artists in a bourgeoning cultural expansion. Nevertheless, I suspect (romantic that I am?) that it is because being creative in artistic ways is a very good way of living. The creative life is good in itself, however useful it might be in other ways. Most artists I have known—such as my wife—talked to, or whose testimony I have read, produce their art because that is what they feel themselves to be most joyous in doing.

Sometimes this joy has the great feeling of "spontaneous flow." Other times it has the satisfaction of being the creator of things that are good just for themselves, regardless of other kinds of worth.

The components of an artistic life, in any kind of art, include building a special dynamic harmony of the sort we have discussed. The artist needs to master materials, including perhaps most importantly the artist's body; the artist needs to cultivate creative imagination of ideal forms for artistic production; the artist needs to cultivate imaginative innovation regarding the possible and imaginative invention to deal with artistic problems. The artist needs to exercise steady and appropriate aesthetic judgment. The artistic life is a series of situations of artistic creativity, and the artist's skills carry over from one situation to the next. Moreover, the artist's maturing creativity, in all these dimensions, grows from one situation to the next. Of course, there are times of uncreativity, when the performing or producing activity is frustrated. The artistic life is rarely an unbroken progression. Some artists claim that their lives are less steady than those of other people, that the artistic imagination makes them misfits, that it leads to psychological and spiritual pain, and sometimes to somatic disease. Because some of the artistic situations in an artist's life are very much oriented to audiences and to the search for recognition and fame, some artists become very much other-directed; acceptance or rejection, fame or ridicule, can lead to emotional roller coasters. Yet even when an artist's life is a personal or social mess when viewed by those standards, if it is artistically productive it still is a work of art itself, a harmony that has the beauty of making things that are enjoyable in themselves through a short or long life of work.

John Dewey's *Art as Experience* is one of the greatest books ever written about the nature of art and the artistic creative process. Nevertheless, many people have noted that it just as well might have been entitled *Experience as Art*. In the latter title lies the meaning that all of life, for everyone, should be oriented to making things that are worthwhile in themselves and to appreciating beautiful things that we did not and could not make, such as sunsets, campfires, flowing streams, flowers, trees, and noisy birds. This was Dewey's larger point: life should be oriented to the things that are intrinsically worthwhile and enjoyable. Chapter 6 began with a long quote from Dewey about the deliberate creation and sustenance of those things that are "neat" pleasures. Since then I have discussed some of the complications involved in identifying and creating the pleasures that are worthwhile in themselves as these have been parceled out in the developed arts. The depth and contrast of beauty in the arts is far more intense in the long run than that found in walking on stilts (although the problems of balance for the stilt walker might be intense enough in the moment). As we become aware of the complexity of beauty in intrinsically good artwork in practices and artifacts, it becomes apparent that multidimensional cultures are necessary for even those festivities no more subtle than would find entertainment in walking on stilts.

For each of us to look upon life as the creation and enjoyment of art, including the enjoyment of our lives as our own artistic creations, requires learning how to see life, or at least portions of it, as embodying beautiful ideal forms. This involves composing the functions of our life's components as to have narrowness and width, vagueness and triviality, as to achieve both depth and the focus of contrast. The appreciation of this means learning to pay attention to the immediate qualities of life, knowing that those qualities are beautiful harmonies with the harmonic structure of densities gathered with complexity and simplicity. To live life artfully requires attention to focus and depth, to easily neglected connections, to sensitivities that must be learned through inquiry and openness to the utterly unexpected. Dewey would say that the "meaning of life" is how well life is lived as the creation and enjoyment of things that are beautiful and worthwhile in themselves.

The primary thesis of this book is that goodness is a function of form wherever form obtains. Form is a harmony that achieves some density of being by virtue of how it composes its various essential and conditional components according to its functions of narrowness, width, vagueness, and triviality. Because any form relates internally to any other thing with respect to which it is determinate, its compositional functions determine how it is located in an existential field with respect to those things. Part I began the analysis of this by showing how any form, and anything with form, has the goodness of its harmonizing the components in the way that it does, with its pattern, its components, its location in an existential field, and its overall goodness, including the valuable elements in its relations.

Part II has extended the goodness in form to the analysis of beauty, the kind of goodness in form that is good in itself, however it might be instrumentally good or bad elsewhere. We find beauty all throughout nature because anything natural is determinate and has form. Art is one kind of beauty found within nature. We must resist the temptation to think of art as in opposition to nature, creating a false distinction between the "natural," meaning what happens on its own, and the "artificial," meaning what people introduce into nature. Art production and enjoyments are natural activities. The human capacities to interpret and appreciate it limit the appreciation of beauty in nature. Among the beauties of nature are those in humanly produced art, and most of part II focused on art. Although the goodness of beauty in art is extremely complicated, involving the dual perspectives of audience and artists in defining the situation of experiencing art as beautiful, as well as the depths of symbolism, context, and a host of other elements, it is still the goodness of the art as such (which includes the appreciability of the art). In this respect, all the goodness in beautiful nature, including art, consists of the thing's own harmony rather than the harmony's influence on something else.

PART III

Goodness in Obligation and Personhood

I want now to complicate the hypothesis about goodness by attending to obligation and personhood, topics more complex than the goodness a thing has in itself that is the object of art. Among the things essential to personhood, I shall argue, is how people relate to the world in ways in which they are under obligation. People of course have many kinds of components and put them together in countless complex ways. Historical and ancestral conditions, biology and environment, social and civilizational structures, simply *give* most of these components to people.

Nevertheless, an honorific connotation attaches to the label of "persons." In the honorific sense, persons are what they are by virtue of what they do with what they are given. We judge people normatively, not by their given conditions, but by how they respond to them. In senses that I shall explore in this part, persons are under obligation to relate to certain things and therefore are under normative judgment, even if no one judges them. Persons are responsible for how they respond. Only beings who are responsible in this sense, even if they utterly fail their responsibilities (most of us fail them, but not utterly), can be called persons. Conversely, when we refuse to hold people responsible, we dehumanize them. We objectify them as merely mechanically moving as the products of given conditions. In matters of normative judgment, we reduce them to mere victims of their antecedent causes. Persons have a developmental trajectory, of

173

course, beginning as infants with no responsibility and perhaps living long enough to become incompetent in responsibility; exactly where personhood in the extended sense begins and ends is a matter of controversy. The topic of this part, however, is the special goodness in being human persons. Many other values in being human exist, and persons are much more complex than I shall discuss here, including in matters of civilization. These matters of obligation, however, are among the most important essential components of personhood.

I shall explore four cases of goodness consisting in a two-term relation yielding obligation. A two-term obligation relation is a harmony that relates two or more harmonies. In these cases, one harmony has a goodness of its own, the set of conditions to which a person is obligated to respond. A second harmony in the two-term relation also has a goodness of its own, the goodness of the person harmonizing through time. In the two-term obligation relations, however, the goodness in question is that of the harmony of the relation between the two included harmonies, something over and above most of the ways by which the two harmonies relate together. To recur to an example from the previous chapter, when musicians, actors, or dancers establish rapport with one another, a special kind of relation comes to be over and above other relations among them. They might move with respect to one another in the same space, in coordinated times, according to the same score or script, and still not be in rapport. Rapport is a special kind of harmony over and above many others that gives a special excellence to the performance, which is a harmony in itself over and above the performers, though containing them as components. Of course, the rapport in itself is something to which each of the performers relates so that it becomes a component of their individual performances. We judge performers themselves by how easily, quickly, and deeply they can enter into rapport with each other. Sometimes, particular performers establish relationships so that they easily enter into rapport with each other but not so easily with other performers. The rapport itself is a component of the performance as a unified work of art. How persons fulfill (or do not fulfill) their obligations is like how performers develop (or do not develop) rapport with one another.

Without suggesting for a moment that the following are the only kinds of goodness that consist in two-term obligation relations, in this part I shall discuss: the goodness in interpretations relating truly or falsely to their objects (chapter 9); the goodness in responsible decisions and actions relating morally or immorally to the situations they address and affect (chapter 10); the goodness in conforming, comporting, and composing oneself rightly or wrongly in one's situation, including the social and natural issues on one's watch, which is more about crafting oneself in relation to the world rather than merely choosing among the world's possibilities (chapter 11); and the goodness in being virtuous or not in relation to the goodness one might obtain within one's situation considered globally (chapter 12). These are basic kinds of human goodness: being true, moral, right, and virtuous. Of course, these goods are complicated, for instance, in the extent to which they are borne by individuals, groups, or societies, or in respect to the kinds of things to which the person or persons bearing the goods are related. These goods also overlap and modify one another. Subsequent chapters will explore some but by no means all of these complexities.

In the discussions to follow, I shall develop special meanings for truth, morality, rightness, and virtue. Truth and virtue have common-sense meanings that serve nicely to orient the special points I want to make about them. Rightness is a strange word here that has to do with relating to the large contours of the world, a point that will have to be explained (in chapter 11); it is more unintelligible than misleading at this stage of my argument. Morality, however, can be misleading at this point. What I mean by the term is any kind of decision making that determines both consequences of action and the goodness (or badness) of the chooser as chooser. This is far broader than a commonsense understanding of morality as having to do with better and worse choices that can be scaled together in principle. Morality in my usage also means the choices we make between alternative possibilities that are simply different kinds of good, not necessarily better or worse than one another. Career choices, for instance, can be among equally "good" kinds of careers, but they determine the chooser to have the character of one who chooses this versus that career. Many choices in how to live are of this broad nature. Kant had a much more restricted notion of morality, having to do with imperatives for choice, not simply options among different possibilities. My discussion of Kant in chapter 10 will show why his notion of morality is too restrictive and that categorical imperatives should not be understood his way. By morality I mean obligations regarding choice.

The decisive mark of these goods, in contrast to that of beauty, is that they involve a dyad in the relation: true, not false; moral, not immoral; right, not wrong (this is perhaps the most confusing goodness to sort); virtuous, not vicious. I need to add many qualifications to this. For instance, someone can be true, moral, right, or good in some respects and not others. Beauty is not in a dyadic relation to ugliness because the ugly is just a disappointing form of beauty; the dyadic obligation relations relate two harmonies, one of which should conform in some sense to the other. All these dyadic relations are mediated a thousand times over. Human life is extremely ambiguous and even ambivalent in respect to how we judge it: true here, false in that respect; moral in one sense but immoral in another; well engaged here but disengaged there; good in this way, bad in that way. Because of these ambiguities, it is often wise not to judge people much, not even oneself. The Christian religion says serious judgment belongs to God alone, and many Christians believe that God just throws up His or Her hands and is merciful and forgiving to everyone.

Nevertheless, despite the ambiguity and the wisdom in refraining from judgment, these goods are extremely important in discerning the worth of human life. They are among the most important lumps of density of being in the overall harmonic density of being in a person or a people's life. Despite the difficulty of judgment, indeed the psychological and social hazard of it, a profound sense exists that we are obligated to seek truth, moral righteousness, attuned engagement, and overall virtue. To suppose, or hope, that "anything goes" is to accept a life aesthetically flattened. Many people complain that relativisms of many sorts do lead to this flattened life.

These four kinds of two-term goods stem from what is indeed an ultimate condition of human life, namely, that we live under obligation. Obligation points differentially to both harmonies in the two-term relation. On the one hand, it points to what persons should do regarding that to which they are obligated to respond. On the other hand, it points to the responding person as having personal worth based on the response. Over and above all that is given to human life, we give ourselves normative characters by the responses we make in obligation.

In an important sense, the core of obligation comes from the fact that we make ourselves better or worse (in four different senses) by how we respond, and therefore we define ourselves normatively in those responses. We do not need an elaborate Kantian theory of rational consistency of will to know that the reason we should follow our obligations is that we make ourselves worse people by not doing so. Of course, we can choose to be worse persons, ignoring obligation or directly thwarting it. Religious notions of the will to sin are relevant here. However, the plain fact is that to do the worse makes us worse persons in that respect, and to do the better makes us better persons. Lying under obligation thus determines both terms, the object side to be made better or worse by the person's actions, and the person side to be a better or worse person.

Part of being human is that we face alternative possibilities in the future over which we have some modicum of control and about which we decide, individually or conjointly. This means that, in different ways for each of the goods, we decide for what we actualize and are responsible for that. We often mediate these decisions by the rituals that constitute the natural and social fabrics of human life. We are cognitively responsible for what we believe or affirm in interpretations, for what we choose and do in moral matters, for how we engage or fail to engage the issues of our watch, and for what we become. Each of these defines our own character insofar as it also defines what happens in actualization. To have to respond is to live under obligation to choose well, and we meet or fail those various senses of obligation in terms of how we act within the situations of those two-term relations.

At this point I need to raise an objection to my way of thinking here. Some people, especially personalists, argue that we must recognize some irreducible trait of personhood on which to base a fundamental claim to human dignity. Without that irreducible trait, personhood might be denied to people who are so broken as not to have achievements in truth, morals, rightness, or virtue. For personalists, upholding irreducible personhood makes transcendental subjectivity an attractive position, defining personhood outside the context of anything empirical. The point of this is to defend the dignity of persons even when they do not achieve the high traits we associate with personhood, such as being true, moral, right, and virtuous. Many persons are too young, too old, too disabled, or too disadvantaged to have much dignity in the facing of obligation, and personalists, along with many others, would like to be able to attribute dignity with attendant rights to them anyway. The sketch of personhood I make here stresses achieved dignity rather than a priori attributable dignity.

I sympathize with this objection. Nevertheless, I believe that lying under obligation in its varying dimensions is what is essential to making a person a person, allowing for a vast array of differing conditional components. Here are several qualifications. First, lying under obligation is not the same as fulfilling the obligations in any way, shape, or form. I've never known anyone who failed all obligations, but then I've led a sheltered life. You are a person if you have obligations, even if you do not fulfill them. Second, all human lives arc from their beginning until their ending, and serious obligations are in the middle when people engage the various aspects of their environments, societies, projects, and so forth. I would say that a person lies under obligation when too young to have relevant obligations yet and when too old to have them still. Therefore, we protect the very young before they grow into obligations because we assume, or at least hope, that they will lie under obligations and engage them. We protect the debilitated and the very elderly when they can no longer manage lying under obligation because they once did and deserve the dignity of the whole life. Third, notice that this does not decide just when human life begins or when it ends, and hence leaves open debates on such issues as abortion and euthanasia. Fourth, although my suggestion that personhood stems from lying under obligation is a philosophical hypothesis subject to further discussion, it can function as a "moral a priori" criterion for claiming human dignity with rights for persons, given the qualifications here. I would stress that whether a given individual actually does lie under obligation is an empirical matter and can be problematic in borderline cases.

Great worth comes in creating beauty and in being beautiful. No obligation attends creating beauty and being beautiful, however, except in unusual circumstances. Obligation does attend to being cognitively true, moral, authentically engaged in right ways, and virtuous.

CHAPTER 9

Goodness in Being True

Goodness as Conformity

That our interpretations of things ought to be true almost goes without saying. The commonsense meaning of interpretation is that it says how things are. The qualification "*almost* goes without saying" comes from the fact that interpretations need to be interesting as well as true, and sometimes that they be interesting is more important than that they be true. I could give a true description of a square inch on the surface of my desk that is one inch from my pen, another true description of the spot two inches away, another three inches away, and so forth, accumulating scads of true interpretations of virtually no interest. We should not waste attention on interpretations of no interest. On the one hand, we direct our interpretative attention toward what is important for our own purposes and habitual valuations; many things are interesting because of our intentionality. On the other hand, we direct our interpretive attention in response to what looks interesting on its own, to what elicits, charms, or commands our attention. Most interpretations are a combination of these. Sometimes it is worthwhile to direct interpretive attention to what we interpret falsely simply because it stimulates our imagination and gets us to thinking in new ways. In addition, sometimes, great but dangerous worth is to be found in a fantasy life that is misconstrued as real life. Nevertheless, in the long run, and not a very long run, it is important for pragmatic reasons that our interpretations aim to be true. Our interpretive apparatus evolved to enable us to take in what it is important to know to get along in life.

I have a stronger thesis to push in this chapter, however. Not only is it pragmatically helpful to interpret things truly most of the time, but we are essentially under obligation to conform ourselves interpretively to the world. Acknowledging exceptional circumstances, to be a human person is to be under obligation to be true in interpreting the world and affairs of life. The key to arguing this point is the obligatoriness of certain kinds of conformation.

The root of the goodness of the basic two-term relations discussed in this part is that one term, the personal one, conforms to the other. A person has the goodness of holding a truth when the person's relevant belief affirms of its object a relevant character of the object, conforming belief to object in a certain respect. A person is moral when choices are for the greater goodness in the alternatives, conforming to the relevant character of the goodness-laden possibilities. A person is righteous when engaged with the contours of life in ways that are appropriate to the character of those contours, conforming engagement in appropriate ways to them. A person is good when the achievements of life more or less embody the good possibilities for that life, conforming actual achievement to relevant ideals regarding possibility. I shall flesh out these highly abstract statements shortly. It is apparent from them, however, that the relevant harmonic goodness has two terms: the way the agent under obligation conforms and that to which the agent conforms.[1]

In the earlier chapters of this book, I interpreted harmony to mean that a determinate thing is a harmony that relates in its own nature to all the things with respect to which it is determinate. Its goodness consists in the density of being it can achieve in the ways by which it composes those components in functions of triviality, vagueness, narrowness, and width, achieving elegance of contrast and depth. At the level of concrete life, many of the most important harmonies have specific definite characters, such as human beings related to one another or to social and natural elements of their environments. The goods of truth, morality, rightness, and virtue, as reflected on here, are goods to be achieved by human beings relating to other things truly, morally, rightly, and virtuously. Only human beings, we usually think, have the internal and social character to be valuable in these ways. Not everything in the world is appropriate to be the object of morality or rightness; many things might be the object of beliefs that should be true but in fact are irrelevant to any human belief. The virtue achieved in a life involves relating to relevant ideal possibilities, but not all possibilities are relevant.

Conformation does not necessarily mean mirroring or being like that to which a person conforms, although sometimes it can mean that, as when choristers tune themselves to the same pitch and timbre. Conformation means taking the other into account and comporting oneself appropriately. "Appropriateness" connotes the goodness–quality of the relation, and the kind of relation involved determines the kind of appropriateness. Choristers who are supposed to be singing the same note aim to tune their pitch and timbre. Choristers who are supposed to be singing different notes in harmony aim to tune their sounds to the intervals between their pitches. A soloist singing above a chorus aims for a timbre that has more overtones than the chorus in order to stand out even when singing the same pitch or in harmony.

Conformation in a person can be radically different from the thing to which the person conforms. Consider the case of truth, which I will discuss in more detail in the next section. Truth is a function of belief or interpretation. An interpretation, according to the prag-matic approach I follow, is an action or a habit of action that takes its object to be as its sign says in a certain respect.[2] Suppose a person believes that the barn across the field is red. The barn is the object interpreted and "red" is the sign. The respect in which red is the sign to interpret the barn is color. Few if any interpretations would use the sign "red" to interpret the barn in respect to who owns it, what is stored in it, or how old it is. The interpreter has purposes, values, or goods that largely determine in the moment the relevant respect of interpretation. The interpreter has to have a semiotic system that defines red relative to other colors, that governs the use of the term red relative to other colors, and that has qualifications dealing with how a barn that is red in the daylight looks black at night, or green if the interpreter is wearing green-tinted glasses like Dorothy in Oz. With all those qualifications, the interpretation that the barn is red is true if the barn is determinately red and not some other color. Within the cultural limitations of what the sign "red" means, it is either true or false that the barn is red, a dyadic relation within the triad of the interpreter interpreting the object with the sign.

But what does truth mean here? I defend the view that truth is the carryover of goodness from the object into the interpreter in the respect in which the sign stands for the object and as qualified by trans-formations of biology, culture, semiotic systems, and purposes.[3] Readers of this book have a good idea now of what goodness is and how it is resident in form. The barn with its red surface is a wooden structure covered with red paint. Light is reflected off the paint, passes through the observer's pupils, is absorbed by their retinas, and is processed by the vastly complex visual nervous system. The original perception that says the barn is red comes from a particular perspective relative to the barn. The mental image produced is classified as red within the inter-preter's semiotic system, and the person's culture determines that things such as barns are noted and sometimes described in terms of color. The interpreter has some special purpose, such as distinguishing the red barn from blue and weathered gray buildings adjacent in the field. The *situation* of interpreting the barn includes all the relevant causal elements in the carryover from the barn in the field to the interpreter. The purposes or intentions of the interpreter determine what is rele-vant to the situation, reflecting the resources of the semiotic system and the goods in the culture of selecting out buildings for notice. When the situation calls for truth, the interpretation is under obligation to conform to the barn's color. In the interpretive situation, the semiotic system, cultural classifications, and the interpreter's interests of course condition the interpretation. Nevertheless, given all that, the barn is either red or not. The interpreter's interpretation should conform to what the barn is in respect of color. The barn itself has the chemi-cal composition of painted wood, and the paint has the character of reflecting light in a certain spectrum. The person's interpretation has a biological, cultural, semiotic, and purposive structure, none of which is painted wood. But the interpretation conforms, if the barn is red and not some other color, because that is the appropriate way for a barn to be interpreted in respect of color in this culture with this semiotic color classification and for these purposes. The appropriateness is the way the person's belief about the barn's color is determined by the nature of belief or interpretation, the interests in interpretation, the cultural and semiotic systems at hand, and the nature of the barn in respect to color.

Aristotle said that truth is the carryover of the form of the thing into the form of the mind, leaving the material of the thing behind. I say that truth is the carryover of the goodness of the thing into the interpreter's experience, which includes the interpretation being made, in the respect in which the interpretive signs stand for the thing. Although on the theory I am putting forward to you the goodness of something is carried in its form, the form that bears the goodness of the red barn in the barn is very different from the form that registers the difference in the interpreter. The complex harmony of the situation of barn-color assessing is what carries the goodness across from the barn to the interpreter through many steps. Many of those steps might not be structured as interpretations, contrary to what Peirce might say. Unlike Cartesian dualists (Aristotle was a proto-Cartesian dualist in this respect), I do not think truth involves getting the form of the wooden painted barn into the nervous system and subjective thinking of the interpreter so that the interpreter includes red wood. Rather it involves getting whatever is achieved as a good in the red barn, as involved in a situation of being interpreted with respect of color by this interpreter from the perspective of purpose (in cultural context, with semiotic systems, etc.), into the experience of the interpreter so that the interpreter knows this respect of the goodness of the barn and can act accordingly. For instance, the interpreter can pick out the barn from a group of barns with non-red colors. The situation of interpreting includes the real barn and the interested interpreter, and all the things that lie in the transformational route involved in the interpretive situation. The barn is not merely something in the mind of the interpreter, as Cartesians are caught saying. Or, perhaps we should say that the mind of the interpreter is not something in the interpreter's head but is the whole situation in which the harmony of the interpreter includes all the realities interpreted and involved in interpretation. Perhaps it is appropriate to say that the attentive mind of the interpreter is across the field where the barn is. The truth relation in this interpretation is the situation in which the interpreter conforms to the reality of the barn's color by thinking it is red.

Conformity in morality means, roughly, that the putative moral agent interprets the goods in the alternatives correctly and chooses to actualize the better ones, at least the better ones for the agent's purposes. The moral situation is one in which the agent's potential actions define a situation with real differences in goodness concerning possibilities. In contrast to most cognitive situations, moral situations are determined by problems of the will. In the *Meditations*, Descartes attempted to turn cognitive situations into moral ones by saying that possible judgments, for instance that the barn is red, that it is blue, that it is gray, need to be affirmed by the will before there is a truth claim. This is true for situations in which there is cognitive inquiry into how to interpret things, not just interpretation arising out of interest and habit of interpretation, glancing at the barn and thinking that it is red.

Conformity in rightness, as I use that term here, means that the person engages things according to their natures, as the person interpretively discerns them and in that engagement takes up an appropriate stance toward those things. Perhaps this is just to be in awe of them, or to fight them if they are evil, or to work on a friendship with them, or to learn to live in environmental support of them. In many respects, morality can be viewed as a species of rightness. Conformity in rightness, however, is the building of a life that is appropriate to the large-scale structures of one's natural, social, and personal environments.

Conformity in virtue has to do with building a life that is appropriate for the ideals that are appropriate for that life's situations. More on this in chapter 12.

The rest of this chapter will focus on the obligation of truth.

The Goodness of Truth

If truth is the carryover of goodness from the object to the interpreter in the respects in which the signs stand for the object, subject to the qualifications of the interpreter's biology, culture, semiotic systems, and purposes, what is the goodness of truth? Or, what are the goods of truth? Or, what are the dimensions of goodness in truth?

A beginning of an answer to this question is to observe that interpreting things truly allows for an orientation to those things that

takes into account their natures. At its fanciest, this Platonic and Confucian observation is that the function of knowing is to guide life.
Interpretation aimed at truth is fundamentally practical reason, letting
us know what the important things are and how to foster, protect, or
achieve them. This was the lesson of Plato's *Republic*, and it stands in
contrast to Aristotle's view of practical reason. For Aristotle, practical
reason is more a function of imitation of good models than Plato's
complicated vision of training the rulers, or one's own soul, for the
sake of living well. For Aristotle, cognitive knowing is of the highest
sort, where reason is a bit like "thought thinking itself" (as in book 10
of the *Nicomachean Ethics*). Thought thinking itself, as approximated in
human knowing, is something worthwhile in itself, the highest good
possible to man (probably not to women, in Aristotle's view), and that
for the sake of which practical reason arranges for a safe and leisurely
life. For Aristotle, the highest good of human life is the contemplation
of eternal truths, for which practical reason is a means. For Plato, the
highest good of human life is finding the right harmony of factors
to maximize the good possible for individuals and societies. Reason,
including theoretical and dialectical reason, is the means toward that
decision making and guidance. The common view of many philosophers is that Plato was the abstracted theoretical thinker whereas
Aristotle was the practical one. Nevertheless, the reverse is true. Plato
recognized the allure of pure contemplation but said (in *Republic*, book
7) that the contemplator, who escapes the cave of illusion and sees the
world of pure forms, needs to be dragged back down into the cave to
advise others. I agree with Plato. One of life's many beauties, in the
sense of things enjoyable for their own sake, is theoretical contemplation, my mathematical friends tell me. However, a beautiful life, one
good for its own sake, is a complex harmony that needs construction
over a lifetime by many decisions guided by good interpretations of
the world. Confucius agreed with Plato on the importance of thinking
for practice and held up the sage as the ideal.

Just about all living things interpret the world around them and
survive because they interpret that world truly enough to be well
oriented. An amoeba moves toward something it interprets as food and
away from something it interprets as poison. The higher animals have
complex nervous systems for perceiving, interpreting, and responding

to zillions of things in their environment—prey, predators, dangerous weather, where to find water and shelter, whom to have sex with, and how to take care of offspring.

Human beings evolve highly complex semiotic systems of gestures, words, and thought patterns that allow them to detect what is good, bad, satisfying, and frustrating. Our interpretations allow us to note and attend to the goods of things in the environment of obvious practical importance. One of the most important kinds of things to know about are those that give us social solidarity and staying power, cohesiveness in our social and political groupings, and an orientation to moving throughout a terrain that sustains us across the seasons. For this reason, very early human beings developed stories about their group that let them pick up on the things needed for social solidarity and identity. The stories were not necessarily true in a modern historical sense, but believing them incorporated into the group and individual experience what is valuable in the context of life for such social cohesion. Very early people developed conceptions of their neighborhood, indeed of the cosmos, that gave them an orientation about the place and time in which they existed.

By the time of the Axial Age, the philosophers and theologians had developed ideas of the cosmos as a whole, defined by one or a few principles. These large-scale philosophies conceive all people to be related as being human and that goods such as love, justice, equality, and mutual respect are among the most important personal and social features to cultivate. The religious wisdom of the Axial Age religions is that the nature of the very cosmos is such that human life is lived better when people conform to life's situations with love, justice, and equality or mutual respect, seen as "All under Heaven," as the Chinese put it. Call these early large-scale interpretations of the world myths, legends, proto-science, theology, or philosophy as you will; they are summary interpretations of what there is in the world and situations of human life that should guide the formations of human characters, rituals, and societies. The different early cultures of the world had wildly different signs or conceptions of how the world hangs together, the nature of space and time, and what their history was. They had different, but not wildly different, conceptions of what love, justice, and equality or mutual respect consist in. The Axial Age ideals were laid down on top of social organizations of ingroup-outgroup competition and conflict and we have not thoroughly institutionalized them even today. The ingroup-outgroup "philosophers" also often correctly interpreted what they and their group need to do to survive and flourish in a competitive environment. To live in the world so as to achieve the highest kinds of life means interpreting it as a saint does. To live in the world so as to survive means interpreting it like a soldier. To know how to do both requires interpreting the world like a sage. The harsh pressures of human life in an environment that treats people like straw dogs result in an overabundance of soldiers relative to saints and sages.

In between the interpretations of the world in terms of its most basic matters of worth and the interpretations struggling to survive until morning are the quotidian needs to interpret the world as a place to live. People develop and organize interpretations of the plants and animals in their district, the weather they have to cope with, their neighbors, migrations, changing seasons, emerging and disappearing foodstuffs. An individual running through the forest to warn that the enemy is approaching has to not only interpret the enemy and the threat but how to follow the path, what to dodge, where to hide, and whom to tell. Most of those interpretations are unconscious—the runner just notices them and quickly responds while running, just as a driver on a crowded but familiar road responds unconsciously to a host of signals. Individuals have to interpret everything around them, even the pull of gravity so as to respond with the right muscles to stay upright and move forward. Individuals need semiotic systems learned through ritual behavior and organized in cultural ways of life.

Nevertheless, as Dewey pointed out (as quoted in chapter 6), when the exigencies of life are somewhat in hand, people interpret the world in terms of what gives them "pleasure neat," things enjoyed for their own sake. They decorate the utilitarian with the beautiful. So, interpretations employ signs that pick up on what is valuable for its own sake in experience. Early in human history, well before the Axial Age, people began to ask what things in life are most worth enjoying. When does partying become too much in light of the hangover the next day? When should short-term goods be sacrificed for long-term ones? Cultures answer these kinds of questions in different ways, but they all complexify their semiotic systems and cultural stores of interpretations so as to be able to discover what in their natural and social environments yields what they can approve as the more important goods in life.

Many of the most important interpretations of the environment for human life are the causal ones, knowing how things in the world work. What kinds of things there are and how they work are objects of science, with myth being the stuff of proto-science as well as having kinds of truth and wisdom science lacks. Because our interpretations so often are practical and receive quick feedback, superstition in many instances can be set aside for reinforced common sense. Knowing how human-scale things work raises questions of larger patterns of causation that gives birth to science in the modern sense. Because of the very great importance of understanding things, scientific knowledge now often is sought for its own sake, not just for technological applications or for warding off disaster. Knowing is itself indeed beautiful, as Aristotle argued and Plato worried about. One of the most important things to know about human life is that the more it is conformed to the nature of the goodness-structure of the world, the greater is the achievement of harmony in human life. Understanding life is not the only great achievement of human beings. People can be great in their density of being while understanding little or having false interpretations of most things. The understanding a person has is itself a harmony integrated with other components of the person; but as a harmony itself, understanding has its structure of narrowness, width, vagueness, and triviality. A person understands certain things with great focus and sharpness and integrates these things more or less widely; the person understands other things vaguely so that the differences between them do not count; some things are dismissed as trivial and not understood at all. Philosophy is the work of taking responsibility for the harmony of one's own understanding of diverse things.

In what sense or senses are people obligated to know things truly, as best as possible? It would seem that people are not morally culpable for having false interpretations, the way they are morally culpable for their choices and actions. We make all sorts of qualifications in judging the obligation to know things truly, such as not having the means to know, not being of an age to know, and not having the culture or semiotic resources to know. Even taking all such qualifications into account, however, interpretations connect directly with actions, for which we are morally culpable. They at least provide the orientation to what is real and important on the basis of which decisions are made and actions taken. So it is important for parents to be informed about what is poisonous, to the extent it can be known, when they feed their children. Sometimes it is not possible to know about this, as evidenced by scientific debates about the virtues of various diets. However, it is obligatory for parents to do the best they can to know about the food they feed those in their care. People often say that in political matters everyone is entitled to his or her own opinion. This might be right when the opinion is about how to develop guidance in a complex situation that can go several good or bad ways. Nevertheless, it is not right that the opinions should not be informed by the best interpretations of what is true in the situation. The goodness of truth is that it is obligatory to know the truth so much as is possible insofar as interpretations guide opinion, shaping decisions and actions. Of course, this is complicated because political issues often are addressed by people in conflicting cultures, with different semiotic systems, and perhaps different short-term purposes. Historical and scientific literacy would seem to be obligatory for voters today.

Nevertheless, knowing a lot of science and history might not guarantee that voters know what is valuable in things. The goods noticed in science and historical narrative might not be the ones important in the moment. The truths in scientific and historical interpretations might not be the ones needed for good political judgment. The question of what truths we need is not just about human thinking. Though including that, the question is about what there is in the world that we should know in order to conform our lives, including the political dimensions of life, to what is valuable in the world. This is a question about the nature of the world.

Being True

The formula that truth is the carryover of goodness from the object to the interpreter in the senses discussed earlier does not adequately convey all the dimensions of truth. That formulation applies mainly to individual interpretations, or connected families of interpretations such as interpreting all the things that are across the field near the red barn, including stinky barnyards, noisy machinery, and squawking chickens. We have many thick or connected sets of interpretations, such as our general understanding of our family and friends. Think of the complicated set of interrelated interpretations involved in driving a car—watching the direction and tilt of the road, feeling the road's surface, attention to speeding up and slowing down, the sideways tilt on curves, the interpretation of what other drivers are doing, thinking about the signs and signals, all these and a thousand more kinetic interpretations are usually smoothly integrated. An unexpected pothole or an errant driver, or a shriek from a passenger, suddenly can prompt a new direction of attention. The carryover formula works well to help us understand these families of interpretation. What does it miss? It misses the sense that the interpreter should be true, not only the interpretations. I will explore this subtle point in this section.

Although this is not the place to elaborate a full theory of interpretation, two foci are involved in situations of interpretation.[4] One is the perspective of the interpreters who, with purposes, intentionality, and so forth, select the object to interpret and in what respects, along with all the relevant mediating circumstances and causal connections. That selection of object and respect of interpretation is sometimes and to some degree conscious, as in choice, but far more often and perhaps to some degree in every interpretation is constituted by other factors of valuation in the interpreter. My point is that the interpreter, not the object selected, determines most parameters of the interpretive situation. In a situation of interpretation, the interpreters constitute part of their own nature by the interpretations that carry across what is important into their experience. The second focus is the environment of the object. This environment includes the object but also a lot of that to which the object relates by the character of its own harmony with narrow, wide, vague, and trivial functions. Indeed, most often the environment offers many objects in various relations. Some people have called such an environment "affordances" that can call forth multiple interpretations at once.[5] The complex of affordances offers an interconnected set of possibilities for interpretation and action. Driving down a busy highway is a complex of affordances that afford interpretations of the road, its pitch, the traffic, the kinetics of the car, the other drivers, and so forth. The driver makes interpretations all together in response to the connectedness of factors in the environment. In the evolution of human semiotic systems and interpretive behavior, individual interpretations such as propositions are not worked out one by one. Rather, the complex of interpretations develops according to the connectedness of the important things in the environment. In the wild, we distinguish prey from predators, note conditions for fight or flight, map the passages through the environment, distinguish plants and other physical features, adjust to the quality of light, and so forth, more or less all at once and together. The complex of affordances is a condition that calls for evolutionary adaptation by means of making the relevant multitude of interpretations in connection. Agricultural activity requires interpreting the many conditions of nature but also the social conditions of cooperation, tool using, and so forth, a matter of natural and social affordances. Domestic life requires multitasking of enormous complexity, with the situation's affordances calling forth a multitude of relatively connected interpretive responses: if your domestic interpretive responses are not sufficiently integrated, the soup can boil over while you rush to prevent the baby from falling down the stairs. You can go into a large party with a multitude of sights, sounds, and smells, interpreting the identity of many people at once, and immediately be able to sense that on one side of the room there is great tension and on the other is gaiety. I use the phrase "and so forth" frequently here because we all know these kinds of connections, though perhaps without realizing what we know—knowing with affordances.

As Peirce and others have pointed out, what interpreters need is complex signs that can mirror the many things going on at once, signs, for instance, coordinating the senses, or the muscles in driving, or the emotions in going into a complicated party. Many animals have what Peirce called indexical signs that point them to the things in the environment they need to grasp. Higher animals also have iconic signs that map the complex environment for them. Human beings as well as many animals have complicated symbolic signs or conventional semiotic signs that allow for communication while reacting to the environment's affordances together through time. The connectedness of the environment exerts natural and cultural evolutionary pressure for people to develop the signs for interpreting what is valuable in the environment and important to know for the many aspects of human life. It is not just that smart people are more successful in developing signs that pick up better on what is valuable. It is that the character of what is valuable in the world and important for human life pushes people to become smarter and rewards those that do. The character of the world rewards better cooperation, better communication, and better tools for discernment and response, as well as predation, parasitism, and cheating among social organisms.

I do not mean to suggest that there is a monolithic complex environment. Many environments exist for individuals and many different approaches and interests in the environments. The physical and social environments are constantly changing. So people are erratically shifting from one interpretive set of iconic, indexical, and conventional semiotic systems to another, often with little organized connection among them. Whereas it is true that there is a large existential field with all sorts of connections and disconnections, human interpretation is always oriented to situations in which only some things are relevant for interpretation, and in relation to only some other things.

In contrast to this division of the world that human beings interpret is the question of the internal organization of the interpretations. Assuming that interpretations are rarely made one by one but rather in a complex situation of many affordances, most people, just in order to survive and have at least minimal social life, master the interpretive signs and strategies for many different common situations, such as eating, dressing, relating to family members, work of various sorts, and the like. In each of these situations, individuals can master the interpretation of the relevant affordances with at least enough truth to get along. Nevertheless, we value highly those people who can master the relevant truths in a situation to a high degree. We call an outstanding baseball shortstop a "true" shortstop. We call an outstanding cook a true chef. We call an outstanding leader a true leader. These people cultivate their lives to have and employ the interpretive apparatus to get to the important truths of these situations. Nevertheless, the true shortstop might be a poor cook, and both the player and the chef might be confused, ignorant, and harmful leaders.

Is it not an ideal good for human life to integrate the common situations so that one is true to them in connection with one another? You "live in the truth," to use that old phrase, when and to the extent that you can integrate the many situations in the various domains of life so as to be whole in interpreting what is valuable in life. To be sure, many different kinds of interpretation exist. In our day, scientific interpretation is extremely important for getting at what is valuable beyond ordinary comprehension, and the ideal of being able to connect the different domains of life in which there are multiple situations gives rise to the search for universal principles; this has been an ideal since the Axial Age. However, this is only one kind of interpretation. A different, though related, kind of interpretation is that which lifts up what is important for life to attend to. What is it wise to know in times of war and times of peace, prosperity and poverty, quick change and quotidian steadiness? Earlier I spoke of the sagely integration of the interpretive skills of the saints and those of the soldiers. Knowing what is important in life in general is a kind of "being true" to the world. Even this second kind of interpretation might lead to overemphasis on cognition in interpretation. Because interpretation takes the goodness of what is interpreted into the interpreter's life and responses, there is a kind of interpretation that emphasizes the responses, the muscular read-iness, the habits of shifting attention, the virtues of steadiness, focused constancy, and flexibility of will in changing circumstances. Of course, many variations exist in these rough models of the scientist, the sage, and the agent in interpretation. These vary within and among cultures.

Nevertheless, together these and similar models of conformity to the world in interpretation indicate a goodness for human life that is generally appreciated, the goodness of being a "true interpreter." Insofar as we are obligated to be true in this general sense, we are obligated to pursue the truth in as many venues as possible and to become people who are loyal to the pursuit of truth. To be sure, countless situations exist in which interest in the truth of a situation legitimately suppresses or trivializes other interests. A soldier charging in battle should not stop to reflect on a unified field theory, and a physicist struggling to make sense of dark matter should not stop to cook or play baseball, except to relax the mind for better scientific thinking. However, there

does exist the ideal of being true to the world, in the sense of grasping what is good and important and reacting correctly, as a cultivated
trait of human nature.

Is "being true" an obligation? As mentioned before, being true is
an obligation in a moral sense insofar as the truth of interpretations
bears upon morally freighted actions. However, another sense of obligation exists that applies to being true in conformal interpretation of
the world as such, insofar as that is possible. How people interpret the
world is part of their character. If they interpret the world well, they
are good interpreters; if poorly, then bad interpreters. One of the necessary components of human life is having the interpretations crucial
for survival. To flourish means surviving well. Surviving well means,
among other things, constituting oneself to have interpretations that
harmonize with the world. Few species have the capacity to attempt to
respond to the world, or to "their world" as such. For human beings,
this kind of conformal response is possible. If it is possible to respond
by "being true," and also possible not to respond that way, then being
true is the better alternative, and the obligation exists to choose it. This
obligation can have great practical force when culpable ignorance and
biased denials complicate the choice to be true or not.

My argument in this section has been, first, to note that individual interpretations come in what I called "families," such as the
situation of driving a car in traffic. Such a situation involves many
interpretations integrated together by integrating signs. On the side
of what is interpreted is what I called "affordances," namely, the connectedness of things in the world so as to afford the possibilities of
interpreting them together. We interpret the world according to the
feedback we receive sometimes from the world's affordance. Second,
I have pointed out that many situations exist of such affordances and
human interpretive responses. The integration of these diverse situational interpretations in human experience constitutes what I called
"being true," that is, developing the integrative interpretive signs with
life so that the world appears with some integration and the person
attains excellence in being true generally. Only when a person is generally true to the diverse affordances of the world does that person
have a world. Otherwise, the person has only relatively unconnected
situations of interpretation. The personal integration of interpretive

abilities across diverse situations depends on there being real connections in the world among its diverse affordances. If you force a subjective integration of your experience by confining things to some simple integrative principles, you live in an illusory world. If you find how the diverse affordances of the world really hang together, or fail to hang together, you can relate to the world in truth. All such truths, of course, are fallible.

The Obligation to Inquiry

Being true in the sense I just discussed sounds as if it were a static achievement. It cannot be that, however, because interpretation is always fallible. Our interpretations are always vulnerable to correction, enlargement, and reassessment. Therefore, the good of being true sustains itself only by translating itself into a life of inquiry. More modestly, because we are true only in certain domains of our lives, we need to be in the mode of inquiry in those domains. Yet, ideally, we should be able to connect and harmonize all or at least most of the domains of our lives. The obligation to inquiry then is on the verge of connecting domains whose connections need harmonizing. My claim here is an extreme one: we are obligated to cultivate the practice of inquiry throughout our lives. We should live as if we can take nothing for granted even though we inevitably take for granted most of the ways we live in the world.

This is an extreme claim because it is obviously absurd. Charles Peirce is the founder of the pragmatic mode of inquiry, a version of which I defend here with modifications. Jay Schulkin, the philosopher-neuroscientist, has written eloquently in several books about the value of Peircean inquiry across many disciplines in the sciences and humanities.[6] Nevertheless, Peirce said, in his late (1898) essay "Philosophy and the Conduct of Life," that on vitally important topics we should trust our biological and cultural instincts because our inquiries are always too fluid, tentative, and fallible to base a life on.[7] Most philosophers believe Peirce could not really have meant this, but Richard Atkins has shown that he truly did.[8] Furthermore, Peirce pointed out, to inquire about everything is quite literally impossible. We have to assume nearly every interpretation we have of our world in order to focus on inquiry into anything specific. Ongoing life works on our habits and rituals (though Peirce did not think much about rituals). Inquiry means that we question that into which we inquire, and we cannot question everything at once. Therefore, we cannot possibly live as if we can take nothing for granted. That would be absurd!

Peirce announced his theory of inquiry in his early (1877) "The Fixation of Belief," in which he argued that inquiry arises only when something causes us to doubt a belief.[9] He ridiculed Descartes's pretense to doubt everything (finding that he could not doubt his own existence as doubter) as being mere paper doubt, doubt on paper, not in real life.[10] We live with a vast store of beliefs guiding physical and mental behavior and only inquire when something casts doubt on a belief, interrupting the activity guided by the belief. Doubt is an irritation and inquiry is the attempt to remove the irritation. In that essay, he considered four ways of removing the irritation and fixing unsettled belief. One is the "method of tenacity," holding on to the prior belief despite the doubt. Another is the "method of authority," removing doubt by appeal to authority. A third is the "a priori method" by which doubt is removed by appeal to what is supposed instinctual. With these three methods, if there was doubt in the first place, it will return to defeat the settledness of the belief. The fourth is the "scientific method" in which beliefs are treated as hypotheses and tested in various domains with modes of inquiry analogous to laboratory science. Peirce elaborated his "scientific" method of inquiry all his life and connected it with his studies in logic. The "a priori method" condemned in the early essay sounds much like the defense of habit, sentiment, and instinct defended in 1898; he had come to appreciate both the corrective power of evolution by 1898 and the fickleness of the actual practices of science. In his early article, Peirce indicated that the motive for inquiry on the analogy of science was to scratch the irritation of doubt and settle belief that would guide behavior. In the later article, his motive was the desire to avoid the error of conforming behavior to adventuresome hypotheses that might be half-baked.

My argument, however, is that we are under an obligation to pursue inquiry or become inquirers because of the obligation to be true to the world. A special kind of goodness exists in the two-term relation of being true to the things to which life should conform. Of course, we can choose to ignore this kind of goodness as many if not most people do. However, we will have chosen for ourselves an identity that fails to acknowledge and address this kind of good. Perhaps that is not so bad. We fail obligations all the time. Nevertheless, it does fail an obligation that is basic to what it means to be a human person.

To say an obligation exists to inquire and to cultivate the skills of inquiry perhaps is too strong. Perhaps instead we should say that some people are curious and others are not, and that the curious ones should become inquirers. Is it not a fault, however, to be incurious when something exists in our environment relative to our comportment about which it is worth being curious? If it is a fault, then we are under obligation to do right by the possibility of inquiring. Because inquiring is possible, and that possibility has a value, the choice between inquiring and not inquiring is a choice between alternative possibilities. Sometimes, of course, many options more important than inquiring force themselves upon us. The greater obligation is to choose the possibility with the greater good. The issue here, however, is whether there is an obligation stemming from the personhood trait of being true.

The obligation to be an inquirer comes not from the environment alone that could be investigated, nor from a person's personhood in general. It comes from a combination of these in a harmony that is a two-term relation. Each of us is a person but with particularities of our environments, as well as of our personal identities as growing through time. The content of the obligation to inquiry is determined at various stages in life through our interactions as persons with our environments. Overall, however, our personhood is determined with regard to being true by how we cultivate that changing set of obligations over time.

Peirce was right that no one could doubt everything at any one time. Inquiry always has to focus on something about which we can be curious, propose hypotheses, and test the alternatives. To do this we have to presuppose a whole host of assumptions about defining our world and interests. Inquiry is a highly focused activity requiring a supportive background. At any given moment, whether focused in inquiry or on something else entirely, we operate with the assumptions built into our habits, our personal histories, our socialization, our rituals, and the cultured structure of how we pay attention to things.

Nevertheless, our obligation to inquiry comes in layers, as it were. Suppose in fact that you are a biologist engaged in an experiment about certain effects of dopamine. To set up the experiment, you have to know the literature about dopamine and the effects it might regulate, and so having read up you treat that literature as assumed guiding beliefs for orienting your inquiry. The scientific literature itself is vetted within a scientific community with peer review, which assumes that the peer reviewers are competent. Moreover, you assume the journals publishing the literature to have good taste and reflect the garnered expertise of the scientific community. Science is expensive and depends on funding agencies that have their own agenda; if you and your scientific collaborators think that your science is value-free and morally objective, then the values that underlie your community, its journals, colloquies, as well as your own laboratory, are largely those of the funders. For the sake of doing your experimental inquiry into this aspect of dopamine, you work with all those layers of beliefs as assumptions that allow you to move forward. Nevertheless, every one of those layers is itself questionable and you probably have questioned each one at some time or another. Are the peer reviewers for whom you write fair, or do you worry that your hypothesis steps on someone's toes? Journals become associated with large-scale programmatic directions; does your research challenge those directions? Does your research question what skills are needed in order to make good scientific judgment in good taste? All scientific fields are skewed to the interests of funders; sometimes those interests are genuinely shaped by what looks promising, but sometimes by other considerations. As a reflective enough scientist to read this book, you know that assumptions have to be made in order to carry out any inquiry, but any level of beliefs assumed in this simple dopamine experiment can itself be brought into question by focused inquiry. To be a good scientific inquirer you have to be ready, under appropriate circumstances, to question and inquire critically into any level of those beliefs built into your scientific culture. That is part of your obligation as a scientist.

As a person, you engage in a great many different contours of your environment structured by social institutions with belief systems.

Only a very few of those engagements would count as inquiry rather than other forms of activities. Nevertheless, as you form your personal identity throughout the many phases of life on many different planes, it is possible to develop the character of critical assessment of how well you relate in your conscious and unconscious habits and beliefs to what the goods and ills are of things. Suppose your society has the educational and economic institutions that allow you to train as a scientist and, upon critical reflection, you are grateful for that. Many people are unaware of the educational and economic institutions that give them their advantages, and so are not grateful; shame. Suppose also that the educational and economic institutions that benefit you are also racist and oppressive to people in other social conditions. If your gratitude looks only to what your society does for you, it is of a selfish sort, well placed in your case but still selfish. Do you not have an obligation to become aware of what those institutions do to others and so enlarge your critical assessment? This might require considerable inquiry, calling into question the assumptions of your scientific elite to see how it has many effects. The educational funding recently poured into STEM (science, technology, engineering, mathematics) is ruining art and music education and is making the humanities seem unprofitable. Do you not have an obligation to look into this? The obligations you have as a scientist are different from those of your neighbor who is a music teacher and his husband who works for the gas company. Furthermore, your training as a scientist probably brings the nature of inquiry to more prominence in your thinking—you are a professional inquirer in a highly ritualized profession inquiring about just the prescribed things, and they inquire only when something prompts their attention to do so. Nevertheless, they too live under the obligation to think and consequently behave truly about the world, or at least their parts of it.

In conclusion, I want to insist, contrary to Peirce in some moods and contrary to most conservatives who think inquiry is unsettling, that there is a special two-term harmony between individuals and the contours of the world in which they live that consists in interpreting it truly in conscious thought and the habits of conforming to it. This harmony is not alone between the world and the individual at any given time but is in the developing ways by which the individual practices inquire into what the world really is, given the fallibility of our interpretations and interpretive constructions. The way to be true to the world is to be an inquirer into it, in the multitude of ways that exist of relating to the environments, one's self, and the possibilities for all.

The choice to be true is an obligation that leads to the choice to be righteous, the topic of chapter 11. Before that, however, I want to examine the goodness of morality.

CHAPTER 10

Goodness in Being Moral

Morality as a Two-Term Relation

The pertinent relations involved in morality are those between a moral agent and the environment lodging the moral issues. Of course, in most important senses, moral agency is not a merely individual affair with one moral agent. Most of our moral actions are conjoint actions in which people act together. Moral actions are usually elements in a complex situation in which other moral agents are acting, so that the moral actions are somewhat integrated harmonies, or discordant disharmonies, of many moral agents acting within a common existential field. Achieving the ability to act conjointly with others so as to share responsibility is an excellent virtue. Nevertheless, temporarily for the sake of argument here, we can begin by making the reductive abstraction of talking about a moral agent as if the agent were only an individual, not a group acting conjointly.

A person's moral actions, based on decisions about the possibilities for actions, and decisions about participating in conjoint actions, contribute to the character of the individual. We commonly think this when referring to actions where the whole responsibility falls on the individual. However, even in cases of people acting together, each individual is responsible for his or her participation and thus accrues elements of moral character from that participation. One aspect of personal agency in the two-term relation in morality between the agent

202   Metaphysics of Goodness

and the surrounding issues is that moral agency creates moral character in the agent as well as affecting the goodness–laden consequences of the morally freighted action within the world. This is hugely important for understanding moral obligation.

Thus, a dual effect comes from any morally relevant actions by an agent. On the one hand are the moral consequences of the action in the world, often having to do with the effects on other individuals, sometimes in life and death matters. These consequences include how the moral action affects the goods in the rest of the situation. Moral action is not just about the moral agent. It is also about the consequences. On the other hand, moral action, depending on its nature and quality, determines the moral character of the agent. So when we think about moral character, it consists in large, though not complete, measure in the moral character the agent gives himself or herself by being the one who chooses and acts on the alternatives at hand with their respective goods.

Immanuel Kant was committed to understanding morality solely in terms of the constitution of the moral subject. This is similar to his attempt to define the worldliness of the world, and its necessary conditions, solely in terms of the constitution of the knowing subject. In morals, Kant argued that the determination of the moral will rests entirely on the possible consistency of an act of moral will.[1] The primary way of determining whether a possible act is in accord with the categorical imperative that constitutes one's duty is to attempt to formulate a description of the act into a universalizable maxim for any moral agent in the same or at least a similar situation. If the act can indeed be formulated as a maxim, for instance, "lie when it will get you out of trouble," when you are tempted to lie to get out of trouble, then you have to ask whether it can be universalized. Kant said it cannot be universalized, because if everyone lied to get out of trouble, no one would believe what anyone said in troubled times, and therefore it would be impossible to get anyone to believe a lie. Only a believable lie is a lie. Therefore, the only maxim about lying that can be universalized is something like "never lie when it would get you out of trouble." Lying in most other circumstances is also contrary to the categorical imperative for the same reason: if it were universalized, lying itself would become impossible and society would have absolutely no trust.[2]

Now part of Kant's reasoning here is that we can have synthetic a priori knowledge only of the conditions of subjectivity, the subjective will in the case of morality. If we tried to determine our duty by looking at the world to see what the most valuable alternative is, we could never have certain knowledge. Moreover, in looking at the world, we need to regard ourselves as wholly determined by mechanical psychological factors, not as free agents. If we did not assume a complete determinism in empirical matters, we would not be able to distinguish empirical reality from mere subjective fiction, Kant thought. However, if we consider ourselves as subjectively free moral agents, then we can regard the empirical field of action *as if* we and others were moral agents. Then we can imagine willing so as to treat others as ends in themselves, not as means only, even though we know that we know people to be merely determined processes in larger processes of nature, not ends in themselves. What we know, thought Kant, has to be set aside, or radically reinterpreted, so that we can consider our wills as effective in an *as if* world. Thus, Kant thought that moral considerations should deal only with the structure of the subjective will and with what we can will universally and consistently.

Nevertheless, Kant's arguments about the transcendental subjectivity of the synthetic a priori in morals, or what he called "practical reason," are no better than his arguments about the transcendental subjective conditions of theoretical knowledge. He thought that only transcendentally subjective will could give us categorical imperatives, that is, imperatives that define our duty rather than determining it hypothetically. To the contrary, I argue, obligation consists in part in the fact that the moral quality of our choices determines the moral quality that accrues to our character. We *ought* to choose the best alternatives because that will make us the best choosers and to choose anything less would give us a worse moral character. The categorical imperative can be reformulated as an hypothetical imperative: if an agent chooses A, it will give the agent the moral character of being the chooser of A, whatever that character is. The reason one ought to choose the best alternative is that nothing else is the best choice and does not make for the best chooser in that regard. This leaves for empirical inquiry the analysis of moral situations to determine what is best. The difficulty of moral analysis is the realistic situation in which we face moral choices and in which we must act. Kant's morality of universalizable maxims is simply out of touch with the moral situations in which we live.

A positive way of looking at Kant's philosophy is to say that Kant found a way to defend moral freedom in an intellectual world that assumes determinism as a prerequisite for scientific thinking. With the deterministic assumption, people are merely automata and thus not morally responsible for anything. In his theory of knowledge of the empirical world, put forward in his *Critique of Pure Reason*, he affirmed the determinism required, he thought, by science. In his theory of moral subjectivity and the categorical imperative, in both his *Critique of Practical Reason* and his *Foundations of the Metaphysics of Morals*, he affirmed the human freedom necessary to admit moral responsibility. He kept these strictly apart by saying that morality does not apply in the empirical world. The American pragmatists adopted the defense of freedom and creativity, especially as developed by some of the romantic Kantian idealists. The pragmatists simply ignored the distinction between deterministic empirical knowledge and free moral knowledge and will that applies to an *as if* realm. They thought instead that human beings are natural organisms in a natural environment with some freedom and creativity but circumscribed by the circumstances and human resources. Peirce, James, and Dewey all worried that if a person does not exert creativity within the range of free options, it is perfectly possible for the person practically to accept being determined, and hence not a responsible person. For the pragmatists, how much order and of what sorts are empirical questions, not something that needs to be assumed a priori. The pragmatists were right.[3]

Thus, the other side of the two-term relation of morality is the goodness-laden situations that give rise to morality in the first place. Taking this into account allows us to see that most moral reasoning has to do with analyzing the moral aspects of the situation. Situation ethics is far more important for moral reasoning than focusing on the subjective structure of the will itself. The tradition of situation ethics in the West has come with great force from Plato, and it is the way to categorize the Confucian traditions in Western categories. Stephen Angle gives an excellent account in his *Sagehood* of the education of the would-be sage in learning how to analyze the complex situations of moral weight, with layer upon layer of coherences and incoherences. Many Western philosophers interpret Confucian philosophy as virtue ethics, harping upon the emphasis on education of the sage. Nevertheless, the sage's virtues are in being able to engage in concrete detail with the exigencies of the situation; sagacity is in the main a heightened ability to perceive layers of connections and disconnections and to imagine how things might be different. The situation side in the two-term relation of morality poses the problems of discerning what the goods of things are, what the alternatives are, what might be done about them, and how to imagine all these things together. The quality of moral actions has to do with how much good and harm they do, including, but usually only as a small part, the good and harm they do to the character of the moral agents.[4]

Obligation with Freedom

Obligation comes upon us because we face situations in which the future offers us options that differ in the goods they would actualize. William James reminded us, in his essay "The Will to Believe," that options are living or dead, forced or avoidable, and momentous or trivial.[5] Although we know that we make most choices conjointly with others, so that options are for several or many people at once, and that we sometimes negotiate decision making, let me follow out James's case where there is individual choice among options available to that individual.

By "living or dead," James meant to distinguish options that really might be chosen from those that realistically cannot be chosen. His own emphasis was on a person's interest in choosing. He illustrated his distinction by saying that for his audience (members of the philosophy clubs at Yale and Brown universities, all male), it was a living option to become an atheist or a Christian but it was not a live option to choose between being a theosophist and a Muslim. In our more pluralistic age, those are all living options for American undergraduate students, and many more exist to choose among as well. James had in mind the exercise of free will regarding life paths. In cases of morality, however, often we face options we would very much like not to have to choose among, for instance choosing the least of evils. Kant, for instance, worried in the *Foundations for the Metaphysics of Morals* that we should be suspicious of our motives if we in fact want to do what we have decided is our duty. We can be much more confident in our moral reasoning, he thought, if our duty is in conflict with what we want, what is attractive, or what serves our interests. I have argued that the relevant goods in the options of choice lie in those possibilities as such, not in any consistency of will; so obligation, or duty, has to do with what is best. Kant was right to note that sometimes, however, especially in moral situations, what is best is what we would much prefer to be a dead option. To make James's point relevant, a dead option is one that we really cannot choose, even if we thought we could. Sometimes in moral situations, those options we would much prefer to be dead are indeed living and the best that we can choose. We should think of a dead option instead as one that really is not a possible future even though we might mistakenly think it is.

Freedom has as one of its features the power to seek out what seemed to be a dead option and find ways to make it live. Freedom in part means the creativity and imagination to figure out how to make what seemed a dead option living. Perhaps there is a way around what seemed the only living option to a better one. Moral creativity, which Kant and his deterministic colleagues did not believe in for real empirical action, involves the power to find good living options among the real possibilities that we had not noticed, or that we can make possible by some intervening action. James's distinction between living and dead options is in the end the distinction between real and unreal possibilities, and with what we can do to affect real possibilities, insofar as we can discern this.

His distinction between "forced or avoidable" options seems more straightforward. We can avoid some options and cannot avoid others. A forced option is one we cannot avoid. A painter has the option of coloring a certain shape red or blue but can avoid the option by making only a line drawing with no color, or not making any art at all. Once committed to painting in color, however, all the shapes to be colored involve forced options. Beth Neville has argued that art classes should be required in grade school and high school because they model situations in which people are forced to make choices and to reason about the best ones to make. Learning art is practice at learning the morality of forced options. Learning to make art is practice at the exercise of responsible freedom where not much of moral consequences depends on the failed experiments, at least in school. Moral options, unlike whether to create a work of art, are all forced, a point that I shall explore in the next section.

James's distinction between "momentous and trivial" options is extremely important as a defining element of morality. Moral choices are important as well as forced upon us. In moral situations, what we do makes an important difference to what happens. If it is not important or momentous, we should not take it as a matter of morality, I contend. There are two main lines of objections to this contention, however. Some Kantians, who worry most about the effect of the choice on the chooser and use that effect to define the content of the categorical imperative, would say that even in an "objectively unimportant" situation, the agent is obliged to choose morally. Because lying is always wrong, when someone fishes for a compliment about his or her appearance, a Kantian would always render an honest verdict. However, for the sake of the courtesy rituals underlying human life, it might be better to include lying, or at least dissimulation, about things like that. Self-righteousness in small matters is annoying.

The other line of objection to my contention that only momentous things are the province of morality is the claim that there is a moral responsibility to play the rituals of the small things in life. The momentous rituals of courtesy that enable social relations thus bring an obligation to ritual lying on occasion. With this objection I would wholeheartedly agree but emphasize its main point: the rituals of social life are momentously important, even those that seem the most trivially conventional. Whether our ritual of greeting consists in shaking hands or bowing with hands pressed together is trivial. Nevertheless, it is momentous that we have rituals of greeting that we can play with those whom we meet, however different those rituals are in each case. The Western tradition has greatly underestimated the moral importance of playing rituals well, and having good rituals to play, in the building of social means of containing conflicts, satisfying diverse and competing interests, and making possible many of the institutions and practices in which high civilization consists. One of the most living, forced, and momentous arenas of morality is the correction, maintenance, and skillful playing of the rituals that constitute so much of civilization.[6] The point here is that morality has to do with choice among options that are living (whether we like it or not), forced, and momentous.

Freedom to choose among options has two elements, the reality of the options to which our apparatus of choosing must conform and the creativity of our choices and actions. As I have argued, the future has possibilities that allow of alternatives and the alternatives have different goods. Where the future does not allow of alternatives, we do not have freedom of choice and action: whatever happens has been predetermined because what has been actualized already does not have alternative possibilities. However, so often in human affairs, and across much of nature, the past does not determine completely what can happen in its future. Many spontaneous things decide among open options in nature. In human affairs, that spontaneity can take the form of choice and action based on choice.

In human choice, "spontaneity" is not merely random or arbitrary selection. Rather, human beings can insert themselves so as to analyze the future possibilities, frame them into coherent options for choice and action, and then deliberately choose one way to go within the option and pursue it. The person might ignore the whole situation and let other forces, inertial ones or the agencies of other people, make the decisions about what happens and carry those decisions out. Nevertheless, an individual can insert himself or herself into the situation by a creative act of making himself or herself a relevant agent. Whether a person does that is itself often a moral choice. Sometimes, of course, it is better just to go with the flow; other times it is very important to take up an agential role. Nearly always, the choice of whether to take up such a role is a moral one, that is, living, forced, and momentous. So part of moral choice is the free and responsible creation of oneself as a moral agent involved in determining what happens.

The other side of moral creativity involves the analysis of the situation and its options. First, though we inherit goodness-categories and habits of valuation for interpreting the future possibilities, part of moral creativity is to try to look at things more critically and from other points of view. The Confucian tradition of sagehood elaborates this point in depth: the sage does not merely see with old eyes but creates new eyes, new points of view, and new categories for understanding. A good sage, a moral sage, does this creative analysis so often that it becomes second nature and appears almost spontaneous.

Second, moral creativity also includes creating new possibilities within the limits of what the future can hold that would not exist without creative intervention. That is, we can augment the options for choice by actions that change the situation, perhaps involving more people, perhaps protecting otherwise vulnerable people, institutions, and other things of value. Adept moral agents are creative in making new and better options. Some moral philosophers like to invent moral dilemmas that do not allow time for this kind of creative response, for instance, having to choose between switching a speeding train onto a track that will kill one friend or onto another track that would kill five strangers or villains. However, most of our moral situations are not like this split-second decision making. They allow rather for many complex layers of venues of creative action.

In this section, I have tried to make two main points. First, freedom in morality forces itself upon us because the future gives us choices to make that are living, forced, and momentous. Even if we choose not to make choices in a certain situation, this is a choice among options for choice and has whatever goodness it has, determining the agent's moral character. Second, freedom is not only in making a bare choice but also in the creativity of choosing, the creativity of new ways of understanding the goodness-laden options at stake, the creativity of intervening to change the options themselves.

The pragmatic tradition from Peirce, James, and Dewey has emphasized the importance of imaginative creativity in being free moral agents. Those philosophers did not worry much, nor should we, about theoretical arguments to the effect that we are mechanistically determined and that freedom is therefore an illusion. They cared not a fig about debates about "compatibilism" between determinism and free will. Nevertheless, they cared greatly about the moral sloth of letting ourselves be determined by onrushing events rather than exercising the difficult arts of moral creativity. As James tried to put it but was nearly always misunderstood, we make ourselves free in the sense of being effective moral agents, hopefully for the good, only if we exercise our freedom to do so. James emphasized the psychological side: if we sit in our depression and feelings of hopelessness, we make ourselves unfree, but we should instead create ourselves, by the exercise of our free will and grit, to be moral agents. The Confucians among us would emphasize the very great difficulty of making ourselves into creative moral agents—and the obligation to do so.

Obligation without Freedom

Much as we should prize and cultivate moral creativity, a sense exists in which morality bears a special kind of unfreedom. A moral dilemma or situation for action has elements that are simply given and that we cannot escape. An artist is free in being able to avoid artwork, or, once committed to a work of art, to choose what elements to take up and what not. Artistic creativity consists in large measure in finding new resources, or new ways of deploying resources, to fulfill ideal goals that themselves change in the process of artistic production. In a moral situation in which you are a relevant agent, you cannot simply choose not to get involved without that being a moral action on its own with consequences that determine your moral character as well as make a difference to what happens. Similarly, many choices have to do with how to shape your life where you are more or less free in what to take up. Decisions about career, family, lifestyle, cultural enjoyments and commitments, and many other things are heavily value-laden and have powerful consequences for the actual world, and yet they are not moral decisions in any narrow sense. You can be free to be a financial accountant or a sports announcer, so long as those are living options in the sense that you really could become either one. Perhaps you can do both at once, although most of us have to make serious decisions among careers that are not compatible at the same time. Beyond yourself, you will make a significant difference to your friends and family, your neighborhood, some of the institutions such as schools and healthcare facilities, and various kinds of cultural life. Only in some rare instances in creating a life are there significant moral dimensions, for instance, a need to go to war as a soldier when demanded or to give up music for medicine because of a momentous social need that others cannot fill. Chapters 11 and 12 will explore these kinds of normative relations with the situations of life to which we should conform in one way or another, in these instances, conforming by making something new and significant.

Although the lines between moral situations are not sharp, it is helpful to point out three primary kinds: moral obligations to the environment, both natural and social; moral obligations to people in special relations such as family members, colleagues, and friends; and moral obligations in emergencies.

Moral obligations to the natural environment are coming to greater prominence in our consciousness, especially with the sudden awakening to climate change. One way to understand moral obligation to the natural environment is through ritual. Rituals are the ways we behave habitually so as to accomplish something needed for life and civilization (topics I will discuss more in part IV). For instance, how people procure food is ritualized in diverse ways in each culture. Some are hunter-gatherers, some farmers, some anglers, many in much more complicated and complex rituals of food gathering and preparation. These economic practices are all culturally learned and most usually are practiced together with others as conjoint actions. They engage the natural environment, with effects that are significant for the stability, growth, or diminishment of elements in the surround, including plants and animals, water sources, climate, durability, change, and habitability. What is true for rituals of food production is true for rituals of dwellings and public buildings, rituals of commerce and travel, and a host of other dimensions of human life. Human beings have developed the vast ritual systems of diverse civilizations so as to accomplish human goals, such as having nourishment, safety, the arts, and a good life. However, the rituals also involve altering the environment in sometimes significant ways, as in farming practices. A moral obligation exists to develop and play rituals the goodness of which includes the goods involved in altering the environment. Often we think of rituals as only involving interactions among people, neglecting how our interactions with nature are also ritualized. Our rituals with nature are critical, even as they involve actions with people as well. Because rituals with nature bind us in causal patterns with nature, there is a moral obligation to attend to rituals with an eye to the goods involved in the whole ritualized situation. The moral part of this is that we are obligated to conform to what should be a good ritual situation, and our moral character develops in part by how we attend to rituals with nature.

Similarly, often special obligations exist with regard to other people. An obvious case is obligations of parents to children, of friends to friends, and of neighbors to neighbors. In business, employers have obligations to employees and vice versa. Political life includes obligations of citizenship and of various offices to one another and to constituencies. The morality in these kinds of obligations comes from the relations, not from the specifics. The relations are regarded usefully as defined by rituals, those of family life, friendship, communal life, economic life, and political life in the preceding examples. The rituals are the social patterns, the playing of which constitutes the relations. The ritual interplays define the relations. No particular moral obligation obtains for parents to feed their children beans versus apples for dinner tonight. Nevertheless, a moral obligation does obtain for the parents to provide good food and care generally. The moral obligation is to be good parents as delineated through the multitude of domestic rituals. With regard to friendship, few moral obligations obtain to do this or that, but a moral obligation does obtain to be a good friend, however the rituals and emergencies at hand define that. Not to play whatever rituals define the care involved in friendship is immoral. With regard to community life, neighborliness has many alternative rituals that can define it, most of which do not have moral dimensions, but to be a good neighbor, whatever rituals are involved in your particular community, is a moral obligation. In respect to economic life, the ritual relations are extremely complex. Often in unjust societies (and what society is wholly just?), the economic rituals ought to be changed. Sometimes these are moral matters of justice. Nevertheless, always a moral obligation obtains for individuals to do the right thing regarding the rituals of economics that involve, work, distribution, changing the earth, shaping trade with others, and the rest. To complain that you are treated unjustly and rebel against the economic institutions and rituals at hand does not absolve you from finding some rituals to strive for in order to conform to what would be good in ritualized economic relations. Politics is also a moral matter with regard to playing rituals that make for good political life; the specifics might not be moral, but the obligation to be political in ways that make for social good is a moral obligation. The general principle defining morality here is the obligation to relate to the rituals defining, for better or worse, your relations to the environment in which you act. We are morally obligated to attend normatively to the rituals that relate us.

The rituals by which we interact with the world in our local environments do not necessarily define moral obligations in emergencies. If someone is in trouble and needs help, a moral obligation to help obtains even if there is not ritualized regulation of responsibility. If a natural disaster is about to occur, moral obligations exist to help mitigate its effects on the larger world. Moral obligations also exist to prevent natural disasters that seem to be arising. At present, moral economic and social obligations exist to change the ways by which human beings disrupt the environment, for instance, by causing global warming and bad climate change. However, there is also an emergency moral obligation to fend off the destruction of the environment for its own sake, which might be met by changing people's ritualized relations with nature negatively impacting the environment.

Social contract theorists such as Thomas Hobbes and John Locke thought that people live in a state of nature in which they are all free and have no obligations until people establish a social contract in which they distribute obligations and responsibilities.[7] I say rather that, in an imagined state with no social contract or organization, total moral responsibility falls on everyone to do something about whatever is obligatory, that is, in need of being done. Everyone is responsible for feeding every child until there are family rituals that assign specific responsibilities and release others. The creation of organized society channels responses to what ought to be done generally through rituals that cultivate vast interlocking matrices of responsibilities making possible the great institutions of civilization. Without ritualized social orders, there is only chaos in which everyone is responsible for everything that ought to be done, thus a moral failure in nearly every respect.

"Emergency" means "a matter arising" that is not naturally taken care of by the rituals and anticipations at hand. Organized societies develop special institutions to handle emergencies, such as police and

ambulance services. We have a moral obligation to foster such institutions for emergencies. Nevertheless, even with the best of situations,
matters will still arise that ipso facto establish you as the one who
can do something about it and that constitute for you a moral role.

Achievement of Responsible Identity

All through this volume, I have stressed the point that goodness lies
in the formal nature of things that have goodness, not in projections
we make on objects we value. The latter has been the view of much
Western moral thinking, especially Locke and Kant. Of course, for us
to recognize goodness in things, we have to discern it and therefore
need interpretive schemes and practices. Moreover, we have needs and
interests of our own that direct our discernments of goodness. The
appreciation of goodness is never just a simple reading off or mirroring
of the goods resident in the things of the world. Nevertheless, I have
stressed the residence of goodness in things to push back against the
common subjectivism that attempts to limit goodness to the valuing.

In moral theory, transcendental subjectivism of Kant's sort takes
the form of having a morally good will; morality does not have much
to do with the effects agents have on the goods of what happens.
Against this, I have argued that morality has to do with conforming
to the relations with things that produce what is best, under certain
circumstances. Now, however, I shall relent somewhat and focus on a
subjective side of morality, or what might seem subjective.

The thing with goodness that we affect most often, thoroughly,
and steadily through life is ourselves. In a strict moral sense, we give
ourselves our moral characters by the moral choices we make throughout life, with all the twists, compromises, and misjudgments in the
ambiguous circumstances of life. But we define ourselves in many
other ways too: by the friends and associations we make; by how we
relate to family members, creating and destroying family institutions;
by our jobs, career choices, and places of residence; by the myriad
ways we construct our lives, often for a long time and through many
phases. If we create and enjoy beautiful things, we add those things

to our identities. If we fail to create and enjoy beauty, that makes us something too.

A special dimension to morality consists in the moral obligation to give ourselves a responsible identity. All the two-termed kinds of relations we have to the world already embody obligation: the obligation to conform to the world appropriately. The self-identity kind of moral identity is our relation to that other set of obligations, the obligation to make ourselves good people in relation to those other obligations. Kant would love the point that, in this dimension of morality at least, we have the obligation to develop the identity of being good at fulfilling our obligations of whatever sort.

Let us beware of the tendency to think of personal identity too individualistically. We are not subjective centers of intention that relate to others only as objects. We are cooperative people forming identities together. Our identity is not like that of a substance bearing properties but rather is a harmony integrating all the things to which we relate, as described in part I. The identity of any one of us is a dynamic harmony growing through time that composes the components of our personal harmony in functions of triviality, vagueness, narrowness, and width. Our composition changes through time as things become more or less important, as they emerge into our relevant environment or pass out of it, as our interests change and mature. At nearly all times, who we are and should be is a function of many people acting together in various situations. So we should not think about identity too individualistically. Nevertheless, however conjoint most of our decisions and behaviors are, each of us has a special moral responsibility to make ourselves responsible for fulfilling obligations, moral and otherwise.

To sort out aspects of personal identity in non-stupid ways is particularly difficult because it has two sides; personal identity is a harmony of these two sides. One side, the subjective side, consists in the dynamic harmony of us personally moment by moment and through time. This is how we manages our relations with all sorts of things that have their own harmonic identity. Our subjective identity is not always very tight—sometimes we are little more than a chaotic jumble of attempts to bring affairs to a determinate shape. At other times, we achieve very great focus, with a maximization of narrowness

and width in personal identity. Some of us do not have much cumulative unity through time, and one of the graces of human life is the
ability to get over and leave behind some aspects of personal identity.
This is more complicated than just moral guilt, praiseworthiness, and
blameworthiness. Nevertheless, through the duration of our lives, we
have a dynamic harmony, or a harmony of momentary or episodic
harmonies, for which we are responsible themselves, however conjoint
much of life is with others.

The other side, the objective side, is the identity we have in
terms of the effects we have on other things, institutions, and people.
I have been a teacher and, although I tried to teach truly and treat
my students well, taking responsibility for the content of what I teach,
I cannot exercise responsibility for what my students do with what I
teach them. That is their responsibility, part of their respective subjective
identities. I am vain enough to hope that what I taught is important
enough to affect their lives on many levels and for a long time; this is
foolish vanity, however, because my teachings can be taken up in ways
disastrously detrimental to the lives of the students. Nevertheless, what I
taught my students is just as much part of my identity as those things
that remain within my personal harmony of responsibility, despite the
fact I have little or no control over those effects.

Similarly, I have effects on the institutions within which I live:
family, work, and all areas of conjoint action and enjoyment. In some
respects, I am responsible subjectively for these effects; but in other
respects, the institutions and shared life have dynamics of their own that
give different compositions of my effects. As a biological being, I have
significant effects on the natural environment: my metabolism alone
has a huge footprint over time. To some extent, I can be personally,
that is, subjectively, responsible for these effects in many of the ways
discussed earlier. Nevertheless, in a great many respects, these effects
on the social and natural environments beyond myself are not within
the powers of my responsibility. Still, they are parts of my identity, my
cumulative identity within creation over time. My subjective responsibility for fulfilling obligations ends with death. The objective fallout
of my identity carries on long after.

Perhaps we are tempted to limit personal identity to what we
can harmonize responsibly within our subjective identities and say that

what people, institutions, and nature do with our effects within them is simply not us. However, that would be like saying that our genetic code, our family birth-order position, the givens of our circumstances from the local to the global, the accidents of our watch, are not part of our identity. To be sure, we harmonize all these things more or less well within our ongoing subjective identity. However, a lot of that is simply given and we have to take it as partly defining what we are. From a subjective moral point of view, what is most important about our moral identity is what we do with what we are given. Nevertheless, our identity is not limited to what we do but also includes what we are given. Similarly, our identity includes what other things do with what we give them.

Consider Abraham Lincoln. Subjectively he did many things but died in 1865; there is no more subjective harmonization for him after that. Objectively, however, he has had an enormous effect on subsequent affairs down to this day, a genuine hero and model. His legacy, as we call it, is as much him as his subjective harmonizations. His policies and perspicuous "heart" are much more important than his achievements at dental hygiene, for instance, over which he probably had very much responsible control. Lincoln's identity is even more important in its objective legacies than in its quotidian subjective achievements. Adolph Hitler is a model of an opposite moral sort. Most people are far more modest than Lincoln or Hitler in their objective identities. Nevertheless, those objective identities are as much part of who people are as their subjective identities that harmonize within their own individual dynamic harmonies.

The moral obligation to ourselves as achievements of responsibility is limited to what we can harmonize within the dynamic harmonies of our lives. This includes the efforts we can make to insure that our objective identities are as good as they can be, modest in their demands on the natural environment, helpful in their contributions to social environments, given to beauty and to contributing to good lives in the societies and civilizations around us. We have a moral obligation to make the relation between ourselves and our obligations of various sorts to be as good as possible, and we are moral failures to the extent that we neglect this self-cultivation. The Confucians have understood this kind of moral obligation with great depth.[8]

In this chapter, I have developed the hypothesis that morality is the obligation we have in choices that are among living, forced, and momentous options. Other kinds of obligations obtain for our choices, but those among living, forced, and momentous options constitute what we usually think of as the moral. The hypothesis includes a defense of free will among options that are not antecedently determined. Moreover, free will includes the creativity to develop the possibilities that frame our options. We are morally obligated to improve our options where we can. The hypothesis also includes an analysis of how moral options are given, in contrast to those we choose to have. This distinction marks a major difference between artistic creativity and moral obligation. Finally, I have argued here that one of our moral obligations is to create ourselves as good people, especially good at fulfilling moral obligations. We have an obligation to ourselves, insofar as our identity is amenable to our control. Nevertheless, our identity, and thus our cumulative goodness or value, includes objective effects on others that we cannot control. Our normative identity is more than that for which we can be responsible.

CHAPTER 11

Goodness in Being Right

How could you have followed the arguments here about obligations to truth and morality without feeling that they are absurd abstractions from the rich textures of life in the living? No one simply "makes an inquiry"! We move into inquiry in an explicit sense only by refocusing attention on other things. No one simply "makes a decision"! We decide things for the most part while doing a great many other things. Surely you have thought of these irresponsible abstractions! Nevertheless, we abstract in order to simplify, and we simplify in order to do something. Abstractions are the tools of practical reason. Nevertheless, it is necessary to put these forms of obligation into a more realistic context of human life. The things we do under whatever obligation are set within larger orientations to the main contours of life. We relate holistically to those contours, and our inquiries and decisions find their places within those orientations. How can we understand this?

Beyond the goodness of being moral is the goodness of being right, as I shall use the term "right." The goodness in being right is the goodness of those harmonies that relate us individually to the world in its important humanly relevant contours. These harmonies are components of our own subjective and objective natures. The things to which we relate, of course, are internal conditioning components of us in certain respects, and most of those things also have careers of

219

their own. "Being right" is a strong term, too strong in some instances, because it suggests a sharp contrast between being right and being wrong. Often the most relevant question is whether we relate this way or that way, not how well we relate. Nevertheless, even in these instances involving much free choice and the inertia of accidents, still a sense exists of appropriateness, or inappropriateness. Morality, to be sure, is a subcase of right relations focusing on choice among possibilities, although other kinds of relations exist that involve appropriate and inappropriate orientation. Being right is a two-termed relation between us and the contoured world in which we live. Moral choices among possibilities do not always deal with the contours of life.

The goodness of being right is in our relations with the basic contours of the world and our various life situations. Permit me to shape the notion of "contour" as a term of art. A contour, as I use the term, is a harmony in the world of many things to which we relate such that our relation to the harmony as such is important. We relate to a great many things, most trivially, many vaguely, and a great many without connecting them significantly to much else. For instance, to relate to our toothbrush and bath mat is not very significant so long as the relations serve health. To worry about rightly relating to the brush and the mat is philosophical overkill, so long as we relate rightly to hygiene and health. The brush and mat are tiny elements in the contours of hygiene and health. Nevertheless, taking care of hygiene and health is an important contour of life for most of us. It fits with many other contours of life, some common to most of us, others idiosyncratic to each or only some of us. Life has its contours and understanding the important contours of life is important for grasping how to live rightly or wrongly, appropriately or inappropriately, to the world. The contours of the world relative to us constitute some of the main humanly important structures.

Four dimensions of the goodness of right engagement of the contours of life structure this chapter. The first is the nature of engagement as such. The second is the appropriate engagements of the actual contours on our watch. The third is that aspect of goodness that accrues to human character in engagement of life's contours. The fourth is the achievement of finite identity in the engagement of those contours.

Engagement

"Engagement" is the word I use for what Dewey called "transaction" and sometimes "interaction." The point he was making with those terms was that the fundamental relation of a person to the world is that of an organism to its environment. He meant to distinguish his position from the transcendental claim that the relation is that of a subject to a complex of objects in the world. Objectivity, in that Cartesian-Kantian tradition, means how things in the world appear within subjective consciousness. Descartes had adopted the term "objectivity" from medieval philosophy, in which it meant the reality of things for knowers in contrast to the reality things have in themselves (which medieval philosophy called "formal reality"). For Dewey and the other pragmatists in different terms, knowledge, consciousness, and other traits of subjectivity are activities that arise in some higher organisms by virtue of their interactions with their environment.

I use the term "engagement" to speak of this interactive natural process in the case of human beings. It carries a connotation of being able to engage or disengage, or be unengaged, which is important in considering being right with the world in its relevant contours. Whether and how, including how well, we engage is the first condition we will consider of the goodness of being right with the world.

If we were in thrall to a substance cosmology, it would be appropriate to think of a person as an individual relating externally with the environment. Dewey's terminology allows for this interpretation, although he did not hold to it consistently. In my alternative cosmology of harmonies, the complex harmony of a human being already includes relations with the relevant things in the environment. Those environing things are conditioning components of the person, even when their function is so trivial that they might not even exist as far as they bear differentially upon the person. Their function might be so vague that their real characters are subordinate to covering characteristics, just as the blue of the sky substitutes for all the meteorological events above. Other components of the environment function in narrow and wide ways to punctuate foreground and background elements, all with their goods including the goods constituted by the ways in which they are together. The environment in this sense is internal to the person's harmony, with its elements internally related. Of course, the person harmonizes those conditional components with essential ones, those expressing continuity of DNA and other bodily elements, continuity of culture, continuity of personal projects, and the rest. Among the most distinctive essential integrating components are those of agency, will, and intention. Human beings interpret the world using multileveled semiotic systems that help orient responses to things so that the things plus the person's responses to them are integrated in the person's harmony.

At this point it is worth reminding ourselves that the metaphysical force of this cosmology is that each determinate thing is a harmony that is internally related to all the things with respect to which it is determinate and at the same time has essential components that give it its own being. Each harmony that plays roles in a given harmony is also external to that harmony by virtue of its own essential components. Therefore, we can say that things are both external to each other and yet related to each other. The relations at the metaphysical level are internal so that each harmony includes among its constituents its relations and their relata, and, at the same time, the relations guarantee that their terms do not reduce to one another. Things can be both related and external to one another so that each harmony has its own being. Some people have difficulty conceiving this because they assume what Whitehead characterized as "the fallacy of simple location," namely, the assumption that things exist only in themselves such that their relations to one another make no difference to their natures.[1] The cosmology I defend here assumes (with many arguments given elsewhere) that things have multiple locations, places where they come to be and places where they enter into other things with respect to which they are determinate.[2] Some people have difficulty conceiving of multiple locations because they assume that "locations" are places in a field that has its own being independent of the things in it, with some locations here and others there, or now and then. If this were so, then the things would have their locations entirely separate from one another except for the structures of the field that are external to the things in it. Then all relations would be external to the natures of the things related, "atoms in the void." However, the cosmology I advocate argues that the harmonies that take on existential location constitute the existential field of space and time. Being "here and now" is a thing's existential location because it integrates other things as being "there and then" relative to itself. Other things define their own existential location by what they do with the first thing, putting it earlier and distant; their natures include the first thing as being earlier and distant in the ways they compose their components with triviality, vagueness, narrowness, and width. The existential field is not a container but the matrix of conditioning relations among things as their harmonies integrate their determinate relations. Abstract and "metaphysical" as this point is, it is crucial to recognizing the goods in right relationship with the world. It allows a distinction between a person and that person's world, without making the person an atom subjectively representing the world in its subjective consciousness and not really relating internally to the things represented.

The goodness of relating rightly to the world inheres in a two-termed harmony that includes persons and their environing world. These terms are internal to one another, with the person occupying places within the world and the world constituting conditioning components of the person. Nevertheless, the world has its own contours, its own harmonic natures, its own connections. These contours might not register in what the person takes in of the world. The person might trivialize or dismiss with vague substitutes what is really important or valuable in the world. The person might mistake the goods of what is important in the world that is registered and value them inappropriately. The things in the world that become components of a person are not necessarily treated within the person as they deserve to be: a toxin ingested as food is very badly integrated in the person. Therefore, the problem of engagement is how to engage the world according to its nature. This is not to say that everything is to be related to positively: toxins ought not to be eaten; enemies ought not to be embraced vulnerably. Nevertheless, the character of how a person comports himself or herself to the world depends on grasping just what the world is worth and how.

People are dynamic harmonies, which is to say they are constantly changing. They relate to the things in their environment differently depending on the time of day; they approach some things that later they push aside. Because people are dynamic harmonies, constantly reforming momentary processes to deal with new things, the big question is how to harmonize with this or that thing next. All living things are dynamic harmonies in this respect. However, we human beings anticipate the future with symbols that articulate multiple possibilities. The important forms of human harmonies are dynamic ones of setting up new harmonic states and processes. If we human beings were static harmonies, we would not ask how to engage our world. The question would be only how we are mutually implicated with things in the world. But we are dynamic harmonies in a dynamic world, and some of the most important dimensions of human harmonies are those that have to do with our intentional activities toward things in the world. We engage the world in many ways on many levels, and moral engagement is only the surface.

What we engage in the world are its contours, as I have called the matter, following some ideas and terms of Justus Buchler.[3] We do not engage the world item by item, but by movements in this contour and movements in that contour. Health and hygiene is one kind of contour, family life another, neighborhood affairs, educational affairs, even world-historical affairs. These contours are characteristics of kinds of harmonies that unite other harmonies within the world. They are what they are, really, insofar as they unite those harmonies of the world. We relate to those contours insofar as we can discern the harmonic nature of them. Thus, we must interpret them in terms of our semiotic systems in most cases, although elemental recognitions of the contours of some things do not involve complicated semiotic systems. A toddler relates to the contours of gravity while standing and running with only a little learned semiotic habits of how to stand and move.

The goodness of being right in relation to the world thus depends on some accuracy with which we engage the world according to its own nature, not mistaking toxins for food. Interpreting the nature of the world in its relevant contours is a vastly important problem in itself. However, my interest here is in calling attention to the issues of engaging the world as we understand it.

Some people (but not all of us) are so seriously unenterprising as to engage the world hardly at all. They live off inertia from what their immediate background culture and society have given them. They apprehend little of the complexity and depth of the world, with its blends and contrasts of goods, and just get along, until they do not get along anymore. Other people are in denial about engaging many important contours, for instance, their families, or issues of health, or social responsibilities. Many reasons exist for such kinds of denial. Some are psychological, some have to do with the difficulty of problems in the world, and some have to do with traumas of pain, or rejection, or failure. Many people retreat when they should engage. The theological virtue of faith is, as Paul Tillich said, the courage to be in an engaged relation when there are many reasons to despair.[4]

The first dimension of the goodness of being right is the goodness of engaging as such, perhaps irrespective of whether the engagement is appropriate or inappropriate. To be a human being is to lie under the obligation to engage the world as such, in its relevant contours to one's life.

Appropriate Engagement with the Contours of the World

The second dimension of the goodness of being right is the goodness of engaging the world as it is *appropriately*. This obviously has two parts, as befits the goodness in a two-term relation. The first is the understanding of the world as it is and the second is the meaning of "appropriate" responses.

In a literal sense, "the world as it is" includes all the harmonies that are determinate with respect to one another and that together constitute an existential field set within an ontological context of mutual relevance. In this literal sense, any harmony, such as a person, relates to all those things with respect to which it is determinate. Any harmony composes its components so that they function trivially, vaguely, narrowly, and widely. For all practical purposes, a harmony is indeterminate with respect to those things that are trivial for it. Whitehead was wise to point out that making certain things trivial can mean that they do not count, but it also means that the harmony has possibilities for composing itself that it would not have if it did not trivialize those things. He said that the trivializing or "negative prehension" of those things itself affects the subjective form of the harmony, which I have called its composition.

The "world as it is," so described, does not call attention to the dynamics of most of the existential fields in which we operate. We relate to things as past and future, and as contemporaries with whom we share the selective actualizations of future possibilities. Actualized goods already exist that give the past and environing world its goodness-laden structures, and these goods are constantly shifting in their relations, and hence are goods among themselves, as we advance with actualizations of future possibilities. Some harmonies with which we relate are future possibilities, and those possibilities shift as they come closer to their moments of decision and actualization. We also relate to many harmonies as our contemporaries in the moving fields of actualization. We do not really have to worry about engaging the entire world all at once, but rather only those things that come up relevantly within the spheres of our lives.

In this volume, I have talked frequently about how the existential field is divided into "situations" in which we engage particular things through relevant causal and other factors. The perspective of the person interpreting or engaging something defines a situation, and some situations have multiple perspectives involved. In this sense, the world relevant to a person's experience consists of all the situations in which the person is involved.

However, the world, as it is relevant to living rightly with regard to it, is defined by its own contours, not merely as a function of a person's situations defined by their perspectives. Those contours are relevant to human life, but they are not much determined by the perspectives of particular human intentions. The contours have their own harmonies that provide causal backgrounds and foregrounds for engagement. The contours making up human health, for instance, include subcontours of hygiene and nutrition. The contours of hygiene have to do with externally cleaning the body and internally cleaning the teeth and, especially for some cultures, cleaning out the digestive tract. Certain aspects of the contours of cleaning the body have been known for a long time, for instance, those that involve visible grime and those that involve objectionable body odor (although what is objectionable is itself somewhat variable according to cultures). Now we know about microbes relative to the hygienic contours and the importance of cleaning up some microbes that pass on disease, foster skin lesions, and so forth. Even now, of course, we do not understand the full scope of the contours of human hygiene and doubtless are missing a lot. Moreover, the ways we now engage those contours are subject to correction and improvement—better soaps, more effective antibiotics, elimination of harmful hygienic practices, and discovery of new aspects of the contours of hygiene. Part of a right engagement of the contours of hygiene is interest in improving our knowledge and technologies of engaging cleanliness. However, parts that are even more important have to do with taking care to address hygienic issues steadily and responsibly according to the best knowledge we have. For individuals, this means, among other things, finding out what the best practices are. Engaging the contours of hygiene is only one of the many areas of engagement, and in many circumstances it is not the most important. A person or family under conditions of starvation often would have to sacrifice engagement with hygienic contours to engage the contours of nutrition. The point here is that the structure of the contours to be engaged is in the nature of things, not much with the constructions of human intentionality as subjective projection. Subjective projection of appreciation of sunsets can set up the objective, environmentally structured situations of sunset watching; there are strict causal conditions in such a situation that are determinate parts of the harmony of appreciation of a beautiful sunset. But the real natural structures of the main contours of human life are far more determinative of what people need to conform to in order to be right with the world.

The contours relevant to human life are, to be sure, mixtures of natural nonhuman conditions and human structures. Human knowledge affects the structures of hygiene contours and what people prize in different kinds of cleanliness. Economic systems and cultural and personal food preferences partially determine the structures of nutrition contours. The personal, social, and natural elements in the contours of life are mixed and yet really determinate (or partially indeterminate and ready for determining) such that to engage them requires engaging what they really are, insofar as that can be known.

Some phenomenologists are fond of thinking about experience in terms of what they call a "lifeworld," by which they mean the world as registering in human consciousness, subconsciousness, and perhaps other structures of subjectivity. My point here is that the real world is what the contours of life are irrespective of whether they are re-represented in consciousness in ways phenomenologists might call a lifeworld. In fact, engagement includes the obligation to conform the experiential or representational lifeworld to the real lifeworld. Our intentions and interpretive habits direct our engagements and therefore need semiotic representations of the real contours of life. Hopefully, our representations of the world are so geared to engagement that there are many pragmatic tests that provide feedback and correct our subjective representations of lifeworlds.

Having discussed some aspects of what contours are and what they are not, I now want to ask: What are the main contours with respect to which we should be engaged? No a priori philosophical answers to this exist save that the contours structure the conditions for human life. Bottom line biology sets contours for human life, and these include nutrition, safety from the elements including clothing and housing, and social organizations that allow for and foster repro-duction. We can imagine primitive jungle and savanna circumstances for these biological contours, but we can also imagine what these contours might be for astronauts within a long-term space station, and those contours would be quite different. I am not privy to the sex life of astronauts on station, but if they were to live in an artificial space station on Mars for generations, they would have to create and engage reproductive contours. Civilized societies develop cooperative arrangements for food, safety, and reproduction, and hence there are complicated, deeply layered, and ritually structured contours of social life and politics. Furthermore, the biological leisure afforded by coop-erative social life in turn affords contours of enjoyment and artistic life, both creativity and appreciation. The enormously complex, deep, and contrastive goods borne by the harmonies of high civilization with their diverse pockets of intensity or density of being all have contours to be engaged. These contours differ radically from time to time, place to place, culture to culture, and community to community.

What those contours are needs to be determined by the individ-uals who engage them. People's native cultural habits provide the pri-mary forms of instruction, and there is a self-reflexive need to engage the contours of education that teach how to engage. In the long run, relative to the contours for sustaining and fostering the fulfillments of human life in high civilization, the contours of education, contours of education upon contours of education, are among the most important contours to engage. Here lies one of the most important justifications of "liberal education": to teach and learn how better to engage the important contours of life.

The contours I have discussed so far have been those that are generally steady for human flourishing, those of biology, social organization, and the arts that are enjoyed for their own sakes. Contours of crisis and change also exist, with which engagement is obligatory. The weather changes and so food production must adapt. Barbarians come over the hill and threaten social organizations. Tsunamis flood the coast. War destroys institutions. These are the affairs of our watch, and things such as this occur on every watch. They are contours of life that call for engagement. Organized societies develop institutions for engaging crises and change. Nevertheless, these institutions themselves are vulnerable to crisis and change. All of these things are needful of engagement. We fail our obligation to engage them when we do not.

Of course, it is not only possible but common for us to fail to engage these contours of human life. Few of you reading this book fail to engage the contours of your hygiene and nutrition, at least most of the time. Most of you, however, know people too depressed, disabled, or senile to engage them, people who need external prodding to bathe and eat. People refuse to pay attention to their domestic contours and fail to be responsible in their family. People neglect their community's institutions such as schools and hospitals. People live in denial about their political situation and basic social conditions. People live in beautiful towns and never look around them. People live near museums and never enter them, near concert halls and never attend. People could have a social life full of enjoyment and do not put out the energy to engage it. People could have friends and lovers but retreat from social contact to extraordinary degrees. People who fail to engage in some or all of these ways are not just *them*: they are *us* sometimes. All of us, most likely, are uneven in our engagements with the world and sometimes seriously fail. Under stress, we sometimes prioritize things in order to finesse certain contours—when starving, cleanliness, is not a priority for life.

Being right with life and the world is an obligation stemming from a two-termed relation between the world in which we live and our engagement of it. We are obliged to engage the contours of our world and, to the extent we do not, we fail that obligation. A special goodness exists in fulfilling that obligation, and we miss an important possible human goodness when we do not. The extent to which we engage the contours of our lives determines part of the goodness of our personal identity, to which the discussion now turns.

Engagement as Self-Constitution

Two terms are important in the relation of being rightly engaged with the contours of the world. One is the contours of the world. Being right with the world means engaging it as it is, to the extent that we can know and appreciate that. The other term is we ourselves who engage. We are obliged to engage well, even if we do not fulfill that obligation. Part of that obliged engagement is creating ourselves to be good at the engagements of our watch. Self-creation as engagers consists of at least three connected tasks. One is educating ourselves about just what the contours of the world are, the point at which we left the previous section. The second is developing the normative judgments necessary to make appropriate responses to the world's contours. The third is to cultivate ourselves to have the creativity to engage effectively. Although by no means the whole of what it means to be good people, these tasks are extremely important aspects of the achievement of human goodness.

Regarding education, learning about the structures of the world's contours is vastly important, as argued earlier. This means a great many different things, however, in different contexts. Surely for our time it means an obligation in a society to carry on scientific investigation with a heavy investment of social resources. We should undertake scientific investigation of all aspects of the world's contours with good institutional judgment about what to study next. Although only a few people would themselves be scientists, part of the obligation to education in being right with the world is that individuals should educate themselves in relevant sciences and use that knowledge to form their judgments. The negative side of this is that people who reject scientific findings and the importance of scientific inquiry because of political, psychological, religious, or other biases are failing the obligation to engage the world responsibly. Contemporaries who deny climate change because they benefit financially from fossil fuel industries are guilty of bad engagement of the world. People who deny biological, including human, evolution are guilty of the same thing; they are in denial of what the world really is. To be sure, science is fallible and what it pronounces true today proves false tomorrow in many instances. Yet, as Peirce argued so well, scientific inquiry is the most efficient way of finding correctives to false beliefs.

Education in critical thinking, however, is very important in addition to scientific understanding. Science by nature is reductive, and criticism is necessary to understand both what it leaves out of account in the reductions and what that exclusion means for biasing our understanding of the real world engaged. Whitehead called philosophy, in one of its functions, the "critic of abstractions."[5] Most other areas of modern or late modern life have elements of criticism. We have the social sciences and also social critics, political sciences and also political critics, anthropological sciences and cultural critics. The arts are all expressions of beauty and in some ways and degrees are enjoyable as such, as I argued in part II. We also have critics in all the arts to say just how a work of art is beautiful, what is obscured, how the effects are obtained, and how art objects stand with regard to the depth and contrasts of reality they exhibit. Cumulatively, the various skills and arts of criticism constitute a side of wisdom, a knowledge of what goods are constituted, excluded, lifted up, and obscured by the scientific and artistic endeavors to grapple with the nature of the world. The nature of the sciences and the critical disciplines has had many forms and still does; they are in constant change. In our late modern context, they are evolving and shifting boundaries in exciting ways.

Another side of wisdom is vision, a way of seeing the whole of some contours of life. This is also associated with philosophy in its system-building modes. Philosophical systems are intellectually constructed conceptual platforms from which a vision of the whole is possible. A good system is one that leaves out nothing that occurs in experience. Anything must be understandable as an instance of something in the vision. This is particularly important relative to the sciences because of their reductive nature. Systematic philosophy cannot be reductive at all—everything must fit in, and the discovery of some aspect of the world that does not fit into a vision is good reason to change the vision. In addition to fitting everything in, a vision has to make everything coherent, which means developing a harmony to the vision that has goodness. A given set of components can be put together in different ways, and some ways are better than others. The better philosophers are those with the better harmonies of the things within their vision. Not everyone in a society is a philosopher, of course. However, everyone needs both critical and visionary philosophy in his or her repertoire of responses. In the past, religions have provided various kinds of critical and visionary orientation to the world, but religions seem less effective these days in much public learning. Society needs to sponsor the critical arts and philosophy in these senses and build them into the culture so that they give orientation to everyone regarding what is real, especially relative to favored ways of describing the world. For a society to be heavy on scientific representation of what is what and light on criticism and vision is to shackle and misdirect the possibilities of genuine engagement of the world among its individuals.

The move from the obligation to know to the obligation to make good judgments about what is appropriate in response to the world is an extension of education. It involves character development as well as knowledge in the senses mentioned. In Plato's ideal curriculum outlined in the *Republic* (books 5–7), following the studies of the arts and sciences, especially mathematics and military strategy, the students are sent to the colonies where they can practice developing good judgment without endangering Athens with their immature mistakes. The formulation of policies on a grand scale goes beyond merely understanding the situation. It requires understanding what the long-range goals ought to be and how to get there from the situation at hand. In Plato's vision, this was supposed to be political guidance for the whole city-state.

In the contours of hygiene, judgment for responding to current practices requires normative judgment of what is most appropriate. The goals of nutrition are not as obvious as they seem, since there are competing notions of health, and of how health relates to the contours of individual freedom where people might be free to eat unhealthy things, for instance. To be able to engage the world appropriately requires serious development of capacities for judgment of what goods are at stake, how these goods relate to what the world is, and what the various goods are along relevant contours. Many people forsake the obligation to develop good policies for life and hence fall back on inherited policies. In many ways, this is sufficient in a flourishing society where at least somebody in authority is taking that kind of responsibility seriously. Nevertheless, even in the best of societies, an obligation exists to commit oneself to the goods that determine appropriate engagements in the important contours of life. This is part of the overall obligation to be right with the world.

Building upon both education and the need for good judgment regarding what is appropriate for engaging life is the need for the character of good *agency* in engagement. This means, on the one hand, that we have obligations to organize our personal selves to be good at engagement, free from denial, as free as possible from ignorance, and free from misleading, false, or inadequate goals. On the other hand, it means also developing the skills to engage effectively, which usually means learning to act in concert with others to engage the issues on our watch. At the root of engaging the world with others is skill and finesse at the playing of social rituals. To engage the world usually entails engaging it with others, with their education, their judgments of appropriateness, and their characters. What a pity it is that so many people who fail to engage life effectively and thoroughly do so because they cannot live conjointly with others! Most often, this is a failure to play well in the rituals in which so much of social life consists. To be able to engage the world well, to be right with it, requires achieving a deep and contrastive structure of the self as agent.

I have argued here that being right with the contours of the world requires developing the character to engage them so as to be relevantly knowledgeable and wise, ready with good judgment, and skillful at the agency of engagement.

Engagement as Finite Limitation

Søren Kierkegaard is the most famous philosopher to make a point we all understand implicitly, namely, that freedom of choice involves having options among which to choose.[6] If we choose one, however, those other options disappear and we are committed to the choice we have made, which is to say we have lost our freedom to choose otherwise. Of course, we can be vacillating choosers, never really making a choice. This is the predicament Kierkegaard thought many of us are in: unfree because we are incapable of making a real choice and following through, no matter how many options are open to us.

Engaging the world requires making choices and acting upon them. Indeed, choosing is not a merely internal mental event to be distinguished from action—choosing is the beginning of action; continuous action in the world is the living out of choosing. In continuous action, we sometimes are tempted to abandon the choice, to temporize. Sometimes, especially in complex conjoint actions with others, there is a constant process of reconsideration. As conditions change and new matters arise, new tacks are needed to keep the long-range intended action on track. Aristotle's admirals start the action rolling when they decide to do battle on the morrow, but how they do battle is a matter of constant tactical redeployment of forces. This is not so much a shift from the original decision but a management of the temporal complexity of choosing in the first place as the action plays out. It is also possible to undermine an original choice by tactics that really serve a different choice and its strategy. Admirals do not win many battles by vacillating on whether to do battle.

To choose does two things. First, it causes what we choose to happen, insofar as that depends upon our choice; this is a matter of structuring the actual world. Second, it gives us the character of being the choosers of what we choose, with the elements of goodness-identity tied to the merits of our choice. We can avoid giving ourselves such a character by refusing to engage. I have mentioned earlier some common reasons for such refusal. Perhaps even more common than those is the hope that we can maintain our freedom by not choosing, therefore always retaining the character of not having chosen this or not having chosen that but always being able to choose anything. To retain this character, which Kierkegaard called "fastidiousness after the finite," is to choose a character that can never be free. Such a character can never make a choice.

What Kierkegaard says about individual choices holds as well for the multitude of choices required for engaging the world in its relevant contours. To engage life in the ways described in this chapter and in many other ways is to give ourselves serious finite identities. Although we are always individuals interdefined in social and natural ways, we individuate ourselves by how we engage. This is an important sense of creativity, self-creativity, in our works of engagement. To the extent that we do not engage, we are constituted mainly by the influences upon us and the ways by which we manage to put these together. To the extent that we do engage, we take responsibility for how we relate to those influences and constitute ourselves as responsible in those ways.

As I have said, many contours of life exist, and they differ some-what among us. No one paradigm of self-creativity exists. Moreover, most of us are engaged in some, not in others; engaged with depth and intensity, engaged barely; engaged now but not in the future. Life is in constant change, and so is the texture of our engagements. For many of us, life has a number of existential crises where we choose to engage better, or to withdraw, sometimes doing one, other times the other; often we vacillate. Nevertheless, over time we develop habits of engagement or disengagement. Some of us deeply engage life most of the time, like Zorba the Greek. Others engage less. A great many of us (not those reading this book, of course, but others) are so beaten down by life that survival trumps engagement in nearly all respects, and many even give up on survival. Bob Dylan has sung about many of these people. But he has also sung about those who engage despite being beaten down.[7]

The goodness of being right characterizes the relations between us as human beings and the world in which we live. Without "being right with the world" in any significant sense, we are of course con-ditioned by it, both individually and as we live together. Nevertheless, over and above those kinds of conditionings we can engage the world with our own creativity, achieving something of the goodness of being right with the world, conforming to its contours and acting with a sense of appropriateness to those contours. To be sure, we might be mistaken about the real nature of the contours, as when we do not know that our health is affected in part by microbes we cannot see. We might be unwise with regard to the goods and goals we choose in trying to make appropriate responses. But to engage with reasonable conformation to what is what and with some wisdom about what is appropriate to do about this is still possible. To engage in that way in an instance is to actualize ourselves as choosers. To do so over time, and over many contours, through a lifetime, is to achieve a beautiful human goodness of being right with life.

The goodness of being right with life in this sense, a goodness in a significant two-term relation, is an aesthetic one. This is so because it is a harmony with aesthetic coherence, of the sort analyzed in respect to form in part I of this volume. Many relations exist between us as individuals and the world in which we live; but this one, based on engagement, is a special kind of goodness. To say that a person who achieves a life of habitual engagement is beautiful makes great sense. Some of this beauty is in being moral, which is a goodness of its own. Nevertheless, the beauty of being right with the world is more than morality.

Because the goodness of being right with the world is an achievement that is good for its own sake, it is a kind of work of art. People can be nudged toward this kind of engagement, but even the most favored, the most cultivated, the most educated, can fail to engage. Each of us must achieve this for ourselves, in concert with others but in ways that define our own identity. A life of being right with the world is a part of life that is achieved by art. It is beautiful in itself, however much it has goods and harms in relation to many other things. Furthermore, being right with the world is enjoyable in itself for its own sake. Walking on stilts is a minor art of living. Being right with the world is major.

CHAPTER 12

Goodness in Being Virtuous

Conformation to the Ultimate Content of Life

Whereas the goodness in being right is a function of our relation to the world in its contours most relevant to human life, the goodness in being virtuous is a function of our relation to life itself in its deepest meaning. This relation includes and goes beyond being true, moral, and right. Human virtue, as I use the term, is a two-term relation between us and the life we live. Virtue's goodness consists in the kinds of harmony involved in that relation. This complex thesis, though subtle, is difficult to explicate because the metaphors through which we approach it are slippery. In addition, in the Western tradition we associate "virtue" with Aristotle's philosophy, according to which virtue is a property of persons, a point I greatly complicate. On my hypothesis, by contrast with Aristotle's, virtue is a property of a relation between persons and life in its deepest meaning for them, the Mandate of Heaven for them, as Confucians would put it.

What is the content of "life" in a thesis such as this? What does it mean for us to be alive in the cosmos? Saying what is alive versus inanimate is hard enough in science these days. However, the thesis here is about the other end of the spectrum of life, not how it emerges from nonliving or prelife forms but rather about the fullness possible to human life, its most expansive achievements, how it functions as the most intense achievement of virtue within the cosmos given the conditions for human life. My hypothesis is that the content of life is the harmonization of five projects of obligation stemming from the ultimate conditions for human life. After rehearsing these five projects, I shall describe briefly the rule that generates them from metaphysical or cosmological considerations. The goodness in being virtuous is a matter of religion.

The goodness of "being virtuous," as I develop that term of art here, is the goodness in harmonizing five projects relative to the ultimate conditions of human life: righteousness in choice, integration of the components of the self, loving engagement of others, achievement of a goodness–identity, and consent to the radically contingent givenness of life.[1] Obligations to truth, to moral decision making, and to being right in relation to the basic contours of life are involved in these projects and in the virtuous harmonization of them.

Reflected upon from many angles in this volume, an ultimate condition of our lives is the common necessity to choose among alternative possibilities, each of which has the goodness resident in its form. This is the human perspective on the ultimate cosmological condition that any determinate thing has form, which we face in choosing among the forms of possibilities. To be sure, we need to interpret the real goods of our possibilities, and this interpretation depends on our semiotic systems and our imaginative development of them: we only interpret the possibilities in certain respects. Furthermore, most of our choices and actions are conjoint with others in certain respects. Nevertheless, part of being human, an ultimate part behind which we cannot go, is the responsibility to choose well. I have discussed this as the obligation to be moral and emphasized its role in personhood.

Every developed religious tradition has complex problematics of righteousness. Codes and learned habits exist of applying certain signs and symbols to elucidate what is at stake in the possibilities. We have developed disciplines of choosing and acting effectively by ourselves and with others. We have assessed failures of all sorts, from moral failures to just plain mistakes in judgment and commitment. All religions have problematics for dealing with failure, including rubrics for punishment and mercy as would make sense in the general mythology of the tradition, programs of reeducation, and rituals for excluding and then perhaps reincluding miscreants within the community. Vast cultural differences exist among how religions have developed the problematics of righteousness.[2] Nevertheless, because the ultimate condition of having to make choices is as unavoidable as having to have cultural responses to weather, every religious tradition has to develop something.

In this volume, I have raised many situations for choice, including choosing about beauty, truth, morality, and existential engagement. These are among the huge overarching kinds of choices. Quotidian life is filled with countless numbers of other choices, such as what to wear today, which way to walk, when to rise and sleep, and how to greet neighbors. Choices fill daily life, many of which occur almost automatically out of habit, but that could be otherwise and therefore we are somewhat responsible for such habit-guided choices. Part of being virtuous is how we address this general obligation to choose well and what to do about it when we do not.

Regarding the self, every person has components that function in a superabundance of harmonies on many levels. As understood by biology, the human body is not just a product of DNA and circumstances but organizes itself with extraordinary complexity, especially in the neural system. We need to relate to the bodies we inherit and develop them through the accidents of life. We also have social contexts such as family, neighborhood, economic systems, and educational institutions and opportunities to which each of us needs to relate in harmonizing ourselves. We have our specific neighbors, friends, enemies, and accidental human interactions to deal with. Perhaps most important, we have the causes of suffering to deal with, genetic and acquired diseases, traumas physical and emotional, disasters of nature and of human wars and depredations. How are all these to be integrated into a harmonious self?

Different religions have quite different models of the self that makes for wholeness. The Western religious traditions give high place to the integrity required of an agent or actor in history. The South Asian traditions give high place to negating agency and letting the self just be, finding release into a greater reality for many forms of Hinduism and giving up on any own-being of an underlying substantial self for many forms of Buddhism. East Asian religious traditions regard the self as extremely intimate with the rest of reality, harmonizing with the Dao for better or worse in Confucian and Daoist senses.

These summary generalizations barely suggest the many varia-tions and cases that fall outside what I have listed. Nevertheless, every religious tradition has some ways of coping with the fact that human wholeness does not happen automatically and is an ultimate condition for every person, within or without a deep cultured tradition. Most traditions have multiple competing responses. Within the Chinese tradi-tion the Daoists have often counseled to conform to the inertial forces of the Dao, registered in yin and yang changes; Confucians have often said to fight back to defend the human sphere, building granaries in anticipation of bad harvests and dikes in anticipation of flooding. Just as any determinate thing has to integrate its components, so human beings need to integrate themselves, not just finding some way of fit-ting the components together but doing so in ways that recognize the components' own goods. Finding wholeness is an ultimate problematic of human life. Being virtuous is a function, in part, of how well we address this problematic. What we do with regard to wholeness is somewhat, though not completely, a matter of what we choose about wholeness and its constituents. However, it does not reduce to the problem of righteousness. The kind of self we have affects how we make choices, but it does not determine those choices completely. The problematics of righteous choice and integration to wholeness require harmonization in a good life.

Engagement with others recognizes that the other things in our world have natures and careers of their own, and we should not con-sider them to be merely functions of our own interests or those of our group. Therefore, we need to relate to them not only in relation to what they mean to us but also in terms of appreciating and respect-ing their own nature and goods. The justification for considering this an ultimate condition for human life is the metaphysical point that all determinate things, we human beings in this case, are determinate with respect to other things that are partly external to us. In our own harmonic constitutions, we compose our own natures by giving our conditioning components functions as narrow, wide, vague, and trivial. Our own harmonies require some such kind of composition. Yet the things that function as our components have their own harmonic natures with their own goods. Therefore, in addition to considerations of the functions of those things in our own harmonies, our own harmonies, in order to be good, ought to be composed so as to respect those other things. The things we trivialize or vaguely transmute should not be harmed by that. Living in the Boston area, I relate specifically to many people here, but the vast majority of residents of the area I treat vaguely as "Boston area residents." In most of my life, I pay little or no attention to them at all, trivializing them. Nevertheless, part of being good is that my citizenship should be respectful of them, and where needed I should respond to their needs. I completely trivialize the inhabitants of planets other than Earth, if there are such, and this is just fine. However, I should not support dumping waste into outer space that might pollute their territories. A general way of stating this aspect of being good is that we should behave in ways that are respectful of all the things in creation, in all the world, the Ten Thousand Things. This does not mean that we should always support them—some things we should destroy. Nevertheless, our comportment toward such "others" should always be respectful and appreciative, even if what we appreciate is a threat to our civilization that we should try to thwart.

In our time, two main projects of proper engagement of others have become prominent. One is the engagement of other people, especially people not in our ingroups. This has been an ideal since the beginnings of the Axial Age, and current events have shown that recent political turns inward have exacerbated the issues with such engagement. From the Axial Age onward, however, most major religious traditions and civilizations have had something like the Golden Rule and the imperative of compassion, love, and justice toward all human beings, not only our ingroup comrades.

The other project is recognition of the integrity of the environment. This became prominent in the dominant cultures of the world when it became apparent that human practices were fouling the human habitat. Now we have come to see that nature is such an interwoven ecology of ecologies that we need to respect and honor just about everything on its own terms at once. These are complicated issues, often pitting human development against protection of the environment. Nevertheless, part of what it means to be "virtuous" is to live in such a way as to be respectful of the environment. The word "compassion" nicely addresses both proper engagement of other people and the proper engagement of nature and social institutions because it suggests assuming their place somehow, seeing the world from their perspective, taking up how they should achieve their virtue from the standpoint of their own-being, insofar as we can symbolize and empathize with that.

The next ultimate condition of human life, addressing which is part of what it means to be "virtuous" in the expansive way under discussion here, is the need to address the meaning of human life, both personally and within the cosmos. What is the goodness of an individual's life? What is the goodness of human life as such? Does the cosmos itself have goodness and what is the place of human life in this? Many formulations of this question come from the world religions and from secular philosophic reflection. Some religions formulate this question in terms of the goodness of personal life as matters of salvation or damnation, others as matters of ultimate liberation or enlightenment. Other sections of this chapter will elaborate this ultimate condition of human life and how addressing it is part of "being good."

The final ultimate condition of human life is that we exist at all. All the major religions have expressed wonder at this and have many ways of approaching and accounting for it. I have defended the view that the existence of determinate things is the product of an "ontological creative act," but this is not a ringing phrase. As I mentioned before, there are three main families of symbolic systems to express this. The theistic one elaborates the model of the person as agent or creator, with all the variants within the theistic traditions. Most of the responses advocated by the personification model are matters of worship and gratitude. The second family of metaphors focuses on consciousness, stripping the notion of person of the very elements of agency and will promoted by theism. The determinate world is contingent on things arising from some proto-conscious base, for instance, Brahman or the Buddha-mind, something like consciousness that is either super real or super empty. The third family of metaphors has to do with spontaneous emergence, as in the Dao that cannot be named or the nonbeing that gives rise to the Great Ultimate, and so forth. Perhaps we can call this dimension of ultimacy on the human part "ontological faith," although the "faith" language is not universal.[3]

The Harmony of Virtue

"Being Virtuous" in the sense I intend is a complicated two-term relation between us and the normativity of us being in the world. "Being right" is the two-term relation between us and the relevant contours of the world we live in. Being virtuous includes this but also goes beyond to include our own normative identity within the world to which we relate. In this point, I am trying to articulate a widely felt sense of obligation to be not only true, moral, and right in engaging the world but to be as virtuous as we can. This is a conformation of ourselves to the most comprehensive ideal for ourselves given our unfolding place in the world. The next section will discuss the significance of this identity. The topic of this section is the integration of dimensions of ultimacy and the goods involved particular to this integration.

How we relate to the ideal of virtue for ourselves is a complex harmony that is especially significant for the overall harmony we achieve in our value-identity. Like any harmony, it has many determinate components, and here I want to focus on the five dimensions of ultimacy sketched previously. The question is how we harmonize, for better or worse, the ultimate obligations of choice, wholeness, compassionate engagement, meaning, and deference or consent to the contingency of existence. In any person's life, a de facto harmony exists that integrates these ultimate dimensions of life. Sadly, these dimensions can be neglected and addressed so poorly that the harmony of them is rather poor; although everyone has a degree and kind of virtue, most people's virtue is not of a high quality, that is, a harmony that has value on its own.

Living under the obligation to choose well obviously underlies all the other obligations. What we do about our own wholeness, our relations with others, our struggles with meaning, and consent to (or dissent from) the contingency of existence involves choices and in all instances we should choose well. The problematic of righteousness, however, focuses on choices relative to the field of future possibilities, given our actual situation, and in concert with other people and forces making selective actualizations. In a given situation, say, Aristotle's admirals contemplating a sea battle on the morrow, the field of possibilities embraces goods that affect a great many things, including the possibility of victory. They need to decide what to do by assessing their enemy's strength and tactical deployment, their own resources, weather, and such like. Nevertheless, with regard to their own wholeness, each admiral needs to take into account issues of personal safety as well as honor. With regard to respectful engagement and compassion with others, each needs to assess obligations to the groups whose navy they are and how to be respectful of enemies; what is the cost in environmental resources of going into battle? With respect to meaning, is victory or flight part of a meaningful history, or do human affairs ultimately come down to what the Greeks interpreted as the whims of the gods and what we might call dumb fate? How is the commitment to fight or not related to the consent the admirals give to their contingent existence? The harmony of the choices made includes all these components in functions that might be narrow, wide, vague, or trivial. I would imagine Greek admirals giving fairly high importance to considerations of their own honor and of their responsibilities to their city-state, with less importance to their personal safety, even less to respecting their foes (usually barbarian Persians or Sicilians), and hardly any to how the forests might be depleted by the loss of many ships. On the other hand, if the example were the Roman emperor Marcus Aurelius contemplating battle against the barbarians, I would imagine that questions of how the possible future deals with the meaning of life and the contingency of existence would be quite important for him. He would have deep respect for soldiers on all sides and likely would dismiss his personal honor and safety as childish concerns.

Although concerns for wholeness of the self appear in many choices we make moment by moment, they have a problematic harmony of their own. Our lives have many components, frequently difficult to harmonize. A congenitally sick person is likely not to be a great athlete, although there are remarkable exceptions. If we are raised in squalor with no one to care much about us; if we have no formal education or, worse, miseducation; if we are among minority groups oppressed in the larger society; if our time is one of upheaval and chaos—we have many strikes against us. Perhaps we deserve pity and no one should expect us to be "virtuous" people. Many of us are inclined to excuse people in these sad conditions and not expect them to fulfill serious obligations—to truth, morality, rightness of engagement, or virtue. (Of course important questions exist about who is to judge in these matters.) Yet sometimes extraordinarily virtuous people arise out of such conditions. That this is possible is part of human dignity.

The quality of our success in developing integrated whole selves, whatever that turns out to be as articulated in one culture or another, is very important for how we deal with the other obligations. Part of our self is our education, and we are under obligation to be educated well for the decisions we make. Part of us is our acquired abilities to act well in various circumstances. If we are psychologically immature or pathological, it affects our abilities to choose well in situations of choice, and to relate to other people. If we are suffering, that can inhibit our choices, our relations with others, and our sense of the meaning of life and the goodness of existence. So part of the obligation to wholeness is to come to terms with suffering, a point that dominates Buddhist thinking. To deal with the multitude of obligations and opportunities of life is difficult with a poorly developed self, one without wholeness and balance.

How well we engage others with compassion, both other people and various aspects of the environment with which we can interact directly or indirectly, is a matter of obligation in itself. It also affects the choices that are open to us. To choose benevolently is hard when we roil with hate for things. To make choices that favor the environment over self-interest, which sometimes we should do, is hard if we have little or broken respect for nature. The problematic of engaging others according to their deserts is a polar struggle between selfishness and compassion for others: our personal interests versus the interests of others that claim our attention, our ingroup's interests versus the outgroup's interests, human society versus the natural environment. Erring on the side of selfishness can lead to bad choices, a malformed self, a perverted sense of life's meaning, and an incapacity to consent to contingent existence as such.

How we find meaning in life is also a matter of obligation in itself. How well we attend to this problematic affects our obligations to good choices, to cultivating a whole self, and to relating well to others. The problematic of finding meaning in life is a polar struggle between despair and hope for engaging life with meaning. If there are no frameworks for articulating the meaning of life, our engagements with others, pursuit of self-cultivation, and practice of choosing well become unmoored and drift. It is so easy to give up on life and thus give up on addressing the obligations in the ultimate conditions of life. Most of us despair sometimes, but our cultures provide all sorts of symbols of meaningfulness. Our existential lives cope with issues of despair and hope. To the extent that we cope well and live lives of hope and faith so that what we do and become counts for something, our attention to the other dimensions of ultimate obligation can flourish.

How we relate to the contingency of existence is our basic religious stance, affecting everything else we do. Do we live in basic affirmation, negation, or ignoration? Living in affirmation or gratitude for existence is a little like having hope. Many situations exist, however, in which we have no realistic hope and simply give up on life, or at least some part of life, as having meaning. Yet paradoxically we still can affirm our existence as hopeless. Sometimes we think we should engage the ground of existence—God, abysmal consciousness, spontaneously creative nothingness, as if it were an other; this is especially so when the ontological creative act is symbolized with personifications. Nevertheless, nothing is really there as an ontological other because all determinate things that might be other are themselves products of the ontological act. Acceptance of the contingency of existence is the condition for engaging with anything other. Acceptance of the contingency of existence is the condition for the project of cultivating the self. Acceptance of the contingency of existence is the condition for taking choice seriously. Negating the contingency of existence undermines all those other projects. Ignoring it, as most people do even when they engage in the activities of religion, makes people vulnerable to having all life's projects be nothing more than wind.

So, would it not be good if we could just always choose well, develop a healthy self, engage others with compassion, enjoy confidence in life's meaning, and worship the source of existence? Sadly, life does not work out that way. These dimensions of ultimate human obligation are complex in themselves and always involve compromises in coming to harmony. Taken together, they also involve compromises.

They are components of the harmony of being good that have to be composed in functions of narrowness, width, vagueness, and triviality. Sometimes choices to fulfill obligations to those who depend on us require belonging to supportive groups that are themselves bigoted with regard to others. Sometimes compassion for others requires downplaying the pursuit of our family's interests. Sometimes we ought to sacrifice our lives for some other good that seems greater. Sometimes we need to compromise the cultivation of our self, in its career and potentials, because of the needs of the situation. Sometimes our choices are simply mistaken and result in the ruination of everything. Sometimes the best that we can do is still bad. Sometimes we do the worst that we can do and have to live with that. Sometimes everything else has to live with the worst that we can do.

If the harmonies that would make up a virtuous life are rich enough in density of being, tragedy, failure, and harm exist under optimum circumstances when things go seriously wrong. Especially is this so when our choices are bad, we are not up to the task, our neighbors are simply unlovable, life has lost its meaning, and the ground of existence is a perfect storm. For everyone, this is somewhat true.

Therefore, the pattern of being virtuous, which integrates our lives regarding the five ultimate conditions of obligation, includes narrow contrastive elements that focus these tragedies, failures, and evils. A virtuous life can take these into harmony. The pattern of being virtuous can have elements of width that embrace the bad with the good. The pattern of being virtuous can rise vaguely above tragedies and guilt. The pattern of being virtuous can identify with things from the perspective of which those tragedies and guilts are trivial. To be virtuous does not mean to be successful. It means to make the best of all this. To be virtuous has among its narrow contrasts those that sharpen tragedy, failure, and evil.

Virtue-Identity

Being more or less virtuous is an important part of a person's identity. As I have tried to make evident throughout this volume, however, our identity is not a set of properties that characterizes us like the properties of a substance. As harmonies, we compose ourselves of many components that contain and relate to many other things. We are harmonies that foreground many things, giving them prominent functions of narrowness and width, and constitute ourselves against and within backgrounds of things vague and trivial. I do not "have" my identity and you yours, exactly. You are part of my identity (vaguely placed as a reader) and I am part of your identity as the author you are reading. The role of being good in our respective identities requires greater elaboration of the thesis that things are harmonies, that we are harmonies.

Earlier I argued that a person's identity has a subjective part and an objective part. The objective part is who the person is for other people, for the institutions of life, and for the many layers of nature the person influences. This follows the medieval usage of "objective" to mean an object for a knower, a usage carried on by Descartes and made hugely important by Kant. As a teacher, my objective identity includes what I have taught students and how I otherwise have influenced them. Strictly speaking, these aspects of my identity are components of the harmonies that the students make of themselves. My objective identity also includes my influences on family and friends; I have been active in shaping the institutions within which I have worked. In two or three generations, most of the specifics of my influences will be subordinated vaguely under subsequent personal and social structures. Students will forget where they learned my lessons, memories vaguely will replace direct influence and then themselves fade, and my environmental footprint will generalize into aggregate calories burned and chemicals returned to the soil.

The subjective side of identity is more clearly associated with what we think of as personal identity, that is, the ways the subharmonies through time and the overall dynamic harmony of our lives integrate our components. We are, after all, harmonies of our own, different from other people, from our institutions, and from vast elements of nature, even though we relate internally to those things. To say those things are internally related means that they function as components in our own harmonies, trivially, vaguely, narrowly, or widely. Yet those things have their own harmonies as well, not only functioning as components in us. We have our own essential components that integrate the things that condition us within our own harmonies. Those component harmonies have essential components of their own. The subjective side of our identity through time, or at any given time, is defined by how our own essential components determine the integration of all our components.

The easiest way to understand this regarding human life is to look to those essential components that constitute us as centers of intention, of action, will, thought, and the other faculties associated with subjectivity. In a general sense, these are the mental functions that Descartes contrasted with bodily functions, with mental and bodily functions ascribed to different kinds of substance. Kant made this far more specific when he defined transcendental subjectivity in terms of the activity of synthesizing components of experience according to the transcendental unity of apperception so that it is always "I" who synthesizes this with this, that with that. "Center of intention" is a vague term that encompasses centers of synthesizing in categoreal consistency in knowledge, in constituting the consistency of will so as to be free, and in constituting the consistency of something like aesthetic judgment, to use Kant's main topics. The idealist tradition stemming from Kant has elaborated the primacy of such centers of intention in defining subjectivity or the integrative element of human identity.

The American pragmatic approach has a more naturalistic bent. We human beings involve vastly dense layers of integration that only sometimes reaches the organization level of centers of intention. One strain of harmony that is essential to my identity is the influence of my DNA on my bodily functions, growth, and decay throughout my life. The DNA is unique to me and is essential to my identity but is far from itself being a center of intention, even though it enables me sometimes to exercise conscious and agential centers of intention (a tree's DNA does not enable the tree to have centers of intention like a human's). When I was an infant, the rituals of my family life, including learning how to move, sing, speak, and play, began as rather external conditions that were integrated with my DNA functions by low-level biological processes. Soon, however, they became essential components so that I related to a great many things in terms of those rituals, eventually taking charge of improving or at least changing some of them. Sometime in adolescence, I took responsibility, usually without realizing it, for how I behaved in response to the things in the environment and the accidents of life, at least in some aspects of life. At sixteen, I was responsible for driving a car well but not for voting well, which had to wait until I was twenty-one. By the end of adolescence, I, not my parents or schools, was responsible for how I was true, moral, right, and virtuous, though I was immature, inconsistent, and often bad at how I fulfilled those responsibilities. By that time, to some degree or another, my parents, schooling, and DNA had become objective in their identity within me and I took them in by essential components that made them part of my own subjectivity. Well, sometimes I did this and other times I lapsed into childishness. Sometimes I was aware and conscious of what was going on; at other times my attention wandered or went to sleep. Sometimes now in my old age I am a high-functioning center of intention and other times I lapse into uncentered intentions. Sometimes I let intentionality just go to sleep and what Aristotle would have called "vegetative" functions are about the highest kind of harmony I have. In my study is an easy chair that looks out onto our garden. Sometimes as I sit there, I read and think about super-intellectual, centered, philosophy. Sometimes I have moments of minor creativity. Other times I forget about that and just enjoy looking at the garden. Sometimes I dose off completely. In view is a garden statue of the Buddha and I can reflect on how he would say that centered, conscious intentionality is an illusion, which justifies letting it go in sleep. Sometimes in wandering reverie, I reflect on Rickard's rules for measuring age: in late middle age we count how many pages we read per nap, whereas in old age we count naps per page. My seriously centered intentionality is episodic and my identity wanders from sharp focus to the trivialization of anything like centeredness. All of this, however, is my identity, moment to moment, through durations, and cumulatively through life. As such, its integrating elements are essential components producing my subjective identity even when it is far from centered in the idealists' sense. Kant himself did not say that human beings are always functioning according to the centered integration of *transcendental* subjectivity, only that they achieve knowledge, morality, and judgment when they do so, however episodically.

How does being virtuous relate to identity? Surely, it is a function of our subjective identity because we exercise responsibility in attending to how we live in the overall life-project of doing justice in a more or less harmonious way to our choices, wholeness, engagement of others, acquisition of meaning, and responsiveness to the contingency of existence. The integration of these ultimate dimensions of life is rarely a matter of conscious intention for most people. Who would even have thought of them in the terms I have used to describe them here? Who would have thought much about the life-project of relating these things? For the most part, we are conscious only at certain times of the stresses of relating choice to the interests of the self, or of how difficult it is to have compassion for certain people because we have unhealed wounds because of them, or of other problems of harmonizing the agonizingly demanding narrow shock points of personal existence. Even though we do not often directly intend the project of "being virtuous," our habits and cumulative lesser projects constitute a kind of harmony that functions as an essential component in putting our lives together. How virtuous we are in this sense, and how we work at aspects of it, are essential components of how we put our subjective harmony together.

Would it not seem that what other people, institutions, and the natural environment do with the ways we influence them are *not* measures or components of *our* virtue? Precisely because this is a matter of their essential harmonizings, not ours, what they do with our influences is a function of their virtue (insofar as they are people), not ours. Nevertheless, do I not have a responsibility to make my lessons clear and relevant enough that my students do not misunderstand or misuse them? Do I not have a responsibility to make sure that, to the extent possible, my use of and influences upon the institutions of my society improve them? Do I not have a special responsibility to the environment to minimize my negative impact and maximize my contributions to its flourishing? Of course I do. These responsibilities are part of my direct engagements with these things. My life with its influences has the cumulative goodness, positive or negative, that comes from how I influence other things in their own, other, natures.

My identity as "being virtuous" presupposes all these ways of being true, moral, and right with the contours of life. Nevertheless, it is a project on top of all those to integrate them so that my life coheres to some extent in the ways its little elements relate to the ultimate conditions of life. My virtue as a person thus is a harmony laid on top of and integrating the various ways of being true, moral, and right. Relative to virtue, *how* virtuous I am is a complex matter of how well I integrate all these things.

The downside of this sense of identity, regarding how virtuous a person is, over and above being true, moral, and right, is that there are so many ways to fail. With all good intentions, a farmer might introduce crops that are supposed to improve the ecology of the fields but that turn out to be disastrous by inviting pests that ruin valuable plant life. Despite the good intentions, the farmer's identity includes the devastation of the pests. Despite my careful lessons, students might employ them to support bigotry. And then there are all the ways by which the hang-togetherness of my obligations to the harmony of the ultimate conditions are faulty, filled with missed opportunities, and committed to things that block important densities of being that otherwise would be possible.

The goodness of being virtuous, in the senses discussed here, is the goodness achieved in the harmony we make of integrating our lives as oriented to the five dimensions of human ultimacy. Just as each of us is true, but perhaps not very true or as true as we could and should be; moral, but not as moral as we should be; right in relation to the contours of life, but not all that right; so we are virtuous in harmonizing what is ultimate but often not very virtuous or as virtuous as we could and should be. These are all important elements in our personal identities.

Virtue and the World's Goodness

Virtue is a good that we as individuals have insofar as we relate with some patterned harmony to the ultimate conditions of human existence. How virtuous we are depends on the depths and contrasts of the ways by which we harmonize our various engagements with things insofar as they relate to choice, self, others, meaning, and existence. Most everything in life relates to all these ultimate conditions. Even if we are seriously deficient in harmonizing them, they fit together in some pattern or other. The pattern might be minimal connectedness, a complexity without simplicity, perhaps, or a simplicity without complexity that fails to register the differences among the ultimate conditions. Nevertheless, no matter how deficient we are in living in relation to the ultimate conditions, we have some virtue. Everyone is virtuous in some way. Some of us, however, are so bad at being virtuous that it makes sense to call those of us in that condition just plain "vicious." When we judge people in estimation of their character, we say that some are bad, some are virtuous in mediocre ways, some are very virtuous, and some few are superlatively good. Of course, many ways exist to achieve the harmony of virtue—this way, that way, and some other way. Often we cannot scale these as better and worse, just different. Yet what is fascinating about people is their virtue, in degree and kind. We think we understand and appreciate people when we understand the harmonies that relate them to the ultimate conditions of choice, self, otherness, meaning, and existence.

By analogy, we speak of a virtuous community or a community's degree and kind of virtue. We can do this because communities sometimes have cultures, or a spirit, that serves to foster the harmonious living with reference to the ultimates of human life. Such a culture nudges individuals within it to be virtuous according to the culture's models. Yet often individuals within a society reject or poorly absorb the cultural elements that would relate them to the ultimates in that culture's ways. Roughly speaking, however, we can say that a community has a level and kind of virtue because of (1) its institutions for educating choices; (2) its models and supports for self-development and wholeness, especially dealing with suffering; (3) its ritualized and promoted ways of relating to the environments of nature, institutional connections with other communities, and with individuals outside the community; (4) its literatures and other arts that articulate meaning; and (5) its religions. Every community needs some education and inquiry for choices, economy and domestic life for selfhood, politics for relating to others, intellectual life for meaning, and religious life to relate to existence, and all of these need some kind of mutual compatibility, preferably harmonies that build up harmonies upon harmonies. Many communities are rather bad in this regard. Yet high civilizations built up super harmonies to achieve goods far beyond what we have discussed so far. Part IV will take up this topic in detail.

The question inevitably arises, however, whether, beyond individual and social virtue, a goodness to the whole cosmos exists that is akin to virtue. Many people would like to think that the world as a whole is good. Theists sometimes want to consider the world as an artifact of God and to judge the quality of God by judging the quality of that artifact. However, the world of created things is not a whole. It does not have an overall determinate pattern within which all things harmonize as components; the created things only fit together de facto and not everything fits everything else. Rather, the very meaning of determinateness is that things are determinate with respect to other things that are somewhat external to them. To be determinate is to be determinately different from other things. Therefore, it is better to say, with the Chinese, that the world is the Ten Thousand Things. Various harmonies exist that relate to one another by their conditional components in an existential field. The only unity of the cosmos is that every determinate thing is created by the singular ontological act of creation that has no determinate nature of its own to unify what it creates. If it did have such a determinate nature, the act would have to be in a deeper ontological context of mutual relevance to relate it to the other determinate things it is supposed to harmonize. So there can be no harmony of the whole, no determinate one for the many, no beautiful cohesiveness of the cosmos, only pockets of order, partly connected densities of being.

What this means for our human identity is that no determinate perspective is possible from which the unity of our subjective and objective elements of identity can be registered. In fact, given the exteriority of things to which we are also internally related, there is no unity to our identity. One can see the panic behind the European philosophic tradition's insistence on the transcendental unity of apperception, the obsession with finding centeredness that would define personal identity. However, the metaphysical, aesthetic, and obligation-framed model of personal identity is that the self is not and cannot be fully unified. Our identity exists fully only in the ontological creative act, and there only as part of the entirety of creation. Religiously, this is not unusual. We have identity only in God, not in a comprehensive harmony that is our true self. We have the subjective unity of what we do harmonize as part of our identity, but this is not the whole of who we are; we are also our effects. The Buddhists would say that there is no ontological self at all, only the dharmas as they come and go. The Hindus would say that the belief in an underlying self needs to be relinquished so that the individual self dissolves in liberation. The Chinese would say that we should just attend to our duties as they arise on our watch and be prepared to honor ancestors no matter how good or bad they are. Perhaps we should look upon ourselves as future ancestors, to be accepted or forgotten in our various parts and influences.

Part IV

Goodness in Flourishing and Civilization

With part IV, we come to the goods found in social relations. As I shall review in chapter 13, the kinds of goodness mainly discussed in parts 1 and 2 are those found in harmonies themselves. The goodness discussed in part III is that found in relations between human beings and aspects of our environment in which we have obligations. Both of these suppose that there are goods achieved in social relations that connect us with the natural, social, and personal environments. These are the harmonies within which we can flourish as human beings.

Chapter 13 elaborates the differences among kinds of goodness that Peirce would classify as Firsts, Seconds, and Thirds. It goes on to sort some of the confusions about how we speak of human flourishing. Social relations bear cultural relations but do not reduce to them. Cultural relations bear the kinds of harmonies that have civilizational goodness but do not reduce to them. The historical evolution of society, and of human relations with nature, makes the employment of categories like these confusing; in some respects, the best we can do is point out the confusions. Would we not say that Imhotep's Egypt was a high civilization? Would we not also say that the level of flourishing for nearly everyone in his civilization would be uncivilized today? Human flourishing is almost more complicated than one can imagine.

Chapter 14 begins the first of two lines of thought as to what makes us flourish, namely, the achievement of ritual. I present a Confucian theory of ritual and show it to underlie much of what we mean by human flourishing. Ritual is a crucial component of culture, stability, and the foundation for creativity. Nevertheless, so often rituals define social relations such that some people flourish more than others, indeed at the expense of other people's flourishing. We need to conceive rituals therefore as bearing moral weight that should be subject to constant evaluation and criticism. In this light, we need to think of rituals as constantly dynamic, always changing and often for better or worse. Given the problems of conflict in global society, the goodness of conflict-resolving rituals is greatly to be prized and is obligatory for political institutions.

The second line of thought about what makes civilized life flourish is about creativity. Chapter 15 begins with a thematic reflection on initiative. Even just the faithful playing of rituals requires initiative. In a civilization, however, initiative is not just getting started and doing things. It is the making of a person's life. In civilizations, especially high civilizations, a crucial good of civilized harmonies is that individuals are encouraged and supported in taking the initiative to shape their own lives. Because there are so many ways to shape a life, and so many different models of worthy lives to emulate and fashion to our idiosyncrasies, the good of shaping one's life is extremely vague. That vagueness is part of its goodness: each life made is unique. Beyond the value in a civilization of shaping one's own life is the goodness of creating beauty for its own sake and for all to enjoy. In a civilization, we prize beauty of all sorts, from decoration to the creation of great works of art. Civilized people are aesthetes in the noblest possible sense of this word, although different civilizations have different sensibilities regarding what beauties to appreciate and encourage for artistic celebration. Beyond the civilized social structures that celebrate beauty are those that celebrate creative initiative as such, which I call a spirit of creativity. Whitehead was getting at this with his notion of zest in a civilization.[1]

Chapter 16 returns to the notion of civilization, distinguishing descriptive and normative aspects of the theory of civilization developing here. The relation of civilization to culture provides one of the crucial issues when it comes to the dynamic of civilization. Civilization is achieved in bits of initiative and lost in bits of decay, mixing good and tragedy. Each civilization has its own special character, reinforced by the spirit of the civilization, a concept further to be developed. The development, enjoyment, and loss of a civilization's spirit is different from spirit in an individual, although individuals participate in the spirit of a civilization. The civilization with a particular spirit calls forth energy. Its structures are energized, and this is more than merely the sum of energetic initiatives from individuals. Civilized structures are harmonies that have special character and energy of their own. Individuals are components in these structural harmonies, and so is the natural environment and layer upon layer of ritualized institutions. Nevertheless, civilized structures are harmonies in their own right with their own integrity, stemming from their own essential components. They have their own special kinds of goodness that I shall explore in this part. The emphasis on creativity throughout this volume bespeaks the proximity of this philosophy to the romanticism we associate with Herder, Schleiermacher, and Goethe. For them, a society is good to the extent and in the ways it promotes individual creativity. To have the initiative and creativity to craft one's own life is a great good. Nevertheless, individual creativity is by no means the only factor to be considered in assessing the social structures that make or break human flourishing. The goodness of social structures, and indeed of civilization, is not confined to making individuals creative. Flourishing is not only creativity. To bend the point to a formula, flourishing is closer to the enjoyment of beauty in the conditions of life than it is to being a self-creating individual. This point should affect the ways you read chapters 15 and 16.

CHAPTER 13

Goodness in Human Flourishing

Goodness in Contexts

If you thought the goods in determinate forms per se, in determinate harmony and the arts, in obligation and personhood were complex, gird yourself for more complexity in human flourishing and civilization. So far I have had to tack between abstract, clearly defined concepts and lists of illustrations, hoping to make progress. With human flourishing, however, we come to levels upon levels of conditions for flourishing, zillions of interlocking structures of civilizations, and hundreds of thousands, perhaps millions, of different contexts and tastes for flourishing. Although in this part, I shall introduce some new abstract technical terms, by and large the topics about which I shall speak are objects of gesture that are accurately indicated only some of the time. So we need a new orienting structure to hold the conversation together.

As mentioned several times, Charles Peirce's ideas of Firstness, Secondness, and Thirdness are both simple and extraordinarily fecund for understanding great metaphysical distinctions within things that often are otherwise so deep as to pass notice. Minimally defined, Firstness is anything that is what it is without relation to anything else; Secondness is anything that is what it is by virtue of distinction from something else, sheer otherness; Thirdness is anything that is what it is by connecting two or more things.

261

To take a leaf from Peirce's book, the theory of beauty presented in part II is the study of goodness as it is good in itself, goodness as Firstness. The theory of art presented in part II is the study of goodness as humanly produced for its own sake, for enjoyment in itself, also Firstness, whatever other goodness it might have. The theory of goodness as normative for human life, the topic of part III, is the study of goodness in a two-term relation in which people are obliged in some sense to relate normatively to something: truth, morality, rightness, and virtue. This is a matter of Secondness, juxtaposing something in reality to our interpretations, decisions among possibilities, appropriate conformation to life's structures, and self-constitution.

With part IV we move to the goodness achieved in the contexts in which we live, the harmonies that mediate all the things we do. This topic is the Thirdness of goodness in relation to human life. These are the harmonies that constitute our families, the communities and larger societies within which we live, our cultures, our civilizations. For the sake of shorthand expression, I shall summarily call all these "civilization." For the most part, all these kinds of mediating and contextualizing harmonies are elements within civilization; I will make some qualifications as we go.

Up to this point in the argument, I have emphasized the distinction between the goodness inherent in things because they have form and the goodness that we see in those things when we interpret them. Our interpretations are always only in certain respects and are biased by our own interests and limited by our semiotic resources. There are the real goods in things and there are our valuations of them, which are always fallible. A third term in the distinction is goodness in the sense of those things we prize, insofar as we interpret them. "Human goods" are the things we hold dear, that we strive for, that sometimes we enjoy for their own sakes, as when we value having art. Human goods sometimes are normative, as when we strive to be true, moral, right, and virtuous. Human goods include those we prize for the civilizational contexts in which we live. Because so many modern Western thinkers have denied that goods really reside in things that have form and insisted instead that goodness is nothing more than the imposition of human valuation on a world of natural, valueless facts, it has been necessary to emphasize this distinction.

However, the goods of civilization muddy this distinction. Of course, there are real goods in the harmonies that make up civilization. The goodness of an economy that allows people to live is real; a healthy economy is a high goodness, really and irrespective of whether people recognize that. People *interpret* the economy as being valuable in certain ways, although not everyone thinks of the economy as such, sometimes only with the aspects of whether they have a good enough job. People furthermore can *prize* an economy as an ideal for the possibilities at hand, sometimes only wishing for a better job, sometimes thinking of things that would make the economy more just, steady and secure, abler to grow, and so forth. In this last case, people have signs that they construe as ideals for what the economy should be, sometimes broad and utopian, other times specific to themselves personally, and most of the time in the middle of this scale of ideal thinking. The muddle comes because the goods of many of the harmonies in civilization are actually achieved because we strive for them, and the goods of the actual structures are in constant tension with regard to whether they can be sustained, or improved. Of course, not all people are cognizant of the fact that they exist within a civilization for better or worse. Many people do not appreciate how much of civilization is of human artifice, or the fact the human artifice alters the natural environments for better or worse. Nevertheless, most people are aware with at least partial self-consciousness of the ways their contexts enable freedom and equality, pit freedom and equality against each other, or should be altered for greater freedom and equality. Because living in a civilized context is a maelstrom of dynamic processes, the relation between the actual goods, perceived goods, and hoped-for actualization of possible goods is in inconstant flux. The perception of what is valuable in our civilizational structures is greatly affected by whether we perceive those structures to have embodied what we had prized and hoped for, or whether they still fall short, or whether what we had previously enjoyed has collapsed. Such perceptions might be true of the real goods or they might miss what is really going on.

The goods in the harmonies that constitute the structures of civilization are fundamentally those that enable human flourishing. Human flourishing is the center. I do not mean human flourishing in the sense meant by secular humanism that aims explicitly to discount transcendent elements. Part of human flourishing is engagement with the ultimate conditions of life, including the grounds for obligation, the ultimate dignity of the human self, engagements with others as others, the search for ultimate meaning, and coming to terms with the sheer arbitrariness of existence itself. Human beings do not flourish only for their own sakes. Other goods are also involved. A civilization might be destructive of the environment. Certain microbes might be well served by a civilization that keeps human beings around for the microbes to live in or on. But for the most part, the goods in the structures of human civilization are those that make for human flourishing. The next two sections expand on the notion of human flourishing in social terms. Here I want to make a point about the metaphysics of the civilizational context.

A civilization, with the people within it, is a small part of the broadest ontological context of mutual relevance. As such, it has many harmonies defining cosmological contexts of mutual relevance, where things condition one another to create causal fields. Considered as within the ontological context of mutual relevance, the institutions of civilization involve individuals whose definition does not come completely from those institutions or causal relations. The individuals also have their own integrity. It is tempting, perhaps, to regard civilization as the largest basket of human life containing all other elements of the human. Or if not civilization, then civilization plus a biological context, or global context, or solar system context, all of which contexts causally affect human flourishing in ways we are beginning to understand.

Nevertheless, we need to resist this temptation to totalization of context. The causal relations and resulting harmonies are what they are. Each person within the context takes those contextual elements as conditional elements that they must compose within their harmonies, with some elevating functioning as narrow, wide, vague, or trivial. But each person also has his or her own individual essential components. The same holds for every amoeba, tree, and shooting star, although our interest here is in human flourishing.

Given this point, it should also be said that the uniqueness of a work of art is not contained completely within or reduced to the components of a civilization. How an individual is or is not true must take into account the conditions of civilization, but it does not reduce to that. An individual's moral life is a component of civilization and has civilizational elements among its own components. However, the morality does not reduce to that. The same is to be said about an individual being right. The contours of existence include those of civilization and other contexts, and they contribute components to the individual whose obligation it is to be right. But that obligation does not reduce to context. So too with goodness: all people with their individual and collective goods are components of the civilization within which they exist, but that membership does not exhaust them. Although people within a civilization internalize much of that civilization, and themselves are located within the civilization, they are not simply located within that civilization: they have their own integrity, for better or worse.

While starting four chapters on goodness in civilization, it might seem anomalous to emphasize the integrity of individuals and of human enterprises over against civilization. Nevertheless, a deep-seated fallacy is common in our ordinary reflections as well as our philosophies, namely, that things can be wholly contained within other things. We commonly believe that when something is in something else, it is nothing more than a part of what it is in. However, the theory of harmony developed in this book, regarding goodness, shows this to be a fallacy. Each thing is a harmony with conditional components that might very well locate it within some larger harmony, or within a number of different harmonies. Yet each harmony also has its own essential components that give it its own-being. If it did not have its own-being, it could not hold a place within a larger harmony. Among other roles, the essential components of a thing connect it immediately with the ontological creative act; the conditional components of a thing connect it mediately with the ontological creative act in harmonies of the components themselves. In this crucial sense, each harmony has its existential heart, however much it is also a component in something else. In fact, only because it has its existential heart as a harmony of its own can it have the standing to be a component in something else. Not to recognize this is to commit what I call the "fallacy of total containment." This relates to Whitehead's "fallacy of simple location," which would say that a thing is reduced to the place that it is in existentially and cannot be a component in something else except by being wholly contained within that thing. Both of these are related to the "fallacy of substance ontology" widely criticized by process thinkers of many kinds and cultures. Harmony ontology, which holds that everything determinate is a harmony whose form gives it goodness, rejects all three fallacies. (Granted, the front line of the rejection is simply to label them as fallacies, which calls attention to them as questionable assumptions.)

In this discussion of goodness, therefore, it is important to begin with the recognition that the goods in civilization both enable and coordinate the goods in beauty as such in human life, the goods in beauty as produced and enjoyed by human art, the goods of truth and living in the truth, the goods of morality, the goods in being right, and the goods in being virtuous. Yet, the goods in civilization do not exhaust those other goods. Even when civilization fails miserably, those other goods can be achieved in human life in their respective harmonies. This is the first qualification of the shorthand claim that all the structures of human life can be contained within "civilization."

Civilization

A second qualification of the claim that civilization is the embracing structure for all structures that are part of human flourishing is an historical one. Many forms of human existence have flourished that are phylogenetically more primitive than civilization. The word "civilization" comes from the Latin *civitas*, meaning "city." A civilization has "politics," which comes from the Greek *polis*, meaning "city." Important differences exist between civilized city life and tribal life on a small scale. In small-scale tribal life, people relate to one another according to family connections and assorted kinship roles. Moreover, in small-scale tribal life people know one another personally, perhaps not well, but through their kinship roles at least. Conflicts are interpreted in family terms and resolved, if indeed they are resolved, by familial authority structures of which there are many kinds. In a city, by contrast, there are too many people for everyone to know one another, and the roles for interaction include those of citizenship (*civitas* again) over and above familial roles. As I shall argue in chapter 14, people in a civilized city interact according to many rituals over and above family rituals. In large-scale tribes, of course, there are too many people for personal face-to-face acquaintance, and roles of authority become too distant to be based on family models. The sheikdoms of the Middle East today are civilized like cities and have internal politics that transcend family connections, although they might follow family models.

From the standpoint of the historical rise of civilization, what is important about cities is not their location in one place but the fact that they contain many different kinds of people together, people of different families, different and sometimes sharply bounded social classes, sometimes different ethnicities, and different languages. Some civilizations are nomadic with no fixed city, such as that of ancient Israel before it settled around Jerusalem. Even ancient Israel had rules for treating the slaves and foreigners in their midst, a pretty sure sign of civilization in the sense of different kinds of people living together in such numbers as to require many kinds of relationship other than family ones.

One of the marks of civilization is the readiness of the central authorities to employ police (from *polis*) to suppress the feudal disputes of tribalism. Families in close proximity easily get into feuds with one another, leading to violence that threatens the safety, economy, and culture of the larger group. The move to police is a move to treating people as citizens of the whole, not merely as members of families. Just as nuclear families suppress or control the will of individuals for the good of the whole, so tribes subordinate nuclear families to the good of the tribe; civilizations police the tribes for the good of the larger community, a city or a traveling nation.

The line between tribal and civilized societies is jagged and porous. Some civilizations carry the family orientation over into ruling families. Chinese civilization from the third century BCE to the twentieth has modeled nearly all kinds of social structures on family metaphors. Americans sometimes think of George Washington as the "Father of the Country." In small tribal groups, slaves and foreigners can exist who are known personally in their roles and not treated impersonally as a class. Transitions from tribal organizations to civic ones are slow and uneven. Transitions back the other way, from modern democratic civilizations toward tribal or at least nativistic organization also occur, in haphazard and partial ways. The move from tribe to civilization might not always be progress.

At the other end, civilizations become more and more complex, with greater achievements of things of goodness. With wariness about untoward colonialist implications, we can speak of "high civilizations" when there is significant writing, relations to other civilizations (as well as uncivilized barbarian tribes), a regard for all human beings as worthy of respect regardless of whose ingroup they belong to, an assumption that the cosmos has some kind of unity under one or a few principles, and the rise of elite thinkers and artists as well as rulers. These are the conditions used by Karl Jaspers and others to describe the Axial Age.[1] The Axial Age arose with the widespread rise of empires that forced different language groups together with an imperial language and often dislocated people from their ancestral lands, graveyards, and holy places. Nevertheless, remember Imhotep the architect, who was also the chancellor of Egypt under Pharaoh Djoser (reigned 2630–2611 BCE), a physician, and a high priest; would we not say that he represented the Third Dynasty as a high civilization two millennia before the Axial Age? All these categories are very slippery.

I note the rise of "civilization" in order to point out that there has been human flourishing under conditions that were by no means civilized. Hunter-gatherers can flourish. Early agriculturalists can flourish. Groups that are naturally or deliberately homogeneous in many respects can flourish. Furthermore, within groups that flourish there can be individuals or subgroups that do not flourish, slaves, for instance, or women, or sexual minorities, or left-handed people, or disabled or ugly people. The structures that make for flourishing do not accomplish that uniformly.

So we must recognize the relativity of flourishing and the meaning of "civilization." In some civilizations the economic system, flourishing according to its own lights, can support only a small number of people and then with some of them struggling along. On the other hand, Xunzi in fourth-century BCE China envisioned a huge civilization with significant differences among social classes but with solid economic sufficiency for even the poorest class.[2] We think of the classical period in ancient Greece as the very paradigm of high civilization with its playwrights and philosophers, sculptors and architects, and a technology of warfare that lasted with little change for nearly a millennium. Some of the institutions of contemporary democracy began there. But by contemporary American standards, the health care in ancient Greece was atrocious and the easy acceptance of slavery seems deeply immoral. The goods of individualism in one civilization versus the goods of group solidarity in another might make each seem barbaric to the other. It makes sense to identify the flourishing or failure to flourish of a social group by measuring its own institutions in comparison with other contemporary institutions: ancient Athens had great health care for its time and place. On the other hand, institutions in a society can very well support the flourishing of some people but at the expense of others, as in cases of slavery or a sharply class-divided society. Finding the language to discuss what flourishing means and how there can be goods achieved in civilizations as such is extremely confusing.

Fortunately, the theory of goodness as resident in the form of harmonies offers a way forward. We can define a "social harmony" as one that (1) has people and many other kinds of things among its components, but whose essential organizing components are not individuals, and (2) makes possible harmonies that are important for the individuals by virtue of the relations within the social harmony. Social rituals are obvious examples of social harmonies, and the next chapter shall be devoted to them. Social governance structures such as a kingship polity or a democratic polity are social harmonies. In a kingdom, the person of the king is crucial and determinative of how the kingdom is set up and governed, but the social harmony is the structure that provides the office and its supports. Social harmonies can be as local as a family structure in which people play parenting, filial, and other roles. Economic structures are social harmonies. Cultural conditions such as language and the handing down of lore about how to conduct economic business or maintain shelters are social harmonies. Social harmonies involve many kinds of components besides human beings, such as the materials for food and shelter. Cultural harmonies include educational structures, the arts, literature, and social worldviews. But the reasons to call them "social" is that they make it possible for human beings to be the kinds of harmonies that bear human goodness. Economic social structures make it possible for people to eat, be clothed, and have careers. Cultural social structures make it possible for people to communicate with one another, build and appreciate the Taj Mahal, enjoy landscape paintings, and be moved by Beethoven. In many instances, the social structures important for human flourishing, relative to this or that society, are those that make up the contours of life regarding which people are obligated to be right.

Flourishing

Now we can consider some generalizations about the social harmonies of flourishing that are obvious once said. They need to be qualified beyond simple statement as soon as we apply them to cases, but such qualifications can help frame a broad vision (the "width" function in philosophy) of the diverse things we need to keep in mind as we consider our own civilizations. Perhaps the classic attempt to do this is Plato's construction of the elements of a political state in books 2–4 of the *Republic*. He said there are structures that satisfy appetite, namely, the economic ones that he imagined growing from primitive to rich to decadent conditions. He discussed military structures that call upon spiritedness or aggressiveness to protect the goods that satisfy appetites and also structures of government that order the state to keep it rich and safe, calling upon educated reason and experienced political skill. Plato's account shows Socrates playing with deep ironies in this account—book 8 gives a radically different picture of political realities. The story of the ideal state has been an orienting model for Western thought for millennia. What are some of the social structures for flourishing?

Consider first the dimension of biological survival and reproduction. With very few artifacts, hunter-gatherer societies can flourish, finding food and shelter in a round of places, raising enough children to maintain a population fit for the niche, building educational experiences around apprenticeships and initiation ceremonies, providing protection from predators and foes, and finding leadership among recognized personal qualities as well as offices coming from stages of life and dominance. Such societies are exceedingly vulnerable to natural conditions such as flood, fire, or drought that ruin their subsistence round of travel through territory, or diseases that kill off their prey, or the advent of new and powerful predators and foes. In the event of such disasters, hunter-gatherer societies do not flourish. They may perish. In these dire circumstances, different social harmonies are desirable. For instance, the people might settle on high ground or learn to build dykes and store grain, they can invent better hunting tools, agricultural life can be developed with increased supplies of food, and so forth. In such conditions, the people can flourish at new levels. If neighbors raid their agricultural fields, they can develop the social structures of a militia or army. With such division of labor, social structures can support more people and the social structures of towns and cities can grow. With flourishing depending on the cooperation of significantly different social roles and classes of people, complex political structures are needed, and these might be powerful enough to force some people, for instance, slaves, to work to make the other people flourish while they themselves do not flourish. The way this story is usually told, the move from hunter-gatherers to agriculturalists, to city-states, to empires, is as a move of progress in human flourishing. But as flourishing is enhanced at higher levels for some people, it might be stymied for other people.

Considering the dimension of the arts, remember Dewey's dictum that the simplest people deck themselves before they clothe themselves, and that they sing and make a game of drudgework. Again, a story can be told of the evolution of ever more complex forms of art to make the depth of human aesthetic pleasure greater and its focused pleasures sharper. Walking on stilts can be supplemented by acrobatics and eventually develop into Olympic gymnastics. A twenty-first-century American musician can flourish at a given level with no more instruction than apprenticeship to a more accomplished musician; learning to read music leads to greater breadth and depth of musical performance, especially if it is still accompanied by concentrated apprenticeship. However, we should remember that the fact that some forms of art are more "developed," in the sense of a more complex social structure, does not make them necessarily more valuable in an artistic sense. Artistic goodness has to do with the depth and contrasts achieved by the compositional functions of components as to narrowness and width, vagueness and triviality.

Given the multifariousness of contexts for flourishing, what it means to flourish is relative to the context at hand. One can flourish or not in the context of hunter-gatherer health care or twenty-first-century Boston health care. Poor health care in Boston, one of the most concentrated centers of tertiary care facilities in the world, cannot be excused just because it is better than hunter-gatherer care.

Flourishing for any given individual is extraordinarily complex to understand, even for the individual. Of course, the fundamental contours of life, as discussed in chapter 11, are basic, and they have many diverse manifestations depending on the person's culture and society, or cultures and societies. In just about any social location, the social structures can make or break flourishing with regard to (1) biological conditions, (2) economic conditions providing means of taking advantage of many dimensions of life, (3) cultural conditions for providing access to assorted traditions, (4) cultural conditions for making and enjoying the arts, (5) educational conditions that give the individual access to what should be learned to flourish in various dimensions or that give the individual access to what is of special interest to learn, and (6) religious conditions that allow serious religious practices and deep spirituality. These are some of the contours of life within which people can flourish or not, depending on their structures, that are common in "developed" countries today and that have different manifestations in the different civilizations.

More personal social structures also affect flourishing. Families might be normatively defined by family rituals typical for their general social and cultural situation, but the ways those rituals are played might make or break flourishing. Most people flourish only if they have some friends, a few intimate friends, more collegial friends, and capacities to interact in friendly fashion with a wide range of people. Social circumstances might make it difficult or impossible to have intimate friends, such as a job that requires constant traveling with no home or regular personal location. One might live in a hostile environment that precludes any kind of friendship. There are special circumstances that require friendship for flourishing. For instance, college students flourish when they have classmates and roommates with whom they can develop quick but deep and enduring friendships; often these friendships arise between people with very different backgrounds, although sometimes it is impossible for a person to find such a friendship structure in which to live. Personal lives involve specific careers, sometimes several of them at once or serially. The social conditions have to be just right for people to flourish to any deep degree, and sometimes "career" means "onerous, hopeless, oppressive, and killing job." Personal aspirations are not limited to goals for careers. Suppose someone wants to be an athlete but has no athletic ability except walking on stilts, and the person's society does not practice or allow stilt walking: that aspiration cannot flourish there. Personal aspirations are highly diverse and often idiosyncratic. People cannot flourish with their aspirations unless the social structures and important relations among harmonies supply the right conditions.

I have spoken of the conditions for flourishing as being social structures, that is, social harmonies that have some kind of stability for the duration. However, sometimes people need unique conditions in order to flourish. They need to meet the right person at the right time, or have the right problem occur where they are at the right time, or have an historical opportunity that fits their aspirations. Some people fail to flourish in life because they did not receive the right word of encouragement at the right time, and gave up. Many of the problems of our educational systems in advanced countries is that young children are given ideas about ideal opportunities but no one is there to give them the right push, with the result that they collapse in despair, frustration, and self-destructive behavior. Of course, many aspects of personal flourishing are simply matters of individual interactions. Here I am calling attention to the social conditions that make those interactions happen or fail to happen.

As mentioned, most of the social conditions for flourishing are steady social relations. I shall analyze these in much detail in the next chapter as forms of ritual. However, as a kind of counterbalance to what can be achieved through ritual are the social conditions that make for creativity and invention, for zest and gusto, for a life filled with enthusiasm: narrow foci of interest connected with wide forms of integration. A flourishing civilization is where people can flourish by taking part in such matters of "spirit." I shall discuss this in chapter 15.

Flourishing is uneven. In a given society, there might be conditions for great economic flourishing for everyone but an impoverished set of aesthetic conditions. For a given individual, certain contours of life might enjoy great flourishing but others are lacking. In a given society, the social conditions might be such that some people flourish very broadly while others are oppressed as slaves, disenfranchised as women, or excluded from most venues of life because they are disabled. One of the ideals of most civilizations is that everyone gets to flourish in the ways appropriate to them.

The Global Context of High Civilizations

Alfred North Whitehead's *Adventures of Ideas* is one of the most important philosophy books of the twentieth century and it ranks with the best of any century. By "philosophy" here, I do not mean metaphysics, cosmology, or logic, in all of which fields Whitehead is well known. Rather I mean philosophy as in philosophy of life, a wise understanding of the human enterprise. The first part of his book, which he called sociological, traced the development or "adventure" of ideas into history, giving his reading of the evolution of civilization. The story of civilization, according to Whitehead in the terms chosen for his chapter titles, begins with the invention of the idea of the human soul and moves to the humanitarian ideal (the ideals I have associated with the Axial Age civilizations). Civilization then develops aspects of freedom until freedom ideally applies to everyone and transforms power in society from force to persuasion. Power as persuasion leads to foresight, which Whitehead associated with science. In the fourth and last part of the book, he names the ideals that characterized what he called "high civilization": truth, beauty, truth and beauty together, adventure, and peace. Obviously, Whitehead's thinking has deeply influenced the book you are reading.

Nevertheless, in one respect this book is a radical departure from Whitehead. A child of his time, as I am of mine, Whitehead viewed civilization as Western civilization. He mentioned others with great respect, but Western civilization for him is civilization, with "civilized experience" (to use another of his favorite phrases), and all other civilizations are civilizations to be noted for their differences and idiosyncrasies. In his preface, he lists eight books that have principally influenced his thinking, and they are all about Western cultural history and philosophy.

Now we are sensitive to many of the limitations of Western colonialism. Just how the great civilizations of the world have developed is an empirical question, and scholars know much more about that than was known in the Western academy in Whitehead's time. I am sure that if Whitehead were living now, he would correct his seeming assumption of Western civilization as the paradigm for all. He would probably argue that there are certain metaphysical or cosmological ideas that should be registerable in all civilizations, and he promoted his own cosmology. The arguments for his own cosmology, in *Process and Reality*, mainly come from criticizing cosmological ideas in the West, not those arising in South Asia or in East Asia. Nevertheless, he would say that cosmological matters run across all civilizations. I have used his technical ideas of vagueness, triviality, narrowness, and width to develop the cosmological theory of beauty in this book.

Yet we can still raise questions about his understanding of civilization. The stories of civilization appropriate for South and East Asia, and the Americas beginning in pre-European contact times, are not the same as the story of civilization in the West, assuming that Whitehead had the West right. Moreover, although his characterizations of the ideal of civilization are original, profound, and inspiring, they show the underlying assumptions of the most prominent Western model of ultimacy, the metaphors of God as a personified agent creator. For Whitehead, civilization's ideals have to do with the flourishing of agency. In South Asia, however, the fundamental metaphors for ultimacy begin with personal experience, as in the West, but move to divest the model of person of precisely the aspects of agency so important in the West. Consciousness is purified so that its contents come and go without any attachment or control. The gods that Hindus and Buddhists believe in, in their different ways, are themselves subject to the higher laws of Karma and are not ultimate. Or rather, they are reconceived as ultimate by being divested of all agency. The ideals of peace as release from clinging and from the need for life trump the Western ideals of peace as harmonious interaction. Freedom is to get to die, not to achieve something. In East Asia, the fundamental metaphors for ultimacy are hardly personal at all but have to do with spontaneous emergence of processes that need to be brought into harmony. Ideals of spontaneity and the coping with forces that need to be harmonized come to the surface of East Asian civilizations rather than those of truth, freedom, and peace. Harmony is the principal recurring theme in East Asian civilizations and is more important than freedom in the other two senses mentioned. Beauty is an ideal that cuts across all three great families of civilization, interestingly, though with different paradigmatic ideals of beauty.

To do better than Whitehead, therefore, we must be sensitive to fundamental differences among the world's civilizations in how they nuance their ideals for the social conditions of flourishing. To note that they have different institutions and social structures is not enough. We need to attend to differences in the goods achieved through these different conditions.

Whitehead's strategy was to give a genetic account of civilization, telling a developmental story from early to late. My strategy is the opposite, to take note of our present circumstance and work backward to sort its roots in different manifestations of structures for flourishing. Many reasons lie behind this switch in intellectual strategy. One of the most important is my conviction that we live in a global society tied together by a great many kinds of causal connections—economic, military, internet, travel, climatic, and the like. These causal connections are different in different parts of the globe, but almost everyone relates to just about everyone else through some direct or indirect causal connection. Defining "society" through causal connections, we can recognize that we have a global society that, in loose and lumpy ways, ties together more local societies with tighter orders. The locality of subsocieties is not necessarily geographical, although there are geographically discreet societies. A subsociety might be those people who communicated in projects over the internet, versus those who do not connect much with the internet or at least not on the same topic; a subsociety might be people sharing in a global religion that have much in common despite different cultural indigenizations; a subsociety might be the global academic community. Despite living in a global society and in perhaps a number of subsocieties, we do not have a global civilization. Indeed, we have many civilizations, each with its structured contours of life that provide both ideals for flourishing and fulcra for criticizing actual social structures. For our own flourishing, as discerned by our philosophy, we need to identify our own social location on the globe and come to appreciate in critical, responsible fashion all the civilizational structures and ideals to which our location gives us access.

Whitehead was satisfied with his own location as solidly within the Western civilization that he traced, while acknowledging, learning from, and appreciating other civilizations as other than his own. Our situation, at least mine, is different. My birth and early education was in the American Midwest (St. Louis, Missouri), and I went to college and graduate school learning almost exclusively Western materials. However, early in my teaching I began interacting with East Asian cultures, especially China, Korea, Japan, and Singapore. Through teaching and travel, I came to identify with Confucianism as well as my original Methodist Christianity and am recognized modestly as a Confucian philosopher by other East Asian scholars. My house has a room filled with photos of my ancestors. The study where I write is crammed with books, of course, and computer equipment. But it also has a large wooden statue of Jesus, a collection of crosses and crucifixes, a small collection of Orthodox icons, a large framed rubbing of Confucius from his hometown, three reproductions of Chinese landscape paintings, a large scroll reproducing a passage from Wang Yangming in his own calligraphy, three framed pieces of calligraphy done by Korean artist-monk Po Ban, a book cover drawing of Laozi by my wife with calligraphy by Po Ban, a hanging scroll of calligraphy by a contemporary Confucian friend, a framed reproduction of contemporary Confucian calligraphy, photos of family members, a framed print by Leonard Baskin, two watercolors by my wife as well as framed originals of book covers she has designed, two wooden carvings (Indian and Indonesian) of Ganesh (patron god of philosophers), a wooden carving of Shiva/Shakti (left and right sides, respectively), a bronze dancing Shiva, a bronze Korean bell, a small bust of the Kamakura Buddha, a fourth-century Chinese roof tile, a marble bust of Augustus Caesar, a fired clay Daodai, two large etchings of dragons by my wife, a wooden carved dragon, and a large fired clay dragon (we call the room the "Dragon Room"). These are not merely souvenirs of travels: they are tokens of the civilizations and cultural resources to which I have access. They are what make me me. Starting from my study, my roots tangle throughout the world and go back very far. Therefore, the quality of my flourishing is a mixture of many civilizations, harmonized in various parts in functions of narrowness, width, vagueness, and triviality. These illustrations deal only with the religious and philosophical dimensions of my life and flourishing. As to the dimension of health, I am a type 1 diabetic with an insulin pump, parts of which come from China, and I practice taijiquan. Within "my harmony" are a great many places on Earth and times of diverse histories. So it is with most people who are likely to read this book. You readers probably are as entangled as I, except insofar as you are younger.

It would be possible to tell genetic stories of civilizations, starting from their roots. We could divide civilizations according to their political embodiments, as Samuel Huntington did in *The Clash of Civilizations*. Or we could divide them according to basic metaphorical themes, as I have done in distinguishing those whose root metaphors for ultimacy are personification, purified consciousness, and spontaneous emergence. But it is better to start with our own situation of a global society with various positions that each of us occupies, reaching back into many civilizations and subsocieties of causal interaction. This will facilitate a contemporary conversation about the social conditions for flourishing.

CHAPTER 14

Goodness in Rituals and Institutions

The thesis of this chapter is that human flourishing is *enabled* by good rituals. The thesis of chapter 15 is that human flourishing is *exercised* by creativity.

A General Theory of Ritual

Western thought, and to some extent South Asian thought, has tended to exaggerate the difference between the natural and the human. One consequence of this is to understand ritual most often as mere human artifact and indeed often as artificial, not fully real, and not at the heart of human potential. East Asian thought, however, principally Confucianism, has viewed the human as a specialization within nature, emphasizing continuity throughout nature including the most sophisticated human achievements. All the Confucians have recognized the pervasiveness and importance of rituals, although they have interpreted rituals in different ways. The great ancient theorist of ritual was Xunzi, whose thought I have developed in contemporary terms and do so here.[1] By ritual here I mean any general pattern of behavior, from cognitive to overt behavior, in which individuals play roles relative to other individuals, social institutions, and nature. This is an extremely broad conception of ritual and is congruent with pragmatism's emphasis on semiotically charged behavior. In my usage of the term, any semiotically shaped behavior is ritual play. Liturgists think of ritual in terms of ceremony; that is but the tip of the iceberg. Anthropologists think of ritual in terms of the boundaries and authority structures of social groups; true enough for some rituals. Speaking to others or oneself in a language with a vocabulary and syntax is ritual action. Learned ways of farming are rituals for working with the earth. Learning to stand and play against the pull of gravity is learning a ritual.

Xunzi pointed out in his essay on Heaven or nature (*Tien*) that nature (or Heaven) endows us with our biological capacities and with emotional, cognitive, and voluntary capacities.[2] However, nature does not endow these in their appropriate connections. Their connections all come from learned, human meaningful behavior. This is to say, semiotically shaped culture lies at the heart of the human. Whereas Westerners tend to associate ritual with religious or court rituals, the Confucians see rituals as extending throughout the whole of human activity in interconnected ways.[3]

Human biology has evolved so as to be able to move in all sorts of ways. But elementary movement always has to be learned in some specific ways. Unless disabled or abandoned, all human infants learn to stand. Standing requires ritualized habits of using muscles to counteract the pull of gravity. East Asian babies learn to stand with their feet more or less parallel, whereas Western babies learn to stand with their toes angled out at about forty-five degrees. Walking involves learning rituals of moving through space, usually toward an adult. East Asian babies learn to put their toes and heel down at about the same time, whereas Western babies put the heel down first with the toe afterward; in exaggerated form, East Asians walk with something close to a shuffle and Westerners with a goose step. Most young children can make sounds; Aristotle noted that babies babble in the phonemes of their parents' language. Communication through language is a universal human capacity, but each language is a different ritual for doing so. Family life for raising children and living domestically is required for human life, but the ritual cultures for this are different. As noted earlier, rituals exist for working the earth and finding wild game that differ from group to group, relating them to nature differently. Rituals for social life differ among groups and in concentric circles around any individual's group memberships. Rituals exist for cooperation and finer rituals for friendship. Rituals exist for expressions of social authority and government, and these differ greatly among groups. Of course, religious and political rituals exist, sometimes even the same rituals for both dimensions that we have come to distinguish. Many rituals are unconscious, but some are explicit ceremonies to be understood in their own terms, often backed by rituals of mythologizing; most rituals are unconscious until their practice requires attention.

This understanding of ritual derived from Confucianism under-scores the sense in which we should think of human beings as har-monies rather than substances. Because rituals require interacting with other things in nature, usually also with people, we relate internally to those other things in patterns of narrowness, width, vagueness, and triviality according to our composition. If we think of ourselves as self-contained substances, the interplay with other people and things through rituals is a kind of external relation. But if we recognize that we are harmonies mutually determining one another, then our ritual interplays are internal to who we are. A baby is defined ritually by habits of relating to the pull of gravity as parents do; a beginning speaker connects internally with the semiotic systems in a language and with people who speak that language. With this understanding of ritual, no opposition exists between loyalty to a group and personal self-interest; there are only questions about what and where harmonies are to be enhanced in the social existential field defined in part by mutual conditioning through playing roles in ritual structures.

Most rituals are complex interactions that involve multiple play-ers in diverse roles. Thus, the rituals in which we play roles define us intrinsically. A ritual is like a general pattern of roles, like interactive dance steps with several dancers. Each step has to be taken in an indi-vidual way and many different individual ways can fulfill the general role within the ritual. As in social dancing, rituals can be played well or poorly. Maturation in ritual play involves learning to individuate oneself in the role. In a given community, for instance, there might be a general pattern for how boys should treat their fathers, and every boy in the village can follow the pattern. Yet each boy comes to treat his individual father somewhat differently from the ways the other boys treat their fathers, in part because their fathers are different and in part because the boys make themselves different by the ways they individuate themselves in this ritual. Although ritual playing is not the whole of life, it is involved in nearly every aspect of life. Hence, the virtues that allow for excellence in ritual playing are important for being human, as the Confucians have emphasized. A great part of human virtue is skill and sincerity at playing the important rituals of life. Nearly everyone can speak. Only some speak well.

All of this discussion of ritual should be understood as a specification of harmonies important for human life. A ritual is a social structure involving nature and other people. It exists as a general habit of the social environment. The ritual is a real part of the social structure even when it is not being played. The playing of a ritual involves the persons who play the diverse roles as components, though usually not the only components. The many individual players are components of the ritual itself, both as potential players and as actual players. The playing of a ritual takes time, and of course the ritual itself is a component in all sorts of other rituals and social structures.

For each of the players, the rituals are components that the person has to harmonize, and a deeply important kind of harmonization of personal life is how the person balances out the many rituals in a ritual matrix. We have ritual relations with each of the members of our family, and often there are integrating rituals connecting these rituals. We have ritual relations in our economic life and in relation to the various institutions of our community. Going through the day, we play in many rituals at once and move from ritual to ritual serially as well. Rituals tend to cluster in various domains of life. I have a set of rituals for home life, with chores and regular activities, and with interactions with my wife, children, grandchildren, and neighbors. I had a different set of rituals for work where I interacted with students in class and elsewhere, with colleagues, took care of my office, and served on committees. I have rituals for integrating my domestic ritual roles and other rituals for how I behave at work as a professor. The integrating rituals have their own tones and styles, and these differ from one another. My wife lets me know quickly if I slip into treating her as I treated my secretary; fortunately, I have never treated a secretary the way I treat my wife. I had a half-hour drive between home and work along a beautiful but curving, narrow, and fast road; the rituals of driving the car, both mechanical and emotional, helped mediate between the domestic and academic ritual complexes. Much of life's acquired poise is learning how to move from one ritual complex to another, balancing them, and when they compete for paying attention, prioritizing them.

Although most ritual playing is unconscious, automatic, and habit driven, rituals often do not work.[4] Dysfunctional families are obvious examples of this. Sometimes this is because one or more of the players in the ritual dance do not play well or fail to play at all. Think about how we strain to keep an even temper and continue playing our rituals as best we can at work or at home when others are causing trouble. Sometimes the rituals do not fit the circumstances. Consider how difficult it is to take part in a one-parent household using the rituals that require two parents. Or think of how inappropriate the rituals of an academic honor system are for a student population that embodies a ritual culture of cheating when they can. Much of our ordinary lives focus on getting the rituals in which we are involved to work.

Sometimes, of course, the rituals are just plain bad. The ritual structure of a dysfunctional family, for instance, might include making one of the family members into a scapegoat, which is terrible for that person; sometimes the therapeutic cure for family dysfunction is to identify the actual rituals that are in play and deliberately change them. On a broader scale, a racist society is filled with rituals that reinforce and play out that racism. Some of the rituals are overt, such as deliberate segregation in education and housing. Others are unconscious, such as ritual ways of eye contact, demanded habits of deference, reactions of hostility when a person acts uppity, and racially biased expectations of excellence. People can be firmly committed on moral, religious, and legal grounds to overcoming racism but still unconsciously play in rituals that perpetuate racism. Most economic systems of rituals work for the benefit of some people at significant cost to others. That is just the way the system of rituals works in the economic sphere. The rituals in many societies are abusive to women. One of the most important domains of moral effort is the analysis and amendment of the rituals that structure a society.

Rituals in Human Flourishing

For all the evils they might embody, however, rituals are what make human life possible. They are the source of flourishing where people flourish. More important, however, rituals are the enablers of social life at all levels.

Without rituals of family life, sexual reproduction would be possible in the abstract but families could not function. Human beings could not have evolved to bear children whose amazing capacities require a long childhood of care and nurture if there were no family rituals that define and habituate such care. Some family rituals are such that only certain members of the family flourish, such as males as opposed to females, or the firstborn, or the most beautiful. Families rarely can live alone and need to be involved in rituals of community life. Although many different forms of community life exist, no community life would be possible without the rituals. Primitive rituals of cooperation make possible cooperation on the hunt, or in growing crops. More sophisticated political rituals make possible much more efficient social organization. Without rituals of education, education would not take place, whether it is the first-person handing down of lore in peasant societies or the education of a university elite.

The ancient Chinese were so impressed with the importance of ritual for defining human life that they developed a slogan, "Heaven, Earth, and the Human," that Xunzi cited.[5] Roughly speaking, for them Heaven represented the principles of harmonization, Earth represented all the stuff that changes and needs harmonization, from crass material things such as stones to subtle things such as human thought and appreciation. The Human, for them, meant, among other things, everything that involves semiotic or meaningful organization, that is, everything that involves following some kind of ritual form. To make their point in modern evolutionary terms, human beings evolved by developing the ritual activities that constitute a certain kind of human practice, such as family life or speaking in a language. This is the important sense in which ritual is what enables human flourishing, or life as human in any sense.

Ritual formation of a practice that constitutes part of human life does not mean that the practice is mechanical or necessitated. Playing the ritual of speaking in English creates the possibility of communicating in that language. Nevertheless, it does not determine what you say in English; you decide that on various other grounds. Nevertheless, some things are easier to say in Chinese than in English, and vice versa. Language expresses and shapes thought forms, and different languages do this differently. Metaphors develop differently in different languages and sometimes translations are difficult. We do not translate between languages by translating each into a third language but rather by rehearsing how to fulfill intended expressions or communications in each language with different linguistic forms. Sometimes we find easy equivalences between languages. However, even where we would expect it to be easy, sometimes it is not; any native English speaker who has tried to follow directions in English for assembling a machine written by a Japanese engineer understands this. So nuanced are some linguistic habits in a language that creative transformations of a language in poetry are almost impossible to translate without a thousand footnotes indicating differences in language forms. A poem is a harmony in a language with narrow, wide, vague, and trivial components that stretch far beyond its own words with associations that connect far across the language. Other languages have different kinds of association. I cannot imagine how the poems of Gerard Manley Hopkins could be translated into Chinese, except in their ideas; those poems so often have such a material feel to their language that the ideas are not the important parts. Still, with all the complexity of the mixture of the medium and the message, as Marshall McLuhan pointed out, the language itself usually does not tell you what to say in it, only how to say what you want. The ritualized habits of walking do not tell you whether to walk first to the drug store or the food market. The rituals of family life do not determine how the oldest child does in school, although they put pressure to perform within certain limits.

All human flourishing requires the development of the practices within which people can flourish and, as noted in the previous section, the practices in any given social environment determine what flourishing might consist in. It is possible to flourish in an American town where everyone speaks English and no one speaks Chinese if you speak English, but if you speak only Chinese you will not flourish easily in that town until you learn English.

Nevertheless, because rituals are social structures that usually involve a number of people, they do not always promote the flourishing of all the players equally. Our social habits involve evil and oppression as well as flourishing. In this age of heightened sensitivity to structural evil, such as racism, the oppression of women, and bigotry against sexual minorities, it is easy to view the rituals that embody that evil in a negative way. That we are so tempted requires us to think first of the positive enabling of possibilities for social life that rituals provide. A given family ritual might be oppressive of the women in the family, but it makes family life possible. Without family life of some sort, there would be no women to oppress or men to be oppressors. A given society might be filled with rituals of racism. However, it enables the possibility that different races can coexist; the alternative is war, genocide, or ethnic cleansing.

One of the ideals that developed with the Axial Age is that of equal flourishing. If possible, it is ideal and normative for those with the capacity to make a difference to transform ritual structures so that the level of social life they make possible allows for the more or less equal flourishing of all people involved in the social relations. In some societies, the family rituals make it simply impossible to imagine that women not be required to do the menial work while the men have more leisure. Perhaps the family rituals can be reimagined so that women's work is regarded as equally fulfilling as men's, though it is hard to keep this from being simply hypocritical. Some strategies for change would allow women to have the same jobs men do, working outside the home (exclusion from public life is a common form of oppression of women); this requires massive changes in other parts of the society. Sometimes strategies for change involve discovering and cultivating some special potentials in women not relevant to their oppressed work in the household or in the jobs more typically done by men. However, all this is difficult and involves defining flourishing for women in ways many traditional societies do not support. Nevertheless, within my own lifetime, in the communities in which I have lived, the places assigned to women have changed dramatically for the better.

The first step in correcting the injustices in social rituals is to understand them precisely as rituals. They are not merely bad conditions, or simply unjust. Rather, they are functions of rituals that connect people together in the ways that constitute a complex society. The playing of family rituals connects necessarily with the playing of economic and political rituals. The social location of a given community is a function of rituals of intergroup association, among other conditions. Groups exist within groups, leading up to national and civilizational interactions. We do in fact live within a roughly interacting global society. We need then to understand the complex connections among the rituals such that they support one another. Or perhaps they do not support one another when they should.

Critical moral analysis, therefore, needs to employ the analytical tools that can see what rituals are in play, what kinds and levels of social life they enable, and how changing any one ritual might have systematic consequences throughout the whole system of rituals. This mode of analysis of the harmonies of society has been common in the Confucian tradition since his own time. Now, however, it needs to rise to the level of sophistication that modern science and the multifarious approaches of historiography can provide. Noting the systematic inter-connections of rituals to constitute complex social structures, plus the vast matrices of rituals that any individual plays, indicates how difficult it is to change rituals. Surrounding rituals that depend on a certain one to be played can put huge pressures on the ritual not to change. Conversely, a broken or badly played ritual has consequences throughout the system of rituals. To be sure, the relations among different ritual structures in a society are not all systematic. Many are adventitious. Moreover, great power exists in certain individuals to make a difference breaking through ritual structures. Nevertheless, moral analysis needs to take very seriously the ways in which rituals in a society interact to reinforce or obstruct one another.

One contribution of this discussion ought to be to show how rituals are harmonies of various sorts that create a social reality that includes individuals. The goodness of the ritual is whatever goodness accrues to the harmony it has, composing some things to be narrow focal points of goodness; others to be broadly integrative, holding goods together; others to be vaguely representative of things otherwise dismissed; and yet others to be dismissed into triviality without much if any representation. The analysis of goodness in harmony, applied to social rituals, indicates how the components of ritual and their form together constitute the goodness of the rituals. The goodness of any ritual depends in part on the goods of its components. Hence, the ritual system of a society is the interlocking of many achievements of goodness, negative as well as positive goodness.

Institutions in High Civilization

We should pay special attention to those rituals that constitute social institutions. Now in Western societies it is common to distinguish many dimensions of life that constitute our civilizations. For instance, we distinguish the economic from the political, the educational, the artistic, the literary, the religious, and a number of others. Academic specializations address different dimensions of life and their institutions, although in retrospect we see that the ways we distinguish those dimensions and their institutions often come from the state of the art of those disciplines. The nature of the scientific and academic disciplines is constantly changing, which changes the conception of what they study.

Some scholars like to trace these institutions of social life back to original sources. For instance, some cultural biologists like to think of the origins of religion in primitive societies as forces that fostered group solidarity and thus gave an adaptive advantage over groups that had little religion and hence little adaptive advantage. Explaining the biological adaptability of the early practices, celebrations, feastings, storytelling, and the like, some scientists think they are "explaining" religion; insofar as they appeal to adaptive advantage for a robust social authority structure, however, they are explaining the origins of politics. Those same practices are the primitive origins of educational institutions, and of the arts. In fact, all social institutions arose from those few, compact, practices of early human beings in their groups. For the purposes of our own understanding of the goods in social institutions, it is better to start with the distinctions we now commonly make and work back to their historical development. Even here, however, there is not much agreement across civilizations as they stand now. For instance, societies with a heritage in modern Europe with its history of wars of religion are comfortable distinguishing political from religious institutions, which is not true of Islamic societies whose political authorities are conceived in close relation to religious authorities.

To be sure, many of the institutions of civilized social life are related to and dependent on one another. Most institutions have some cost and therefore depend on economic practices, some of which are institutionalized. Many institutions have authority structures and therefore depend on political dynamics. Religion integrates responses to ultimacy in just about every dimension of life and therefore has components that come from all and in turn often affect all other dimensions or set of institutions. Each institution is a harmony whose existence and expression in social practices contains as components all the other institutions, with particular structures of narrowness, width, vagueness, and triviality. The interrelations among social institutions, and the goods each achieves (for better or worse), invite exploration in terms of how the institutions are components in one another and how each has its own essential ways of composing its components.

Civilized societies differ among themselves in the kinds and states of institutions they have. I do not mean to promote here a scientific analysis of our global situation with regard to the main institutions. I mean only to offer reflections on some of the main institutions that characterize our global situation with the point of showing how each is the actualization or habituation of something of goodness in civilized societies.

Consider the family of economic institutions. Working the earth and various elements in the natural environment for food began as ritualized habits of various sorts in early groups. Specific technologies developed in modern times that are not themselves habits as much as they are deliberate programs, and now food technologies are constantly changing. Economic institutions include research and experimentation into improved ways of finding nourishment. The institutions of research and experimentation themselves reflect institutionalized ways of relating to nature, some of which we now regard as exploitative and dangerous. In addition to the economics of nourishment, thousands of institutions exist for manufacturing items that play roles in modern societies. These are not the same for all societies, and yet the spread of scientific modernization has brought most of them to remote lands all over the globe. In addition to the economic institutions of production are those of distribution, of trade that gets the produced goods to those who want them. Trade is facilitated by money, which is built on all sorts of institutions such as banks, governments, industries for mining gold and silver, stock and bond markets, betting on futures, and the like. When the habits of thinking and practice that guide our activities here become objects of conscious attention, we call them institutions. Among the institutions of economy are those that distribute wealth, making some rich, others poor, and most in between, with many shifting in their degree of wealth. Because most people have economic needs to work and economic institutions of production and distribution change and move from place to place, people move their places of residence today almost as much as they did in the days of hunter-gatherers.

When it comes to economic institutions, we have come to prize the achievement of certain goods in those institutions. For instance, the institutions of most modern societies strive to produce enough food for everyone, enough clothing and shelter, enough wealth to support communities that allow access to the arts and pleasures of life. Sometimes we are aware only of needs to improve systems of distribution of wealth so as to give everyone enough; sometimes we aim to approach equality. But we also need means of production that do not ruin the environment, that allow for gracious living, and that call forth ingenuity and creativity among people so that working makes for a meaningful life. Because most of our economic institutions are not wholly just, we are conscious of the need to improve where we can the functioning of ritual habits and deliberately sustained organizations. But, given their interdependence, these institutions are hard to change.

Consider another family of institutions already mentioned, those having to do with good health. Some of these have to do with finding and cultivating nutritious food and the habits of eating a healthy diet when there is choice. Other institutions of health have to do with living well, getting exercise, having work that is appropriate to age and physical condition. Other institutions of health have to do with the education necessary to live in healthy ways. Vast institutions exist for the repair of health when people are sick, hurt, or disabled in one way or another. Until recently, the ritualized habits most people have within the institutions of health have often been unconscious. Now we can see important differences in results of different ways of life, nutrition, and the rest.

Consider the institutions of religion. Although this is a controversial claim, I say that religion is engagement with ultimate matters in five domains of ultimacy, as already mentioned. Perhaps foremost is engagement of the sheer contingency of existence, which in most cultures is expressed in institutions of worship. Worship is not only in religious membership organizations but also in various kinds of meditation and artistic activity, dancing, singing, and the like.

Second, religion engages the ultimate boundary conditions of having to make choices among alternatives with different goods, giving rise to the institutions of truth, morality, authentic living, and goodness. These institutions include educational ones for understanding what is best but also penal institutions for punishing or correcting those who choose badly in some senses. These institutions are not religious only but are religious when they function as ways of engaging the fact that we live under obligation.

Third, religion is the engagement of what it means to be a self, which includes the institutions of mental and spiritual health, of reconciliation with family and society, and of coping with suffering, institutions such as hospitals and summer camps. These institutions also are not religious only but are religious in the ways that becoming a self is an ultimate condition of human life.

Fourth, religion engages the ultimate condition of interacting with other people, with institutions, and with nature more broadly speaking; this interaction has integrity in its own goodness and existence that extends beyond the roles those things play in our own lives. This is most forcefully addressed in the interactions of things outside our ingroups. Of course, there are ingroups within ingroups, such that the latter become outgroups in certain circumstances. A local community is an outgroup to our family, and in turn the larger body politic is an outgroup to a local community. These distinctions of group identity are drawn in many ways and often have nothing to do with religion. But when the others demand recognition for standing on their own, that is a religious ultimate and the institutions that shape our responses are religious institutions.

Finally, are the ultimate conditions defining the meaning and
goodness of life, of our individual lives and our lives together in context. Those conditions are represented by narratives and cosmologies
as well as by founding events and holy places. They were to articulate
questions of the meaning of life.

The common sense of ultimacy constitutes a pressure for harmonizing the institutions that deal with the five ultimate conditions.
Sometimes we have large institutional harmonies that consist in traditions of thought and practice that deal with all five: the great religions
of the world such as Buddhism, Christianity, Confucianism, Daoism,
Hinduism, Islam, and Judaism (to list some alphabetically). Within each
of these, however, are competing traditions. We practice religion within
some social venue, and often these are institutions such as churches
and denominational organizations. We can appreciate such institutions
for their politics, and the political analysis sometimes can bracket out
analysis of how well the institutions serve the engagement of the
ultimate realities. Nevertheless, insofar as these institutions and organizations serve to enable or make possible our engagement with the five
ultimates, they are religious. Insofar as they are cut off from ultimacy,
even though they bear religious names, they are better analyzed in
terms of their politics, or the quality of their medicine.

These remarks serve only to illustrate the interlocking ways by
which different institutions achieve social goodness in relation to one
another, acting as components in each other and spreading out in family resemblances. Late modern societies have complicated forms of politics, for instance. American institutions distinguish within government
between legislative, executive, and judicial branches, with protections
to allow each to be a corrective to the others. This is not the only
form of late modern government, however: witness that of China. The
American model has a kind of thematic normativity that is expressed
in at least lip service to the distinctions between those branches, even
when other models in fact are in play. This is because there is widely
perceived goodness in the kinds of institutions that distinguish those
perceived branches, what American constitutional thinking calls "balance of power."

Late modern societies have many institutions besides those discussed here. My point is that all of them are social rituals that are

harmonies containing components in patterns that both interrelate them and allow each to have its own essential components so as not be reduced to others. Most ritual institutions are very long lasting and have material components such as buildings and other venues. The large-scale social rituals often contain as components many material things. So, governments have government buildings, many employees, and usually instruments of organized force such as police and armies. What makes them institutions, however, is that people play in their rituals so that the economy creates wealth for better or worse, the health of the people is secured for better or worse, the ultimates of human life are engaged for better or worse, and people are governed for better or worse. The capital building is not part of government if the government does not use it in the rituals of governing; it could be sold for a museum. A denominational structure with its buildings and employees is not part of religion unless it functions in a ritual that engages ultimacy. I have used the word "institution" here to indicate those structures in a society that make possible the complex inter-actions of social life in more or less steady and approved ways. The rituals that relate individuals to more local and accidental aspects of their interpersonal, social, and natural environments are not institutions.

The final question I want to raise in this chapter is what kinds of rituals and institutions tie societies together.

Rituals in Global Society and Civilization

For the time being, it is safe to say that we have a global society defined by important interactions affecting everyone, but not a global civiliza-tion. We have many civilizations with somewhat indistinct boundaries relative to one another. Each civilization itself is a rough harmony of many cultures. The cultural pluralism of civilizations dates back to the Axial Age when multicultural empires in China, South Asia, and West Asia forced people of different cultural backgrounds to live together.[6] To some degree, the different cultures in those early empires were able to maintain their integrity. Roman polity, for example, facilitated the different languages, religions, and political organizations of the con-quered people so long as they also acknowledged the Roman emperor, paid taxes, and gave at least lip service to the Roman gods. So people had multiple levels of identity, one as citizen of the empire but others as citizens of their cultures. Each culture too was an amalgam of subcultures, of different city cultures, of tribal cultures. Citizenship or "membership" is itself a harmony of somewhat discrete and sometimes competing kinds of memberships. Various memberships or citizenships are among nearly everyone's components that they need to integrate well or poorly in their lives. To combine memberships in various levels of social harmonies in a good way is one of the ideals for civilization.

Just as the Axial Age arose within empires that forced many cultures together, our own history in the last three centuries of Western colonialism has done that as well, but on a global scale. The British, French, Spanish, Dutch, German, and in a somewhat similar way the American empires spread around the globe. Often their colonies abutted one another. Each of these empires had its own language and forced that language on top of the colonials' languages. The British colony of India was itself already an empire, compressing many cultures together. It had been unified as an empire under Buddhist, Hindu, and Muslim imperial powers at different times, each leaving some of its distinctive civilizational marks. As the twentieth century progressed, the main differences among the European imperial centers gradually fell away, although their different linguistic heritages lasted in their colonies. In fact, Europe integrated those powers into the European Union. As a result, we now regard that colonialist period mainly as Western imperialism, not British, French, and the others.

The Islamic world had many polities since its beginning in the seventh century, ranging from serious unity across the whole to somewhat nativistic enclaves of ethnic power, though all relating positively to the myths of Islamic unity and reverence for the land, language, and person of Mohammed. Nevertheless, the Islamic world was diverse enough that the rise of the Ottoman Empire made it a culture-crunching empire much like the European ones. By the end of the nineteenth century, the Ottoman Empire was in competition with the European empires and Russia. As it disintegrated about that time and during the first decades of the twentieth century, its colonies became colonies of the European empires.

The Japanese empire had a different history, beginning only with the Meiji Restoration in the mid-nineteenth century. With its defeat of Russia at the Battle of Tsushima in 1905, Japan established itself as the dominant sea power in the Western Pacific. It quickly colonized Korea and Taiwan (Formosa) and settled a large military establishment in Manchuria as a buffer against the Russians. It never completely colonized the whole of China but treated the northeast as under its colonial hegemony. Thinking of itself as having an empire, Japan thought itself under attack by the American empire and in turn waged a suicidal war on America and its allies in the Pacific. As a colonial power, however, Japan must have done something right because its two main former colonies, (South) Korea and Taiwan, are major economic forces in the world today. Most of the colonies of the European empires that were still under colonial rule at the beginning of the twentieth century remain economically and politically problematic.

Today among postmodern thinkers, it is fashionable to decry Western colonialism, treating it as a great evil (Japanese and Ottoman colonialisms are not much at the center of attention). The accusation is that modern Western civilization came to represent the cultures of the colonies in the terms of Western culture, forcing Western categories on the understanding of the colonies and not appreciating or prizing those aspects of the native colonial cultures that thus fell out of view. This is surely true: the cultures and civilizational structures of the Western powers were imposed on the colonies to a large extent, and only in the last two centuries have strong movements arisen to identify colonialist distortions and seek to correct for bias. This is especially true in the areas of science, capitalistic economics of several sorts, and the technology resulting from both. It is also true in education. In fact, the greatest anti-colonialist writers such as Edward Said and Talal Asad have lived within Western academic institutions, written for Western academic audiences, and published in Western academic venues. Generally, these anti-colonialist writers are part of a Western philosophic discourse deriving from Hegel and Marx and are committed to cultural pluralism. Their attack on colonialism is in behalf of recognizing the distinctive character and worth of the colonies' own cultures, advocating cultural or civilizational pluralism over against the dominance of Western civilization that eradicates the civilizations of the colonized. The other people who also are against colonialism argue for their own land's cultures to be revived and protected from domination usually are conservative nativists who reject cultural pluralism. The anti-colonialism associated with postmodernism is itself a very Western phenomenon. Insofar as it is used to defend the different cultures of the former colonies, it is another form of Western imposition.

Surely, the empires of Western (and Ottoman and Japanese) colonialism have been violent, bloody, hugely destructive of older social forms, and morally atrocious from our point of view. The same was true of the early empires in China, South Asia, Greece, and Rome. Had we lived then and not been representatives of the imperial centers, we surely would have decried the wars of aggression and the maintenance of imperial military establishments.[7] We would have lamented the cultures that did not survive the pressures to integrate different cultures. Nevertheless, those Axial Age empires did develop civilizational forms to live together in tolerable harmony with different cultural ideals. They taught us that we should respect every individual as human in ways that take precedence over respecting them as not being in our ingroup. They taught us that we live in an integrated world under common principles of nature and that in some ways we are all connected. Each of these empires, and their offshoots, had different forms for these teachings, but we can now see their commonality.

Can we now look upon modern colonial history in at least one positive light, namely, that it has imposed upon the world some working conceptions of global economy and political interconnectedness? It has imposed upon the world an elite Western culture that prizes cultural differences, even as it distorts them into Western categories. Can we not celebrate that the resistance to colonialist distortions and destructions of colonies' cultures made possible by a liberal Western academy that prizes pluralism and empiricism in looking at different cultures? Can we not advocate for academic learning around the world, based on Western models that teach humane learning and scientific inquiry? Humane learning and scientific inquiry are both committed to the vulnerability to correction of their own views. I ask these rhetorical questions to indicate that there is power in those ideals of Western civilization.

I stress the point that, although we have a global society, we do not have a global civilization. Western civilization now is a dominant culture imposed upon the globe, more or less, but opposed by the rising consciousness of other civilizations and colonial cultures. The United Nations was founded on the model of the United States with a republican legislative assembly, an international judiciary, and an executive secretariat. However, the founding fathers of the United States belonged to a common liberal, Christian and humanist, European literate class and they had sufficient dominance to impose that culture on the hordes of immigrants from other cultures. The African Americans were written into the constitution usually as slaves, and the Native Americans were just pushed aside and mostly slaughtered.[8] In the United Nations, the sense of republican representation envisioned for the General Assembly is not shared by all the civilizations mentioned, nor are the ideals of individual rights, nor the sense that leaders are accountable to their people. The weakness of the United Nations is indicative that it is a surface ideal for a global society with competing civilizations that differ greatly in what they prize about human flourishing.

Are there any forms of social harmony that can alleviate the conflict, destructiveness, and horrors of a global society in which rape, war, poverty, and disease are so prevalent despite being vices in the eyes of every civilization?

Let me introduce another aspect of the Confucian approach to ritual that I have been developing. Western anthropological approaches to ritual have emphasized the roles that rituals have played in setting the boundaries and identities of groups. The rituals of one culture distinguish it from other cultures. The Chinese approach, however, sees rituals precisely as ways of relating to outgroups. Family rituals integrate different generations, genders, and responsibilities. Village rituals allow families to live together. Xunzi explicitly said than any society has different social classes, each with its own interests and sense of identity over against the others, and he said social rituals are required precisely to have those social classes that are nearly always on the edge of conflict live together successfully.[9] Success means that each class is viable economically (for Xunzi), each has protection against enemies, and each is protected in its rights and means to carry on its own ways from generation to generation. Success does *not* mean that peasants should like the gentry or the aristocracy, or that the literati should like or even much respect people from any of the other classes. Nevertheless, the social rituals are effective without common agreement or appreciation if they keep the social classes in balance. Social rituals do indeed define ingroups. Nevertheless, more importantly they define relations with outgroups. They provide ways of getting along in some harmony with other ingroups that are outgroups to yours. Now, a high civilization is one in which the social harmonies that allow for the coexistence and flourishing of ingroups create new levels of harmony that themselves define ingroups of appreciation.

My suggestion is that the different civilizations now in conflict in our global societies need to seek out new ritual forms that allow them all to flourish, pretty much on their own terms, while developing their own conflicting interests. These need not, indeed cannot, be the rituals of just one civilization imposed on the rest, as the West has tried to impose the rituals of democratic civilization on the rest. How do we conceive the rituals that bridge gulfs between civilizations? Partly by analogy with existing rituals. Partly by trial and error. Partly by the models of heroes of reconciliation such as Nelson Mandela. All of these involve creativity, not just the imposition of a previously developed social order with its matrix of goods in its ritual harmonies. This is the topic of the next chapter.

Let this chapter conclude with a caution, however. The Confucians have always known that sometimes there is just no way to bring things to harmony. Sometimes the forces of nature cannot be tamed with dykes and granaries. Sometimes conflicts between people cannot be mediated without violence and destruction. No guarantee exists that the violence of our global situation can be alleviated by new global rituals that allow people to coexist in difference. Every civilizational unification also involves, inevitably, the destruction of units that simply cannot survive in the harmonized civilization. Civilization means the loss of those things that cannot sustain themselves in the conditions of harmony with others.

CHAPTER 15

Goodness in Creativity and Spirit

The thesis of the previous chapter was that ritual makes human flourishing possible, especially civilized flourishing. The thesis of the present
chapter is that human creativity is the exercise of actual flourishing
made possible by a ritual base. Creativity is even more complex than
ritual life. Indeed, the very playing of rituals often requires creativity.
To be sure, at the cosmological level the sheer passage of time involves
creativity because each present change makes an advance on the past.
But here I mean human creativity, with the intent, conscious or not,
to make something new and good. I introduced creativity as a topic
in part II, especially in chapter 8, in connection with artistic creativity.
The present chapter explores many other areas in which creativity is
an essential feature of human life insofar as life flourishes in those
areas. The first topic is creativity as taking initiative.

Initiative

The rituals we play for the most part constitute the good structures of
human life. Sometimes we shape ourselves by rituals in such elementary
ways that they become unconscious habits. We take for granted our
habits of relating to gravity and our social situation such that we stand
and walk in learned ways that have come to seem wholly natural and

require no initiative from us now. But what better example is there of initiative, striving to make something new, starting something up, than a baby struggling to stand and take a step? Infantile intentionality might not be on a par with that of parents taking the initiative to care for their family according to family rituals, but it is on the way. A ritual itself is a general habit that characterizes the environment but that has to be acted upon when appropriate.

Nominalists might think that rituals have no reality except when they are being actualized, but they are mistaken. Even when not acted upon, the social reality of a ritual is that it is a structured way of acting that is appropriate when the occasion calls for it. The occasion's call might be a prompt to which we respond unconsciously. Nevertheless, some initiative is involved to move from the possibility of playing a ritual role to actually playing it. In Western societies, most of us would automatically take the hand of someone in greeting when that person extends it; that is a mainly automatic initiative. If we intend to snub the person in a situation of greeting, then it also takes initiative not to take the extended hand. Most of the rituals of which we are aware do require something like deliberate initiative. To engage the earth by planting a garden requires the initiative of actually digging. To engage the rituals of education requires the initiatives of going to school on the part of both students and teachers in order to play their respective roles. To play the rituals of enjoying art requires the initiative of going to museums and looking, or to concert halls and listening. To play the rituals of health care requires us actually to brush our teeth. To engage in the rituals of lawmaking requires someone initiating the lawmaking process.

The previous chapter discussed how rituals provide vague guidelines for the ritual interactions that players have to make specific in order to play them at all. In addition to actually initiating ritual play, individuals need to initiate the education rituals of perfecting their ritual play. Such education rituals are for learning how to play better, to play with appropriate attention to the specific details of the other players and the social structures constituted by the play, and of learning to play various rituals with a personal style that reflects how the individuals balance out their playing of their other rituals.[1]

Much, but not all, of personal maturation consists in learning how to individuate and perfect the important ritual roles we play. I am a college professor and have been for a long time, albeit now retired. The rituals of classroom teaching have evolved over my career and I have adapted to the evolution more or less well, less well with regard to the use of recent high-tech equipment. In addition to the adaptation to new classroom rituals, however, I have somewhat improved in my classroom style. When I began, I taught seminars almost exclusively by asking questions, frustrating some students who wanted to hear something from me; recently, my seminars require student seminar reports, questions from the students and me about the reports, and also mini-lectures by me on matters arising. When I began, my lectures in large courses were overprepared by my current lights; I focused too much on what I thought should be in the minds of the students by the end of class. Now I have learned to feel the student moods and signs of understanding or confusion; humor is helpful; sometimes I stop for questions, even in a large class. Moreover, a major component of classroom rituals is my use of language. Speaking, of course, is itself a ritual that I employ to get across what I hope the students will learn. But I have learned to be conscious of the nuances of rhetoric in how I speak, changing pace, emphasizing the more important points, teaching by surprise sometimes. I am also concerned to model speaking for students, a matter that has gotten more difficult as the distance between my capabilities of academic speech and the speech patterns of students has grown. Over the last twenty years the percentage of students in my lectures for whom English is a second language has steadily grown, requiring appropriate language rituals. In addressing all these problems of initiative in classroom rituals, I feel a constant need for creativity, to which I respond with varied results.

Nearly all the rituals discussed in the previous chapter need some initiative that requires a creative modification of the situation in which the rituals are merely habits ready for actualization. This is so in the rituals of the economy, government, educational systems, religion, the arts, domestic life, and all the rest.

Nevertheless, one of the most important parts of playing rituals is the normative analysis and correction of them. One of Confucianism's

most important contributions to global philosophy is its emphasis on
understanding social structures as built on rituals. Confucianism rightly
stresses the importance of bringing them to consciousness and assessing them and working to deconstruct rituals that have destructive or
unfair consequences. Most of all, progressive contemporary Confucians
promote the development of new rituals that sustain the good in the
old ways of doing things while eliminating the bad, and perhaps at
the same time cultivate rituals that enable even better novel social
achievements. This is true of rituals within the family, the local community, the society, the civilization, and global interactions, true also
of rituals that cut dimensionally across all social groupings such as the
economic, political, educational, artistic, and religious.

Rituals are in constant change. Every time one is played, it is
altered a bit by the way it is played. The structure of ritual accom-
modates to the idiosyncrasies of its players. Because rituals interrelate
so much, a change for any reason in one ritual is likely to modify
another, and people need initiative to make the modification. For
instance, family rituals are modified by changing circumstances in the
economic rituals, and vice versa. The playing of such rituals requires
constant initiative. This is especially true when rituals are deliberately
changed by the power of one party over the weakness of some others,
or by the novel entrance of non-adept players or very creative ones.
We need even more initiative in our efforts to improve our society
by learning to play the present rituals better or by improving rituals.
Perhaps in such times of change, consciousness of the ritual as such
diminishes in favor of the intention not to do it that way anymore
but to do it differently. This still is initiative.

Of course, precisely because social rituals are so intertwined and
are played by so many individuals, and because individuals juggle their
initiatives to play many rituals in their own matrices of connections,
a change in the playing of one ritual by one player can have reper-
cussions throughout the system. For this, among other reasons, rituals
are constantly changing even when there is no obvious proximate
cause. Players need constant initiative to adjust. On the other hand,
rituals are often extremely difficult to change for the better, or for
one's advantage if not for the better, because the changes required
throughout the system are not easy to discern or make. The system

of ritual interconnections itself puts great pressure on individual rituals to stay steady and play their roles in the others. As those of us who have understood the ritual embeddedness of racism in America know, some rituals are particularly hard to change for the better when the rituals themselves are constantly adjusting to maintain homeostasis of the system.

Nevertheless, people concerned for justice, beauty, and other aspects of flourishing can exert great initiative to live through the rituals while improving them.

Life is not all ritual playing, however, despite the fact that we need to play the rituals that constitute our social structures. Each of us has plans for doing things for which the rituals are only the medium. We take initiatives to befriend certain people and cultivate the friendships through various circumstances. We take initiatives to build homes and families, to beautify our neighborhoods, to cope with disease and ill health. We find many things to be interesting and seek the education to be able to pursue those interests. We love the celebrations of holidays and festivals (even if they do not involve walking on stilts). As we age, we seek out different kinds of friendships, family relations, living situations, and occupations.

In each of these and countless other initiatives we undertake, the means involve ritual structures. Just as the rituals of language use do not dictate what we should say, especially if we aspire to poetry, so the rituals of our social relations do not dictate what initiatives we can take with them. We live in and through rituals so that we can do the things we want to do.

In fact, most people would describe quotidian life in terms first of our initiatives and only secondarily in terms of forming and playing the rituals that provide the structures with which we can accomplish what we want. The following section will lift to attention some of the ways by which we have the initiative to make up our own lives, and the goods involved in this. The section after will say some things about how we come to want the things that call forth our initiative. The moral of this section has been that an elementary dimension of human flourishing is taking initiative within and beyond the channels of the roles of the rituals constituting the social structures within which we live. To be alive is to be on the initiative.

Making a Life

Our discussion of what it means to be a human being began abstractly in terms of a harmony of components with the goodness achieved by composing those components with narrowness, width, vagueness, and triviality. That stage of analysis nailed down the claim that we intricately relate to other things, not as substances in a container but as harmonies of those other things in relation, plus our own essential components. Then the discussion moved to how the pull of beauty motivates and organizes us, a topic to which I shall return shortly. In part III, I reflected on the ways in which human beings are special harmonies that compose themselves responsibly (or irresponsibly) by the ways they relate to things truly (or falsely), morally (or immorally), rightly (or wrongly), and well so as to become virtuous (or not so virtuous). In the present chapter I have considered how human beings are social animals, indicating in elementary and illustrative ways how any kind of flourishing—in, through, and above engaging the world with our obligations—employs social structures, the goods that shape kinds of flourishing. The previous chapter analyzed social structures as rituals, human participation in social structures as ritual play, and how rituals are internally definitive in part of personal identity.

Now I want to bring to attention another important element of human goodness, namely, that in significant measure we make our-selves who we are. Of course, we make our lives out of what we are given. We are given the resources of our environment, our complex personal, biological, psychological history, and a host of other givens. We are given the resources of the possibilities open to us individually and together, and ways by which we can recognize and understand these possibilities. Beyond these givens are the initiatives by which we do something with them. Often the "givens to" us are "takens by" us. What is interesting about us is what we do with what we are given. Less interesting are the givens themselves, although the initiatives are impossible without the givens. Any good biography, including our reflections on our own personal identity, involves understanding what we do with the conditions of our lives.

Our essential components are those things within us that take initiative with the things that condition us. We respond with initiative in many parts of our lives. Not everything, in fact hardly much at all, has to do with integrating ourselves into some harmonious overall identity. Perhaps only spiritual heroes have the laser integration called for by Kierkegaard's claim that purity of heart is to will one thing. Most of us lurch through life with at most a few complex nodes of density of being, strung together by having to relate more or less well to changing circumstances.

Yet were not the existentialists right to emphasize the obligations of freedom to will, to take initiative? Beginning with Kierkegaard, finding poetic language with Nietzsche, coming to sharp analysis with Sartre, they reversed Western modernity's obsession with explaining human life by its conditions. Sartre snorted, quite to the contrary, that "existence precedes essence."[2] We are what we make ourselves to be. We are not what others, or the conditions of life, make us to be. What they make us to be is not us; it is an alien essence. There is "no exit" from the givens of life, if we are waiting for something to make us free. Our freedom comes only when we will ourselves to be something, and then our true essence is what we will.

Sartre's bitterness is extreme and, ironically, we can understand him best within the hard conditions of his life during the Second World War after the collapse of the Weimar Republic in Germany and the Great Depression. He was a bitter resistance fighter. Life seemed to him like his friend Camus's Sisyphus: unending repetition of effort with no permanent success. The will of resistance and sheer self-making was the only way out for him. Is not this a bit too heavy for most of us? We find a much more genial pressing of the same point in Ralph Waldo Emerson's happy romantic transcendentalism. For all Emerson's rhetorical flourishes, he had a saner grasp than Sartre of the gives and takes of freedom, but with all the spunk for which Sartre hoped. No wonder Nietzsche liked Emerson.

Two lessons, among many others, come readily from the existentialists. The first is that we do not need to assume that the givens of life completely determine what gives our life resources, direction, and achieved goodness. I emphasize this here and prize my kinship with the happiness of Emerson. In the religious dimension of my life, I am deeply grateful for the existence of the world, including my corner of it. Therefore, I look upon what is given with awe and appreciation.

Yet at the same time, the givens of life can be horrible and niggardly of human resources. For many of us, life begins as a burden that only gets heavier. For those of us so oppressed, life is unjust, unhelpful, and unattractive. What a huge difference exists between those of us born without lasting parents, in poverty, in a culture of violence, thievery, and no hope, and those of us born in loving families with educations that bring out the best in us and economic situations that allow us to fulfill our ambitions! The existentialists pointed out the vast differences in birth and circumstances among people and said, with Heidegger, that we are just "thrown" where we are.[3] Our personal givens are a huge accident. We cannot take pride in our position because there is no reason why we are not in someone else's position. We cannot take credit for anything given us. In a literal sense, our lives are absurd, without justifying reason. This is the first existentialist lesson.

The second existentialist lesson is that the only way to attain humanity in this condition of thrownness is to will ourselves to be what we are. If we can change things—and nearly always we can—then we should take initiative and do so. Even if we cannot change much, we can affirm what and who we are and take responsibility for that identity. The failure of humanity is a failure of will. The existentialists called this a disease, a disease of spiritual death. Rudolf Bultmann and Paul Tillich used this point to reinterpret the Western notions of sin and salvation: sin is living in spiritual death where the inevitable is given, whereas salvation is taking up the gift of life despite these circumstances. Life in this usage means initiative, moving out from the given by taking it with initiative.

The existentialist critique of consumerist culture is acute. As consumers, we think we are free because we have chances to buy things and have a great range of choice in what to buy. Even impoverished consumers can think of themselves as free within their budget. But being enticed to buy, with the freedom to do it, is to be conditioned by the market. This includes the advertising that tells us we are free when we can make ourselves sexy by buying a fast car, or strong and masculine by buying a pickup truck, or sexy as a woman by latching onto a man with a fast car or pickup. To be in a consumerist culture is to be granted choices, that is, *given* choices, and it does not matter much what you choose. The existentialists are right that this is a form of unfreedom.

Freedom is the making of a life, taking the thousands of initiatives necessary to building an identity through time for which one is responsible. Not all people who shape their own lives with authenticity make particularly good ones. Nevertheless, the goodness that comes from the harmony that includes initiative in its own formation is at the essence of what it means to be normatively human. To live badly is better in many respects than not to live in the sense of making a life.

Of course, the existentialists looked at life as if through a small tube and saw only their point about initiative. They did not revel as they should have at all the goods achieved by our bodies, physical circumstances, and the structural harmonies of the ritual interweavings of high civilization. They did not have Emerson's exuberant experience of Nature or the Oversoul, his delight in the direct experience of things rather than through the experience of others. But then, the existentialists lived in societies they thought to be debased, where the creativity of culture had turned sour and only the force of the past made us do what we do. For them, the great temptation to which Western civilization draws us is to acquiesce in the role of victim, or perhaps, if we are lucky, to be among those who have been made happy, not living happily but made by conditions to be happy.

From the existentialists we learn the crucial lesson that to be merely conditioned, and not to take up the conditions on our own initiative, is to be dead. Sometimes this is the image associated with a society formed thoroughly by rituals: we are nothing more than what the rituals make us—rote players, routine living, and spiritual death. To be sure, I have argued that there is enormous initiative required to be players within rituals, even more to be good players, and even more yet to play rituals with the intent to improve them and thus the lives that can be lived through their structures. Still, it is important to balance out the conditioning formation of rituals, essential as they are to the harmonies of socially complex existence, with the need to extend ourselves in initiatives. Our initiatives collectively are the most important of the essential features by which we make up our lives, our identities with others in the world. Initiative is involved in all responses to obligations to truth, morality, rightness, and virtue. Initiative is also involved in much more.

It is one thing to note that daily life calls for countless initiatives and another to address the vast issues of shaping a life. A life has a wholeness to it, for better or worse, which includes issues of personal identity, of modifying our environments so as to live better in them, interacting with people around the accidents of life that cumulatively make up our lives. Very few of us think often of the human task of making our lives through our initiatives or explicitly make the making of life to be an important complex initiative. We are doing it constantly, however, and at the back of our minds as we do this are considerations of how the matter at hand fits into or problematizes the overall task of making up our lives. Sometimes we take only short views about our lives, sometimes longer ones. To take an explicit view on the whole of life as such makes you a philosopher.

The visions and aspirations we have for our lives usually are in the vague background of our engagements of other things. Hardly ever are they cast into complete triviality, and then in cases of sudden emergency where we might have to sacrifice the future for the sake of some overriding personal concern, such as saving someone else. But even in these emergencies when we sacrifice our lives for something else, the motive for doing so includes in the vague background some vision of who and what we would like to be. To undertake any serious risk deliberately includes in the harmonies of those decisions some crucial components that say this is the kind of person we would like to be and that we make ourselves in taking the risk.

So, one of the uniquely valuable dimensions of human flourishing is to have the initiative not only to determine ourselves in essential features but to determine more wholly what kind of person we would like to be. This is not about us in isolation from our social and natural environments. Rather it is about us as we affect those environments and ourselves, and our interactions with those environments as in the two-term norms for relationship. It is about how the back and forth of those causal connections create new levels of social reality in which people can (or cannot) flourish. Perhaps we should keep in mind, on the one hand, the language of taking the initiative to make ourselves the person we want to be and, on the other, the language of making the world a better place because of what we do and become. Both together constitute making our lives.

Civilizations have various models of what a good life consists in, often taken from actual lives construed as paradigms. There are saints, sages, soldiers, great mothers, great fathers, kings and queens, champions of democracy, great artists, musicians, and architects—who would not want to be like Imhotep? The list could go on indefinitely, and each social context nuances the models differently. Civilizations have more to say about what lives are worth making than come from models. Ideals define caste identity in some societies, gender identity, social class identity, artistic or "high" culture identity, and all in various ways. The point is, for any one of us, the lives we can, should, and might succeed or fail to make need to be relevant to the components of our lives, not someone else's. Whereas the ideals of a good life in a given social location are shaped by the paradigms and other conditions that have educative effect, in fact, the ideals lie primarily in the possibilities for the conditions at hand. What the ideal is for making a life is a connection primarily of the actual and possible, with the goods imbedded in the forms of both. Only secondarily should we attend to the ways we think about the ideals.[4] To be able to take initiative to make a life is a very high good of civilization.

Pursuit of Beauty

Having stressed the goods in the ritualized foundations of the social structures we have for human flourishing, and having stressed the goods in the apparently countervailing issues of initiative in small things and in making a life, we now can ask where we get the ideals that can guide the flourishing of society and the making of a life. The answer toward which I have been building is this: the fundamental motivation for initiative in building a civilization for flourishing or in building a life is a response to beauty. Beauty is goodness attractive in itself, as I have defined it. To be sure, the goods in truth, morality, rightness, and virtue justify all sorts of motivations for initiative, but the initiatives are motivated by the beauty in those goods; this is especially so when we grasp the goods in matters of truth, morality, rightness, and virtue after analysis and dialectical vetting. Initiative is fundamentally the responsiveness in an aesthetic act of appreciation. The appreciation is not just the harmony of thinking that something is beautiful. The appreciation rather is the entire organization of the harmonies of harmonies in one's life so as to be able to have the form of the appreciation of beauty wherever it lies in experience.

The ancient Confucian document, the *Doctrine of the Mean* (*Zhongyong*), says that what human beings receive from Heaven, construed as the creative ultimate, is their inner nature or "heart-mind."[5] This heart-mind is an aesthetic capacity to recognize and respond appropriately to the goods of things in their own natures and in their connections, if selfishness does not cloud that capacity. "Sincerity" in the Confucian sense requires both the elimination of selfishness that clouds our vision and biases our actions and the cultivation of skills to apprehend accurately in the layers of connections of things and to act skillfully personally and with others. The Confucian theory of ritual gives structure to all this. The Confucian ideal of Sagehood can be described as the perfection of analytical aesthetic vision and of skills of acting beautifully to harmonize things whose goods need respect.[6]

Plato is famous in the West for being interpreted as saying that we always do what we think is best, and that what we think is best is recognized aesthetically. Because we so often do bad things, he is interpreted to say that the remedy is better education because we are wrong about what we think is best. The entire enterprise of Western education, begun by Plato and his student Aristotle, the presidents of the first two universities in the West, has had an aesthetic force: to better understand things so that we know what is good and worth doing and bad and worth preventing or undoing. Confucius, too, thought that the way to Sagehood for individuals and the way to flourishing for societies was through education, although he had different educational forms for that, not universities.

The riposte in the West to Plato has been the observation that we often know the better, really and truly, and yet still do the worse. As St. Paul wrote to the Roman Christians, "For I do not do what I want, but I do the very thing I hate."[7] The great prevalence of guilty conscience among us testifies to this phenomenon. The Platonic answer to this has been that we mistake the lesser good for the greater good. For instance, we know on the one hand that sexual activity is very complicated in society, with consequences far beyond a given sex act affecting a number of human relationships and social institutions, and with the value of sexual acts determined by how they affect a vast array of harmonies and disharmonies. Yet on the other hand, a sexual opportunity might be so overwhelming in its attractiveness that we allow our lust for that to trivialize all the other components of that sex act, pushing them out of consciousness. We know the greater goodness of regulating our sexual activity with the larger connections in mind, and we know that the attractiveness that inspires lust is of lesser goodness and in some circumstance is a danger to many. Nevertheless, there is a narrower power in the momentary lust in response to an attractive person than there is in the power that puts the wider considerations in context. Sometimes we do not have the discipline to put them both in a perspective that sorts the greater and lesser goods.

The response of Platonists, including myself, to St. Paul is that the reason we do what at some level we know we should not and vice versa is a failure at integration within ourselves. We are attracted to so many different and conflicting things at once that we cannot sort them so as to perceive and be attracted responsively to the harmony that establishes priorities. We might cognitively know the prioritizing harmony in question, but that knowledge is not in the aesthetic form that actually harmonizes us in the relevant ways. Our discussion has made apparent how many levels of harmony there are within us and in our relations of beauty, truth, morality, rightness, and virtue with the rest of the world. The achievement of a life we would want most to make involves extraordinary complexities of self-harmonization, of self-creating initiative, that compose the vast set of complexes in the environment into our nature.

Plato is a good guide here, if we can avoid the common simplistic interpretations of him. The common interpretation is that physical beauty evokes the response of desire. A beautiful person evokes the response of love with sexual overtones. For Plato, the experience of sex does not temporarily satisfy desire but rather stokes it to higher aspirations. We begin with sexual longing for a person's beautiful countenance and move on to loving the person's soul. We then come to love not just any old soul, though any human soul has its beauty, but the wise soul, the courageous soul, the soul that takes after one or other of the gods. This is something like the plot of Plato's *Phaedrus*. From the most beautiful souls, whom we learn to love, we can move to loving beauty itself, the form of beauty. The greatest human aspiration, according to this interpretation of Plato, is to seek union with the form of beauty, meanwhile loving other people by making them disciples of the philosophical pursuit of union with the form of beauty or the form of the good, as Plato calls it in the *Republic*. Plato's *Symposium* is the classical place for this interpretation of Plato's theory, namely, that we are motivated by beauty and perfected the more we rise above beautiful things to the form of beauty itself. The plot of the *Symposium* is a drinking party to celebrate one of the participants winning a prize for a play. The group agrees to water their wine so that they can make speeches in praise of love. Robert S. Brumbaugh has pointed out that the speeches from the beginning of the dialogue represent points of view that ascend the Divided Line that Plato had used to organize kinds of cognition and cognizable objects in the *Republic*: images, common sense, theorizing, and dialectic.[8] Among the *Symposium* speakers is the comic playwright Aristophanes, who provided the hilarious theory of sexual love that says humans were once two persons in one globular body. However, the gods bisected humans after beating them in war so that, ever after, the two separated halves sought each other. Some of the originals were heterosexual, some were both women, and some both men. This explains why some people are homosexual in their erotic pursuits whereas others are heterosexual. Sexuality on this theory is a longing after a lost larger self. The Adam and Eve story has the same point, though without an explanation of homosexuality. Socrates, however, speaking last in the series of *Symposium* speeches, rejects both the view that sex is an impulse and the view that sex is longing for reunion with something lost. Rather, sexual longing is a response to an external beauty, and the better the more beautiful. Citing his divine teacher, Diotima, Socrates says that the highest eroticism is that of the teacher producing good students and that it leads to devotion to beauty itself. The form of beauty itself is the cause of all the lower forms of desire for something beautiful at whatever level. The Neo-Platonic tradition of Plotinus and the Christian and Muslim Neo-Platonists runs with this point that beauty itself is a transcendental trait of the One from which all plurality and determinateness comes.

Nevertheless, Plato's *Symposium* does not leave on the high note of the transcendent forms. Alcibiades breaks in to the party drunk and takes over the proceedings. He is an extremely attractive young man, though irresponsible and a traitor to Athens in the eyes of many. He praises Socrates as the most beautiful of persons, though Socrates is old and ugly. He recounts how he was a suitor of Socrates and sought unsuccessfully to bring him to his bed. The moral of the *Symposium* seems to be that Socrates's discipline in putting first things first and being able to resist the charms of Alcibiades is the greater beauty. Human beauty here, and in other Platonic dialogues, is leading the philosophic life. My argument is in this line, not the Neo-Platonic one.

The argument of this chapter so far is this. Within the given conditions of life, initiative is required to engage life at all, to be alive, to be more than a product of antecedent causes. Initiative is motivated by the attractiveness or beauty of its intended object. Sometimes this beauty is something to which we relate by learned habit and the givens of culture. Sometimes it requires special discernment from among the possibilities for initiative. Nevertheless, with the vast complexities, the coherencies and even more the incoherencies, of where initiatives might go, they need to attain some order of priorities. The problem for initiative is not that there are so few attractive options but that there are so many. Any inherited and acquired culture already has social structures that embody standards for prioritizing things. Rarely are these enough. We are beset by contradictory pulls from short-range and long-range goods, goods for self and goods for others, goods of physical feeling and goods of spiritual accomplishments, goods that others would congratulate us for pursuing and goods upon which others frown.

Moreover, each of us has a unique life situation; we have much in common with people like us in our society, but any society has people unlike us. Our individual lives have different shapes at different times. Things that we see as attractive at one stage in life are not so attractive at another, or during the day versus during the night, or with friends versus at work. We constantly need to achieve balance like a logger trying to stay upright on logs careening through rapids. This balance is itself a kind of harmony that has a perceived beauty. Or if we don't perceive the harmony yet, if we cannot imagine it, if there simply is no way of harmonizing the goods we want to pursue in an order of good priorities and timing, the beauty we seek is an ideal we do not have. Moreover, that ideal would have to keep changing as we move through different situations of life and relate to different people in different places.

Confucius, Plato, and indeed nearly all the ancient philosophers from East Asia, South Asia, and West Asia, in various ways define the philosophic life as the disciplined and learned capacity to make up one's life with proper contributions to the environment and with internalized structures that provide poise and balance regarding how to take initiative regarding beautiful things. Philosophy is a way of life that has a special level of harmony, the harmony of learning to live with beauty. Living with beauty means enhancing beauty. The move to art is an elementary enhancement of the beauty that is worth prizing as such. A philosopher is someone with a dimension of harmonization who, with good reason and relevant erudition, discerns how to make coherent the attractions for initiative with balance and true proportion and has the discipline to do so. Alcibiades saw this in Socrates (in Plato's creation).

So an extraordinary goodness possible for human life is that of a harmony growing throughout of capacities to respond to the beautiful attractions for initiative in a balanced, proportionate, wise, philosophic way. Not all people are philosophical of course, just as many never think much about making a life. Nevertheless, everyone can learn to be philosophical in this sense. I do not mean professional philosophers here, of course, many of whom are not philosophical at all in this sense. Because everyone can learn to develop this philosophical harmony, with its goodness of balancing how each person can respond appropriately to the attractions for initiative, everyone should seek a philosophical education from the university and the college of hard knocks.

The Spirit of Creativity

Yet another dimension of human goodness now rises to attention, an elaboration of what has been said, which I call a "spirit of creativity."

From the tradition of German idealism of Hegel and Schelling, "spirit" has become a general term for the act of first moving out of where we stand into something new and different and then integrating the two. Paul Tillich developed this in Christian terms of life in the Holy Spirit.[9] Whitehead took something very much like this to characterize his notion of creativity: the advance into novelty is the many becoming one and thereby increased by one, which he called the Category of the Ultimate.[10]

I would like to distinguish and relate spirit and creativity in the following way. Creativity is the making of something new. The continuity with what is old comes from the limits of creativity where those exist. For instance, the future possibilities set limits for creativity within time, and what has been created before sets limits to potentiality. Nontemporal creativity, namely, the creation of determinate things as such, is sheer making of novel things, with no limits. My concern here, however, is with temporal creativity.

Spirit, in relation to creativity, is a kind of harmony in which components of width embrace many different instances of whatever it is the spirit of, with only the vaguest quality of what that is. For instance, the spirit of Christmas vaguely is the spirit of joyous gratitude and benevolent giving. That vague spirit is instantiated in parties for children, parties for adults, parties for families, decorations with religious symbols, decorations with pagan symbols, decorations with purely commercial symbols, the making or purchasing of gifts, the giving of gifts, the opening of presents and enjoyment of gifts, the general appreciation of friends and of family members, the efforts to travel for reunions, and a host of other things. Annoyances, grievances, worry about money, and other such negative things are vaguely transmuted and represented with sentiments of forgiveness and magnanimous cheer (at least temporarily) and trivialized until after New Year's celebrations. Each of the items of celebration listed is a kind of narrow focus of the Christmas spirit. The organization of the holiday season provides most of components of width that bind together the narrow points of focus. The organization of local social structures provides most of the rest of the binding components of width, determining who meets with and gives to whom. Each of the narrow foci, the celebrations and the gifts, would be radically different from what they really are if they were not explicitly instances or specifications of the spirit of Christmas. Put more metaphysically, an essential component of each of those instances of Christmas spirit is that the instances are components of the Christmas-spirit harmony.

In a harmony that is a spirit in this sense, the components of vagueness embracing concrete actual instances are extremely important, whereas in many other kinds of harmony I have discussed the vague components are functions of making other things unimportant. A spirit, in this sense, cannot get along without the exercises of actual spirit that illustrate the spirit itself. If there were no parties, no gift giving, no suppression of animosities, there would be no Christmas spirit. Ironically, for Christians, it is not necessary for there to be any actual references to the Incarnation or to Jesus for the Christmas spirit to be real and effective. Many people have the Christmas spirit without being Christians in any serious sense.

Some people will have difficulty in taking this notion of spirit seriously because they suffer from nominalism, the belief that only actual particular things are real. Nevertheless, something is real if it has effects and determines other things. The Christmas spirit is very powerful, organizing people's lives, changing their attitudes at least temporarily, stoking commerce, and having all sorts of effects. Those things would not happen without the Christmas spirit. People in China celebrate the spirit of Christmas in powerful ways these days with very few of them being Christians in motivation. The spirit motivates the extravagant buying and giving in the name of Santa Claus.

The notion of spirit is important for understanding the goodness of civilization, as will be explored in chapter 16. Here I want to comment on the spirit of creativity. A spirit of creativity can be a harmony embracing a group, whether the group is small such as a family, or large such as a civilization, or perhaps even a global society with many civilizations. The spirit of creativity has a vague character that comprises at least four things. First is an appreciation of rich valuable resources among what is given. Second is some critical appraisal of the given such that something is seen as problematic or subject to being improved. Third is the imagination to see what can be done or made to solve the problem or improve the situation. Fourth is the initiative to do something to turn the imagined ideal into an end-in-view and act upon it. This is the vague character of creativity. The narrow nodes in the harmony of the spirit of creativity are the places where creativity occurs. The components of width are those that bind the group in having the many creative nodes together as instances of the vague component of creativity. The trivial components are those that are set aside in both the vague spirit of creativity and the narrow creative instances.

Artists generally, though not always, are creative people. A single artist over a duration has many instances of creativity, perhaps with different media, or different situations of dance or music; the "group" is the many endeavors of the same artist. A colony of artists might be animated by the spirit of creativity, working together and separately, but joined by whatever traits bind them as appreciating creativity together; not all artist colonies are creative, some being merely imitators. A family can have the spirit of creativity, in how the adults do their work, in how the children learn to play and learn, and in how the family functions together at home and perhaps on trips and holidays; many families do not have much spirit of creativity. The spirit of creativity can energize a local community, working to improve its various institutions; many local communities instead are dispirited and slowly collapse as their old institutions fail to enable flourishing. There are times when nations can be more or less imbued with a spirit of creativity.

In American history, we can appreciate this in the periods immediately following the Revolutionary War, the Civil War, and the Second World War. The creativity following the Civil War took three somewhat unrelated forms: the Reconstruction effort, the antireconstruction effort to reinstate the Old South, and the industrial and agricultural expansion of the North, particularly westward. Even the Native Americans had a spirit of creativity in trying to preserve their old ways of life under pressures that ultimately destroyed them; perhaps we should say that post–Civil War America had four disparate spirits of creativity.

Roughly speaking, we can appreciate loose but powerful eras of a spirit of creativity, for instance, the two centuries prior to the Han empire in China, Ashoka's empire in India, and Alexander's empire in

West Asia. We regard the two centuries prior in each case as "classic" periods resulting in empires that developed versions of the Axial Age. Many other examples of people in very large groups with a spirit of creativity exist. The vague spirit of creativity in each instance has attributes peculiar to itself that come from whatever the cultural resources are from which they work.

Extraordinarily rich goods lie in the harmonies that are spirits of creativity uniting a group. Whenever instances of creativity occur, flourishing is enhanced, and the instances occur in part because they are components of the spirit of creativity and that spirit functions as a component in each instance, however unconsciously.

Creativity, however, is a notion that seems particularly important in Western culture. The primary models for ultimacy in the West are creative gods or more usually a creative God. Creativity becomes a human and social virtue in imitation of the metaphors for understanding why there is anything at all. South Asian cultures, however, eliminate precisely those creative agential elements from the metaphors of consciousness developed from human experience. East Asian cultures abandoned the personifying metaphors very early in favor of metaphors of spontaneous emergence. The point about Western bias is well taken with regard to the metaphoric resonances of creativity.

Nevertheless, creativity is also present with different metaphoric resonance in the South and East Asian cultures. Some of the earliest Upanishads signal creation coming from heat in the cosmology of Samkhya philosophy; of the three natural forces, *rajas*, *tamas*, and *sattva*, it is *rajas*, a metaphorical version of kingliness, that is the force of creativity within time. *Rajas* is hot. In later Upanishadic thought, Brahman without qualities gives rise to Brahman with qualities that in turn gives rise to Ishvara, a creating god. Kashmir Saivism conceives Shiva as repetitively moving outward as Shakti in formed patterns or groups, inhaling again and then exhaling to produce temporal continuity. In East Asian culture, the Dao is all about creativity, with an even more pronounced emphasis on creative process than in either other great cultural system, just not creativity associated with human creators.

Thus, the conception of a "spirit of creativity" is cross-culturally fit to describe a certain kind of goodness that can obtain in social structures for groups of many sizes. Not all groups have it, to be sure.

Yet where it obtains, it fosters acts and instances of creativity, each of which abets human flourishing to a degree. The spirit of creativity can be a powerful cause of creativity when it becomes a component of situations that might be harmonized creatively, appreciating what is good in what is given, appraising it with regard to its possibilities, imaginatively aiming at something new, and inspiring initiative to make things better.

This discussion of spirit in creativity paves the way for the discussion of spirit in civilization, which is to come.

CHAPTER 16

The Goodness in Civilization

Culture and Civilization

Alfred North Whitehead said, in *Adventures of Ideas*, that four, or perhaps five, goods animate civilization: truth, beauty, truth and beauty together, adventure, and peace. He recognized that these ideals do not have much philosophic value unless they are undergirded by a philosophy or cosmology that gives them meaning with regard to nature, society, and individuals, and he provided that in *Adventures of Ideas*. His discussion there was a generalization of the more technical discussion in his earlier *Process and Reality*. In one major point the later volume differed from the earlier, namely, that it dropped all categoreal reference to God, a major and necessary part of the system of *Process and Reality*. The only reference to God in *Adventures of Ideas* was one clause of a sentence about Plato's God. *Adventures of Ideas* collapses the religious dimension so prominent in *Process and Reality* into civilization. "Peace," the title and topic of the culminating chapter of *Adventures of Ideas*, is about the grasp of the harmony of the adventure of youth with the tragic beauty of old age, "the dream of youth and the harvest of tragedy."[1] Evil, for Whitehead, was the passing away of achievement, which in a world of constant process and change is a tragic condition of life.[2] The harmony of adventure and tragedy is a "final fact," he said, which is like the religious vision at the end of *Process and Reality*.

I think myself that peace in his sense is indeed a religious vision, not particularly associated with civilization, especially high civilization as he described it. To understand peace as a "final fact" requires a robust philosophy of eternity, which Whitehead denied himself. I have treated what he called "peace" extensively as a religious vision in *Ultimates*, *Existence*, and *Religion* and will drop it out, for the most part, from this discussion of civilization. Yet my previous discussions of beauty and truth owe much to Whitehead's philosophy, and his notion of adventure is close to what I have called initiative. Thus, my project here, in a rough sense and with many qualifications, is an extension of Whitehead's project. To point this out is important because almost no one else, except Paul Weiss, has attempted a philosophy of life in our time.

One important qualification to that Whiteheadian affinity is that I have treated truth, morality, rightness, and personal virtue as characteristics of persons in relation to their world, not as characteristics or ideals for civilization as such. They are the goods of two-term harmonies relating persons to things in their environment, characterizing the relations of persons to something else. Even beauty is in such a two-term relation insofar as we appreciate or create it; this holds also for making oneself a beautiful person. The topic in this chapter is what I call the goodness in the spirit of a civilization. First, some further reflections are required on the concept of civilization.

We should recognize at the outset that the word "civilization" is used both descriptively, taking the use from historians, and normatively as a term of art, taking the use from commencement speakers. Earlier I commented that civilizations are inclusive of several cultures in describing the Axial Age as a time of empires that combined several local cultures together with some common elements and some locally distinctive elements. In this descriptive use, we also can say that larger civilizations include smaller civilizations, just as we can say that larger cultures include smaller cultures. Sometimes this is what we mean by saying that civilizations are large social groupings of different kinds of people. In this sense, civilization connotes the goods achieved in combining the different smaller groupings. Most of these goods are positive, such as those of the Axial Age, especially as seen in distant perspective. Sometimes those goods are negative in that they entail the loss of those positive differences between groups that cannot be sustained when they are combined, perhaps by force, in a larger civilization. The contemporary complaints about "colonialism" have to do with missing what is lost rather than appreciating what is gained in the colonial civilizations, especially the loss of the ability of the colonized peoples to define themselves in independence from the colonizers.

A root meaning of "culture," taken from Western anthropology, is meaning-laden material that can be passed down from generation to generation. A culture in this sense is part of the environment people in a group inherit. Such a culture includes all the social structures that make the cultured society possible, as well as the things of beauty and art, including the means of appreciation and communication. Initiative is required for individuals to take on that culture, and for its institutions to reembody the culture in new circumstances. Sometimes cultures become incapable of sustaining flourishing as circumstances change. We can speak of the culture of a civilization in this sense, complex as it would be. Not all civilizations, however, have unifying cultures.

Whitehead pointed out a normative element in the notion of civilization, as he used that term. He spoke of a civilization being vital when it is full of zest and adventure, such as the civilization of the classical period of ancient Greece. However, the civilization can become repetitive, losing zest and innovation, as he viewed Hellenism to have done. A zestless civilization reduces to its achieved culture at some point and concentrates on maintaining this in changing circumstances. I think this is a vastly oversimplified historical interpretation of the ancient Mediterranean civilizations, but there is something in Whitehead's point. "Culture" does not have the connotation of innovation and adventure, of growth and development. "Civilization" does have that connotation.

Therefore, I propose to define civilization, in contrast to culture, to include its self-making. Civilization is the creation of itself out of circumstances in which it is not yet fully formed. Civilizations are not only dynamic—all cultures are dynamic in that their structures harmonize and cope with constant change—but also growing, adding levels and kinds of harmonies for human flourishing. When we look at Imhotep's civilization or Sargon of Akkad's, we see not only the cultural structures, artifacts, and achievements they created. We appreciate also that they created those things. They advanced upon antecedent conditions. Remember always that any group's social structure enables human flourishing, but often unevenly: some people flourish while others suffer. However, a civilization makes possible new levels of flourishing, new kinds of arts, new kinds of economies, new architecture, new military powers, new kinds of science and philosophy.

Civilization as growth can mean many things. To be sure, it can mean expansion of territory to take in new cultures and the new technologies made possible by their resources, as was the case with Sargon's civilization. In a broad view, the rise of modern European civilization began with colonial expansion, technological innovation, the spread of European culture globally, and more recently the incorporation of former colonies' cultures into European civilization. Imhotep's civilization, however, was not expansionist in that regard but rather innovative with regard to the internal culture of Egypt in arts, architecture, medicine, and political administration. Chinese civilization, in a broad view, has been only slowly expansionist in territory, moving from the unification of the inner states of China in the Qin dynasty slowly down the Silk Road but not into West Asia. Chinese expansionism was always somewhat constrained by the Confucian belief that government needs to be limited to what it can administer in levels of face-to-face relationships. Only lately under the influence of Western Marxism has China adopted colonialist imperial postures toward Tibet, Taiwan, and the islands off its east coast. This is somewhat ironic because its Marxist philosophy originally was supposed to renounce territorial boundaries in favor of international class solidarity—the working class of the world versus the capitalist class. The most serious innovations of Chinese civilization have been the cycles of dynastic civilization that are highly innovative and then that stagnate in repetition and become dysfunctional as changes occur and new pressures arise. Chinese civilization is characterized by the innovations of the Qin-Han dynasties, the Tang, the Song Northern and Southern, the Yuan, the Ming, and the Jing dynasties.[3]

We do not usually call tribal cultures "civilizations" because we know them for their structures, not for their innovations that brought about those structures. Evolutionary anthropologists and historians can note the innovations in tools, practices, and arts from one tribal culture to another but as a chronical of innovative steps, not a process of innovation. We begin to speak of civilization when innovation becomes deliberate because something in the inherited cultures needs amendment or connection.

The Native North American peoples are an interesting case in point. At the time of the coming of Europeans, they had different cultures with different languages and the traits of different civilizations in the Mississippi River bottom, the far west, and the northeast where they practiced settled agriculture. Most of the tribes, however, were mainly hunter–gatherers with tribal organization. With the coming of Europeans, the Native Americans quickly recognized the differences in cultures between their own and the various European ones and began to innovate, unsuccessfully, to sustain themselves. By the time of the great Indian Wars of the 1860s–1890s, major tribes from east of the Mississippi had moved, often unwillingly, to the Great Plains where they tried to patch together a civilization with horses, guns, and innovative hunting methods to keep on the move, hoping to sustain this new way of life against white, expansive capitalism. Without settled agriculture, however, they could not unite efficiently enough to protect their territory from the whites and, where they did settle as agriculturalists, they gave up their nomadic way of life for degenerate reservations. The sad lesson is that the earlier tribal cultures and early American civilizations of the Native Americans could not sustain themselves against or within the highly innovative European immigrant American civilization. Similarly, we know that period in American history more generally for the innovative growth of the Euro-American civilization, at the cost of Native American civilization and without much benefit for the African Americans. The further growth of American civilization in the economically and culturally expansive period after the Second World War did benefit the African Americans, but not the Native Americans.

With these kinds of qualifications and examples in mind, it is possible now to think about the kinds of goods that are possible within civilization in the rich innovative sense and to concentrate on two of these.

Spirit of Civilization: Character

In the previous chapter, I introduced the concept of spirit as a special kind of social harmony. A spirit is a kind of harmony across social elements including people whose form gives great importance to traits that define the spirit vaguely. Included among the components of spirit in this sense are individual persons and various social and natural environmental structures. Depending on the vague character of the particular spirit, the form of a spirit-harmony has all sorts of narrow pockets of harmonic goodness, including persons, that embody the spirit in particular instances and in ongoing continuities. The form of the spirit also has elements that carry the vague traits of the spirit across widely different locations, institutions, and levels of the society. The form of a spirit-harmony is different from the form of a harmony of a person, for instance, or a building, in which the narrow highly defined and the widely connecting components have great importance and the vague components serve to keep vaguely grasped elements at low importance. A person can have a spirit within his or her group as a component of personal harmony. The spirit of that group can have the person's action in accordance with that spirit as a narrow concrete component of the spirit.

The spirit of creativity discussed in the previous chapter focused not on the spirit of a civilization but rather on how an individual can engage a social environment whose spirit coordinates the individual's initiatives with the initiatives of others. The spirit of a civilization is broader than this. It has as its narrow elements mainly the institutions of a civilization, such as various governmental structures, economic structures, technologies, the self-identity of various groups of people, for instance, different ethnic immigrants. Individuals can be particularly influential in creating elements within these institutions, such as inventors like Thomas Edison, and they can be emblematic of innovations in particular areas. However, the chief places of innovation in civilization reflective of the civilization's spirit are in institutions. The components of width in the spirit of a civilization are those that harmonize the institutions with one another.

The vague character of a civilization's spirit takes its definite (though vague) form in part from the social environment of a civilization. For the sake of illustration, please accept my historical account of the formation of American civilization following the Civil War, 1861–1865, to the end of the nineteenth century. Of course, alternative readings of this history exist, but take this one as illustrative of the formation of the American Spirit.

As to government, Americans were self-conscious of being heirs in different ways to the Revolutionary War ideals of freedom, rule by law, and unity as a nation. The Civil War itself had been a terrible test of that unity and Lincoln's Gettysburg Address reasserted the ideal of fourscore and seven years previous. The victorious Union side redefined freedom to include freedom from slavery. Nevertheless, for much of the white South, freedom meant the freedom to reinstate the subservience of African Americans to white plantation culture as had existed during the period of slavery. Freedom for African Americans looked good for the decade of Reconstruction, but it was severely repressed in the South after that. Freedom, however, was very meaningful for the white Protestants of the North who took satisfaction in winning the war but wanted to get on with developing what they construed as their civilization. Freedom also was meaningful for the Irish, Italian, German, Scandinavian, Polish, and other Eastern and Southern European immigrants who came just before, during, and shortly after the war. A strong prejudice prevailed among the white Protestant elite against the Catholics, who in turn had to assert their freedom from Protestant hegemony. Freedom also was important for the Chinese and, to a lesser degree, Japanese immigrants who came as part of the expansion of America to the Pacific. The American spirit covered and energized all these competing projects of freedom.

The main economic structures affecting the rise of the American spirit after the Civil War were the new lands for settling, new resources discovered, particularly gold but also other metals and forests, and most especially new forms of financing. During the Civil War, the Union had developed new forms of borrowing and investing money to build its huge war effort. The Confederacy never was able to adopt this new financing. Investment, risk, the possibility of huge profits, and readiness to accept huge losses and move on, characterized the economic situation. America was not that different from some European countries during this time, although the war focused the economic situation.

Related to this were technological advances having to do with mobilizing for mechanized wartime production. Long-term apprenticeships in crafts became less important and the more efficient, if routinized, work of factory production became more important. Among the technological novelties was the increasing assumption that domestic life could be mobile. People could move to the cities where the factories were, or to the newly opened lands for new farms, or to new towns supporting midwestern and western societies. The transcontinental railroads were important new factors for both economic and technological development, including the technology of mobility.

The self-identities of people include those I have already mentioned, white Protestants, Catholics, European cultures distinguished by languages and some customs, and white Southerners bent on restoring antebellum ways. African Americans attempted to define their new freedom from slavery while fighting off the depredations of the Ku Klux Klan and like groups; for many it meant migrating to the North where there were factory jobs. The factory jobs, however, often were closed to African Americans or the industries were moving west. I have mentioned the self-identity problems of the Native Americans. Many of the Asian immigrants kept very close connections with families in East Asian and only slowly sought to define themselves in relation to the rest of American culture.

The definite but vague spirit of American civilization that emerged after the Civil War thus combined these and other factors. It set great store on the expansion and achievement of freedom and prosperity by economic growth and technological innovation. This spirit was a golden age for those who profited from it, which was just about everyone except the African Americans whose freedom was stifled and the Native Americans. A significant part of the spirit of American post–Civil War civilization is hypocrisy and guilt about those kept from the massive flourishing of the others. This hypocrisy and guilt is present within the felt spirit of the age, even when kept from view. Nearly everyone in America during that period had that American spirit as a component of his or her life, consciously or unconsciously, for benefit or for oppression. It shaped the lives of nearly everyone. At the same time, that spirit had a life of its own, nudging political forms to adapt to expansive progress—government was often (though not always) corrupt and subservient to the rich.

The American spirit did indeed inspire extraordinary efforts and sac-rifices for the sake of freedom in the various competing senses. The spirit also pushed for economic prosperity. By the end of the century, many groups of people had come to define themselves as Americans, participating in the American spirit for better or worse; most of these groups previously had thought of themselves as immigrants looking for a new and better life in America.

This illustration of the spirit of a civilization makes the point that the values achieved by having that spirit are not all good. Some people are hurt and just plain run over by such a developing situation. Probably the rice farmers along the Nile did not want to become brick makers for Imhotep's pyramid civilization, nor did the people of the Balkans want to become tin miners for Sargon. On the other hand, American civilization was vastly richer for its spirit that developed after the Civil War. It was materially richer for nearly everyone involved save Native Americans. It was culturally richer for most people in terms of education and the arts. It was politically richer for the formation of many different power groups that interacted to represent various interests. It gave a sense of belonging to a civilization of Americans that had not existed at the time of the war. The subsequent spread of American civilization around the world through the two World Wars led to widespread flourishing with regard to medicine, health, eco-nomic wealth, and communication among different civilizations. I was in Moscow sharing vodka with some high-ranking Russian intellectuals at the time of the Serbian war against the Muslim states in the former Yugoslavia. They could not believe that I did not identify with the life-and-death struggle for the survival of their Christian Orthodox civilization over against the evils of the Muslim civilization. That was their civilization's view of the Balkan Wars. Mine was the American civilization's view, namely, that the differences between the Orthodox Serbs, Roman Catholic Croats, and Muslim Bosnians and Albanians were denominational differences, to be resolved by religious plural-ism, not the win-or-lose philosophy of the Russians. That American sense of pluralism was a great good created for my inheritance by the American spirit, I remain convinced.

At the time of this writing (2018), the United States seems to have a broken spirit. Political, economic, and domestic partisanship has destroyed many assumed forms of communication. Something similar is true of many other old-line democracies. Does this mean that the spirit of liberal civilizations is gone? Or does it mean that a new spirit is growing that can embrace both the globalism of liberal democracies and the localism of self-affirming particular communities threatened by globalism? I would hope the latter but have genuine fears about the former. Most likely we are in for a century or more of violence about this tension.

Every civilization with a spirit has something definite such as I have described (or mythologized?) for American civilization. There is always some concrete character to the civilization's spirit, whatever that might be and however that might include different institutions and resources as its narrow instantiations. Let me now reflect on two important and complex traits of any spirit of a civilization: energy and creativity.

Energy

By energy here I mean the components of the harmony of a spirit of a civilization from which the institutions, groups, and individuals affected by the spirit derive power to participate in that spirit in their various spheres. The circumstances of their environment are given to them, but the spirit of their civilization energizes them to take up those givens and do something with them in that spirit. Without the spirit of a civilization, institutions, groups, and individuals can let themselves be moved by their givens. Or they can take up their individual initiatives with regard to those givens, or some combination of passive acceptance and more vigorous initiative. With a civilizing spirit, however, they derive power from what is given to do things reflective of the character of that spirit.

The elements given in an environment at any time are all harmonies with specific goods. At one end of a spectrum, certain of those valuable things can be embraced in the spirit as joyful resources. For instance, some of the immigrant groups coming to America in the mid-nineteenth century were encouraged by the pluralism in the emerging American spirit to hold on to their ethnic and linguistic heritage and plant it in new soil more fertile than what they had left in their homeland. The same spirit moved those groups to look on the resources of new lands and new kinds of jobs in America as possibilities for just that planting. These two effects of the American spirit contributed to the specific kinds of freedom that manifested itself in many, though of course not all, places. Freedom for many meant being able to keep and magnify their identity while making it prosper in new ways. For some groups in late-nineteenth-century America, the goal was to let the diverse ethnic identities slip away and have all groups become simply "American," an idea that came to be identified as the "melting pot" theory. Especially the established white Protestants who thought Americans should be like them believed this. Even many of the white Protestants came to view the ethnically different groups as important for economic success and for settling the western wilderness as they shoved the Native Americans aside.

At the other end of that spectrum were groups that saw the "goods" in their environment as very bitter under the aegis of the American spirit. The Native Americans on the plains divided into those on the one hand who came to realize the dominance of the hordes of incoming whites as inevitable, settling on reservations and taking up farming, and those on the other hand who resisted until they were wiped out or finally forced onto reservations. The Native Americans quickly became aware of the emerging American spirit, at least as it bore upon their lives, and that spirit galvanized them to action, some until close to the end of the century. They participated in the American spirit with increasingly ineffective opposition. Nevertheless, that spirit was real to them. It was an important component in the lives of most Native American groups, and their roles as obstacles to Euro-American expansion became an important emblem within the American.

Most energy derived from the spirit of a civilization lies in between joyous embrace—onward and upward—and bitter opposition—resist to the end. Most people see the mix of success and loss in the social transformations guided by the spirit of a civilization, as is obvious in the American case. In a second phase of the development of the American spirit, during the Second World War, the American armed forces latched onto the motto: "The difficult we do immediately, the impossible takes a little longer." This extraordinary optimism carried many American groups through tremendously difficult times.

Nevertheless, it is obviously whistling in the wind. Sometimes even the mildly difficult turns out to be impossible. Life runs over with so many accidents that come in at all angles that the attitude that life is mainly doing what we want is wildly unrealistic. People know this. Therefore, many people participated in the American spirit in the nineteenth century with a sense of irony: go for broke knowing that you might not succeed. The definite but vague character of the American spirit included the energies of high optimism but coupled with the energies that come from knowing the possibility of failure and the need to change direction. In the case of the American spirit, there is a blustery enthusiasm for progress for everyone that internally bears a strong sense of hypocrisy. What was done to the Native Americans is common knowledge. How the freedom of the slaves was betrayed after the war is common knowledge, including among those who worked so hard to betray that freedom and Reconstruction. In 1889, Mark Twain (Samuel Clemens) published his novel *A Connecticut Yankee in King Arthur's Court*, which seems on the surface to be a humorous spoof of romantic images of chivalry.[4] The Yankee transported back to Arthur's court makes fun of a lot of nonsense. However, he secretly industrializes much of England and, when opposed by the clergy and the nobility, goes to war with them. He plants dynamite all through the mountains of England and threatens to separate the nation's ribs from its backbone. When attacked, he hides out in a large cave with his bicycle-riding troops. He strings the surrounds with electrified barbed wire that kills the men in armor who attack. The bodies of the knights, killed by modern means of warfare, decay and ultimately cause disease that kills the Yankee's men in the cave. This book by Twain is one of the first literary works to blast the inhumanity of modern technology and the hubris of the technologists who think they are so clever. The humor at the beginning of the book about having to scratch an itch while wearing plate armor is undermined by the grisly tragedy at the end, where that very armor conducts death by electrocution as each knight reaches out to help his fallen comrade. The spirit of American civilization emerging at this time includes its dark side, the guilt for those betrayed and used up, as well as the upbeat push for progress.

I have written here about the energizing effects of a civilizational spirit on individuals, but most likely the greatest effects are on institutions. The American spirit of progress, freedom, and uplift for everyone had enormous energizing effects on educational institutions, from kindergartens and the early grades through the development of the Land Grant universities. The often-stated ideal was education for everyone. Sometimes the education was directed to certain sectors of life toward which people aimed (or to which they were relegated), for instance, for farming, or the "industrial arts." However, often the ideal motivating educational reforms was to give everyone the capabilities to be whatever they wanted. Before the Civil War, most higher education was of the apprenticeship sort. Afterward was the heyday of "liberal education" that allegedly would prepare the elite for anything. Governmental institutions too took energy from the American spirit, often with the motive of corrupt support of those forces that led to growth, applying the law unevenly and supporting cronyism of those who had the power. The American spirit was extremely powerful in developing social institutions in the late nineteenth century. Of course, similar technological and economic innovations were going on in Europe at the time. They took different forms there, however, because they were much affected by the character of colonialism that infected the spirits of the European civilizations, leading to competition among those civilizations. The American civilization rarely was much affected by colonialist expansion beyond the United States after the achievement of Manifest Destiny; when the Spanish–American War left America with some colonies, people did not quite know what to do with them. The centrality of the ideal of freedom for everyone (with exceptions) meant America was never an enthusiastic colonial power and hence coped with the technology and finance of late modernity differently from the European powers. Generally, the emphasis on universal (if hypocritically applied) freedom in the American spirit led most Americans in the late nineteenth and early twentieth centuries to root for freedom for the colonies rather than for increasing control for the colonial powers.

The spirit of a civilization is able to marshal energy on the one hand because of the depth in the resources given. Depth, remember, is the way by which some harmonies are able to carry on layers upon layers of other harmonies in their form without diminishing their importance. There was depth in vast numbers of immigrants to

America, depth in the martial passions that fought the Civil War, depth in the convictions that government should be democratic, wise, and fair.

Spirit in a civilization on the other hand marshals energy by affecting institutions, groups, and individuals to appreciate the goodness in that depth. When the spirit of a civilization becomes a component in the harmony of an institution, group, or individual, it affects the ways they value the given resources. Without depth in the resources, a belief in something promised by the civilizing spirit is mere fantasy. Without appreciation of the goodness in that depth for carrying out the spirit of the civilization, the resources are useless. Given the great width of the spirit of a civilization, the resources are deep and appreciated in widely different ways. Financiers, farmers, and merchants related to different deep resources and appreciated them in widely different ways, probably not much aware of how the others related to the American spirit. Yet they united in relating in their various ways to the extended characters of the American spirit.

Given that the spirit of a civilization promotes both good and bad consequences in the civilization, it is important to single out the peculiar goods of its energizing elements. Without the energizing elements, a civilization would be only the repetitive maintenance of a culture. What we look for in a civilization is what it contributes that would be lacking without it. A civilization differs from its cultural and natural background environments by what it does that is new, a new level of social reality. The energy in a spirit is what enables a civilization to step out from what was before to what it can achieve on its own.

Creativity

A civilization has not only energy but also creativity. The spirit of a civilization incites creativity in its people, groups, and institutions by the resources it manifests for appreciation in depth. Personal creativity has been a topic in this volume since the early discussion of artistic creativity. Personal creativity appreciates the resources at hand, has a good imagination to see into the possibilities for doing something with those resources, and inquires into how to achieve ideal possibilities. Personal creativity works imaginatively to form the ideal itself through creative activity and has skills at achieving intended results, all of which involve initiative. Artistic creativity is just one special example of how individuals can be creative across a whole spectrum of activities, especially those interacting with elements in their environment and changing the environment. As I argued in the last chapter, individuals can have a spirit of creativity that stimulates them to be creative in many areas of their lives and over long periods. An individual can be creative in some areas and highly conventional in others. In addition, a person can have a creative period and then go into creative doldrums, blocked from imagination, or initiative, or any of the other elements of serious personal creativity.

What is true about creativity for individuals can carry over into groups in most respects. A family can have a spirit of creativity that is effective in some or all aspects of life, at least for a time. A company can have creative periods too, where many facets of the company are prompted to be creative. A spirit of creativity, as happened to the electronics culture in Silicon Valley in the late twentieth and early twenty-first centuries, can stimulate even an industry.

Here I mean to call attention to creativity in the spirit of a civilization, however. The harmony of a civilization-spirit has extraordinary width that embraces areas of concrete life greatly distant from one another. A civilization can have great creativity in some, though perhaps not all, of the arts at the same time that it has creativity in local or larger political organization. At the same time, the civilization can be creative with certain technologies, and with areas of economic organization and finance. A civilization can be highly creative in its educational institutions, not only educational organizations but also institutions concerning what to be curious about, institutions and practices of research. While some of these domains obviously connect, such as technological innovation and economics, those connections might not be tight. Other connections between domains might be slight, such as creativity in painting or music and creativity in political organization or high finance. Often the connections are accidental, as when a new technology provides a new medium for art.

Perhaps special creative spirits exist in each of these domains. However, my focus now is on the creativity in a spirit of a civilization that prompts creativity in those other domains. That civilizational spirit might not have much unifying specific content that the institutional domains and individuals in which it is an important component would recognize. Each person or institutional domain might be unaware, or only vaguely aware, of creativity in the others. Each might not register much about the energies in the others. Yet each does register that creativity and energy are in the air and that their own activities participate in that too. Those who think of themselves, both individually and institutionally, as being in an innovative phase are becoming aware that they are participating in a civilization that is innovative over large areas. Of course, not all parts of a civilizing society are aware of this, or even participate at all in the spirit of a civilization in the making. Many do, however, and the creative energies of that many are components in the harmony of the civilizational spirit itself. The spirit of a civilization functions as a component in the lives of creative individuals and institutional domains only vaguely, usually. It provides a powerful but vague impetus of energy and creativity to those people and domains. As vague, it needs to be integrated with the much more narrow and wide elements in the personal and institutional creativity. Though vague, it can be powerful and pervade many areas of life, harmonizing with the interior harmonies of persons and social groups in many places.

Much of the optimism of the American civilizational spirit in the last half of the nineteenth century and again in the last half of the twentieth century came from the vague but powerful presence of creativity as a spiritual force. The "can do" spirit, the sense that "the difficult we do immediately, the impossible takes a little longer," expresses a general feeling that problems can be solved, that new ways of doing things can be found that get around obstacles, and that this can happen across life. As I stressed earlier, this element of the spirit of a civilization has a mythic character—it is false for many people and with regard to many problems. The underside of this creative spirit is a sense of tragedy: failure would not be tragic, only sad, if there had not been high hope in the first place.

As we can speak of the American spirit in the period following the Civil War, we can speak more generally of the spirit of Western civilization that began in the late fourteenth century with the age of exploration. This led to colonization, along with the Renaissance recovery of an ancient period of emerging civilizations, leading to the Reformation and Counter-Reformation in religion. The development of nation-states came with this, often with the aim of empire. The explosion of modern science, the Enlightenment in philosophy, the social sciences, and letters, and the blossoming of nearly universal formal education expanded this sense of the Western spirit. With this came the conception of the ordinary individual as having dignity and defining humanity (rather than it being defined by heroes or saints), as Charles Taylor has abundantly shown.[5] This emerging spirit of Western civilization took a long time to come out, and its mutual parts often developed relatively independently from one another. Nevertheless, a vague, powerful, sense of energy and creativity shaped it from early on, with that spirit of adventure in many specifically different areas reinforcing the energy and creativity in those separate domains. By the nineteenth century many people possessed a strong sense of the civilization of the West, despite its different languages, despite its competing empires, despite unevenness of political and economic power across Western lands, and despite the fact that North America was both very much part of Western civilization but also desirous of being pluralistic enough to include more than the West as its membership components.

The spirit of a civilization guides the civilization's formation. After the civilization has formed, if the guiding spirit no longer leads to significant innovations, the civilization becomes more like a culture, something inherited and appropriated, but not in-the-building. No clear line exists between a civilization-building spirit and a spirit that continues to innovate only to cope with changing conditions. Nor is there a clear line between failure to innovate enough to keep the culture going and the gradual collapse of the situation. As things begin to fall apart, the spirit of the civilization blows away.

After the Second World War, America enjoyed a renewed national spirit of its own civilization, increased prosperity and increased pluralism with the admission of many new immigrants from Asia and Africa. It fostered special movements to advance women, minority ethnic groups, and sexual minorities. Surprisingly, a nascent spirit for the development of a global civilization began to form in America. At least this was true in some domains. The establishment of the United Nations, building upon American models of government, provided hopeful ideals of political participation for most if not all peoples, as represented by their various governments. Agencies of the United Nations came to promote economic development for all, more or less, an international tribunal for justice, and welfare relief. The fact that member nations could voluntarily opt out of participation restricted the power of many of these agencies. Nevertheless, many people across the globe, not only in America, had hope for a rising spirit of global civilization. After millennia of warfare, Europe united in the European Union, allowing for a common market with free movement from one country to another; its mutual defense agency reinforced NATO. Europe began to participate as a unit internationally in more or less free trade. Then the technological revolution, culminating in the internet, made universal communication more feasible, weakening the boundary restrictions of the nation–states.

For a while, this new technology unleashed great energy and creativity in many quarters and people could dream of an emerging global civilization. However, the very speed of globalizing innovation has left many people in very different kinds of countries behind. At the time of this writing, Britain has voted to leave the European Union, the United States has elected a protectionist populist as president, and several European nations are facing internal forces to go their own way. The Muslim states in the Middle East have turned against each other, and vast migrations out of Africa and the Middle East are taking place as people forsake the possibility of flourishing in their homelands. The current crisis of European civilization is whether it can absorb large numbers of Muslim immigrants in a creative way or reduce to nativistic exclusion. In historical perspective, the twenty-first-century Muslim migration into Europe seems to be of less civilizational consequence than the migration of the Goths into Europe in late antiquity. Whether the current pushback against globalizing technology and economics, and the current failures of civilization in Africa and the Middle East, will block the promising formation of a global civilization is not clear. Perhaps it will fuel the energies and creativity necessary to build a global civilization that is not based so very much on Western models.

Whitehead noted that the root of evil is the fact that nothing lasts and everything perishes in time. The civilizations of Sargon and Imhotep are long gone. Many of the contemporary civilizations are simply fighting to maintain themselves under the radically changing social conditions of the globe. They have become mere cultures in a defensive mode. Even to maintain themselves, they have to participate in a new advancing civilization that can preserve their prized goods in a time of global high-tech interaction that is itself changing with great rapidity. Whether this new civilization is possible is an open question. Its spirit is not powerful now. Perhaps the globe is heading for a new Dark Age. Perhaps it is heading for a new Golden Age.

The problem of impermanence and loss is a religious one, not solely that of human culture and civilizations. Nevertheless, we can say that the goodness of the spirit of a civilization is that it can bring about the energy and creativity to build new dimensions of social life that allow new forms of flourishing. Such a spirit of civilization would maintain and celebrate the rich resources of natural and social environments. Environmentalists, for instance, say that a new global civilization is possible only if we learn to live with greater respect for the ecosystems of the natural environment. Sometimes they model this on ways they attribute to the Native Americans, living close to the soil and considering nature sacred. The Native Americans lost out to the technologically powerful American spirit of the nineteenth century, however. That phase of the American spirit trampled the natural environment as something only good for the satisfactions of human interests in freedom, wealth, and power. If the environmentalists are right, perhaps that mechanistic high-tech society will have to humble itself to a yet unimagined civilization that lives integrally with nature. Without some civilizing spirit, however, the rushing changes of contemporary life will become chaos and just about any kind of human flourishing will become "solitary, poor, nasty, brutish, and short."

The startling contrast between high hope and deep worry I have just expressed comes from the astonishingly high complexity of interrelation charted in this volume. The abstract metaphysical truth that things are harmonies, if my hypothesis is correct, means that any important good requires that things hold together, and that if they do not, the good is impossible or lost. With a rough scheme, this book has examined increasingly complex and important goods, beginning with the ubiquitous good of beauty. Beauty is the goodness of things in themselves, regarded as their own harmony. Art seeks the good of making things to enjoy for their own sake. The goods of human achievement in the face of obligation are at least those of being true, moral, right, and virtuous. The goods of human flourishing set the contexts for the other goods registered in human life. These for the most part are the goods of civilization, structured most often in ritual and energized by creative initiative. That these goods are so interdependent, and thus fragile, should alert us both to the Confucian anxiety to do the best we can and to tragic gratitude for what we have that shall pass. With anxious attention to our best initiatives and gratitude for what is passing, we wait for the arising of a new civilizing spirit, knowing that we cannot command it and that it might never come.

Notes

Preface

1. See James Miller's *China's Green Religion: Daoism and the Quest for a Sustainable Future,* and also his *Daoism: A Short Introduction* and *The Way of Highest Clarity: Nature, Vision and Revelation in Medieval China.*

2. Assuming that many English-language readers of this book are not steeped in Confucianism, I recommend as a general introduction John H. Berthrong's *Transformations of the Confucian Way.* Wing-tsit Chan's *A Source Book in Chinese Philosophy* contains many of the important texts. Joseph Chan's *Confucian Perfectionism: A Political Philosophy for Modern Times,* along with Stephen C. Angle's *Sagehood* and his *Contemporary Confucian Political Philosophy* show that Confucian philosophy has contemporary relevance. For the Daoist side, see James Miller's *Daoism* and *China's Green Revolution.* Bibliographical details about all the citations in this book are given in the bibliography that follows.

3. For an excellent introduction to Neo-Confucian philosophy, emphasizing its contemporary relevance, see Stephen C. Angle and Justin Tiwald's *Neo-Confucianism: A Philosophical Introduction.* I have learned less from the philosophies of South Asia because in various ways they believe that a strong concern for goodness is spiritually problematic in some deep sense.

4. I have elaborated this theory of harmony from other angles in *Ultimates: Philosophical Theology Volume One,* especially part 3.

5. See Angle, *Sagehood.*

6. Charles S. Peirce developed his theory of the categories of Firstness, Secondness, and Thirdness throughout most of his long life. Perhaps his most elegant statement is in his letters to Lady Welby, printed as chapter 32 in *The Essential Peirce,* volume 2. See also his Harvard Lectures, chapters 10–16 in that volume. In the *Collected Papers,* see CP 1.284–544. For an excellent

introduction to Peirce's categories, see Gary Slater's *C. S. Peirce and the Nested Continua Model of Religious Interpretation*, especially chapters 1–3.

7. See Slater's *C. S. Peirce and the Nested Continua Model of Religious Interpretation*.

Part I. Goodness in Harmony and Form

1. I have discussed Aristotle's conception of goodness, in contrast to Plato's, in *Reconstruction of Thinking*, chapter 2.

Chapter 1. Goodness in Experience

1. *Reconstruction of Thinking, Recovery of the Measure*, and *Normative Cultures*.

2. On the significance of ecosystemic and ecological metaphors, see James Miller's derivation of these notions from Daoism rather than Western biological science in *China's Green Religion*, chapters 1–3.

Chapter 2. A Metaphysics of Form as Goodness

1. I develop this flipped contrast between Plato and Aristotle in *Reconstruction of Thinking*, part 1. The relevant texts are Plato's *Republic*, in which he argues that theorizing, dialectic, and philosophy are for the guidance of public and personal life, and Aristotle's *Nicomachean Ethics*, book 10, in which he argues for the life of contemplation.

2. See his *Process and Reality*, parts 1 and 3.

3. See his *Process and Reality*, 24 and 228.

4. Whereas Whitehead analyzed these notions in reference to actual occasions, in *Process and Reality*, 110–15, my analysis is in reference to harmonies. Actual occasions in his sense are a special kind of harmony.

Chapter 3. A Cosmology of Form as Goodness

1. I have used "vagueness" in two ways. In the previous chapter I used vagueness in Whitehead's way to indicate how a given harmony can substitute for a variety of other harmonies within the composition of an inclusive harmony. Thus there is a kind of causal tracking from a many to

a one with regard to the functioning of components in a harmony. In this chapter I use vagueness in Peirce's way to indicate a category that can be instantiated by many different possible specifications, some of which might be contradictory to one another.

2. For a study of Plato on unity, see Robert S. Brumbaugh's *Plato on the One*, which is mainly an analysis of Plato's *Parmenides*.

3. For brilliant studies on unity or oneness in Chinese thought, see Brook Ziporyn's *Ironies of Oneness and Difference: Coherence in Early Chinese Thought: Prolegomena to the Study of Li* and *Beyond Oneness and Difference: Li and Coherence in Chinese Buddhist Thought and Its Antecedents*.

4. However, see the very metaphysical *Beyond Oneness and Difference* by Brook Ziporyn.

5. The notion of finite/infinite contrasts is technical and important. For its use in symbolizing ultimate conditions, see my *The Truth of Broken Symbols*, especially chapter 2. For its use in defining ultimacy, see my *Ultimates*, especially chapters 3 and 10.

6. All of this I discuss at length in *Ultimates*, part 3.

7. *Process and Reality*, part 1, chapter 2; part 5.

8. Charles Hartshorne, *The Divine Relativity*.

9. Stephan Koerner, *The Philosophy of Mathematics: An Introductory Essay*.

10. I have argued this at length in *Eternity and Time's Flow*.

11. See Hartshorne's *The Divine Relativity* and *Creative Synthesis and Philosophic Method* and Ford's *The Emergence of Whitehead's Metaphysics: 1925–1929*.

12. Se F. Bradford Wallach's *The Epochal Nature of Process in Whitehead's Metaphysics* and Auxier and Herstein's *The Quantum of Explanation: Whitehead's Radical Empiricism*.

13. He called them "genetic division" and "morphological division," respectively. See *Process and Reality*, parts 3 and 4.

Chapter 4. Testing the Theory

1. *The Essential Peirce*, volume 1, 29, in the essay "Some Consequences of Four Incapacities."

2. Terrence Deacon says that this is the unfortunate consequence of saying that all causation is mechanical and from the past; cognitive science needs to account for forward-looking intentionality. See his *Incomplete Nature*.

3. See the first chapter of *Process and Reality*.

4. See G. E. Moore's *Principia Ethica*, especially chapter 1.

5. I have analyzed how experiential images arise out of nonexperiential conditioning in *Reconstruction of Thinking*, part 2.

6. See *Process and Reality*, 24.

7. I defend this at length in *Recovery of the Measure*, part 1.

Part II. Goodness in Beauty and Art

1. Thomas Hobbes argued for a strong central government to control the use of force and violence; he thought that people are naturally aggressive and prone to preemptive fighting. In the absence of central control, he said:

> In such condition there is no place for industry, because the fruit thereof is uncertain, and consequently no culture of the earth, no navigation nor the use of commodities that may be imported by sea, no commodious building, no instruments of moving and removing such things as require much force, no knowledge of the face of the earth, no account of time, no arts, no letters, no society, and which is worst of all, continual fear and danger of violent death, and the life of man, solitary, poor, nasty, brutish, and short.

Leviathan, book 8, chapter 9. Although I do not concur with Hobbes that strong government is what guarantees these modes of human flourishing (ritual is the remedy that leads to flourishing I shall argue in chapter 14), he gives a good list of flourishing and its opposite. I shall return to part of this quote at the end of this volume.

Chapter 5. Beauty in Form

1. See Smith's *Forgotten Truth: The Primordial Tradition* and Nasr's *Knowledge and the Sacred*.

2. See Nasr's *The Philosophy of Seyyed Hossein Nasr*, The Library of Living Philosophers, for Huston Smith's essay, "Nasr's Defense of the Perennial Philosophy," and my "Perennial Philosophy in a Public Context," as well as Nasr's gracious replies to both articles.

3. See Angle's *Sagehood* on this point.

4. Wing-tsit Chan translation in his *A Source Book in Chinese Philosophy*, 98. Although the reference to feelings makes it seem as if the topic were human experience, the point is a metaphysical one about the cosmos containing heaven and earth. Equilibrium means creativity prescinding from its creatures and harmony is the result of creativity, the termini of the ontological creative act (brazenly to read my metaphysics back into ancient Confucianism).

5. For a scholarly study of the recalcitrance of things to harmonize, see Franklin Perkins's *Heaven and Earth Are Not Humane: The Problem of Evil in Classical Chinese Philosophy*.

6. See Odin's *Tragic Beauty in Whitehead and Japanese Aesthetics*.

7. Whitehead's account of genetic concrescence is in part 3 of *Process and Reality*.

8. Whitehead's summary account of God is in part 5 of *Process and Reality*. However, his account of God providing subjective unity weaves throughout part 3.

9. I argued this at length in *Creativity and God*. See an extended elaboration of this criticism in *Defining Religion*, chapter 13.

Chapter 6. Beauty in Art

1. John Dewey, *Experience and Nature*, 69–70, the beginning of chapter 3.

2. *Dewey, Experience and Nature*, 70–71.

3. See Peirce's remarkable essay, "A Neglected Argument for the Reality of God" in *The Essential Peirce*, volume 2.

4. See Weiss's *Nine Basic Arts* as well as *The World of Art*.

5. Weiss also wrote about sport as the pursuit of excellence. See his *Sport: A Philosophic Inquiry*. See, as well, Jay Schulkin's *Sport: A Biological, Philosophical, and Cultural Perspective*.

6. For a long defense of this audacious claim, see my *Ultimates* and *Defining Religion*.

Chapter 7. Arts as Observed

1. See *Bob Dylan: The Lyrics 1961–2012* and also Christopher Ricks, *Dylan's Visions of Sin*.

2. See his *Modes of Being*, one of the masterpieces of twentieth-century metaphysics.

3. See Weiss's *First Considerations*. For that volume, he invited some younger philosophers to criticize him and I contributed an essay, "In Defense of Process," in which I presented an early version of my theory of harmony as opposed to his defense of substance. In his reply, he defended his position and took me to task for joining up with a "school," process philosophy, to get myself an audience. Alas, my ruse did not work. The process philosophers ignored me for years because of my rejection of the various process

theological conceptions of God in *Creativity and God*! Weiss was a wonderful teacher and critic.

4. See Gadamer's *Truth and Method*.

5. Plato's *Phaedrus*, 264d, in R. Hackforth's translation, in editors Edith Hamilton and Huntington Cairns's *The Collected Dialogues of Plato: Including the Letters*, 510.

6. See Tracy's *The Analogical Imagination*.

Chapter 8. Arts as Created

1. See Dewey's *Experience and Nature*, 88–92.

2. This usage pervades *Experience and Nature* and *The Quest for Certainty*, as well as many of his other writings. I rarely use "intentionality" in the refined philosophical sense of "aboutness" but rather always as associated with purposefulness.

3. See the splendid discussions of coherence and harmony in Angle's *Sagehood*.

4. To counter the common view, sometimes sponsored by Daoists, that Confucians are naïvely melioristic, see Perkins's *Heaven and Earth Are Not Humane* and Michael David Kaulana Ing's *The Dysfunction of Ritual in Early Confucianism*. See also Miller's *China's Green Religion*.

5. Because not everyone thinks of gardening as an art, indeed a fine art, I recommend William Howard Adams's *Gardens through History: Nature Perfected* for convincing justification of that classification, as well as a beautiful survey of many kinds of gardens.

Chapter 9. Goodness in Being True

1. Whitehead had a different meaning for what he called "conformation," or "conformal feelings." See his *Process and Reality*, part 2, chapter 4, "Organisms and Environment." For him, a feeling is conformal in the sense that it arises in the concrescence of an actual occasion in such a way that the emerging occasion conforms initially to the actual occasion it feels and out of which it arises. Less technically, as one moment emerges it has to conform to what was actualized in the previous moment out of which it emerges. True enough, Whitehead emphasized how the emerging moment can distort radically that to which it initially conforms. Whitehead used his notion of

conformation to account for the expression of power through time, in that a succession of moments is such that each conforms to the character of the preceding one. I prefer to use the notion of conformation to mean the larger attunement of one thing to another, typified by performers with rapport.

2. My points here and in the next section reflect the pragmatic semiotics of Charles S. Peirce. He said:

> A sign, or *representamen*, is something which stands to somebody for something in some respect or capacity. It addresses somebody, that is, creates in the mind of that person an equivalent sign, or perhaps a more developed sign. That sign stands for something, its *object*. It stands for that object, not in all respects, but in reference to a sort of idea which I have sometimes called the *ground* of the representamen.

This quotation is from CP 2.228. Good explanations of Peirce's theory of interpretation, in its initial stages, are in the two famous essays "Questions concerning Certain Faculties Claimed for Man" and "Consequences of Four Incapacities," which are among most anthologized of Peirce's writings, including CP 5 and *The Essential Peirce*, volume 1. I have summarily interpreted Peirce's semiotics in *The Highroad around Modernism*, chapter 1, and at greater length in *On the Scope and Truth of Theology*, chapters 3–4. My use of Peirce differs from the representation of Peirce in T. L. Short's magisterial *Peirce's Theory of Signs*. To summarize his argument all too quickly, he interprets the early Peirce, whom I quote in this note, as a kind of postmodern semiotician for whom signs interpret signs that interpret signs ad infinitum with no real reference; he prefers the later Peirce, whom he sees as holding to semiotics as moving physically from the object to the sign to the interpretant, thus obtaining real reference. But I doubt the truth of that account of forward-moving process. Rather, I see interpretations as taking signs to stand for objects. Whitehead seems to me to be better than Peirce at interpreting the forward movement of process, only some aspects of which involve interpretation.

3. That formula is analyzed and defended in detail in my *Recovery of the Measure*, especially chapters 1–4.

4. I developed a systematic theory of interpretation in *Recovery of the Measure*.

5. James J. Gibson introduced the term in psychology and philosophy in his "Theory of Affordances." For a use of the term in a way close to my own, see Nathaniel F. Barrett's "Toward an Alternative Evolutionary Theory of

Religion: Looking Past Computational Evolutionary Psychology to a Wider Field of Possibilities."

6. See especially Schulkin's *Naturalism and Pragmatism.*

7. See *The Essential Peirce,* volume 2, chapter 4.

8. See Atkins's *Peirce on the Conduct of Life.*

9. See *The Essential Peirce,* volume 1, chapter 7.

10. Peirce held this critique of paper doubt long through his career. David Rohr points out this passage from the late (1905) essay "What Pragmatism Is":

> Philosophers of very diverse stripes propose that philosophy shall take its start from one or another state of mind in which no man, least of all a beginner in philosophy, actually is. One proposes that you shall begin by doubting everything, and says that there is only one thing that you cannot doubt, as if doubted were "as easy as lying." Another proposes that we should begin by observing "the first impressions of sense," forgetting that our very percepts are the results of cognitive elaboration. But in truth, there is but one state of mind from which you can "set out," namely, the very state of mind in which you actually find yourself at the time you do "set out,"—a state in which you are laden with an immense mass of cognition already formed, of which you cannot divest yourself if you would; and who knows whether, if you could, you would not have made all knowledge impossible to yourself? Do you call it *doubting* to write down on a piece of paper that you doubt? If so, doubt has nothing to do with any serious business. But do not make believe; if pedantry has not eaten all the reality out of you, recognize, as you must, that there is much that you do not doubt, in the least. Now, that which you do not at all doubt, you must and do regard as infallible, absolute truth.

My point is that a person seasoned in being "in the truth" understands that even things that are not robustly doubted are still fallible and that therefore alternative ways for things to be might exist, even when we feel no evidence for them.

Chapter 10. Goodness in Being Moral

1. See Kant's *Critique of Practical Reason* and *Foundations of the Metaphysics of Morals.*

2. Kant discussed lying in the *Foundations of the Metaphysics of Morals,* the *Critique of Practical Reason,* and the late *On a Supposed Right to Lie from Altruistic Motives.*

3. I have studied freedom and determinism at great length in *The Cosmology of Freedom,* especially chapters 5–7.

4. Angle is among the philosophers who regard Confucianism as a kind of virtue ethics. Roger T. Ames, however, in his *Confucian Role Ethics,* argues that Confucian ethics is about playing roles well. See also Siufu Tang's *Self-Realization through Confucian Learning: A Contemporary Reconstruction of Xunzi's Ethics.* My own position on Confucian ethics is to stress the learned capacities to analyze situations and think about them imaginatively, not relying so much on preformed virtuous habits and roles. See my *The Good Is One, Its Manifestations Many.*

5. See this delightful but easily misunderstood essay in William James, *The Will to Believe, Human Immortality, and Other Essays in Popular Philosophy,* 1–31.

6. I will develop this point at length in part 4. See also my *The Good Is One, Its Manifestations Many,* chapters 4, 10, 11, 14, and 15.

7. See Hobbes's *Leviathan* and Locke's *Second Treatise of Government.* I have treated this point about reversing obligation in the social contract in *The Puritan Smile,* especially chapter 3.

8. See my *The Good Is One, Its Manifestations Many.* Many Confucians and interpreters of Confucianism have tried to represent the tradition as focusing mainly on the cultivation of the self. This is a lopsided representation, missing the need to discern what is good in the field of action. But it is an important part of the truth about Confucianism.

Chapter 11. Goodness in Being Right

1. The critique of simple location is a major theme of Whitehead's *Science and the Modern World.*

2. See, for instance, my *Recovery of the Measure.*

3. See Buchler's *Metaphysics of Natural Complexes,* especially chapter 2.

4. See Tillich's *The Courage to Be* and *Dynamics of Faith.*

5. This is a basic theme of his *Science and the Modern World.*

6. Among his many works that treat this theme, see *Purity of Heart Is to Will One Thing.*

7. For a critical study of Dylan's songs, see Christopher Ricks's *Dylan's Visions of Sin.*

Chapter 12. Goodness in Being Virtuous

1. This theory of religious problematics of righteousness, wholeness, engagement of others, and value-identity as a condition for meaning is developed at length in my *Existence*, part 1.

2. This point about the diversity of religious responses to the ultimate conditions of life is explored at length in my *Religion*, especially parts 2 and 3.

3. Ontological faith is a theological concept I explore at length in *Religion*, especially part 4.

Part IV. Goodness in Flourishing and Civilization

1. A theme of his *Adventures of Ideas*.

Chapter 13. Goodness in Human Flourishing

1. See Karl Jaspers, *The Origin and Goal of History*. See also Robert Bellah's *Religion in Human Evolution: From the Paleolithic to the Axial Age*.

2. See Xunzi, *Xunzi: The Complete Text*, chapter 19, "On Ritual."

Chapter 14. Goodness in Rituals and Institutions

1. See *Xunzi: The Complete Text*. For recent general commentaries, see Paul Rakita Goldin's *Rituals of the Way: The Philosophy of Xunzi* and Kurtis Hagen's *The Philosophy of Xunzi: A Reconstruction*. For my recent treatments of Xunzi on ritual, and my own extension of his ritual theory, see my *The Good Is One, Its Manifestations Many*.

2. See Edward J. Machle's *Nature and Heaven in the Xunzi* for an excellent book-length analysis of this point.

3. I have argued this point in detail in *Normative Cultures*, chapter 7.

4. For a masterful analysis of dysfunction as understood in early Chinese ritual theory, see Ing's *The Dysfunction of Ritual in Early Confucianism*. Although he construes ritual more narrowly than I do, referring to performances, he notes dysfunction coming from the ritual player's lack of skill, ritual structures that do harm, and natural and social forces that overwhelm anything a ritual might accomplish.

5. *Xunzi*, chapter 17, "On Heaven."

6. Jaspers himself thought that the development of empires that forced different peoples together came toward the end of the Axial Age and that the initial phases of the Axial Age were city-states that fostered independence. I insist on the importance of dealing with different kinds of people for the development of concepts of universal humanity, justice, compassion, and living under common conditions.

7. See Adrian Goldsworthy's *Pax Romana: War, Peace and conquest in the Roman World* for a story of the viciousness of the Roman Empire to its conquered people, a surprising reversal of our usual reverence of the *Pax Romana*.

8. Peter Cozzens tells the tragic story of the Indian Wars in his *The Earth Is Weeping*.

9. *Xunzi, chapter 19, "On Ritual."*

Chapter 15. Goodness in Creativity and Spirit

1. For an expansion of the point of this and the following paragraph, see my *The Good Is One, Its Manifestations Many*, chapter 11.

2. See his *Being and Nothingness*.

3. See Heidegger's *Being and Time*, especially chapter 5.

4. Of course, we interpret the ideals for making our lives only with the signs at hand, or those that can be conjured poetically. Those signs are how we engage what is real. They are among the things that are real, and therefore we need to have educational dimensions to the possibilities for the initiatives we make so as to understand things more truly. But the goods in the harmonies that constitute as life as we would make it lie in the forms of the real actualities and possibilities.

5. A readily available English translation of the *Doctrine of the Mean* is in Wing-tsit Chan's *A Source Book in Chinese Philosophy*, chapter 5.

6. This one-paragraph interpretation of Confucianism is expanded at book-length in my *Boston Confucianism*.

7. *Romans* 7:15b. New Revised Standard Version.

8. See Brumbaugh's *Platonic Studies of Greek Philosophy: Form, Arts, Gadgets, and Hemlock*, part 1. I gratefully follow Brumbaugh in my interpretations of Plato, and in being a Platonic rather than Aristotelian interpreter of Plato and Aristotle.

9. See Tillich's *Systematic Theology Volume III*, part 4, "Life and the Spirit."

10. See Whitehead's *Process and Reality*, part 1, chapter 2, section 2.

Chapter 16. The Goodness in Civilization

1. Whitehead, *Adventures of Ideas*, 381.

2. The best brief account I know of tragedy in Whitehead is Elizabeth M. Kraus's "God the Savior." See also the brilliant extended account in Odin's *Tragic Beauty in Whitehead and Japanese Aesthetics*.

3. For more detail, see Yuri Pines's *The Everlasting Empire: The Political Cultures of Ancient China and Its Imperial Legacy*.

4. See Mark Twain, *A Connecticut Yankee in King Arthur's Court*.

5. See Charles Taylor, *Sources of the Self: The Making of the Modern Identity* and *A Secular Age*.

Bibliography

Adams, William Howard. *Gardens through History: Nature Perfected*. Photography by Everett Scott. New York: Abbeville Press, 1991.

Ames, Roger T. *Confucian Role Ethics: A Vocabulary*. Honolulu: University of Hawaii Press, 2011.

Angle, Stephen. *Sagehood: The Contemporary Significance of Neo-Confucian Philosophy*. Oxford: Oxford University Press, 2009.

———. *Contemporary Confucian Political Philosophy*. Malden: Polity Press, 2012.

———, and Justin Tiwald. *Neo-Confucianism: A Philosophical Introduction*. Cambridge: Polity Press, 2017.

Atkins, Richard Kenneth. *Peirce and the Conduct of Life: Sentiment and Instinct in Ethics and Religion*. Cambridge: Cambridge University Press, 2016.

Auxier, Randall E., and Gary L. Herstein. *The Quantum of Explanation: Whitehead's Radical Empiricism*. New York: Routledge, 2017.

Barrett, Nathaniel F. "Toward an Alternative Evolutionary Theory of Religion: Looking Past Computational Evolutionary Psychology to a Wider Field of Possibilities." *Journal of the American Academy of Religion* 78/3 (September 2010), 583–621.

Bellah, Robert. *Religion in Human Evolution: From the Paleolithic to the Axial Age*. Cambridge: Harvard University Press, 2011.

Berthrong, John H. *Transformations of the Confucian Way*. Boulder: Westview Press, 1998.

Brown, Daniel James. *The Boys in the Boat: Nine Americans and Their Epic Quest for Gold at the 1936 Berlin Olympics*. New York: Penguin/Viking, 2013.

Brumbaugh, Robert S. *Plato on the One: The Hypotheses in the "Parmenides."* New Haven: Yale University Press, 1961.

———. *Plato for the Modern Age*. New York: Collier, 1962.

———. *Philosophers of Greece*. Albany: State University of New York Press, 1981.

————. *Unreality and Time.* Albany: State University of New York Press, 1984.

————. *Platonic Studies of Greek Philosophy: Form, Arts, Gadgets, and Hemlock.* Foreword by Robert Cummings Neville. Albany: State University of New York Press, 1989.

Buchler, Justus. *Metaphysics of Natural Complexes.* New York: Columbia University Press, 1966.

Chan, Joseph. *Confucian Perfectionism: A Political Philosophy for Modern Times.* Princeton: Princeton University Press, 2014.

Chan, Wing-tsit, editor and translator. *A Source Book in Chinese Philosophy.* Princeton: Princeton University Press, 1963.

Cozzens, Peter. *The Earth Is Weeping: The Epic Story of the Indian Wars for the American West.* New York: Alfred A. Knopf, 2017.

Deacon, Terrence W. *The Symbolic Species: The Co-evolution of Language and the Brain.* New York: W. W. Norton, 1993.

————. *Incomplete Nature: How Mind Emerged from Matter.* New York: Norton, 2012.

Dewey, John. *The Influence of Darwin on Philosophy: And Other Essays in Contemporary Thought.* New York: Henry Holt, 1910.

————. *Experience and Nature.* Second edition. New York: W. W. Norton, 1929 (first edition, Open Court, 1925). *John Dewey: The Later Works, 1925–1953: Volume 1, 1925.* Edited by Jo Ann Boydston, with an introduction by Sidney Hook. Carbondale: Southern Illinois University Press, 1981.

————. *The Quest for Certainty: A Study of the Relation of Knowledge and Action.* New York: Minton, Balch and Co., 1929. *John Dewey: The Later Works, 1925–1953: Volume 4, 1929.* Edited by Jo Ann Boydston, with an introduction by Stephen Toulmin. Carbondale: Southern Illinois University Press, 1984.

————. *Art as Experience.* New York: Minton, Balch and Co., 1934. *John Dewey: The Later Works, 1925–1953: Volume 10, 1934.* Edited by Jo Ann Boydston, with an introduction by Abraham Kaplan. Carbondale: Southern Illinois University Press, 1987.

Dylan, Bob. *Bob Dylan: The Lyrics 1961–2012.* New York: Simon & Schuster, 2016.

Emerson, Ralph Waldo. *Selected Writings of Emerson.* Edited with an introduction by Brooks Atkinson and a foreword by Tremaine McDowell. New York: Modern Library/Random House, 1950.

Ford, Lewis S. *The Emergence of Whitehead's Metaphysics: 1925–1929.* Albany: State University of New York Press, 1984.

Gadamer, Hans-Georg. *Truth and Method.* New York: Seabury, 1975.

————. *Philosophical Hermeneutics*. Translated and edited by David E. Linge. Berkeley: University of California Press, 1976.

————. *The Idea of the Good in Platonic-Aristotelian Philosophy*. Translated and with an introduction and annotation by P. Christopher Smith. New Haven: Yale University Press, 1986.

Gibson, James J. "The Theory of Affordances." In *Perceiving, Acting, and Knowing: Toward an Ecological Psychology*, ed. R. Shaw and J. Bransford. Hillsdale: Lawrence Erlbaum, 1977.

Goldin, Paul Rakita. *Rituals of the Way: The Philosophy of Xunzi*. Chicago: Open Court, 1999.

Goldsworthy, Adrian. *Pax Romana: War, Peace and Conquest in the Roman World*. New Haven: Yale University Press, 2016.

Hagen, Kurtis. *The Philosophy of Xunzi: A Reconstruction*. Chicago: Open Court, 2007.

Hartshorne, Charles. *The Divine Relativity: A Social Conception of God*. New Haven: Yale University Press, 1948.

————. *Creative Synthesis and Philosophic Method*. LaSalle: Open Court, 1970.

Heidegger, Martin. *Being and Time*. Translated by Joan Stambaugh, revised with a foreword by Dennis J. Schmidt. Albany: State University of New York Press, 2010.

Herstein, Gary L., and Randall E. Auxier. *The Quantum of Explanation: Whitehead's Radical Empiricism*. New York: Routledge, 2017.

Hobbes, Thomas. *Leviathan*. Introduction by A. D. Lindsay. New York: E. P. Dutton, 1950. Original edition, 1651.

Huntington, Samuel P. *The Clash of Civilizations and the Remaking of World Order*. New York: Simon & Schuster, 1996.

Ing, Michael David Kaulana. *The Dysfunction of Ritual in Early Confucianism*. Oxford: Oxford University Press, 2012.

Ivanhoe, Philip J., and Sungmoon Kim, editors. *Confucianism, A Habit of the Heart: Bellah, Civil Religion, and East Asia*. Albany: State University of New York Press, 2016.

James, William. *The Will to Believe, Human Immortality, and Other Essays in Popular Philosophy*. New York: Dover, 1956.

Jaspers, Karl. *The Origin and Goal of History*. Translated by M. Bullock. New Haven: Yale University Press, 1953.

Kaag, John. *Thinking Through the Imagination: Aesthetics in Human Cognition*. New York: Fordham University Press, 2014.

————. *American Philosophy: A Love Story*. New York: Farrar, Straus and Giroux, 2016.

Kant, Immanuel. *Immanuel Kant's Critique of Pure Reason.* Translated by Nor-
man Kemp Smith. London: Macmillan, 1956; German first (A) edition,
1781; German second (B) edition, 1787.

———. *Critique of Practical Reason: And Other Writings in Moral Philosophy.*
Translated, edited, with an introduction by Lewis White Beck. Chicago:
University of Chicago Press, 1949. German edition of the *Foundations
of the Metaphysics of Morals,* 1785; German edition of the *Critique of
Practical Reason,* 1788; German edition of *On a Supposed Right to Lie
from Altruistic Motives,* 1797.

Kierkegaard, Søren. *Purity of Heart Is to Will One Thing: Spiritual Preparation for
the Office of Confession.* Translated from the Danish with an introductory
essay by Douglas V. Steere. New York: Harper & Brothers, 1938.

———. *Fear and Trembling* and *Sickness unto Death.* Translated with introduc-
tions by Walter Lowrie. Garden City: Doubleday, 1955.

———. *Either/Or.* Volume 1, translated by David F. Swenson with Lillian
Marvin Swenson with revisions and a foreword by Howard A. Johnson.
Volume 2, translated by Walter Lowrie, with revisions and a foreword
by Howard A. Johnson. Garden City: Doubleday, 1959.

Koerner, Stephan. *The Philosophy of Mathematics: An Introductory Essay.* London:
Hutchinson University Library, 1960.

Kraus, Elizabeth M. "God the Savior." In *New Essays in Metaphysics,* ed. Robert Cummings Neville, 199–215. Albany: State University of New York
Press, 1987.

Locke, John. *Two Treatises of Government, with a Supplement Patriarcha by Robert
Filmer.* Edited with an introduction by Thomas I. Cook. New York:
Hafner, 1956. Original edition, 1690.

Machle, Edward J. *Nature and Heaven in the Xunzi: A Study of the "Tien Lun."*
Albany: State University of New York Press, 1993.

McLuhan, Marshall. *The Gutenberg Galaxy.* Toronto: University of Toronto
Press, 1962.

———. *Understanding Media: The Extensions of Man.* New York: Signet, 1964.

Miller, James. *Daoism: A Short Introduction.* Oxford: Oneworld, 2003.

———. *The Way of Highest Clarity: Nature, Vision and Revelation in Medieval
China.* Magdalena: Three Pines Press, 2008.

———. *China's Green Religion: Daoism and the Quest for a Sustainable Future.*
New York: Columbia University Press, 2017.

Moore, G. E. *Principia Ethica.* Cambridge: Cambridge University Press, 1903.

———. *Ethics.* London: Oxford University Press, 1912.

Nasr, Seyyed Hossein. *Knowledge and the Sacred.* Albany: State University of
New York Press, 1989.

———. *The Philosophy of Seyyed Hossein Nasr*. Edited by Lewis Edwin Hahn, Randall E. Auxier, and Lucian W. Stone, Jr. The Library of Living Philosophers, volume 28. LaSalle: Open Court, 2001.

Neville, Robert Cummings. *The Cosmology of Freedom*. New Haven: Yale University Press, 1974. New edition: Albany: State University of New York Press, 1995.

———. *Creativity and God: A Challenge to Process Theology*. New York: Crossroad, 1980. New edition; Albany: State University of New York Press, 1995.

———. *Reconstruction of Thinking*. *Axiology of Thinking*, volume 1. Albany: State University of New York Press, 1981.

———. *The Puritan Smile: A Look toward Moral Reflection*. Albany: State University of New York Press, 1987.

———. *Recovery of the Measure*. *Axiology of Thinking*, volume 2. Albany: State University of New York Press, 1989.

———. *The Highroad around Modernism*. Cover by Beth Neville. Albany: State University of New York Press, 1992.

———. *Eternity and Time's Flow*. Illustrations and cover design by Beth Neville. Albany: State University of New York Press, 1993.

———. *Normative Cultures*. *Axiology of Thinking*, volume 3. Albany: State University of New York Press, 1995.

———. *The Truth of Broken Symbols*. Albany: State University of New York Press, 1996.

———. *Boston Confucianism: Portable Tradition in the Late-Modern World*. Albany: State University of New York Press, 2000.

———. *On the Scope and Truth of Theology: Theology as Symbolic Engagement*. New York: T&T Clark, 2006.

———. *Ultimates: Philosophical Theology Volume One*. Albany: State University of New York Press, 2013.

———. *Existence: Philosophical Theology Volume Two*. Albany: State University of New York Press, 2014.

———. *Religion: Philosophical Theology Volume Three*. Albany: State University of New York, 2015.

———. *The Good Is One, Its Manifestations Many: Confucian Essays in Metaphysics, Morals, Rituals, Institutions, and Genders*. Albany: State University of New York Press, 2016.

———. *Defining Religion: Essays in Philosophy of Religion*. Albany: State University of New York Press, 2017.

———, editor. *New Essays in Metaphysics*. Albany: State University of New York Press, 1987.

Nietzsche, Friedrich. *"The Birth of Tragedy" and "The Genealogy of Morals."* Translated by Francis Golffing. Garden City: Doubleday, 1956.

———. *Thus Spoke Zarathustra: A Book for All and No One.* Translated by Marianne Cowan. Los Angeles: Gateway/Regnery, 1957.

———. *Beyond Good and Evil: Prelude to a Philosophy of the Future.* Translated with commentary by Walter Kaufmann. New York: Random House, 1966.

Odin, Steve. *Tragic Beauty in Whitehead and Japanese Aesthetics.* Lanham: Lexington Books, 2016.

Peirce, Charles S. *The Collected Papers of Charles Sanders Peirce.* Edited by Charles Hartshorne and Paul Weiss. Cambridge: Harvard University Press. Vol. 1, 1931. Vol. 2, 1932. Vol. 5, 1934. Vol. 6, 1935. Vol. 8, edited by Arthur Burks, 1958. Standard citations to the *Collected Papers* are by volume and paragraph number; hence, CP 2.228 would be to volume 2, paragraph 228.

———. *The Essential Peirce: Selected Philosophical Writings: Volume 1 (1867–1893).* Edited by Nathan Houser and Christian Kloesel. Bloomington: Indiana University Press, 1992.

———. *The Essential Peirce: Selected Philosophical Writings: Volume 2 (1893–1913).* Edited by the Peirce Edition Project. Bloomington: Indiana University Press, 1998.

Perkins, Franklin. *Heaven and Earth Are Not Humane: The Problem of Evil in Classical Chinese Philosophy.* Bloomington: Indiana University Press, 2014.

Pines, Yuri. *The Everlasting Empire: The Political Culture of Ancient China and Its Imperial Legacy.* Princeton: Princeton University Press, 2012.

Plato. *The Collected Dialogues of Plato: Including the Letters.* Edited by Edith Hamilton and Huntington Cairns. New York: Pantheon, 1961.

Ricks, Christopher. *Dylan's Visions of Sin.* New York: Harper/Collins, 2003.

Sartre, Jean-Paul. *Being and Nothingness: An Essay on Phenomenological Ontology.* Translated with an introduction by Hazel E. Barnes. New York: Philosophical Library, 1956.

Schulkin, Jay. *The Pursuit of Inquiry.* Albany: State University of New York Press, 1992.

———. *Naturalism and Pragmatism.* New York: Palgrave/Macmillan, 2012.

———. *Pragmatism and the Search for Coherence in Neuroscience.* New York: Palgrave/Macmillan, 2015.

———. *Sport: A Biological, Philosophical, and Cultural Perspective.* New York: Columbia University Press, 2016.

Short, T. L. *Peirce's Theory of Signs.* Cambridge: Cambridge University Press, 2007.

Slater, Gary. *C. S. Peirce and the Nested Continua Model of Religious Interpretation.* Oxford: Oxford University Press, 2015.

Smith, Huston. *Forgotten Truth: The Primordial Tradition.* New York: Harper and Row, 1976.

Tang, Siufu. *Self-Realization through Confucian Learning: A Contemporary Reconstruction of Xunzi's Ethics.* Albany: State University of New York Press, 2016.

Taylor, Charles. *Sources of the Self: The Making of the Modern Identity.* Cambridge: Cambridge University Press, 1989.

———. *A Secular Age.* Cambridge: Harvard University Press, 2007.

Tillich, Paul. *Systematic Theology Volume I.* Chicago: University of Chicago Press, 1951.

———. *The Courage to Be.* New Haven: Yale University Press, 1952.

———. *Dynamics of Faith.* New York: Harper and Brothers, 1957.

———. *Systematic Theology Volume III.* Chicago: University of Chicago Press, 1963.

Tracy, David. *The Analogical Imagination: Christian Theology and the Culture of Pluralism.* New York: Crossroad, 1981.

Tritten, Tyler. *The Contingency of Necessity: Reason and God as Matters of Fact.* Edinburgh: Edinburgh University Press, 2017.

Twain, Mark (Samuel Clemens). *A Connecticut Yankee in King Arthur's Court.* New York: Charles Webster and Co., 1889.

Wallack, F. Bradford. *The Epochal Nature of Process in Whitehead's Metaphysics.* Albany: State University of New York Press, 1980.

Weiss, Paul. *Modes of Being.* Carbondale: Southern Illinois University Press, 1958.

———. *The World of Art.* Carbondale: Southern Illinois University Press, 1961.

———. *Nine Basic Arts.* Carbondale: Southern Illinois University Press, 1961.

———. *Sport: A Philosophic Inquiry.* Carbondale: Southern Illinois University Press, 1969.

———. *Cinematics.* Carbondale: Southern Illinois University Press, 1975.

———. *First Considerations: An Examination of Philosophical Evidence.* Carbondale: Southern Illinois University Press, 1977.

Whitehead, Alfred North. *Science and the Modern World.* New York: Macmillan, 1925.

———. *Process and Reality: An Essay in Cosmology.* New York: Macmillan, 1929. Corrected edition by David Ray Griffin and Donald W. Sherburne; New York: Free Press, 1978.

———. *Adventures of Ideas.* New York: Macmillan, 1933.

Xunzi. *Xunzi: The Complete Text.* Translated with an introduction by Eric L. Hutton. Princeton: Princeton University Press, 2014.

Ziporyn, Brook. *Ironies of Oneness and Difference: Coherence in Early Chinese Thought: Prolegomena to the Study of Li.* Albany: State University of New York Press, 2012.

———. *Beyond Oneness and Difference: Li and Coherence in Chinese Buddhist Thought and Its Antecedents.* Albany: State University of New York Press, 2013.

Index

www.ingramcontent.com/pod-product-compliance
Lightning Source LLC
Chambersburg PA
CBHW030635270326
41929CB00007B/82